# The Mitki
# and the Art of Postmodern Protest in Russia

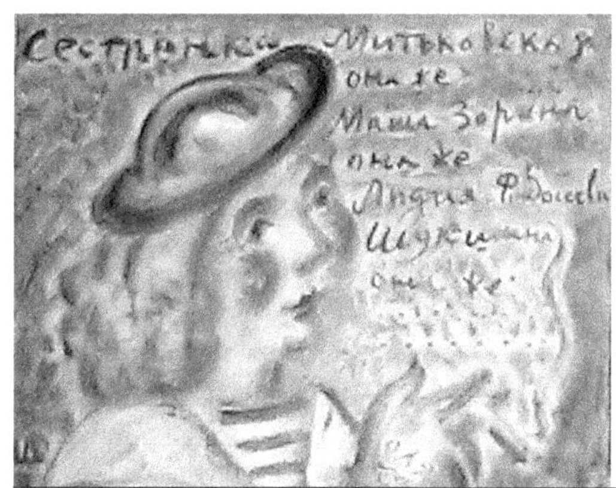

# THE MITKI and the Art of Postmodern Protest in Russia

Alexandar Mihailovic

THE UNIVERSITY OF WISCONSIN PRESS

Publication of this book has been made possible, in part, through support from Williams College.

The University of Wisconsin Press
728 State Street, Suite 443
Madison, Wisconsin 53706
uwpress.wisc.edu

Gray's Inn House, 127 Clerkenwell Road
London EC1R 5DB, United Kingdom
eurospanbookstore.com



This book may be available in a digital edition.

Library of Congress Cataloging-in-Publication Data
Names: Mihailovic, Alexandar, author.
Title: The Mitki and the art of postmodern protest in Russia / Alexandar Mihailovic.
Description: Madison, Wisconsin: The University of Wisconsin Press, [2018] | Includes bibliographical references and index.
Identifiers: LCCN 2017019396 | ISBN 9780299314903 (cloth: alk. paper)
Subjects: LCSH: Gruppa "Mit'ki." | Art movements—Russia (Federation)—Saint Petersburg—History—20th century. | Avant-garde (Aesthetics)—Russia (Federation)—Saint Petersburg—History—20th century. | Art—Political aspects—Russia (Federation)
Classification: LCC N6996 .M54 2018 | DDC 709.47086—dc23
LC record available at https://lccn.loc.gov/2017019396

ISBN 9780299314941 (pbk.: paper)

Segments from chapter 2 are revised versions of material that appeared previously in "In the Heat of the Boiler Room: The Subculture of the Russian Navy in the Work of the St. Petersburg Mit'ki," *World Literature Today* 80:2 (July 2006): 50–57; used by permission of the Board of Regents of the University of Oklahoma and *World Literature Today*.

Lines from W. H. Auden's "Musée des Beaux Arts" in chapter 1 are from *W. H. Auden Collected Poems*, copyright © 1940 and renewed 1968 by W. H. Auden; used by permission of Random House, an imprint and division of Penguin Random House LLC. All rights reserved.

To
HELGA and NICK

# Contents


List of Illustrations ix
Acknowledgments xi
Timeline of the Mitki xv

Introduction: Post Modern, or The Mitki's Chronicle of Russian Leadership 3

1 Glimmer Twins of the Leningrad Underground: The Creation of Dmitri Shagin in Vladimir Shinkarev's *Mitki* 25

2 "Who Is This Heroic Man?" David Bowie and the Mitki's Queering of Masculinity 58

3 Fire Water: Alcoholism and Rehabilitation in the St. Petersburg of the Mitki 96

4 Mosaic Authorship: A Coproduction of Olga and Aleksandr Florensky 126

5 Satire, Sex, and Chance: The Creative Diary of Viktor Tikhomirov 164

Conclusion: Icarus Rising, or The Mitki against Twenty-First-Century Russia 199

Appendix: Vladimir Shinkarev, "In Praise of the Boiler Room" 221

Notes 223
Bibliography 239
Index 249

# Illustrations

Figure 1. Group photo of the Mitki, taken by Viktor Nemtinov in 1989 2
Figure 2. Group portrait of the Mitki, taken by Viktor Nemtinov in 1988 24
Figure 3. Vladimir Shinkarev, *Goethe, "The Sorrows of Young Werther"* 44
Figure 4. Aleksandr Florensky, "A way of having a good time . . ." 62
Figure 5. Vasili Golubev, *The Mitki Send Brezhnev Off to Afghanistan* 64
Figure 6. Dmitri Shagin, *The Little Boat* 72
Figure 7. Aleksandr Florensky, *Little Brothers and Little Sisters* 77
Figure 8. Group painting by the Mitki, *Sisters, or A Woman's Lot* 82
Figure 9. Detail from *Sisters, or A Woman's Lot*, panel by Dmitri Shagin 82
Figure 10. Detail from *Sisters, or A Woman's Lot*, panel by Vladimir Shinkarev 83
Figure 11. Vladimir Shinkarev, *Dancing Alone* 83
Figure 12. Olga Florensky, *The Letter И* 85
Figure 13. Olga Florensky, *The Fearless Aviator Lev Matsievich* 89
Figure 14. Vladimir Shinkarev, "Rainbow Arch, don't drink our beer!" 103
Figure 15. Dmitri Shagin, "Beer" 103
Figure 16. Dmitri Shagin, *Brothers on the Bridge* 104

Figure 17. Aleksandr Florensky, "My wife wanted to punish me, . . ." 119
Figure 18. Olga Florensky, *Night on the Pequod* 133
Figure 19. Olga Florensky, *The Pequod Whale Boat* 134
Figure 20. Olga Florensky, *Captain Ahab on the Whale Boat* 135
Figure 21. O & A Florensky, *Moby Dick* 137
Figure 22. Aleksandr Florensky, *December 24, 2012* 143
Figure 23. Olga Florensky, *Bluebeard* 149
Figure 24. Aleksandr Florensky, "Some kids stuck needles into a masochist . . ." 160
Figure 25. Photo of Viktor Tikhomirov in his studio 168
Figure 26. Viktor Tikhomirov, *Bread and Onion* 171
Figure 27. Viktor Tikhomirov, *Nestor Makhno Throws an Unneeded Woman Overboard* 173
Figure 28. Viktor Tikhomirov, "Wolf, you won't get away from us!" 181
Figure 29. Detail from *Sisters, or A Woman's Lot*, panel by Viktor Tikhomirov 187
Figure 30. The "split" Vasiliev 190
Figure 31. Vasiliev refers to himself in writing as the "Vasiliev Brothers" 190
Figure 32. Matryona/Petko 191
Figure 33. Dmitri Shagin, *The Mitki Write a Letter [to the Oligarchs]* 203
Figure 34. Dmitri Shagin, *Seizure of the Mitki's Studio* 208
Figure 35. The Mitki at the Gavan art opening, taken by Viktor Nemtinov in 1987 212

# Acknowledgments

Although words of thanks are expected at the beginning of any book resulting from a large-scale research project, this one calls for particularly heartfelt expressions of gratitude to a wide range of individuals. Writing a book that focuses on women and men who are still living and highly productive, and whose work spans over three decades and two different countries (the Soviet Union and the Russian Federation), presents a distinct set of challenges. It somehow seems appropriate that I first found out about the Mitki in 1998, from buying a pirated audio cassette of their first collection of music at the Kiev train station in Moscow. I was like many people who found out about the group before the blossoming of the Internet in Russia: I owed the discovery to sheer chance, and a curiosity piqued by the vibrant and distinctly life-affirming aquamarine and deep blue tones of Dmitri Shagin's cover art. Who were these satirical dabblers in paint, print, and sound? Like Yeats's jester, the Mitki tossed up the gaudy "cap and bells" of their collective disinhibition to a public struggling to understand its sudden citizenship in a new country. Already the Mitki were no longer a local phenomenon; information about them was seeping into other parts of the larger complex of Russian popular culture, which in the nineties had an unruliness to it that somehow seemed fitting for the decade that came to be known as "wild." I would first like to thank Sergei Tsytsarev of the Department of Psychology at Hofstra University for putting me in contact with Aleksandr Tarelkin, who eventually introduced me to Evgeni Zubkov in Manhattan. I owe a debt of considerable gratitude to Evgeni, who is a close friend of many of the Mitki. Evgeni's tremendous generosity in introducing me to the group, lending me books from his personal library, and meeting with me at various times remains unmatched by any person whom I have known in my career as a researcher. I would also like to thank Svetlana and Konstantin Vais, of the former InterArt Gallery in Manhattan, for inviting me to their two remarkable exhibits of Dmitri Shagin's work in 2008 and for providing crucial information about prints and canvases.

In St. Petersburg, all members of the group were open to my queries, unstintingly generous with their time, and ever-willing to show me their studio spaces and works in progress. Dmitri Shagin met with me many times, lending me items from his own library and introducing me to other alumni of the nonconformist art movements from Leningrad/St. Petersburg. Vladimir Shinkarev's discussions with me were always illuminating and highly intelligent, even when they did not seem to have a direct bearing on the movement. In more ways than I can calculate, the warmth and openness of Olga and Aleksandr Florensky buoyed the spirits of a researcher away from home. Olga and Aleksandr's comments about the evolution of the movement from the mid-eighties to the mid-nineties gave my writing a much-needed focus and provided the yeast that allowed my project to rise. The hours I spent speaking with Viktor Tikhomirov in his studio afforded me a clearer sense of the movement's breadth. Tikhomirov's gregarious and lively impressions became an invaluable window for taking in the intersection of the visual and literary arts in the city. The spectacular view from the actual window of his studio onto the Church of the Savior on Spilled Blood remains an indelible impression for me, and I have incorporated it into chapter 5 of this book. My conversations in Moscow with the artists Konstantin Batynkov and Nikolai Polisski were very useful in giving context to the earlier phases of the movement, and I appreciate the time they took out from their busy schedules to see me. I would like to thank all the Mitki for their patience for the gestation of this project and for their invaluable assistance. This book would not exist without their participation in it. I would also like to thank Irina Vasilieva, Viacheslav Dolinin, and Alexei Mitin for their time and considerable insights into the movement, and Natalia Semkina for providing me with additional information about two of Viktor Tikhomirov's canvases.

In St. Petersburg, the assistance that I received from people working in galleries, museums, and other organizations was essential for many parts of this project. I would like to acknowledge the generosity and help of Aleksandr Borovsky, the head curator of contemporary Russian art at the State Russian Museum; Aleksandr Nevsky of the Collection at Tsarskoe Selo (Tsarskosel'skaia Kollektsiia) in the city of Pushkin; Tatiana Fedotova of Gallereia S.P.A.S.; and Tatiana Shagina of the Mitki Art Center. In Moscow, Liubov Agafonova of the Vellum Gallery was tremendously helpful in obtaining specific information about paintings from her exhibit "The Arefiev Circle and the Mitki," which ran in February 2017. Vladimir Rekshan, a key player in the development of Russian rock music and the custodian of the Museum of the Realia of Russian Rock Music—located within the Museum of Nonconformist Art, at 10 Pushkinskaia in St. Petersburg—helped me get a feel for the rock scene in Leningrad during the eighties and showed me his remarkable collection of handmade guitars, posters, and Soviet-era scrapbooks. I thank Viktor Nemtinov for answering my questions about his remarkable photographs of eighties-era Leningrad and for providing me with the permission to reproduce three of them. I owe a special expression of gratitude is to Svetlana Moiseeva, the director of House of Hope on the Hill. Dr. Moiseeva was extremely gracious when I visited the House, located in the town Perekiulia to the southwest of St. Petersburg. The House of Hope on the Hill is still the only nonprofit alcohol rehabilitation center within the Russian Federation.

Gwen Walker, my editor at University of Wisconsin Press, has been wonderfully supportive of this book in all its stages. The entire team at Wisconsin was amazing, and I am most grateful to Sarah Kapp, Terry Emmrich, Anna Laura Muenchrath, Ryan Pingel, and Adam Mehring for helping me through the technical aspects of the book production. From the time in 2016 when I was a fellow at the Oakley Center for Humanities and Social Sciences at Williams College, Krista Birch facilitated a crucial subvention for the printing of images, and Mika Hirai in the Williams IT department most capably converted several of them into the correct format. Funds provided by the National Council for Eurasian and East European Research (NCEEER), under authority of a Title VIII grant from the U.S. Department of State, supported the early stages of my research. Neither NCEEER nor the U.S. Government is responsible for the views expressed within this book.

Various colleagues and friends read or heard segments of this project and offered invaluable advice. I would like to thank the following people for their perceptive observations and suggestions during the draft stages of this book: Kasia Pieprzak, Jennifer French, Katie Kent, Alexander Levitsky, Jana Sawicki, Svetlana Evdokimova, Emily Johnson,

Caryl Emerson, Ksana Blank, Jane Sharp, and Elliot Borenstein. Several other people in St. Petersburg freely offered me their assistance. Liubov Gurevich's colossal knowledge about nonconformist art in Leningrad was both inspirational and extremely helpful. Viktor Allakhverdov of the Psychology Department at Petersburg State University assisted me in obtaining archive permissions and introduced me to Iosif Gurvich. Professor Gurvich provided me with a fuller understanding of the current research about alcoholism in Russian culture. Unless otherwise indicated, all translations in this book from the Russian are mine.

I would also like to acknowledge Rostislav Evdokimov and Howard O'Brien, two close friends who encouraged me at very early stages of this project and who have since passed away. *Vechnaia pamiat' (Eternal memory)!*

More than any single person, my wife Helga Druxes inspired and encouraged me to persevere with this project as a book. Her intelligence, unfailing editorial acumen, and thoroughgoing support were crucial for the completion of a project that was a first for me: writing about people who are still active. Our son Nicholas grew up during much of my writing of this book, and his good cheer always grounded me. In more ways than I can say, both he and my wife helped me in moving this project to completion.

# Timeline of the Mitki

1984: *15 Leningrad Artists* exhibition in Ust-Narva, Estonia, containing the work of Vladimir Shinkarev, Dmitri Shagin, the Florenskys, and others.

1984: Beginning of serialization of Vladimir Shinkarev's *Mitki* in the samizdat press.

1984–90: Annual exhibits of the Cooperative of Experimental Representational Art (Tovarishchestvo Eksperiemental'nogo izobrazitel'nogo iskusstva [TEII]), inclusive of the work of Mitki members such as Vladimir Shinkarev, Dmitri Shagin, and the Florenskys as well as works by Timur Novikov and his circle known as the New Artists.

1985: First exhibition of the Mitki in Ust-Izhora, Estonia, containing the work of Vladimir Shinkarev, Dmitri Shagin, the Florenskys, and others.

1987: *Days of Mitki Culture* (*Dni mit'kovskoi kul'tury*) exhibit at the Sverdlov House of Culture in Leningrad.

1988: *Mitki*, first retrospective exhibit at the Exhibit Hall of the Union of Artists, Kuznetskii Most, in Moscow.

1988: *40 Years of the Leningrad Avant-Garde* exhibit at the Gavan exhibition space in Leningrad.

February 15, 1989: Final withdrawal of Soviet troops from Afghanistan.

August 23, 1989: Mass protest of the linking of arms across the borders of the Baltic republics (Lithuania, Latvia, Estonia), representing the desire for secession from the Soviet Union.

1990: First publication in the mainstream, non-samizdat press of Vladimir Shinkarev's *Mitki: Drawings of Aleksandr Olegovich Florenski* (*Mit'ki. Risunki Aleksandra Olegovicha Florenskogo*) (Moscow: IMA Press).

December 25, 1991: Final dissolution of the Soviet Union.

April 30, 1992: Oleg Grigoriev—a prominent figure in absurdist underground poetry in Leningrad and a major influence on the writing and artwork of the Mitki—passes away.

1992: Viktor Tikhomirov makes his first movie, *Grass and Water* (*Trava i voda*).

1992–93: Sporadic publication of the *Mitki Newspaper* (*Mit'kovskaia gazeta*), containing the first publication of poetry by Oleg Grigoriev, Vladimir Shinkarev's *A Papuan from Honduras* and additional chapters of *Mitki*, and essays by Viktor Tikhomirov.

1994: *Mitki: The Retrospective Exhibition: 10 Years of the Movement*, the first major retrospective exhibit of the Mitki, at the State Russian Museum in St. Petersburg.

1995: The Florenskys' exhibit *Movement in the Direction of IYE* at the Borei Gallery in St. Petersburg.

1997: Vladimir Shinkarev writes the final chapter of *Mitki.*

April 11, 1999: Vladimir Shagin—Dmitri's father, a member of the original Arefiev circle of painters, and an important influence on the Mitki's artwork—passes away.

October 11, 1999, to January 11, 2000: Simultaneous exhibits of the Florenskys at the State Russian Museum: Olga Florensky, *Taxidermy*; Aleksandr Florensky, *Modest Architecture*; O & A Florensky, *A Moveable Bestiary.*

2000: First complete published edition of Vladimir Shinkarev's *Mitki*, in his collection *Sobstvenno literatura. Proza, stikhi, basni, pesni* (St. Petersburg: Grand).

2000: Viktor Tikhomirov makes his series of short films, *Mitki: The Flight of Icarus.*

2004: Viktor Tikhomirov films *Sokurov*, his documentary about the filmmaker Aleksandr Sokurov.

April 2005: Break-in and harassment of artists in the group's studio space on Pravda Street in St. Petersburg.

February 2–25, 2006: *Russian Trophy*, the Florenskys' exhibit at the State Russian Museum.

March 2008: Vladimir Shinkarev argues for the dissolution of the Mitki and states his intention to write *The End of the Mitki.*

Fall 2008: Closing of the Mitki's studio space and the opening, with support of the mayor's office, of the Mitki Art Center on Marat Street in St. Petersburg.

2010: Publication of Vladimir Shinkarev's *The End of the Mitki* (*Konets mit'kov*).

2016: Viktor Tikhomirov films *Andrei Kuraev: Direct Speech* (*Andrei Kuraev. Priamaia rech'*), his documentary about the Orthodox priest and public figure.

February 2–18, 2017: *The Arefiev Circle and the Mitki* exhibition at the Vellum Gallery, at the design center ARTPLAY in Moscow.

# The Mitki
# and the Art of Postmodern Protest in Russia

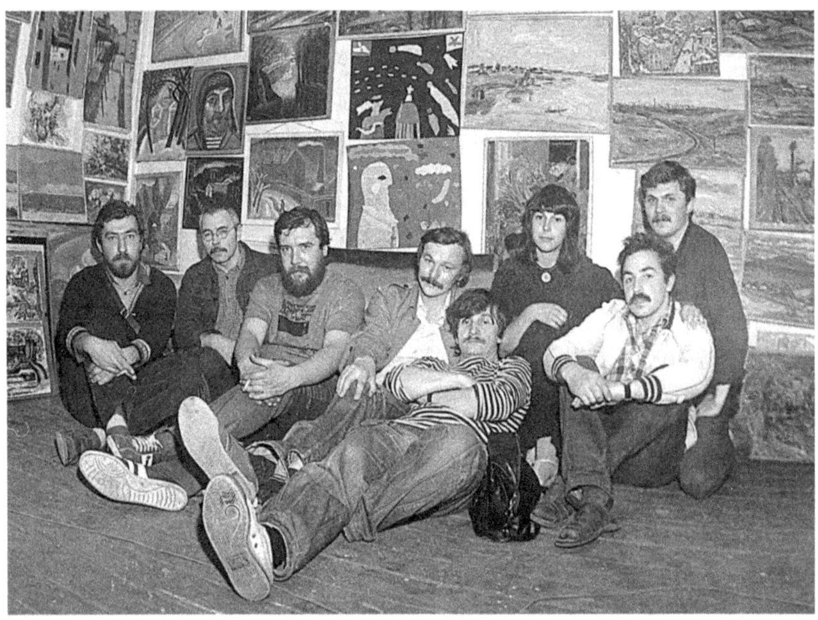

Figure 1. Group photo of the Mitki, taken by Viktor Nemtinov in 1989. *Front left to right*: Aleksandr Florensky, Vladimir Yashke, Dmitri Shagin, Vladimir Shinkarev, Viktor Tikhomirov, Olga Florensky, Andrei Kuznetsov, Vasili Golubev.

# Introduction

## Post Modern, or The Mitki's Chronicle of Russian Leadership

> We can't look at the Mitki outside the context of the Russian avant-garde, which, independently of all sorts of ideological circumstances, always found itself a bit further ahead of its European counterparts. . . . What always significantly helped us was the ideological shaking-up to which we were subjected. A prohibition gives rise to circumvention, and a locked door forces you to climb through the window. Everything that was free in Russia wore a mask. Who dared to speak freely? Clowns, minstrels, and holy fools.
>
> ANDREI BITOV, "The Mitki on the Cusp of Time and Space" (1999)

From the eighties of the last century to the present, political dissent has taken socially dynamic forms within the Russian art world. During the late Soviet period, Leningrad was a city where openings of unsanctioned exhibitions in apartments became an early manifestation of political performance art, highlighting an egalitarian fluidity of assumed identities that went against the grain of puritanical social etiquette.[1] Outside the two major cities, painters and sculptors with unconventional aesthetics maintained personal collections that emerged as nodes within a network of alternative spectatorship. This network paralleled the system of house museums and historical societies that were calculated to connect the Soviet regime's cultural narrative to villages and cities, whose local identities were otherwise at odds with it. In the Moscow metropolitan area, the presentation of unofficial art often took the form of outdoor exhibits, such as the famous bulldozed installation of the Lianozovo group in 1974, which were events calculated to provoke a punitive response from authorities. The Moscow artists and their affiliated theorists and art historian friends, such as Andrei Monastyrsky's Collective Actions groups, endeavored to bring about an interactive conceptualism that decisively razed the fourth wall between artists and the audience at hand. The more ambivalent the audience—bemused and bewildered, if not downright hostile—the better. Painting, sculpture, drawing, and printmaking were media that edged toward the status of adjuncts to a Gesamtkunstwerk, if not accessories to an actual criminal deed.

What has been left out of accounts of the unruly lived theater of Russian nonconformist art is the role and significance of the art collective known as the Mitki. The work of the Mitki includes satirical poetry and prose, pop music, cinema, and conceptualist performance art. The Mitki pioneered the form of politically multivalent protest art that has become a centerpiece of contemporary Russian dissident activism. In the mid-eighties, the untutored style of painting practiced by the Mitki was a provocation, running firmly against the naturalist principles of Soviet art. In his 1995 book *St. Petersburg: A Cultural History*, Solomon Volkov writes that "[the] Mitki embodied a stylized, local variant of Western hippie culture with a strong Russian accent. The main artistic achievement of the group was its ritualized lifestyle," which they led "dressed like outcasts" in "striped sailor shirts [. . .], old quilted jackets, Russian felt boots, and mangy fur hats with earflaps."[2] In fashioning a creative identity that brings together graphic design and a literary production of mock manifestoes with an aesthetic of performance art, the Mitki have much in common with American counterculture groups such as Ken Kesey's Merry Pranksters. Certainly, the Mitki direct their pacifist satire against political authorities in ways that also reveal a close kinship both to European avant-garde movements such as the Dadaists and Situationists. Yet the meaning of the group is much larger than the sum of its affinities and formative influences. The anti-Putin punk performance collective Pussy Riot, sentenced in August 2012 for its protest in Moscow's Church of Christ the Savior, would not have sprung into existence without the example of the Mitki's hybrid aesthetics of image, sound, and act. Pussy Riot's use of balaclava masks, invented by British troops during the Crimean War (1853–56), is particularly resonant with the politicized sartorial identity of the Mitki. Like the Mitki, members of Pussy Riot have worn items of clothing that evoke pivotal military and diplomatic debacles, such as the ill-fated nineteenth-century Crimean campaign. Both Pussy Riot and Pyotr Pavlensky—an artist who uses his body as a canvas for self-inflicted scars that speak truth to autocratic power, and who is currently seeking political asylum in France—use the Mitki's practice of costumed or bodily provocation against normative understandings of patriotism as a means for carrying out public acts of rhetorical ambivalence.

Our best initial strategy for approaching the diverse and wide-ranging work of the Mitki is to think of it as something very much like St. Petersburg today, consisting of a city center that is rich with associations that encompass the dislocations of regime change, collective trauma (most saliently the Nazi blockade of the city), and the narratives of the Leningrad political and aesthetic underground that were no less mythicized *post factum* than the accounts of the city's larger tragedies. As the late dissident historian and poet Rostislav Evdokimov writes, we need to think of the myth of the politically "unofficial" Leningrad as standing in a dialectical tension with the prerevolutionary "Petersburg myth," which possessed its own ambiguous fascination with the consequences of the charismatically autocratic will.[3] The Mitki attempt to draw our attention to the ways in which these two mythological points of orientation are locked in a perpetually unresolved standoff. In making our way through the sites of this conflict and their various conurbations, we need to ask for directions from the work of the Mitki itself. Given the gestural garrulousness that is such an important element of the Mitki's own mythology—and bearing in mind Edward Said's insight about analyzing literary texts based on the generous metacritical cues that they often provide for us—it seems completely appropriate, from a methodological point of view, to use a quizzical stance as a guide for making our way through the multimedia urban sprawl of the Mitki's visual and literary production. As Shinkarev asks in his chapters from *Mitki* written in 1984–85, "In recent times people have been talking about *mitkovian* culture—well, darn it [*dyk*] where can we try some of its fruits?"[4] In our introduction, we will not hesitate to ask the kind of questions that the movement asks about itself.

What does the word *mitki* mean? The answer to that question has as much to do with the mission of the movement as it does with the derivation of the word. Mitki is the plural form of *Mityok,* which is a droll and somewhat childish variant of Mitya, the most common nickname of

Dmitri. The name of the movement can be translated as "little Mityas" and refers to one of its most active participants, the painter and sometime poet Dmitri Shagin. The samizdat absurdist writer Vladimir Shinkarev, who had already gained underground notoriety for his 1980 novel *Maxim and Fyodor*—in which he amusingly traces the unexpectedly lyrical and mythopoeic possibilities of alcohol-induced social dysfunction within a country that officially boasted of having the well-adjusted citizenry befitting a "late" stage of socialism—became the satiric literary voice of the Mitki, while Shagin emerged as a voluble figurehead and public personality for the movement. Shinkarev sketches out the mythology of the movement in his book *Mitki*, which was serialized in several formats and different journals of the underground press from 1984 to 1987. In responding to the increasing renown of the Mitki's Tolstoyan pacifism within the Leningrad underground (*andegraund*), Shinkarev's serial narrative proceeds with a chatty momentum that suggests more the personal documentation of an alternate lifestyle than the compilation of a manifesto for an oppositional political program.

How can we interpret the Mitki? From one perspective, we may regard the group as a parody of both the Stalinist cult of personality and the highly personal, self-referential subcultures of Brezhnev-era dissident groups, with their heated political discussions over kitchen tables and coded slang protecting themselves from eavesdropping outsiders. The dissident as a "loafer," always on the verge of arrest for what the Soviet criminal code termed "parasitism" (*tuneiadstvo*), is clearly evident in the self-image of the Mitki. In their early years, the Mitki's credo of slackerish indolence clashed with the Soviet work ethic of labor, which often conceptualized abjuring one's ego as a particularly important civic virtue. The Mitki seemed to see themselves as people who scorned the Soviet collective in favor of their own. But this ethical choice was not a matter of exchanging one form of de-individualization or self-abnegation for another. As Shinkarev wrote in his early chapters of the book, "The movement of the Mitki does not demand depersonalization or the unification of expressive means"; indeed, "as a *Mityok*, you are not at all obligated to mimic Dmitri Shagin."[5] One could say of the communal spirit of the Mitki what their member Olga Florensky once wrote about the Arefiev Circle of painters and poets (of the fifties and sixties), to which Shagin's father, Vladimir, belonged: for all their self-mythologizing as cultural outsiders, the main hero of graphic and literary work of the Arefiev Circle was the city itself rather than any particular person (or artist, for that matter) who lived and worked in it.[6]

The Mitki established themselves in the mid-1980s, during the first tentative movements of the Soviet Union toward political reform. Like the poets Osip Mandelstam and the Nobel laureate Joseph Brodsky, the Mitki were vividly aware of their multifaceted status outsider selves: they positioned themselves as critics of Soviet expansionist geopolitics while also drawing on the military symbolism of a city that had once been both the seat of an empire and the grievous victim, during the second World War, of Nazi Germany. Certainly, the paradoxical pacifist and Christian-sounding slogan of the movement—that the Mitki's disinclination "to be victorious over anyone" becomes the means for their ultimate conquest of the world—draws attention to what the St. Petersburg-based Russian rock poet and occasional Mitki collaborator Yuri Shevchuk mockingly terms "the injustice of the good," or self-declared and hypocritical virtue, that informed Soviet-era military campaigns in countries such as Czechoslovakia and Afghanistan.[7] Particularly distinctive of dissident life in Leningrad during the seventies and eighties was the cultivation of unofficial and provocative "happenings." Among experimental artists such as the Mitki, these "happenings" often took the form of performances within spaces that would not seem fit for socializing and movement-building, such as in basements or the boiler rooms of buildings. The sweat of performance hung in the air of these spaces, which were often used by rock groups such as Viktor Tsoi's Kino for rehearsals and writing. As Shinkarev muses in a 1991 chapter from his *Mitki*, "The atmosphere of healthy anxiety, and a certain danger" within such spaces seemed to provide a sudden focus to "all emotions and potentials," evoking more the spiritual discipline of a monastery than the drudgery of a production line. "Yet 'monastery,'" he suggests, is "too strong" a term for the boiler room: "here there is no vow of celibacy, and women are invited."[8] Writing her own account of the Leningrad underground's social dynamism in the 1992 poem "A Basement Fairy Tale" ("Podval'naia skazka") Olga Florensky describes breaking into a locked basement only to step into a dream-like yet vaguely sinister interspecies utopia of humans and animals.[9] Her use of the plural first-person in the poem renders the gender of the teller of this tale indeterminate, as if its disappearance was the natural consequence of joining together with beings who are very different from her. The Mitki espouse an ambiguous and at times surprisingly progressive gender politics, and their postmodern political pastiches grapple with the difficult and multiphase transition from the final years of the Soviet Union to the often baffling economic and ideological realities of Putin's Russia.

My research draws on literary, art-historical, and political sources, as well as on extensive interviews that I conducted with Dmitri Shagin, Vladimir Shinkarev, Viktor Tikhomirov, Olga and Aleksandr Florensky, Irina Vasilieva, and other members of the Mitki. I explore the Mitki's project of sabotaging the ideological expectations of much of its Russian audience. Because of their sensitivity to the nuances of various ideological jargons, the Mitki are ideally situated as satirical critics of the language of Putin's Russia, where competing ideological agendas often find themselves in nonsensical alliances during moments of political exigency.

How do the Mitki understand the "postmodern" mission of their movement? As several critics and artist have noted, the term "postmodern" has often been too hastily fitted onto the different body sizes and shapes that comprise the vanguard of nonconformist and post-Soviet art.[10] The art historian and critic Boris Groys has defined the creative practice of postmodernism as a use of the stratagems of repetition, verbal collaging, and aggressive de-contextualization. Supplementing Groys's discussion of postmodernism with Jean-François Lyotard's useful emphasis on the iconoclasm of the "postmodern condition," we may define the postmodernist moment as the "meditation on the desire for the Other that is accompanied by a strategy of delegitimation [*sic*]" through the play with "quotations, 'polystylistics,' nostalgia, irony [and] the 'carnivalesque.'"[11] In creating carefully crafted and internally dissonant pastiches of Russian nationalistic and patriarchal ideology, the Mitki represent the most significant movement of political postmodernism in Russia. In their satirical writing and paintings from the eighties and nineties, they question the wisdom of the unreflective embrace of rehabilitated autocracy that is now a commonplace. In one of his early speeches, Vladimir Putin famously stated, in a ponderous Churchillian locution, that "anyone who does not regret the collapse of the Soviet Union has no heart, but anyone who wants it restored has no brain." It was with this sentiment in mind that he put together what the journalist David Remnick has aptly called a "'postmodern' collection of symbols for the new Russia—some tsarist, some Soviet, some sui generis—[a part of an] everything-to-everyone strategy."[12] The Mitki's preoccupation with reintegrating Soviet ideological artifacts into the rituals of their daily lives, such as the clothing and language of the Russian navy, serves as a prophetic correlative to what Masha Gessen characterized in 2015 as Putin's "retrofitted totalitarianism."[13]

The striking eclecticism of the Mitki's sources—ranging from lives of the Orthodox saints to the brushstrokes of Cézanne and the melodrama of Soviet-era *policier* films, such as *Don't Change the Meeting Place*, and Luchino Visconti's cinema of neorealism—represents the use of postmodernism as a tool for radical demystification, facilitating a direct contemplation of the present moment. I coin the term "postmodern realism" to describe the Mitki's strategy of demystification through a shattering of cultural illusions, by subjecting the ego of the cultural observer to an accelerated barrage of ideological shibboleths. We may apply the notion of the "shattering of the ego," developed by the critic Leo Bersani and the psychoanalyst Adam Phillips in their 2008 book *Intimacies*,[14] to describe the radical de-familiarization that is a crucial element of the Mitki's remaking and revision of received wisdom about national character. In their potent distillation of varied modes of clichéd thinking, speaking, and seeing, the Mitki seek to purge the self of false consciousness, placing it in a position of more genuinely observing, chronicling, and responding to the present. The postmodern realism of the Mitki is, above all, an idea that sets itself the task of enhancing political agency through a renewed contemplation of the interactive physicality of actors that we all are when we enter onto the public square; it is as much an aesthetic playbook for us to reengage in our physical situatedness, against all idealized notions of participatory communities, as it is a bid for coming to a renewed appreciation of the materiality of our lives and the corporeality of our selves.

In the collective work of the Mitki—by which I mean their production as an aggregate, as well as images and texts that reflect shared principles of the movement—we see the attempt to get beyond frozen, cliché-ridden preconceptions, through what the St. Petersburg-based art historian Liubov Gurevich terms the "mosaic" aesthetic of the Leningrad avant-garde. As Gurevich points out, this aesthetic is defined by a notion of a dynamic re-assemblage of a shattered ego.[15] Among artistic groups that identify themselves as culturally Russian, the Mitki are distinctive for being free of anti-Semitism and for acknowledging the important interactions between gentile and Jewish cultures within Russia. The work of the Mitki is significantly indebted to the poetry and painting of Jewish artists who lived in Leningrad from the fifties through the eighties. The Arefiev group of painters in Leningrad formed around the activity of the Jewish painter Aleksandr Arefiev (1931–78), whose work unflinchingly portrays social dysfunction within Soviet everyday life. The aesthetics and social commentary of the Arefiev painters and the

Russian-Jewish Leningrad poets who associated with them, such as Oleg Grigoriev and Roald Mandelstam, were in many respects precursors to the Mitki. The Arefievists' attempt to reconstruct Leningrad and St. Petersburg's identity as a museum of cultural hybridity, in which its residents experience a sense of themselves as spectators as well as participants, resonates with Dostoevsky's and Osip Mandelstam's astringent yet lyrical portrayals of the city. The little-known Roald Mandelstam (no relation to Osip) emerges as a key figure in the development of an absurdist romanticism, emblematic of the Arefievists' consciousness of themselves as nonconformist artists with a pronounced Jewish identity. Of special importance within the milieu of the Leningrad underground was a fondness for heightened role-playing, a theatricalization of everyday life that is strikingly exemplified by the work of the painter and sculptor Mikhail Chemiakin and the photographer Boris Smelov. That the latter was also Dmitri Shagin's stepfather only points to the hothouse luxuriance of cultural production in the underground of the seventies and eighties.[16] In his 1979 vintage silver gelatin print of the young Shagin and his fiancée Tatiana, Smelov has the couple archly look askance at the lens while raising champagne flutes, with Dmitri holding a tea kettle in an oddly emphatic gesture as Tatiana, dressed in a Ukrainian embroidered blouse, cradles a bowl of apples in her lap.[17] Here, the sitters are as much objects in a still life (a genre beloved by both Chemiakin and Smelov) as they are self-conscious actors. Much of the work of the Mitki in general—and of Olga and Aleksandr Florensky's multimedia production in particular—strongly suggests the object excess that Andrei Sinyavsky describes as the signature aesthetic of Nikolai Gogol's fiction, where "decoration" becomes something like "a multitude of small drawers popping out one after another, each jam-packed with life's bric-a-brac and fitted with all sorts of compartments, tiny shelves, and secrets."[18] The Leningrad underground's love of multifaceted performativity—of objects and people freely interacting with each other—was yet another distinct formative influence on the Mitki's development of their collective and synesthetic project.

In the constrictive environment of Putin's Russia, what political identity does the work of the Mitki take on? With their deliberate cross-pollination of militaristic patriotism and a fascination with the cultures of the Russian criminal underground and Soviet-era dissidence, the Mitki represent a highly polished mirror from which much of mainstream journalism in Russia can be refracted and clarified, especially in the shadow of the media dominance maintained by the current government of the Russian Federation. In 2008 Shinkarev used the public forum of the Russian media as an opportunity to announce that he was writing a book about the demise of the movement's bohemian and politically nonaligned principles, titled *The End of the Mitki*. Shinkarev took the highly unusual step of announcing the publication of his next book when he had barely begun it: the provocative book appeared in print only in November 2010, by which time Shagin and Shinkarev argued sporadically (primarily in interviews given to online journals) about the meaning and legacy of the movement.[19] Shinkarev contended that the Mitki had become a social and political "brand," citing in particular the apparent support of the movement's figurehead, Dmitri Shagin, for the policies and public causes advocated by Dmitri Medvedev, who was then president of the Russian Federation. By announcing simultaneously his abandonment of the movement and the publication of the first new book about the Mitki since the final serialized chapter of his *Mitki* in 1997, Shinkarev displayed a shrewd appreciation of the possibilities of publicity in the age of the Internet. Throughout the controversy, both Shinkarev and Shagin have engineered a public image of the artist as a voluble celebrity who uses several different avenues of informational and social media to burnish an already sharply chiseled image. Shinkarev and Shagin's talent for an extensively ramified self-promotion seems quite unusual for people who spent their formative years in the Soviet Union and surpasses in virtuosic manipulation of public response the efforts at self-representation by younger writers such as Vladimir Sorokin, Zakhar Prilepin, and Elena Fanailova.

This book is an attempt to understand the Mitki in a variety of contexts, and as practitioners of a fundamentally performative art. It is not a chronological account, or an examination of how they emerged from the highly diverse world of the Leningrad underground. The creative work of the Mitki represents a critical examination of the contemporary culture and possible legacy of the Russian intelligentsia. Using a palette of ambiguous terms that may be regarded as the literary equivalent of the intermediate tones and the deliberately uncertain compositional boundaries of their fauvist artwork, the Mitki express in the living theater of their broadcast social dysfunction a series of linked questions about social justice in Russia. These questions were largely inherited from the social conscience of the Russian nineteenth century and may be understood as unfolding in the following crucially causal sequence: "Who is to blame?"; "Who lives well in Russia?"; and "What is to be done?" The Mitki began as a movement of democratic horizontality; perhaps it should come as no surprise that the movement of the Mitki "ends" precisely when two of its original members vie for distinct roles or as leaders or spokespersons.

In this light, we come to appreciate the earnestly dissident aspect of a movement that framed itself as a parody of both dissident circles in Leningrad and the militaristic ethos of the post-World War II Soviet Union. Among other things, the Mitki provide a counternarrative to state control and authoritarian leadership. In the present Russian context—of a state that, in the spring of 2017, has resolutely returned to the autocratic fold, with Vladimir Putin and Dmitri Medvedev fully dispensing with the pantomime of change in the corridors of power—the idea of a democratic order that is usurped by one of its members certainly resonates powerfully. One might say that the current changing of the patriarchal guard in the Kremlin is already undergoing a scathing treatment at the hands of the thousands of Russian adolescents who protest both the brazen usurpation of public resources and the undermining of democratic institutions. In their pre-1991 satirical self-mythologization, the Mitki manifest a keen understanding of the situational or aleatory emergence of group identities and social movements, from random and seemingly inauspicious circumstances. An unruly conversation among artists on a bus trip in 1984 produces the name Mitki, from "Dmitri," and a provisional group identity that evolves into a movement serving as a counterpoint to belligerent nationalism; thirty-two years later, the flinging of green solvent onto the face of the oppositional presidential candidate Alexei Navalnyi becomes the ironic emblem of protest. Young protestors in major Russian cities subsequently painted their faces green, as a way of both memorializing their own beginnings as political actors and expressing their solidarity with a figure who, like Dmitri Shagin within the Mitki, is not so much a leader as he is a catalyst for—or node within—a larger network of social connection.

Shinkarev's analogy between the struggle over the legacy of the Mitki and the larger political stage is certainly made even more resonant by the fact that both his and Shagin's first names are identical to those of the two most powerful men in the Kremlin. In his *End of the Mitki*, Shinkarev suggests that the retrenchment of autocracy within the Russian Federation serves as an instructive example of the folly and injustice of any demagogic leadership that makes claims upon a community. Artistic movements and entire nations lose their cohesion and dissolve or end precisely when somebody arrogates to themselves the role and title of leader. By casting doubt upon the morality of even his own efforts at staking a claim as a founder of a group, Shinkarev produces in *The End of the Mitki* both an ironic elegy for the Mitki and a powerful critique of the resurgence of the autocratic tradition within Russian political culture. With this last literary work, Shinkarev offers up one of the most thoroughgoing democratic documents in Russia today, suggesting an absolute incompatibility between collective agency and the very concept of leadership, while also asserting a radical understanding of equality as a diffusion of power across lines of social and gender categories that has the potential to dissolve intersectional modes of oppression. A genuine political movement has either a nominal leader—a person who serves as a coordinator and facilitator of it, rather than an author of it—or none at all. In this regard, Shinkarev's understanding of the Mitki as both a group of artists and a youth movement is closer to the idea recently developed by the African American activist Angela Davis, of a "collectively exercised leadership" in which any given leader plays a role that is recessive and subordinate to the movement itself. As Davis explains, the worship of specific individuals as leaders is a trap, and we need to "adopt a critical stance on the conventional notions of leadership."[20] The fact that some of Davis's own writing was significantly influenced by post-Stalinist models of collective action, and by some of the less orthodox Marxist scholarship coming from the Soviet Union in the seventies, explains both the distinctive contour of her conception of leadership (which decouples the individualism and heroic life stories of leaders from the social movements that they claim to guide) and its confluence with critiques of the Stalinist cult of personality within the artistic underground in Leningrad and Moscow. In Shinkarev's own critique of Shagin's attempts at leadership of a movement that deliberately shunned such hierarchies, we hear more than a little of the dissident Soviet Marxist theorist Mikhail Lifshitz's observation, dating from 1968, that organic leadership can never emerge from a struggle for power, or within a state in thrall to personality cults that frame the figure of leader as a stern shepherd of an otherwise cattle-like and shiftless working class.[21] Notwithstanding Shinkarev's occasional avowals of cultural elitism and positive references to *loci classici* of modern conservative thought such as the work of G. K. Chesterton, in the present political moment his writing is as evocatively anti-authoritarian in its general principles as it is anti-populist in its implications.

While Shinkarev largely eschews the role of leader of the Mitki, there is no question that his books from 1984 to 1997 and 2010 about the movement effectively frame its beginning and its end. In chapter 1 ("Glimmer Twins of the Leningrad Underground: The Creation of Dmitri Shagin in Vladimir Shinkarev's *Mitki*"), I examine the creative evolution of his writing and artwork, focusing on the characterization of Dmitri Shagin as a parody of an autocratic ruler in Shinkarev's 1984–90 samizdat book *Mitki*. In March 2008, Shinkarev declared that the Mitki had run its course. Shinkarev made the announcement in a series of informal press conferences with online Russian journals, some of which were based in the movement's home city of St. Petersburg.[22] Already in 1984, he was contemplating the consequences of postmodernism as a creative practice (manifest in the cult of repetition, verbal collaging, and aggressive decontextualization) in ways that cut across the visual and literary arts. The Mitki is a youth movement devoted to the idea of a pointed disaffiliation from any party, political philosophy, or ideology; for them, such a gesture has the potential to become the purest form of political resistance. From this perspective, Shinkarev's dyspeptic view of cultural decline in contemporary Russia recapitulates his critique of Soviet official culture from the mid-1980s. The graphic and literary work of Dmitri Shagin does, of course, have its own autonomous existence, which is quite independent of any representation of it in Shinkarev's images and words. Each man is, however, vividly aware of the cultural production of the other, and both position themselves as dissimilar twins within the network of creative and personal relations within the group. If we can speak of any primacy of people among the Mitki, perhaps we may do so in this case recognizing the emblematic significance of the connection and intimacy that organically emerge out of dissimilarity and diversity.

Why do the Mitki devote so much attention to themselves as public actors who are molded by traumatized personal identities? In chapter 2 ("'Who Is This Heroic Man?' David Bowie and the Mitki's Queering of Masculinity"), I examine the complexities of gender identity and sexual orientation in the work of the Mitki. The Mitki cast themselves as downscaled and sexually ambiguous versions of the quasi-militarist heroes of Soviet-era official culture. In their representations of a Russian "Little Icarus," Olga Florensky, Dmitri Shagin, and Vladimir Shinkarev underscore the dangers of nostalgia and revisionism, with their accumulated burden of false wisdom that is invariably attained at the expense of an actual past or history. The figure of David Bowie in their work represents a heroic model for protean and restless self-identification. Am I feminine or masculine, Western or Eastern, normative or unorthodox in my orientations? The fact of earnestly asking oneself such questions is no less significant than the provisional answers to them.

What is the possible relation between alcoholism and authoritarianism in Russian culture? The Mitki's dissection of alcoholism—and more specifically the role that drinking played in the formation of their subculture—represents one of the most sustained portrayals of substance abuse within Russian literature, one that is eloquent and arresting for having been launched by artists and writers who were full-blown alcoholics when they wrote and painted their major works. The Mitki have argued that state policies against alcoholism (such as that of Gorbachev's "dry law") only exacerbated problems that they were meant to treat. Yet the Mitki are as ambivalent toward sobriety as they are to alcohol abuse. Here it is important to understand that they perceive an unexpected symmetry between periods of sobriety and the consumption of alcohol, insofar as both states of being represent attempts to shatter conventional, and often highly constrictive and unhealthy, understandings of one's self. What can the disinhibition of inebriation and meetings of twelve-step programs possibly have in common? In chapter 3 ("Fire Water: Alcoholism and Rehabilitation in the St. Petersburg of the Mitki"), I argue that the Mitki perceive alcoholism as a social practice that addresses social problems. The sociality of recovery from alcoholism has, for them, an element of what might be termed creative disinhibition. During the nineties, several members of the Mitki took part in the growing rehabilitation movement within Russia and became closely involved with the activities of the rehabilitation center House of Hope on the Hill (*Dom nadezhdy na gore*) outside of St. Petersburg. The twelve-step program (initially developed in the United States) strikes a balance between individual responsibility and the mutual support of a strong social context and becomes in the graphic art and writing of the Mitki a more clearly etched version of the immediate physicality and unfettered dialogue that embodied the Leningrad underground of the seventies and eighties. In his 1992 *Society of the Spectacle*, Guy Debord asserts that the mass media spectacle is "by definition immune from [real] human activity" and is also "inaccessible to any projected review or correction" and therefore inimical to the very principle of dialogue.[23] For a variety of cognitive reasons (related to the importance of group discussions and verbalization of problems within the twelve-step treatment for addiction), the Mitki have more recently focused on the problem of alcoholism in a way that foregrounds its oppositional synesthetic potentialities, by throwing up the bridges between language and visuality that facilitate the emergence of a social movement into the larger public realm.

In chapter 4, I examine the recent work of the "team" of Olga and Aleksandr Florensky. Much like the British artist collaborative of Gilbert and George, the Florenskys designate their collective work with a name that is reminiscent of a family business or a notary office. Under the eccentric glyph of "O & A Florensky," both artists attempt to foreground a blurring of male and female identity, in a way that draws attention to the possibilities for lambent interaction and play among gendered and individual selves within an artistic "brand." The fact that Katya Florensky, their daughter and now a well-known artist in her own right, participated in one of their recent exhibits only serves to draw attention to the Florenskys' performance of polyphonic creative labor within a cooperative. As the expatriate gallery owner Marat Guelman wryly acknowledged in his public statement for this exhibit of the Florenskys' meditations on Montenegro's landscapes, orthography, and fluctuating history of interdependence with Russia, "We in fact have not three, but rather four, different artists here: Sasha [Aleksandr], Olya, Katya, and 'Sasha and Olya.'"[24] The Florenskys are keen to frame collaboration among artists—whether it be in a social movement such as the Mitki or in what the Scottish psychoanalyst R. D. Laing often characterized as the internal tyranny of family or clan—as a series of tense negotiations between individual autonomy and collective identity.

The link between the deeper appreciation of visuality in all its forms—looking, reading, and observing—and the rehabilitation from addiction emerges as a distinctive feature in the recent work of the Mitki and is particularly evident in Viktor Tikhomirov's highly varied creative productions (chapter 5: "Satire, Sex, and Chance: The Creative Diary of Viktor Tikhomirov"). As the most productive member of the Mitki—and one whose work encompasses multiple creative domains of painting, political cartoons, literary satire, cinema, and social media—Tikhomirov achieves a higher synthesis of the group's concerns about the perils of collective delusions and self-indulgence. Tikhomirov uses the distinctive multimedia profile of his work to communicate an idiosyncratic understanding of autocracy as a social and institutional practice that represents a form of substance abuse. In an interview I conducted in 2005, Vladimir Shinkarev acknowledged the oppositional role of the artistic collective: "There is a difference between the culture of advertisement and a popular culture. Much of the Mitki's work was all about creating a parody of pop culture."[25] Tikhomirov documents what he sees as a genealogy of injustice in the lineage between the political cultures of Leninism and Stalinism. But Tikhomirov also understands quotidian life in the Soviet Union from the end of the Thaw to the early eighties as a break from this ideological continuum of Leninism and Stalinism, and he views the institutions of the late Soviet state as seized up with a profound sclerosis that caused them to retreat from the real lives of people. With this idiosyncratic understanding of the unexpected moral richness of the everyday during the final three decades of the Soviet Union—of interpersonal decency and unmediated intimacy as instances of a kind of emergent "deep state" within the Soviet Union—Tikhomirov positions himself as an opponent of the very category of the political. Yet Tikhomirov also expresses a deep unease with what he sees as the increasingly libertine character of post-Soviet Russia; he problematizes his portrait of the potentialities for ethical and free relations among women and men, asking us to consider the links between personal free license and the acceptance of authoritarianism.

In the conclusion ("Icarus Rising, or The Mitki against Twenty-First-Century Russia") I return to a more extended discussion of the Mitki's critique of isomorphic collectivism, begun in chapter 2 and further developed in the discussion of Viktor Tikhomirov's multifaceted creative output. The heterogeneity of the Mitki's sources and teachers—dissident yet also orthodox Soviet, Russian Orthodox Christian yet Jewish, naïvely folkloric yet imbued with the absurdist voice of high literary modernism—represents a revolt against the group ideal as one in which all members are identical. The Mitki are far more significant as a discursive model than they are as a brand. The group is acutely aware of the danger in becoming a character actor in what Valeriya Novodvorskaya (the former head of the Democratic Union) calls Putin's "comedies of national reconciliation,"[26] and Dmitri Shagin has been outspoken in his support of the punk protest group Pussy Riot.

I would argue that the work the Mitki, produced in their heyday from the mid-eighties to the mid-nineties, anticipates the conflicted status of the artist in a country that has become both consumerist and relentlessly ideological in its appeals to nationalist glory and pride; in their work from that time, the Mitki played with an image of a utopia that was paradoxical, insofar as it was both pacifist in its behavioral orientation and militaristic in its clothing and mock rituals. Many have argued for a fundamental rift in aesthetic orientation between the Moscow and

Leningrad/St. Petersburg movements of artists, a view that Andrew Solomon incisively sums up in the following assessment:

> No one in Leningrad was interested in conceptualism or performance or installations or objects; they made paintings, and though they made them to be meaningful, they also intended them to be beautiful. These early members of the Leningrad vanguard believed in the idea of the masterpiece, in the single work of art, in nature, life, and natural truth. Though the Leningrad artists of this period resembled the [Moscow-based] Lianozovo group, they were more serious, more earnestly engaged with a neo-Stalinist search for the perfect artwork.[27]

While much of Solomon's characterization of the antipodes that the Moscow and Leningrad/St. Petersburg art worlds represented rings true, I would suggest that the Mitki's interest in performative objects, as nodal points on the path to self-examination, brings them close to many goals of the Moscow Conceptualists. In a June 2013 interview, Monastyrsky states that his interest in action objects originated in an appreciation of the hermeticism of individuals during the Brezhnev era, a sense that each person was an ambulatory walled-off city that represented a cosmos of unarticulated feelings and unshared thoughts.[28] While the action object of conceptualism raises the possibility of shattering the closed-off self—the individual within a closed society—it, like the group actions of the Mitki, seemingly has little to say about wider forms of engagement. Yet for all that, the work of the Mitki and the Moscow Conceptualists positively thrums with the yearning for human connection! Both groups draw our attention to actors who are fully able to participate in a happening, regardless of their dispersal across wide and empty spaces. In his recently published memoirs, the artist Viktor Pivovarov speaks of his relations with the Moscow Conceptualists as teaching him a "new understanding of a painting," as something "unbounded" (*razomknutoe*). As Pivovarov explains, a painting takes on meaning only to the extent that it finds itself in a dialogue with the viewer and other artists. According to this understanding, frames accomplish nothing other than to separate and isolate the painting from the world at large.[29] In his 2017 novel *Eugene Telegin and Others*, Viktor Tikhomirov describes the Leningrad youth underground of the late seventies as caught up in events that seethed with "collective behavior." A sesquicentennial updating of Pushkin's portrait of privileged disaffection in *Eugene Onegin*, Tikhomirov's *Eugene Telegin and Others* recreates a time of heady synesthesia and experimentation, offering up an escape from social anomie that eluded Pushkin's ultimately heartbroken protagonist. In Tikhomirov's novel, jam sessions and unofficial exhibits of paintings vie for attention within the same "art-space," and otherwise starkly disparate and sullen young people manage to connect with each other in ways that mirror the stylistic eclecticism of the paintings and music that surround them.[30] Juxtaposing the otherwise very different movements of the Mitki and the Moscow Conceptualists, we begin to see how an artifact can become an event, if not a collective action.

Viktor Tikhomirov, Vladimir Shinkarev in *The End of the Mitki*, the younger artist Irina Vasilieva, and the team of O & A Florensky (as the latter two often refer to their collaborative) have endeavored to preserve and extend the legacy of the movement by imbuing it with a theory of the artifact as a catalyst for what Milan Kundera calls the "longing for repetition," a notion that seems, on its face, to be opposed to the idea of progress and enlightenment. In an early discussion of the symbiotic relation between postmodernism and consumerism, Fredric Jameson drew attention to the considerable potential of postmodernism to reinforce reflexive ways of thinking, through its use of pastiche as a kind of weaponized amplifier of reader or viewer expectations and generalized nostalgia.[31] In the hands of the Mitki, however, the desire for repetition of the past is also a desire for re-experiencing, and therefore potential reexamination. As the St. Petersburg-based art historian Ekaterina Klimova puts it, the presence of "*mitkovian* ideas" in Irina Vasilieva's work results in a graphic language that is reminiscent of the primitive and baseline aesthetics of Russian woodcuts (*lubki*), while also manifesting a laconic yet grotesque monumentality that draws our attention to an everyday reality (*obydennost'*) that is as terrifying as it is beautiful.[32] In his attempt to appeal to our interest in the materiality of a specific object within the realm of the seemingly unremarkable everyday, as a portal for the contemplation of ourselves as paradoxical agents of change, Shinkarev vividly emerges as a theorist who comes close to espousing an aesthetics that recalls the deliberately unmoored experientialism of the Moscow Conceptualists in general, and Andrei Monastyrsky's work in particular.

In his controversial 2010 polemic *The End of the Mitki*, Shinkarev argues that the Mitki began as a movement with a figurehead yet (quite pointedly) no leader. As Monastyrsky and the other participants note in several documents in *Trips to the Countryside*, the ritualistic and carefully choreographed nature of Collective Action would seem to militate against the idea of human intimacy, while raising an awareness of one's status as a bemused observer.[33] Vladimir Shinkarev strikes a similar note in his playfully satirical 2005 pamphlet *Mitkovian Dances*, a purported manual for dancing like a Mityok that references Dmitri Prigov and mimics the Collective Action group's droll instructional essayistic model. He notes that the Mitki's "happenings" from the eighties were often carefully staged parodies of themselves, others, and the very "principle of competition."[34]

Both the Moscow Conceptualists and the Mitki make ample use of patently pseudo-documentary material as a way of drawing attention to the difficulty of capturing live essences outside of their immediate media. Members of both groups compiled glossaries for their group language, which served the purported goal of shielding them from judgmental outsiders and providing the backbone for their worldviews. In both instances, however, the reader of these philological compilations is very quickly made aware that the "language" is essentially a fiction and the dictionary a form of *stiob*, a rebarbative "jamming" of normal communicative patterns and overturning of received wisdom. Most of the vocabulary in Vladimir Shinkarev's "Commentary for the Mitki Discursive Dictionary" (included in his 1991 book-length supplement *From the Materials for the History of the Movement*) is clearly fanciful—as exemplified by the definition of the invented word *ISKUSSTVODEVUSHKO* as a "[female] art historian, who serves the Mitki"[35]—and hardly unique to their circle, as any native speaker would immediately recognize the clear provenance of most of the words in Leningrad student slang and thieves' argot (*blatnaia muzyka*).

In many ways, the work of the Mitki during the eighties and nineties represents a tantalizing extension of the Collective Actions' legacy. In his preface to the *Dictionary of Terms of the Moscow Conceptual School*, Monastyrsky implicitly draws a parallel between the lexicographer's drudgery and the art critic's interpretive work. In writing about contemporary artistic movements that champion nonrepresentability, the critic and the lexicographer are inevitably transformed into distracted bookkeepers who construct incomplete inventories of exhibits and theoretical terminology; they are builders of a grid that is as useful in its supportive angularity as it is expressive in its eccentric asymmetry. Monastyrsky's notion of the documentation of conceptualism as the caprice of introspection tempered by the punctiliousness of fieldwork is arguably an amplification of paradigms from the criticism of the American art critics Harold Rosenberg and Clement Greenberg, who often draped their ornery assessments of specific artists and exhibitions onto the cool armature of a scrupulous chronicling of American Abstract Expressionism as a distinct movement. Quite possibly taking a cue from Shinkarev's modernist undercutting of *soi-disant* "objective" documentary endeavors, Monastyrsky writes that "there is something about the Moscow Conceptual School which resolutely defies museumification," a fact that can "be regarded as a source of either triumph or frustration."[36] In their secondary documentary materials, both Shinkarev and Monastyrsky make extensive use of lists of names and terms, along with drawings of relations among concepts that have limited propaedeutic value. Shinkarev and Monastyrsky offer explanations for the strategies behind their movements that are often more confusing than helpful; in some instances, they draw an almost gleeful attention to the peripherality of the cult of the individual artist-creator to the collaborative practices of their movements. Shinkarev's lists of the movement's members are included in the appendix to *Mitki* and structured in a way that distinctly recalls state security files, with their sterile and hostile categorizations of dissident circles (prioritized according to geographic location and to the purported level of political activity).[37] The chronicler's own account of the movement is, it would seem, tainted with the voice of punitive authority. The Mitki consistently draw our attention to movement politics as a potential miasma for the proliferation of unintended antidemocratic impulses. The Mitki's and the Moscow Conceptualists' quirky self-documentary efforts hint at a lived essence that is very real, if occasionally beyond the ken of the groups themselves. Can any movement or group understand itself? The answer would seem to be no, suggesting that only an outside viewer or reader can parse the significance of a group. In other words, we, the audience, are as much creative actors as the artists themselves.

Perhaps viewing his more recent paintings through the lens of this legacy of the arduous striving for the ideal of artistic collectivism, a few Russians visiting Shinkarev's Facebook page were taken aback by what they felt was the inhuman (*beschelovechnyi*) character of his 2008–11 series of St. Petersburg urban landscapes, titled *Gloomy Paintings*. In a response dated February 14, 2012, Shinkarev rhetorically asks, "Why 'inhuman'? I can understand [using the term] 'shelterless' [*bespriiutnyi*], [but] 'shelterless' is the most human thing of all." He goes on in the same posting to stress that the series is deliberately provocative in character and that he was especially appreciative of one visitor who felt that the very title of the series "for some reason really cheered [him] up," and another who wrote that they reminded him of his childhood dream of becoming a cosmonaut.[38] In keeping with the postmodernist creation of a domain where present and past—and high culture and low—are thoroughly leveled, and where forms of engagement themselves become an art, perhaps "Leningrad Conceptualism" is the most fitting description of the writing, painting, and public actions of the alumni of the movement at the present moment.

The Mitki is a movement of the fleeting gesture and fugitive genre, of the short form in literary production and the small-scale and situational one in the visual arts and social media: the sketch, the vignette, the portrait, and the Facebook post. They use the template of an unorthodox social movement as the point of departure for conceptualizing protest, built on a heightened understanding of ambivalent reader response. But is it truly possible to think of art that has no *fixed* political message as having the character of protest? Is indeterminacy reconcilable with the confrontational character of protest? Among other things, the Mitki ask that we consider the ways in which ideological indeterminacy and incoherence may have the affective features of opposition. Social media sites such as Facebook and vKontakte may open up possibilities for Shinkarev's own interpretive documentation of his work in collaboration with others, of painting as a lever for action and interaction. Social media has become a dynamic new platform for the dissemination of the Mitki's unorthodoxies. Several alumni of the group, most notably Olga, Aleksandr, and Katya Florensky, have posted on Facebook several of their paintings with representations of clearly imaginary postage stamps from a range of countries across the globe, as if to draw attention to the reinsinuation of older and more private or intimate models of communicative technology into new delivery systems.

For the Mitki, social media has emerged as a postmodern mailroom—what we might term a "post modern"—for the establishment of what Pierre Lévy characterized as the "molecular politics" of the "intelligent city" of cyberspace. Writing in 1997—coincidentally, during the apogee of the Mitki's reputation as painters and writers in what Mark Lipovetsky argues is a practice of "half-parodical, half-serious 'holy foolery'"—Lévy argues that such politics spring from the "deterritorialized [*sic*] networks of [the] global economy." Lévy sees such makeshift political orientations more as styles of being than distinct worldviews: they are "rhizomatic processes" that ultimately result in a collective intelligence that suggests not "the formulation of a [explicit political] program," but rather a "way of doing things, the description of a few rules in a new game."[39] As Rostislav Evdokimov notes, for security reasons much of the Leningrad political underground organized itself into semiautonomous clusters, each of which represents a single "egg" or "molecule" within a larger horizontal structure that we may understand as decentered and leaderless.[40] The present-day profile of the Mitki on Facebook and the Russian social media platform vKontakte reflects both a level of interactivity and a principled disaffiliation from any sanctioned political organization within Russia, reinforcing the ideal of a "leaderless" movement that had been the group's founding principle on the eve of the Gorbachev era. In the post-Brexit era of nativism and single-message ideologues, the refusal to answer questions about one's political standing may become the most potent form of rebellion. In a true artistic collective—as in a democracy—there are no leaders and followers, only fellow actors.

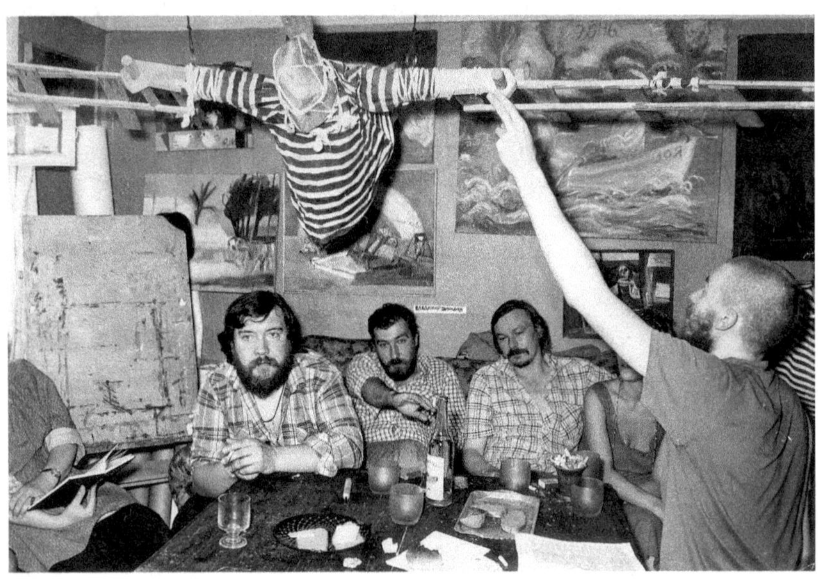

Figure 2. Group portrait of the Mitki, taken by Viktor Nemtinov in 1988. *From left to right*: Dmitri Shagin, Aleksandr Florensky, Vladimir Shinkarev, and Aleksei Mitin (touching a sculpture of Icarus).

# 1

# Glimmer Twins of the Leningrad Underground

## The Creation of Dmitri Shagin in Vladimir Shinkarev's *Mitki*

The early days of guitar weaving started then. You realize what you can do playing guitar with another guy, and what the two of you together can do is to the power of ten, and then you add other people. There's something beautifully friendly and elevating about a bunch of guys playing music together. This wonderful little world that is unassailable.

KEITH RICHARDS, *Life* (2010)

The clever ones already cast their lots on all they see
Locking themselves into bones and their muck
They laugh at those in wild passions still stuck
And sneer at everything that's yours or what's mine

I was given this role
I got a lucky number

YURI SHEVCHUK,
Leningrad-based rock musician and poet (1988)

Dmitri Shagin and Vladimir Shinkarev, the symbolic founders of the Mitki, are well-known for their dramatically self-nullifying declarations and shrewd rhetorical evasions. In a typical passage from his book about the movement (from the chapter titled "The Mitki and the Epoch of the Scientific and Technical Revolution"), Shinkarev asks, "What attitude do the Mitki have towards progress?" "I am pleased to state that the Mitki have staked out the wisest position on this question—that is, they have no attitude towards it at all."[1] Fittingly somehow, Vasiliev Island, the district of St. Petersburg where they live, produces the impression of a sparsely populated crossroads; it is an area of the city with multiple and in some instances only half-formed historical identities. Located in a widened part of the Neva River, with a shape on the map that suggests the wedge of a jagged arctic shelf caught in a current of thawing ice floes, Vasiliev Island is comprised of a jumble of eighteenth-century buildings at one end that gives way to a grid street plan structured according to a series of proposed canals that were never dug. Working in 1716 with the Italian architect Domenico Trezzini, Peter the Great envisioned the island as a central harbor and a fortified redoubt of government buildings, but over the years the original ambitions for the area as the administrative nerve center of the Russian empire were abandoned. Instead, Vasiliev Island became the amalgam of quiet residential streets for the middle and working classes, and the site for academic institutions (such as the Academy of Sciences) that it is known for today.

Although many parts of the city of St. Petersburg evoke the Mitki (such as the address of 70 Griboedov Canal, the address of the apartment where their 1984 unsanctioned exhibition of paintings took place), one site on Vasiliev Island is particularly evocative of the movement, in spite of having no direct connection with its history. Two sphinxes from the Middle East, sculpted in the fourteenth century BCE, flank the front of the Russian Academy of the Arts, near the eastern point, or "spit" (*strelka*), of the island. The sphinxes—whose faces are portraits of Pharaoh Amenhotep III from the eighteenth Dynasty, at different times of his life—produce an odd impression in their location before the Academy. Purchased by the Russian government from Egypt in 1832 and authorized by Nicholas I for their installation in honor of what was then called the Imperial Academy of Fine Arts—and, in the Soviet era, as the "Repin Institute" of fine arts—the sculptures are positioned in what seems a deliberately eccentric manner, facing each other rather than projecting from the front of the Academy entrance. The head of one sphinx is that of a young man with a beard, with an enigmatically neutral expression on his lean, chipped face; the other sphinx, also bearded, represents an older male with a fleshy face, thick lips, and a widely grinning expression. The contrasting pair of sculptures distracts from the solemnity of the Italian baroque façade of the Academy while also sharply contrasting with its style, forcing the viewer to contemplate them, somewhat at the expense of the building it was meant to embellish.

Like these statues, the Mitki are cultural transplants within the present lives of Russian institutions. Alumni of the group have increasingly found themselves in official settings and occasions which they never could have imagined in Soviet times, such as a special ceremony devoted to them during the 2003 tercentenary celebrations of the city's founding. Like the sphinx statues, they have been appropriated to stand before symbols of official culture to which they otherwise bear no relation, and for whom they now have become paradoxical relics that point up the continuity between different forms of imperial glory. From the sixties through the eighties, almost all Mitki received their training in venues other than the Academy, which for over two hundred years has had a remarkably consistent reputation as being highly selective yet artistically orthodox. In contrast to the values of the Academy, the Mitki were educated in institutions and informal organizations that took a more expansive view of traditions of artistic production, such as the Leningrad Higher School of Industry and the Arts (also then known as the Mukhin School) and the Cooperative of Experimental Graphic Art (TEII). Certainly, they were not the first Russian artists to take on the values of this institution. The Russian "Itinerant" painters (*Peredvizhniki*) rallied against the neoclassical aesthetics of the Imperial Academy of the late nineteenth century, in a self-dramatizing emulation of the French Impressionists' spirited opposition to the aesthetics of the Salon. The Mitki see themselves as belonging to a countertradition that defines itself in terms of an improvisational openness and a rejection of any single aesthetic ideology. Perhaps it is no surprise that the Mitki see themselves as heirs to Cézanne as well as the Russian Itinerant painters. Over the course of thirty years of writing (some of it distinctly retrospective in character), they have succeeded in engineering a heterogeneous bloodline of their formative influences, the eclecticism of which serves as an anticoagulant against the stultifying ideals of neoclassical representational art and distinct iconographic traditions.[2] At the same time, the particular nonconformism of the Mitki—their embrace of a frankly rebellious attitude of what Shinkarev in 2010 called a "sympathetic riotousness" or unruliness (*simpatichnoe razdolbaistvo*) embodied in the figure of Shagin, clearly the obverse of his characterization of him in 1984 as a "sympathetic layabout" (*simpatichnyi shalopai*)[3]—contained the seed for movement-building. The Mitki have always been hawkishly keen on establishing their own tradition, which (like the colonialist installation of the sphinxes on Vasiliev Island) faced in directions that pointed not to the entrance into the Academy, but to each other. Their exaggerated love of group insularity is a bid for the formation of creative identity, informed by at least the spirit of political resistance.

Yet as almost all the Mitki now readily and somewhat ruefully admit, they have become their own "name brand," undercutting their status as a group whose original identity was an affiliation of nonconforming artists. In stark contrast with Shagin's childlike fauvist paintings and gregariously Falstaffian public persona, Shinkarev projects an astringent irony and irreverent absurdism in his writing and artwork. As early as 1984, Shinkarev noted the contradictory overall persona of the typical Mityok, based on the public demeanor of Dmitri Shagin: "the face of the Mityok is highly diverse," representing all at once the figures of Hamlet, Falstaff, and the uncouth and tragically passive Russian peasant Anton Goremyka.[4] In his writing about the Mitki from the mid-eighties to the present day, Shinkarev draws our attention to the fact that Dmitri Shagin has always treated his public persona as a carefully maintained construct, expressed in the fact that aspects of his behavior can be understood as an aggregate of Shakespearean and Russian archetypes.[5] Certain aspects of the real-life Shagin's behavior—particularly his talent for self-promotion, currently reflected in his touring with the journalist and semi-retired rock musician Vladimir Rekshan in a musical ensemble with the fey neologistic moniker "Rekshagin"—dovetail with Shinkarev's characterization of him as mercurial and somewhat self-involved trickster. Like Shakespeare's power-conscious buffoon, Shagin is as gregarious in his public bearing as he is shrewd about the regard of others. While his lord and filial surrogate Prince Hal may indulgently call him a "sweet creature of bombast" (*I Henry IV*, II.iv, 326–27), in more unbuttoned moments Falstaff acknowledges the murkiness of his own motives, seeing them as products of a "goodly portly man i' faith, and a corpulent cheerful look, a pleasing eye" who also trades in mild—if nonetheless "lewdly given"—forms of deceit (*I Henry IV*, II.iii, 422–23, 427).[6] In some sense, we may regard Shinkarev and Shagin as emblems for tragedy and comedy in the group's treatment of the difficult yet absurd reality of the Soviet experience, the serious and happy masks of theater in a city whose architecture seems to invite a sense of open-air theatricality.[7] Yet like the relationship between Prince Hal and Falstaff, the question of the location of authority and power—of who is the master and who the novice, who is the parental figure and who the protégé—vibrates throughout the narrative of their friendship. Like the sphinxes in front of the Academy, Shagin and Shinkarev seem to represent two different stages in the development of a single person.

The story of this friendship is fraught with variations on doubleness, deceit, and nonidentical twinship. We feel as if we are invited or encouraged to meditate on the productive ambiguities of friendship—how difference and disagreement may tip over into collaboration and productivity—when we read and see the story of this specific human polarity on the canvas of a group history that began as an oppositional youth movement in the pre-glasnost and pre-perestroika eighties. Another model of partnership makes its way to our awareness from out of the anecdotal thicket of the dealings between Shagin and Shinkarev, and from the clamorous aggregate of their writing and painting. Among other things, we are struck by the asymmetry of creative activity between the two men. The paucity of Shagin's writing—which consists almost entirely of light verse composed with an eye to musical accompaniment, collected into a booklet published in 2002—is dwarfed by the volume and high-wattage modernist ambitions of Shinkarev's wide-ranging textual output, like the dim lightbulb in the vestibule of a building in St. Petersburg that blends into the stronger beam of light cast by a streetlamp. Conversely, in the realm of painting and graphic art, Shagin has been more productive than the perfectionistic Shinkarev, whose canvases eschew the rapid cartoon-like outlines that characterize Shagin's brushwork. Shagin's technique of painting suggests the stylistic boundary-crossings of the French Expressionist Georges Rouault. With their wide and seemingly hurried brush outlines, Rouault's lithographs are almost perversely more evocative of the methods of gouache drawing than they are of the conventions of printmaking from his time. In a similar vein, when we stand in front of a Shagin painting, we see a composition in oil that evokes the immediacy of a watercolor struggling against the hefty swaths of paint imposed upon it. With their stark temperamental and creative differences, Shinkarev and Shagin have always operated less as friends than as partners with dissimilar personal and artistic styles.

The heterogeneous pairing of Shinkarev and Shagin—the projection of them as "glimmer twins" of the movement (in the mold of Mick Jagger and Keith Richards), representing two very different models of masculinity, the dandyish and the crude—serves as a correlative of the Vasiliev Island sphinxes' enigmatically bland and smiling expressions, with the fleshy lips of one of them suggesting a gender ambiguity that has always been a hallmark of the Rolling Stones' lead singer. We pause to think about collaboration as the meeting place between asymmetrical forces, with Shagin as the largely nonverbal and unpolished partner—as a person whom Russians, in an evocative colloquialism, might call *neobtyosannyi* or "rough-hewn," as if the back-and-forth of daily sociability were like a hand plane giving shape to a gnarled piece of wood. Shagin emerges as a Richards to the Jagger of Shinkarev, who cuts the figure of a poised group propagandist and hyper-articulate public face that channels and fronts the transrational and distinctly nonverbal source material (both image- and music-based) of the Mitki's work. Observing the Rolling Stones in a 1972 concert, one journalist saw Richards as "sprout[ing] out of [Jagger's] nightmares," an "evil *doppelganger* [*sic*] or brother to whom [the nominal leader] always defer[s]" in fashioning the "sounds that mere energy and intelligence could not provide."[8] Such a dichotomy of artistic labor also functions as an unexpected guarantor of the heterogeneity within the group, serving as a pressure valve against the onset of deadening conformism and isomorphous sameness. In his 2010 autobiography, Richards himself describes the dynamic between himself and Jagger as being akin to the collaboration of a "pair of weavers," who lose sight of "who's conducting" when they perform together.[9] There is much to be said for the applicability of this principle of heterogeneous reciprocity to the interaction between Shagin and Shinkarev in the early years of the group's existence. This paradigm of collaboration diverges sharply from the Soviet ideal of group identity as a collectivist mass with identical cells; it also is largely incompatible with the conciliar (*sobornyi*) model of community advanced by Slavophiles prior to the Revolution and often reiterated by Russian nationalists in the present day. The latter model, of *sobornost'* or conciliarism, avows to favor the self-sacrificial absorption of the individual into the group. The foundational partnership of Shinkarev/Shagin revels in its awareness of a divided self, creating the conditions that make possible the coexistence of multiple incommensurate identities within a single group. One of the most vivid representations of this model of productive asymmetry in rock music was Donald Cammell and Nicolas Roeg's 1970 film *Performance,* which has Jagger himself playing a pop star who, in a manner somewhat suggestive of Joseph Conrad's *The Secret Sharer*, exchanges identities with a London gangster played by James Fox. As we shall see in the next chapter, *The Man Who Fell to Earth,* Roeg's later film with another pop star (David Bowie), plays a significant role in Shinkarev's sketching out of the group mythology of the Mitki.

The exacerbated dramatization of this tension within the artists' cooperative is no less important to the Mitki than their actual texts, graphic work, and films. It is not for nothing that Shinkarev defines a typical member of the group as being an "artist of behavior within the world" (*khudozhnik povedeniia v mire*), a person who uses actions to bring about a "carnivalization of [daily] life" (*karnavalizatsiia zhizni*).[10] Not noted by Shinkarev is the fact that Shagin himself—both in public, and on page and canvas—is no less caught in this role of the artist as an engaged documentarian whose works take on their full meaning only when he comments on them. Among other things, both Shinkarev and Shagin share a belief that the artist's behavior is a part of the art. Neither has any patience with the notion of the purity of the work of art, of it speaking exclusively for itself. For them, commentary and the free play of the creative worker's metacriticism are essential to any understanding of a painting or public act. As Shagin stated in an interview from 2013, "we [Mitki] want to improve the world."[11] In the same interview, he drew a close parallel between the artists of his generation, who cut their eyeteeth during the heady openness of the late eighties, with the feminist performance art group Pussy Riot. For all their aesthetic, ideological, and temperamental differences, both men regard crafted objects as having a performative dimension and, conversely, public acts as being guided by pictorial compositional principles. As Shinkarev explains in his 2010 polemical memoir *The End of the Mitki*, the slang and behavioral tics of the Mitki were not examples of actual "speech defects" (*kosnoiazychie*) or of the primitiveness of cognitive tools, but rather of a "consummate perfection that [only] resembles imperfection." He goes on to say that in its day the artificial construct of the Mitki's lifestyle represented the ideal of an open simplicity, akin to the compositional sparseness of the nineteenth-century French artist Honoré Daumier's late prints and drawings.[12] As we shall see, the story of the schism between the two men quickly became its own installation of postmodern protest.

The apparent rift in this partnership took place during a lull in the coordinated projects within the group. In March 2008, Shinkarev declared that the Mitki, the group he helped to form in the mid-1980s, had run its course. He made the announcement in a series of informal press conferences with online Russian journals, some of which (such as *Fontanka* and the local edition of *Novaia gazeta*) were based in the movement's home city of St. Petersburg.[13] *The End of the Mitki* is a volume that is over three times the length of Shinkarev's earlier volume and may legitimately be understood as a continuation of the group manifesto. *The End of the Mitki* is clearly the more polemical of Shinkarev's two major texts. The new volume is a fascinating series of observations about corruption and decline resulting from the coupling of personal vanity and opportunistic ideology. Such a pairing reflects the supply-side pragmatism of post-Soviet Russia, as it evolved from its forthright social Darwinism under Yeltsin to the retrenched state nationalism during the Medvedev and Putin era. Every rhetorical flourish evident in Shinkarev's 1986 *Mitki* is audible here: the fragments of an absurdist drama of layabouts and *clochards* in the late Soviet era, the slyly disorienting series of parodies of genres as disparate as children's poetry and Jungian literary criticism, and the subculture's use of a drolly anthropological tone as its public voice addressed to the mainstream. As in *Mitki*, all of these elements are linked by a consideration of volatile personal relations within the group; indeed, one could say that gossip is elevated from mode to method, as a tool for interpretation that draws on the postmodernist aesthetic of what Fredric Jameson calls "the transformation of reality into images, the fragmentation of time into a series of perceptual presents."[14] The new book—an omnibus of varied cultural analysis, political commentary, memoir, and theatricalized score settling—is arresting for its pointed moral critique and eccentric digressive approach. In *The End of the Mitki*, Shinkarev notes that the Mitki, as a "mythological mass youth movement," resemble Plato's ideals or "forms," which "will never die, get sick or grow old."[15] *The End of the Mitki* may be viewed as an extended elegy for the movement, as Shinkarev's valedictory for a movement that abandoned its foundational principle of viewing youth and rebellion as artificial personae, and as a work whose aesthetic recalls Susan Sontag's characterization of camp as a "solvent for morality." At the same time, such artificiality has, as Sontag points out in her famous essay "Notes on Camp," the character of suasion, if not the potential for the facilitation for movement-building. Among many things, camp is "a mode of seduction [that] employs mannerisms susceptible of a double interpretation," involving "gestures full of duplicity, with a witty meaning for cognoscenti and another, more solemn, for outsiders."[16] Not lost to Shinkarev is the fact that his divulging of the group secrets, and the manner in which its members interpret them, results in at least the conceit of undermining cognitive elites. The figure of Shagin in Shinkarev's work, and in his own literary persona, draws attention to this paradox of proselytization when he states that "the Mitki do not want to be victorious over anyone. . . . They'll always be in the crapper [*v govnishche*], in a losing streak . . . (*in a whisper*) and that's how they will win the world."[17]

With his publication of *The End of the Mitki* two years later, Shinkarev's bid for the movement's dissolution was complete. Nested within this announcement, however, was a declaration of a rather specific character: Shinkarev wanted to extricate his work from that of the very self-advertising Dmitri Shagin, who was laying increasing claims as the sole founder of the movement. The divided partnership of Shinkarev and Shagin—and the water and oil nature of their dealings with each other—is evident from the documented beginnings of the Mitki as both a group of artists and a youth movement. Certainly, the two men's battle over the PR of the "brand" of the Mitki echoes the group's playfully confrontational relation to the larger world. Perhaps the most important aspect of this controversy is the way in which Shinkarev's 1984–85 literary text becomes a catalyst for the formation of both a movement and an artists' circle. The art critic Liubov Gurevich has convincingly argued for the strong novelistic qualities of Shinkarev's *Mitki*. Disagreeing with the public statements of a person who served as the basis for a character in one of your texts is one thing; attempting to expunge such utterances from a movement is quite another, especially if the movement in question was decisively formed by the *vade mecum* of a novelistic text. A text like *Mitki*, which quickly finds an audience, cannot be unwritten or effectively retracted—its seal has already been stamped upon the minds of readers. One way of at least modifying a popular text—thereby changing the gravitational pull among its various characters and narrative details, and providing a more critical perspective on them—is to do what Cervantes did with *Don Quixote*: to add to it in a way that imposes a metanarrative perspective onto a problematic protagonist. This is what Shinkarev accomplishes through the publication of *The End of the Mitki*: it is a continuation and completion of the novel he wrote twenty-five years before. Yet if this is so, we need to ask: what is the passional center of this novel's story?

The answer to that question will emerge at a later point in our discussion. Taken on its own terms, Shinkarev's first book about Mitki seems very much like an unfinished work. What emerges from even the earlier book is that Shinkarev understands the Mitki as a project in perpetual development, if not in a distinct evolutionary arc. Counting its numerous appendixes, the earlier volume was written over a period spanning thirteen years, from 1984 to 1997, and in two distinct countries. Like many a cofounder of what was originally a young person's group—whether it be a movement or a band—Shinkarev in *The End of the Mitki* voices concerns about ideological co-opting and commercialization. In Shinkarev's retrospective view, the initial incarnation of the Mitki enables us to date the arrival of postmodernism in Russia by at least seven years before the Soviet collapse. Dmitri Shagin's vision of the Mitki as a marketable "brand" or label essentially sabotages the group's previous creative practice, which called for the transformation of ideological artifacts such as the Stalinist cult of personality into performances of absurdist drama.[18] Here and elsewhere in *The End of the Mitki*, Shinkarev establishes a principled and somewhat counterintuitive opposition between commodification (in all its forms and stages of development) and postmodernism itself. With pungent idiosyncrasy, Shinkarev understands postmodernism as a spoiler for both commodity fetishism and the cult of consumption. Do you see, he asks us, that this is a dead husk of exploited labor—manufactured *ad infinitum*—and not a talisman for shoring up a shattered self? When an object is repeated, it loses its mystique and status as a prized commodity. Postmodernism is a project that contemplates the possibility of democratization, of property losing its value as a determinant of status and personal worth.

Shinkarev writes in *The End of the Mitki* that "the paintings of the Mitki consist of repeated copies [*povtorov*]," to the point that even many of their exhibits had originals side by side with multiple copies of them.[19] The purpose of this, according to Shinkarev, was to find a connection with an audience that desires what it perceives to be a specific image, while the artist in fact produces for them a variant that they cannot perceive as diverging from the original that they demand. Such slight variations create a "subtle rhythm" among the series of copies. Shinkarev goes on to say that while this rhythm is not the reason for the act of recopying, it has an experiential aspect of engaging in Gilles Deleuze's notion of the incessant repetition as an attempt to make good on lost chances.[20] One might also add that Shinkarev is creating here a distinctive synthesis of different conceptions of postmodernism that are often seen as being at odds with one another. Shinkarev demonstrates that the theory of postmodernism is itself a pastiche and therefore no more genuine or real than the artifacts that it seeks to decenter and trivialize. Reading *The End of the Mitki,* we see how ideas in the public sphere awkwardly reach out to each other, in ad hoc orchestrations; we see how Deleuze and Guattari's interest in culture as a decentered rhizomatic network is installed as a generator of Baudrillardian simulacra, which in turn is modified into a maker of catalysts for a Lyotardian euphoria over the demolition of guiding epistemologies. In Shinkarev's 2010 book, Shagin emerges as a diabolical hip-hop artist, sampling the works of others in a manner that suggests a postmodernism without its usefully bracing irony and mockery.[21] In the first chapter of *Mitki*, which Shinkarev wrote in 1984, he describes Shagin with mock-epic drollery: "like every vanguard in a mass youth movement, Dmitri Shagin experiences conflict with society."[22] In other words, the figure of Shagin is merely one of many in a movement that has broken from the central narrative of the country in which he was born and raised. As if to assure the reader that the movement is not defined by what Jean Baudrillard calls "a definitive code, of which [everyone] is a miniscule terminal," in the next chapter, from 1985, Shinkarev writes that "the movement of the Mitki never suggests depersonalization [*obezlichki*] and the unification of expressive means: being a Mityok, you in no way are required to mimic Dmitri Shagin."[23] In *The End of the Mitki*, Shinkarev gives more explicit expression to that Baudrillardian "terror of control [and] the definite code" where the complete lack of inhibition has resulted in us no longer "playing, but rather manufacturing [*upromyslivaem*] the movement of the Mitki."[24] Much like the work of the French Situationists, the Mitki's work ideally engages in a form of play that is driven by guidelines, designed to draw attention to the performance-related and artifice-driven aspects of rebellion; such "play" is ritualistic, expressing a bracing skepticism about the actual possibilities for spontaneity and agency in a world reigned over by what Baudrillard calls a "transfinite universe of simulation."[25] In addition to the wide eclecticism of sources (from post-structuralism, Buddhist sacred texts, and American and Russian pop culture), what unites *Mitki* and *The End of the Mitki* is a panic about the lure of undemocratic impulses within mass movements.

As we shall see, for Shinkarev much of this drama over the integrity of the Mitki takes place in the specific field of activity that he shares with Shagin, as a co-builder of the movement. There can be little doubt that the elegiac understanding of the passage of time—and the corruption of many individuals as they move from the very private domain of a social, political, or artistic circle to the public sphere—is present as a distinct thematic in the early group work of the Mitki. Dmitri Shagin's 1984 poem "Little Icarus" is a meditation on Brueghel the Elder's painting *The Fall of Icarus* that brazenly shoplifts a couplet from W. H. Auden's "Musée des Beaux Arts." Employing a tone and images reminiscent of A. E. Housman's and Siegfried Sassoon's elegiac characterizations of the young (and perhaps callow) hero cut down tragically in his prime, Shagin sketches a picture of alienation that would resonate with his target audience of the Leningrad bohemian underground, while also hinting at the human cost of the still-unfolding Soviet-Afghan war:

Everyone thrives placidly, and with feeling;
All is well for them, others, and for the birds overhead.
Only from afar does the plowing peasant
Hear the meager splash.

The God-bearing man spits on the howl of little Icarus,
For he is taken up with important work.
The sun gives to the earth a noontime sweat,
As a little boat makes its way for bread.

But for the poor little Icarus,
Forgotten by all his brothers,
Only his white legs stick out
Of the cold green waters.[26]

(Shagin, "Little Icarus")

After reading this, we realize that Shagin jettisons the almost icy language of Auden's description of Icarus' fatal plunge:

In Brueghel's Icarus, for instance: how everything turns away
Quite leisurely from the disaster; the ploughman may
Have heard the splash, the forsaken cry,
But for him it was not an important failure; the sun shone
As it had to on the white legs disappearing into the green
Water; and the expensive delicate ship that must have seen
Something amazing, a boy falling out of the sky,
had somewhere to get to and sailed calmly on.

(W. H. Auden, "Musée des Beaux Arts")

One of the virtues of the Mitki as a movement was its ability to transform literary genres such as Soviet-era verse written for children into objects of ironic contemplation. In Shagin's poem, we hear anguish over joblessness, social anomie, and the premature death of a youth who is regarded with contempt by a "God-Bearing" zealot (*bogonosets*) who may be a stand-in for a militant defender of Soviet ideological pieties. In a chapter from *Mitki* dated 1985, Shinkarev names this text as foundational for the movement, in at least two respects. First, he points out that the acute sense of anomie and isolation expressed in the poem (which was not published until the post-Soviet era) reflects the Mitki's awareness of themselves as social and political outsiders; secondly, he notes that various phrases in the poem became absurdist conversational non sequiturs in the daily life of the movement, as in replying to "How's it going?" with the "only his white legs stick out." The most basic forms of communication become somewhat redeemed from their superficiality and banality, through contact with unanticipated statements of a person with fixations on a specific narrative. What is crucial here is an understanding of the Otherness of others, even within the same group. While Shinkarev presents the iconography of Brueghel the Elder's painting as being a part of the mythology of the Mitki, he also underscores that the preoccupation with the painting is distinctly Shagin's and not that of Shinkarev and other members of the group. As Shinkarev wryly notes in one segment from his earlier book (dated 1985), Aleksandr Florensky once observed that Shagin had retold the story of the painting to him as if it were something that took place just five minutes ago.[27]

In both of Shinkarev's books about the Mitki, the eruption of gossip—of mildly sardonic or openly derisive speech that is reported second or third hand—takes shape as a dynamic verbal pastiche, as a chronicle of ideological counterpoint, if not polyphony, within a circle of interlocutors.[28] Shinkarev's notion of the group dynamic as possessing a polyphonic character is especially important here, and later we will consider its democratic ramifications. The reflective sadness of Shagin's affect-driven borrowings from Auden stands in dramatic contrast with Auden's apparent abjuring of any sense of the painting as an objective correlative for the museum visitor's emotional state. Shagin lifts material from Auden's poem as an unabashed celebration of the persistence of narcissistic identification, rendering his perception of both Brueghel and Auden as an occasion for contemplating the often patent absurdity of neurotic fixation. Given the fact that Shinkarev does not acknowledge the provenance of the poem in his 1985 segment from *Mitki*, we might say that he freely shares in the spoils of Shagin's theft. In the same discussion from that book, Shinkarev points out that one of the other phrases from the poem ("everyone thrives placidly") is an echo from a throw-away line from Soviet-era *policier* mini-series *Don't Change the Meeting Place*, the flavor of which is best rendered in the American English of Damon Runyon: "Two young twists are hanging out with Vasya Vekshin, while the crooks are vamoosing!"[29] Shinkarev's transformation of Shagin's poem into a viral meme within the movement—into what Omry Ronen, in his study of Osip Mandelstam's poetry, describes as the "lexical reiteration" (*leksicheskii povtor*) that counterintuitively generates a highly diverse content—is a meditation on the intersection of one text with a variety of others. Shinkarev seems to be saying that there is no single clear-cut provenance—literary, painterly, or cinematic—to Shagin's text.

What we see from all this is that Shinkarev was contemplating as early as 1985 the fruitful consequences of postmodernism as a creative practice (manifest in the stratagems of repetition, verbal collaging, and aggressive decontextualization) in ways that cut across the visual and literary arts. We can argue that the poem above, with its sampling from Auden, manifests what Boris Groys has defined as postmodernism's use of "quotations, 'polystylistics,' nostalgia, irony [and] the 'carnivalesque'" as a way of expressing a desire for another person—in this case, for a beautiful dying youth—which, for whatever reason, cannot be admitted to through other means.[30] In *The End of the Mitki*, we find the first acknowledgment in any of the writing by or about the Mitki that Shagin had transposed lines from Auden's "Musée des Beaux Arts" into his poem. In Shinkarev's view, Shagin's theft was an act of dynamic creativity: "Mitya, to his credit, did not tarry [*ne polenilsia*] in copying out W. H. Auden's 'Musée des Beaux Arts,' only adding diminutive suffixes to the nouns."[31] Yet Shinkarev himself engages in a form of mock dishonesty in his earlier book when he claims that he draws his discussion about Shagin's poetry from an essay by Aleksandr Florensky titled "The Mitki and Culture." Such an essay does not exist. Shinkarev's Borges-like reference to an idiosyncratic scholastic interpretation that is utterly imaginary serves the purpose of reminding the reader of a founding member of the group other than the two men most often associated with it. We hear the distinctive voice of a raconteur whose passionate involvement in storytelling and gentle mockery is quite distinct from the bookish list-making, disjointed observational style, and often salty irony of Shinkarev's own. This imaginary Florensky cannot talk about aesthetics without slipping into an earthy weaving of words. The Mitki are, in the end, an assemblage of different individuals and perspectives, whose only glue is in the performance of a short-lived simplicity. Shinkarev portrays both himself and Shagin as prestidigitators of text-driven realities, alternately failing to acknowledge sources and indicating some where none exist. The buried eroticism of Auden's verse is made more patent by Shagin, who fuses his "polystylistic" word collage with an intensely homosocial desire.

In *The End of the Mitki*, Shinkarev views this synthesis of collage, textual repetition (through the reiteration of Auden's ekphrastic lines about the painting), and propulsive feeling as an example of postmodernism that goes against the idea of any single individual "owning" an artistic movement. Shinkarev argues that the "literate Mityok" understands that postmodernism continues to thrive in the tightly shared space of contemporary Russian culture. "So, if someone gets all bent out of shape from the thousandth iteration of someone else's [*chuzhogo*; literally, another's] joke," the Mityok would respond by saying that such commentary "is the result of cultural illiteracy [*beskul'tur'e*] and ignorance." Shinkarev concludes this discussion by adding the important caveat that such reasoning depends on whether the Mityok has the actual desire to become a postmodernist.[32] In other words, it is more important to be open to the postmodernist mode than it is to be an agitator for it. As he summarizes the legacy in *The End of the Mitki*, the Mitki represent a youth movement devoted to the idea of the apolitical, and are therefore pointedly unaffiliated with any party, political philosophy, ideology, celebrity cult, or (for that matter) artistic movement.

In both *Mitki* and *The End of the Mitki*, Shinkarev renders Shagin's plagiarism of Auden's poem (which was anthologized in a collection of Anglophone poetry distributed by the cultural center of the American Consulate in Leningrad) into a spectacle of postmodern duplication, as a signal example of the disinvestment of literary property. Auden wrote his poem in 1938, in anticipation of the German invasion of Czechoslovakia. Among other modes of discourse, the poem distinctly evokes the tone of a gallery tour, with a somewhat officious museum guide making a valiant effort to bring this canvas to life for a group of indifferent visitors. One scholar has pointed out the possible identification of the poem's speaker with the ploughman, whose vocation and means of operation are reminiscent of the poet's own work of staggered dividends.[33] In his appropriation and distillation of the poem, Shagin renders the ploughman not into an objective correlative of the poet but rather as one of several blinkered normative personalities, whose indifference or hostility to others unlike themselves may be said to facilitate Icarus' drowning. While Shinkarev does level against Shagin the general accusation of idea theft, in regard to taking of credit for the formation of the movement, he curiously avoids such a criticism in regard to Shagin's poem. Shinkarev assesses "Little Icarus" as one of Shagin's best verses, in spite of the presence of unacknowledged material from someone whom Shagin apparently thought was a little-known English or American young poet. In *The End of the Mitki*, Dmitri Shagin plays the role of a consummate postmodernist artist, whose resourceful transformation of found objects devolves into a reflexive mode of appropriation. The lesson we are meant to take from this situation is that no single person—or committee of people—can be said to own others.

But the author of *The End of the Mitki* is clearly interested in laying his own claim to the group's legacy, insisting, among other things, that the Mitki obtained their name thanks not to Shagin himself, but to the title of Shinkarev's first book about them.[34] In other words, the Shagin of this artists' group is first and foremost a creation of Vladimir Shinkarev, who treats Shagin's texts and paintings as Shagin himself does the poetry of Auden, as a territory where other artists can engage in free-range plundering of characters for their own work. The actual person of Dmitri Shagin is irrelevant, present neither in the "here" of Shinkarev's Russia nor in the "there" of Auden's cosmopolitan Christian West. In eccentrically translating Auden, Shagin has created his own version of both that poem and the canvas that served as its object of contemplation, whose elusive character is already patent to a Russian audience that never saw it directly in a museum. Speaking in general terms of Shagin's literary kleptomania, at another point of the book Shinkarev points out that the insertion of material from talented poets such as Olga Florensky and Roald Mandelstam into Shagin's banal or philistine literary production (*obyvatel'skaia literatura*) resulted in a verse with "strong turns of phrase" and beautifully "chiseled" lines.[35] In *The End of the Mitki*, Shinkarev narrates the story of how something is made, thereby helping us to experience, in the words of the Russian Formalist critic Viktor Shklovsky, the process of an object's manufacturing rather than the artifact (*sdelannoe*) itself.[36]

In *The End of the Mitki*, Shagin and Shinkarev emerge as doppelgängers of each other, both avid to lay different claims to the movement in a narrative that loses its polemical character by virtue of what Shklovsky terms the "sense of non-coincidence within similarity" that we find in any artistic text.[37] In their interactions, the two figures recall the dysfunctional pairs of individuals that populate absurdist drama—with their prickly relations and tendency to bicker in situations of palpable dispossession. One exchange, between the characters of Estragon and Vladimir in Beckett's *Waiting for Godot*, springs most vividly to mind as we read Shinkarev's chronicle of the movement:

ESTRAGON: I remember the maps of the Holy Land. Colored they were. Very pretty. The Dead Sea was pale blue. The very look of it made me thirsty. That's where we'll go, I used to say, that's where we'll go for our honeymoon. We'll swim. We'll be happy.
VLADIMIR: You should have been a poet.[38]

The presence of Shinkarev's own Christian name in Beckett's play draws further attention to this subtext in his two books about the movement, as does the fact that Estragon's visualization of the Holy Land dovetails with the cyan-saturated color schemes of Shagin's paintings, and with the longing for departure by sea from Russia, which figures as a leitmotif in Shagin's poetry. Shagin and Shinkarev are not merely figures in the movement: in Shinkarev's prose, they are characters, literary personae for the idea of a partnership in the vein of a friendship gone bad, if not a broken marriage. Shinkarev assesses Shagin as primarily a consummate performance artist rather than a consistently good pictorial artist. And what is a postmodernist artist if not a poet engineer of verbal artifacts and the gestures that accompany them, of what Shinkarev defines as the "prolonged conceptualist happening" practiced by a "mass youth movement," in contradistinction to the "trending high art" aspirations of the performance artists such as the Moscow Conceptualists or (we might add) Marina Abramovic?

Here we see the dichotomy of the verbal and nonverbal artists of the rock music paradigm (embodied in Western pop music by Jagger and Richards, David Bowie and guitarist Mick Ronson during Bowie's "Hunky Dory" and "Ziggy Stardust" periods, and in Russian rock by the Leningrad/St. Petersburg partnership between the earnest Boris Grebenshchikov and the irreverent keyboard player Sergei Kurekhin, during the early to middle period of the group Akvarium[39]) flipped on its head, with Shagin and Shinkarev switching their earlier positions as voluble front man and public relations person and artist of the transrational, or nonverbal. Using a range of rhetorical and stylistic devices in both their painting and their prose, Shinkarev and Shagin compose a portrait of themselves as two different sides of what Lois Gordon, in her 2002 book on Beckett, calls a "fractured self," designed to produce upon the viewer or reader the impression of a failed brotherly relationship in the mold of Cain and Abel, while demonstrating that even dysfunction plays out in what is fundamentally a single "conglomerative" performance. The relationship between Vladimir and Estragon in

*Waiting for Godot* is, she writes, one "in which each plays a well-defined role" that is essential to the other's "well-being."[40] Much of Gordon's analysis of the play seems remarkably apt in describing the living theater of Shinkarev and Shagin's creative tensions, particularly in their dramatization in *The End of the Mitki*:

> It is as though they had agreed that if one player is the man of reason, speaking in secondary process, with the other, the man of feeling, functioning in the primary process, they can minimize anxiety in the ordeal of survival. What becomes apparent, whether they are lifetime friends or the divided consciousness of a single figure (fifty years old), is that the best scripted efforts to surmount the human condition are endlessly precarious.[41]

Gordon's dichotomy of the speaking and feeling actors of the conglomerate self resonates deeply with the division of roles between the two men whose personalities and creative labor have defined the Mitki. Unlike the thespian dyad that we see at the foreground of *Waiting for Godot*—or the one of Clov and Ham in Beckett's later *Endgame*—Shinkarev and Shagin have a more lambent relation to the dichotomy that Gordon describes, with one at different times taking on the persona(e) typically associated with the other. Yet however often they switch their roles, at the end of any given day in the movement—be it in 1984 or in 2010—the dichotomy itself remains firmly in place.

In *The End of the Mitki*, politics and celebrity emerge as first cousins in the same extended family of commodified relations, as embodied by Shagin's abandonment of painting for becoming a player within state power and a "rock star" who sells his own CDs. As a deputy for the town council of Kolpino, Shagin announced to his constituents that he was the person who, in Shinkarev's telling turn of phrase, "minted" (*upromyslil*) the movement of the Mitki. Shinkarev expresses this drive to demystify and dismantle the self-important cult figure in many of his recent paintings as well. In his series *Cinema 2006*, the faces of well-known performers often dissolve into smudges and opaque blurs, powerfully communicating a world of visual shibboleths that has been stripped of any specific profile. In these canvases, Shinkarev draws more attention to the viewer's apperception of the yellowing and frayed canvas screens in theaters and blurry television monitors on which moving images are projected than to the iconic status of the performers embedded within them. What lies behind these representations of mitigated individual agency is a fascination with the idea of a life-affirming collective, of individuals obtaining identity while closely interacting with others. An insular group interacts with the world at large. What happens? In the beginning, there is the shock of contact with another body of work. The response of the subculture to the larger culture is defensive yet expressive of a yearning for engagement. There is nothing, it seems, more frustrating than the isolation of a subculture, just as there is no prospect as forbidding as the one of personal isolation. Far from being texts that are opposed to each other, with one portraying a glorious heyday of a group and the other its decline, Shinkarev's two books about the Mitki (from 1985–97 and 2010) in fact mirror each other in their portraits of compulsive appropriation. We certainly hear the clinical pathologization of the movement in the persona of Evgeni Barinov, the "author" of Shinkarev's 1993 "Mitki: Part Thirteen (An Imitation of V. Shinkarev)." Under the persona of the Venedikt Erofeev-like Barinov (who, like Erofeev, is a writer and manual laborer who dies from alcohol-related causes), Shinkarev writes that the Mitki decisively reject "Tolstoy's injunction that we not be led astray like cattle, and not to join [glorified] party-affiliated gangs [*partinnye kodly*]."[42]

Although several commentators have noted the indebtedness of the Mitki to French Impressionism, perhaps a better way of understanding their work would be to position it as a hybrid of expressionist and impressionist modes of representation. The expressionist dimension of the Mitki's paintings—featuring fantasy-driven tableaux and figures insolently staring back from their canvases in a mirroring of the painter's subjective overreach—engages in a dramatic competition with the object-centered aspect of their work. The representation of theatricalized public and private spaces, characteristic of the paintings of German Expressionists such as Lovis Corinth, Ernst Kirchner, and Max Beckmann (one of Shinkarev's favorite painters), mingles freely with the blended brushwork of Cézanne. In his painting *Goethe's "The Sorrows of Young Werther,"* from his 1999 series *World Literature*, Shinkarev arguably comes close to thematizing the perilous meeting place between these two vastly different points of orientation in visual representation, made all the more pointed by the choice of a German text for its subject.

The unusually translucent oil brushwork mimics (in a possible nod to Shagin's own paintings) the immediacy of watercolors, while the panel borders in comic-book style introduce an unexpected severity to the sketch-like scenes of daily tedium and delusion, which are suffused in swaths of flat yellows, dull browns, and empty spaces of white

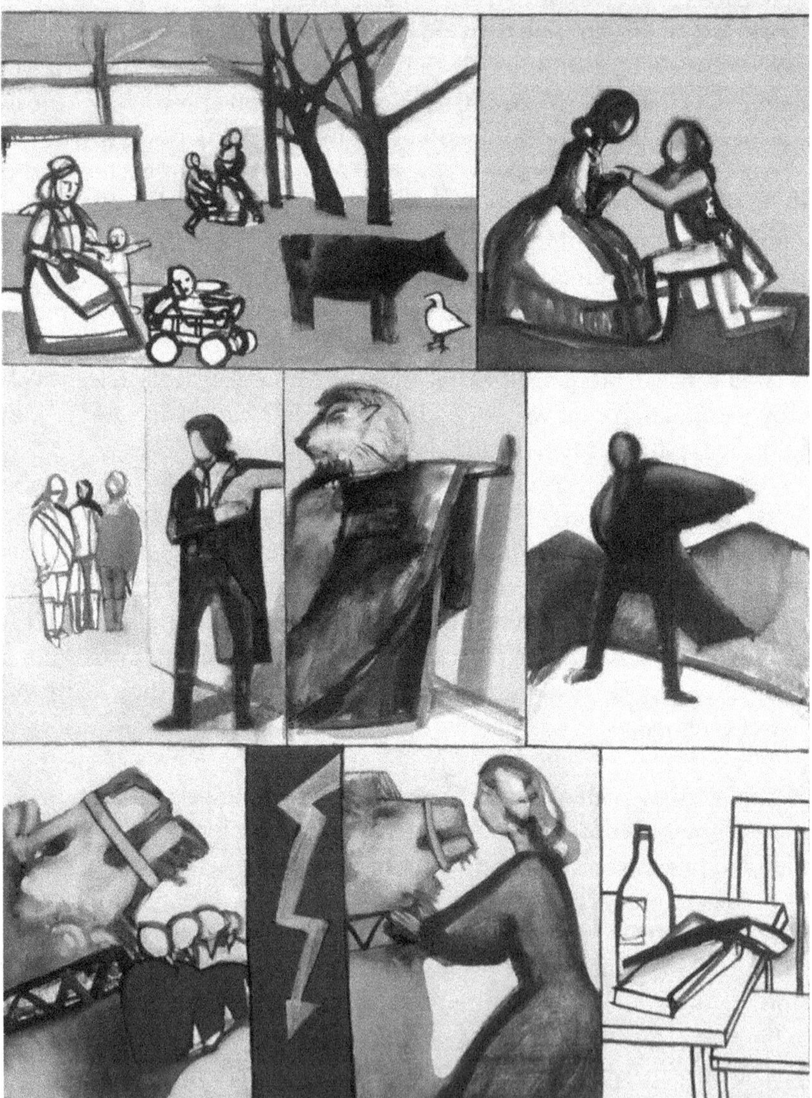


Figure 3. Vladimir Shinkarev, *Goethe, "The Sorrows of Young Werther"* (1999), from the series *World Literature.* Oil, 110 × 76 cm. (Bruno Bishofberger Gallery, Zurich, Switzerland)

suggestive of the simulations of unfinished canvases by German Expressionists such as Max Pechstein. The middle panel of the second row suggests, in the manner of Jean Cocteau's or Ingmar Bergman's films, a surrealist jump cut. Indeed, the entire composition of the painting moves with a cinematic momentum. All this, combined with the most fugitive of smudges on every human face, seems to draw as much attention to the artist's misanthropic and jaundiced eye as it is does to Goethe's novel about an ill-starred infatuation and the pains of unorthodox love relations, which in that writer's day launched a literary youth movement of its own. In his commentary for the painting and the source material, Shinkarev notes that the "dense romanticism [of the novel], with its bolts of lightning and abysses," oddly makes it at once "powerful, highly contrastive, [yet] monotonous." In a dry concluding statement that could also stand as an assessment of the ways in which human affinities, sparking the creation of a movement such as the Mitki, may tip over into codependence, Shinkarev states that Goethe's novel "gives a clinically accurate picture of any form of dependence, and may be useful for alcoholics and drug addicts."[43]

How can we regard partnership as a form of chemical dependency? The answer that Shinkarev's work provides is disquieting insofar as it establishes a tension, if not opposition, between the ideals of friendship on the one hand and partnership and comity within an artistic and social movement on the other. In *The End of the Mitki*, Shinkarev writes that "in those years, we all drank, and when people get sloshed together—they don't have to make much of an effort at playing [at being] the Mitki."[44] Although drugs never played a role in the movement, several friends of the Mitki who were well-known in the Leningrad underground, and in the art and music scene of the nineties, were known to abuse controlled substances. The most tragic of these was the punk-music singer Aleksandr Bashlachev, whom Viktor Tikhomirov and Shinkarev befriended. (Shinkarev designed one of his album covers.) Bashlachev was addicted to heroin and committed suicide in 1998. The association of rock music with addiction in general is strong in *Mitki*. The first chapter makes mention of Akvarium's Grebenshchikov and progressive rock keyboardist Sergei Kurekhin (then a member of Akvarium) as close friends of the group,[45] and a large part of chapter 6 (titled "Further Development of the Myth of the World Catastrophe, according to the Mitki" and written in 1988) is devoted to a series of anecdotes about Grebenshchikov (nicknamed with borderline disrespect as "Grebeshochechok" [itty-bitty comb]) and his various states of intoxication.

Blended with this appreciation of unorthodoxy in lifestyles was a politicized solidarity projected by rock-music practitionership in Leningrad. As Leslie Woodhead observes in his recent book about the countercultural response of Russian youth to the Beatles, much of the Leningrad rock community consisted of a "curious mix of the hippie and dissident," reminiscent of "London in the late sixties."[46] Among Leningrad-based musicians and singers such as Viktor Tsoi of Kino, "Mike" Naumenko of Zoopark (both befriended by the Mitki in the late eighties), and Grebenshchikov himself was an understanding of a band as a music collective that played both with and against its main singer-songwriter. In answer to one Russian rock critic's question, "Have there in your opinion been mutual influences and synthesis between rock music and the *avtorskaya pesnya* [singer-songwriter's song]?" Andrei Makarevich of the Moscow-based band Time Machine replied, "On the level of self-expression, rock and the *avtorskaya pesnya* are very close. Rock music is that *avtorskaya pesnya*, realised in another musical language. The very word *avtorskaya* [literally, authorial; author's or *auteur*'s] describes both genres. With Boris Grebenschikov, for instance, the two genres often interact. Obviously with us too."[47] In a statement that is especially relevant to the Mitki's mode of movement building and collaboration, the Leningrad-based "Mike" Naumenko underscores the give-and-take between author and ensemble:

> Mutual influence . . . Yes, on the level that practically all bands play and sing their own material and the author normally sings the song. Another question is that the lyrics are not always of the necessary quality, but in any case any attempt in this area may be welcomed. It has already been mentioned, but is well worth underlining once more, that however paradoxical it may sound, rock music is a folk music in the most positive sense of the word.[48]

The symbiosis between collective and putative leader that we see in the Mitki is partly derived from the group dynamic that Makarevich and Naumenko describe here, which is also mirrored in the co-creation of the movement by two individuals that is foregrounded throughout Shinkarev's writing about the movement.

We see an illustration of this principle of counterpoint within the group—of the dethroning of the "leader" of an ensemble—in chapter 6 of *Mitki.* Shinkarev juxtaposes two variant texts of the same anecdote, one titled "The Lizard and the Law (as Told by V. Shinkarev)" and the other "The Dragon and the Law (A Myth About Victory, From the Words of D. Shagin)." In the first of these texts, Grebenshchikov prepares for a tour of the United States. His son Gleb loathes a lizard that was given as a gift to his father and that seemed to have come from abroad. Gleb abuses the animal and almost succeeds in drowning it. Grebenshchikov and his wife, Liuda, save the animal from the clutches of their young son and nurse it back to health. Waking up with vicious hangovers the next morning, Boris and Liuda go in search of lizard, only to discover that their son had succeeded in killing it. "Gleb, Gleb! Do you remember how the lizard was a living thing, how she played with you, and now it lies here choked to death. . . . How could you do such a thing?" "Such is the law!" Gleb responds. The version of this anecdote by "Shagin" is less a retelling than it is a politicized interpretation. Shagin notes that 1988 was both the millennium anniversary of the Christianization of Russia, and the Year of the Dragon. In a moment of misplaced patriotism, Grebenshchikov's son was enraged that someone considered the latter to be more important than the former:

> Let's imagine what fear and anguish Gleb Grebenshchikov must have felt, seeing in his home a living, actual dragon—the living embodiment of the antipode to the Christening [of Russia]! . . . The three-year old child . . . saw that his parents had surrendered to the wiles of the Dragon, and that therefore all negotiations with them—and all points of clarification—were useless.
>
> So Gleb Grebenshchikov, in order to save his parents from sorcery, at his own level reprised the victory of St. George.[49]

With these variant accounts, Shinkarev offers up a demonstration of multiple authorship within a collective that has a nominal leader. Who is the putative author, or pretender, here? It may be the author of the book; it also could be the man after whom the movement was named. Both accounts foreground an anxiety over foreignness, possibly combined with a Russian wounded sense of pride during a year of increasing privations and the Soviet Union's undermined international status. Far from encouraging solidarity, such rents in the fabric of the nation's self-image encourage a range of responses. As Shinkarev asserts in *The End of the Mitki*, the group represents a cross-section of Russian culture. The performance of Russianness becomes, very quickly, a mode of self-examination and criticism, if not protest.

Notwithstanding the competitive nature of this friendship, in Shinkarev's writing there is certainly a strong suggestion that he and Shagin are, in various ways, intertwined, both in their codependence as individuals and in their relation to the movement. In these two volumes, in *Mitki* and *The End of the Mitki*, Shagin is a painter who uses his paintings and poetry as advertisements for himself; he is also, in those texts, quite clearly the creation of Vladimir Shinkarev. The first book represents the portrayal of a group in its euphoric days of a largely seamless collective identity, whereas the second consists of a representation of a family drama, with two parents dissolving their union and arguing about the custody of their children. The reported speech of Dmitri Shagin within Shinkarev's text also begs the question of its authorship, in an expansive mode that is necessitated by the leitmotif of internal contestation that is so insistent in Shinkarev's prose. If we assume that the book *Mitki* engendered the wider movement that it documented in its humble beginnings, we may think of the fledgling movement as the author of the book. Who, then, is the real author of that book, among those who are portrayed in it? Is it Shinkarev, the person who sat down to sift through the materials at hand, and to comment on them in the distinct personal style of a medieval scribe compiling a chronicle? Or is it the person after whom the text is essentially named? Both Shagin and Shinkarev are, after all, characters in the text, with the nominal author referring to himself and his wife (who at one point chides him for spending time with those "damned" [*pogannye*] Mitki) by name. Sensing this tension between author and eponymous protagonist, Andrei Bitov takes note of the importance of the idea of effaced or blurred authorship to the experience of reading Shinkarev's first book about the Mitki, which he likens to the tendency of some audiences to identify protagonists as the actual authors of the novels in which they appear: "The name of the author and hero become ambivalent: wasn't it Don Quixote who wrote Cervantes; Robinson Crusoe, Defoe; and Schweik, Hašek?"[50] Not lost to the Russian reader who reads both *Mitki* and *The End of the Mitki* is the additional significance of Shagin's Christian name: like the character of Dmitri in Pushkin's *Boris Godunov*, he is a pretender to the throne.

Bearing in mind that the titles of both books contain Shagin's name in the diminutive and pluralized forms—and in the spirit of brokering a compromise between "Shagin" and "Shinkarev," each of whom contributes in different ways to the social movement and the artistic group—perhaps we need to think of authorship here as multiple, or at least as a form of close collaboration. The homosocial element of the relations between "Shagin" and "Shinkarev" in Shinkarev's prose becomes more palpable when we consider the subtext of the exchange between Estragon and Vladimir in *Waiting for Godot*. Estragon wistfully sees himself and his partner in a life of crushing poverty as going on a honeymoon, where they will swim in the Dead Sea. Similar cadences of yearning for reconnection with another man outside of the borders of the Russian Federation can be found in Shagin's poetry from the nineties. In his 1997 "Trip Around the World," Shagin imagines "swimming in the Mediterranean" and yelping with delight as he picks lemons in Sardinia, but eventually he finds himself musing about his friend the poet and singer Aleksei Khvostenko, who lives in Paris:

But in the North—in Paris—
Our brother man Khvost lives,
Sipping away at red wine
And softly singing:
Old Man, O Old Man,
When will we meet again?
Old Man, O Old Man,
The globe is round all the same.[51]

In his chronicles of the Mitki, Shinkarev uses texts of the actual Shagin as the basis for his literary representation of him. As Shinkarev notes already in *Mitki*, the tone of Shagin's voice is best preserved in his poetry. What Shinkarev does in both books about the Mitki is to place Shagin's voice in a dialogue with others, in a way that had not occurred in the early days of the movement. In a segment from *Mitki* added in 1988, Shinkarev prefaces an imaginary monologue by Shagin (which mimics his phrasing and wide-eyed provincialism, portrayed in earlier anecdotes and in the quotations from Shagin's poems) with the statement that a dour or sad ending to any number of stories can be disarmed by its antithesis, in the form of the *mitkovian* archetypal myth of the victorious hero. This myth serves as constant counterpoint (*postoiannyi kontrapunkt*) to the "polyphony of the myth about catastrophe."[52] It seems that Shagin's voice, taken by itself, is not compatible with the multivoicedness of the actual Mitki. For Shinkarev, Shagin's voice represents a spirit of authoritarianism. We may understand the tension between the character of Shagin on the one hand and the actual functioning of this group of artists on the other, as an opposition between the monologue and plurality, seeing it particularly in light of Roland Barthes's statement that the "philosophy" of the One perceiving the plural as an embodiment of "Evil." As Barthes explains, the traditional moralistic literary work sees the polyphonic or pluralistic text as taking as "its motto the words of the man possessed by demons (Mark 5:9): 'My name is Legion, for we are many.' The plural of the demonical texture which opposes text to work can bring with it fundamental changes in reading, and precisely in areas where monologism appears to be the Law."[53] Within the context of the stories of "The Lizard and the Law" and "The Dragon and the Law," it would seem that Shinkarev (who is well-versed in poststructuralist French theory) identifies Shagin's version of the anecdote about the killing of the lizard by a boy—the son of a fellow traveler of the Mitki, no less—as a justification of stultifying authorial intolerance of otherness (be it personal or geopolitical) that Barthes identifies as a marker of "theological monism."[54] Certainly the coy, lambent tone of the version of this anecdote "as told by V. Shinkarev" would seem more open to the playful irony and experimental relativizing that Boris Groys and others identify as the positive aspects of postmodernism. Shagin, on the other hand, shares the view of the intolerant patriot who regards the authorial word as law. Perhaps there is not as much of a tonal gap between the *Mitki* of the eighties and nineties and *The End of the Mitki* twenty-plus years later. In both volumes, a tendency toward overreach, if not hubris, defines the character of Shagin, to which Shinkarev's self-representation provides an initial, or provisional, counterexample.

Shinkarev's comment about the "polyphony" of his version of the anecdote is also a reference to the literary critic Mikhail Bakhtin's theory of polyphony. Bakhtin understood the concept as a hallmark of the genre of the novel's democratization of community. Dostoevsky's novels are notable for the way the author's voice operates as merely one among many within the text: "The author of a polyphonic novel is not required to renounce himself or his consciousness, but he must to an extraordinary extent broaden, deepen and rearrange this consciousness (to be sure, in a specific direction) in order to accommodate the consciousness of others"; this author must enter into the same domain of "dialogic activity" that the voices of others inhabit.[55] By familiarizing ourselves with Bakhtin's notion of literary polyphony and discourse-based (as opposed to strictly musical) counterpoint, we begin to see more clearly that Shinkarev recreates Shagin as the author of the Mitki:

> The essence of polyphony lies precisely in the fact that the voices remain independent and, as such, are combined in a unity of higher order than homophony. If one is to talk about individual will, then it is precisely in polyphony that a combination of several wills takes place, that the boundaries of the individual will can in principle be exceeded. One can

> put it this way: the artistic will of polyphony is a will to combine many wills, a will to an event. . . . The image of polyphony and counterpoint only points out those new problems which arise when a novel is constructed beyond the boundaries of a single monological unity, just as in music new problems arose when the boundaries of a single voice were exceeded.[56]

Polyphony serves as an example of counterpoint in two senses: it is evident in the contentious relations among all characters in a text (none of whom has legitimate claims to the promise of a final word), and it represents a rebuke to the egoism of the authorial self who seeks to make characters into mere objects of authorial will. As the Leningrad/St. Petersburg art critic Liubov Gurevich shrewdly notes in her essay "Vladimir Shinkarev as Tempter," the artist wrote about the movement in the style of on-site reportage that cumulatively took on the character of a novel. What we see in *Mitki* and *The End of the Mitki* are two segments of a novel about two novelists: one who glorifies the monologue or the stand-alone, unrebutted speech (Shagin) and the other who attempts to construct a movement that acknowledges polyphony. Yet both men stand outside of the novelistic creation that they have engendered and over which they have less control than they would like to admit.

Commenting on Thackeray's *Lovel the Widower*, Eve Kosofsky Sedgwick argues that glorification of "atomized male individualism" comes with an abjuring of the "nuclear family," a "demonization of women, especially mothers," and an eschewing of any possibility of deeper intimacy—sexual or otherwise—among men.[57] What we find in Shinkarev's writing about the Mitki is an exploration of the intimacy that exists within the heart of a youth movement; his work also impresses upon the reader that social movements are informed by creative and artistic affects, as well as by the yearning for social connection. The Mitki is a social movement with strongly pacifist meanings; it is also an artistic collective with an aesthetic agenda of leavening postmodernism with neo-impressionism, expressionism, and naïve primitivism in the vein of Henri Rousseau and the "Jack of Diamonds" circle in Russia. We see that an artists' group functions under the sway of desire, with artists coming together, cathecting each other and the ideals of their program. Such a movement may reach a point of passionate focus from which it can precipitously decline. The rediscovery of human connection with others at the cost of the narcissistic ego—the recovery of a sense of shared purpose—is followed by the splintering of the group, as a result of waning feeling. What finally follows is the struggle over legacy, the fight over what might be regarded as the symbolic stand-in for progeny. Shagin emerges as both a monologic novelist and a derided maternal figure in the vein that Sedgwick describes as being highly characteristic of atomized male fellowships. In one especially revealing moment of acknowledged maternal surrogacy in *The End of the Mitki*, Shinkarev writes that "there are only two people in my life, at whom I have had the effrontery to yell: my mother and Mitya," noting with apparent chagrin that "you can't just yell at your mother—she's just too old."[58] Shinkarev's sudden shift in generalizing about the idea of "mother" as someone whose age precludes her from being the object of verbal abuse begs the question of the category that Shagin may belong to.

A provisional answer to this question is that Shagin, like his mother, represents a figure who is a relay station for the idea of authorship as something that originates outside of the person who handles the language and does the actual writing. Here, we come back to the dichotomy of the glimmer twins, of the articulately cerebral figure caught in a creative tension with the powerfully affective *naïf* and "nature boy"; of the speaker and the doer, the artist and his muse. In both *Mitki* and *The End of the Mitki*, the figure of Dmitri Shagin becomes an object of grim fascination, an example of both a coruscating mythmaker and a possible reflection of the writer compiling these chronicles of a youth movement in its ascendance and decline. In Shinkarev's writing, we see a literary equivalent of the unresolved dialectical tension between work that avows to focus on the qualities and physical setting of the object of contemplation and the emotive state of the person who composes a portrait of them. Shinkarev's extended personal digressions in *Mitki* (such as his inserted essay "In Praise of the Boiler Room," which makes only scant reference to the group and which is included as an Appendix to this book), the numerous hiccup-like personal asides (such as "I am writing these lines late in the evening at a trolley stop"),[59] and the clearly serial nature of the volume, all point to an endeavor of navigating between apperception and incandescent impressions on the one hand, and the highlighted obdurate subjectivity of the solipsistic documentarian on the other. In his 2010 exposé of Shagin's rapacity for sole ownership of the movement, Shinkarev writes of an incident in Paris with Shagin during their first trip abroad in 1989, highlighting a moment of revelation that illuminated his own state of mind as much as it did Shagin's:

We entered some sort of boutique with mirrored walls, finding ourselves amidst all sorts of finery. All of a sudden, I saw my reflection in a mirror—a disheveled person, bloated from drinking—and next to me, an utterly grotesque Mitya: wearing a sailor's shirt with wide splotches of dried sweat, large-breasted (*sisiastyi*), oily clumped hair, and completely covered in a layer of grease like a baking dish in a restaurant serving *chebureki*. Black pores were visible on his face, which had puffed up from the heat; his teeth were stained, with white flecks of food showing on them.

The patrons hurriedly abandoned the boutique, without even noticing Mitya himself: such was the heavy stench emanating from him.

With weary malice I found myself thinking, now he would view himself in the mirror and somehow come to his senses. He would wipe himself clean, straighten his shirt, and close his slack jaw, for starters; that Mitya would notice his reflection, and be mortified. "How awful and disgusting I look!" he would cry out with unfeigned ecstasy, transfixed by the sight of himself.

That's how one should react! That would have meant taking a coherent stand on things. I also looked like a Mityok—unshaven, in a sailor's shirt—but was all the same a bit shamefaced [*stesnialsia*], and afraid about seeming completely disreputable and *ridicule*. But is it possible for Mitki to be ashamed [*stesniat'sia*] of being *ridicule*? Let hapless yuppies feel ashamed: a Mityok has nothing to be ashamed of!

1989 was the year of the Mitki's apogee, and Mitya was in his peak form, perceiving his appearance as an invaluable cultivated asset.[60]

It should be noted that Shinkarev is more interested here in contemplating Shagin as a character within the fiction of his writing about the Mitki than he is in describing any actual person. As Liubov Gurevich argues, it was in Shinkarev's first book about the movement that Dmitri Shagin received his artistic representation in the eyes of others, and that representation subsequently took on a life of its own.[61] Shinkarev understands the Mitki as a pose that may transform itself into a person: such is the power of this variety of group identity, with its emphasis on mimicry of a highly specific behavioral model. In Shinkarev's reckoning, Mitya is aware that the group persona of the Mitki is a conceit, yet he cannot perceive the extent to which the cultivated archetype has taken over his entire being, as if his self has been hollowed out by this form of role-playing. Especially important here is the slippery range of meanings covered by the verb *stesniat'sia*, which can mean to be ashamed, shy, concerned, shamefaced, or simply hesitant to do something. It seems that artifice and choice is a prominent aspect of this lingering sense of shame. What if I decide to go down the same road that Shagin took and still travels upon?

The possibilities for transformation would seem to include a gender dimorphism, signaled here by Shagin's hypertrophied breasts, as denoted by an adjective derived from the vulgar Russian word meaning "tits" (*sis'ki*). In the same chapter of the book, Shinkarev explains that 1989 was the year that the Mitki ceased to be a strictly Leningrad-based movement and became a product for export. Sensitized to Shinkarev's use of postmodernist applications of Bakhtin's theories, which postulate the impossibility of privileging any single voice in the polyphonic novel, many readers would notice the affinities between Shinkarev's description of Shagin's grotesque body and Bakhtin's conception of the representation of the earth in Rabelais's fiction as a symbol of one's native mother, devouring in order to give birth yet again.[62] Shagin becomes for Shinkarev a ravening matriarchal figure of almost sinister appetite and productivity, cultivating a plethora of images for the group's marketability outside of Russia and the Soviet Union. Yet this model, as it turns out in Shinkarev's metacritical allegorical treatment of this shaming incident in Paris, is not desirable either in the West or in Russia. The performance artist has ceased to perceive his behavior as a performance and has instead fully embraced the stance of entitled boorishness that he formerly merely played at. As Shinkarev scathingly puts it at one point of *The End of the Mitki*, "In the worst case scenario, [Shagin] would have been a businessman or a politician" rather than an artist.[63] It would seem that the maternal model of leader—of an authority figure as a nurturer as well as punitive father figure, embodying the dichotomy within Russian political culture of *rodina* ("Motherland") or hearth and home on the one hand and the administrative state or *otechestvo* ("Fatherland") on the other—lends itself to this transformation of the ironic, shape- and gender-shifting performer into a control-obsessive owner, custodian, and presumptive author of a mass movement.

What we see in *The End of the Mitki* is Shinkarev's understanding of the current state of the group, as mired in nostalgia. Shagin would like the group to remain in the pictorial aesthetics and behavioral patterns that it cultivated during the time of economic stagnation and ideological inflexibility in the final years of the Soviet Union. With both that era and the shocking era of untrammeled acquisitiveness from the nineties already having receded well into the past, the *raison d'être* of the group seems to have vanished. Shinkarev sees himself mirrored in Shagin, whose presence became a part of present-day Russian urban folklore thanks to the books Shinkarev wrote about him. The entire episode in the Parisian boutique can be understood as an inverted version of Jacques Lacan's signal concept of the "mirror stage," where the infant comes to a sudden realization of their autonomous ego and liberating separation from their mother. Shinkarev's probable engagement with Lacan's ideas here is pointed up by two details. First, there is the location of the Parisian boutique, which seems the ideal place for demonstrating a theory that posits mirroring as a form of renewed self-conceptualization. It somehow does not come as a surprise that Lacan himself, according to one biographer, had "a passion for fabrics not far removed from fetishism."[64] Second, Shinkarev's understanding of his reflection as a cause for consternation points to what Lacan characterizes as the mirror stage's ambiguity in relation to the figure of the mother: the child's jubilation in recognizing a coherent, graceful self in the mirror takes place at the moment when he "is still trapped in his motor impotence and nursling dependence."[65] In keeping with the dialectical tension that Lacan recognizes in this pivotal developmental moment of the child, Shinkarev sees in this reflection the superimposed image of a male figure lurking in another part of the room, who mimics the properties of a mother figure. One thing is certain: this reflection does not embody the speaker's idea of a desired adult self.

In Shinkarev's *Mitki* and *The End of the Mitki*, Shagin and Shinkarev become a team of performing troubadours that presents the story of their group—in all its moments of enmity, pettiness, and intervals of fellow feeling—to the world at large. In the second book, Shinkarev recapitulates the movement's central ideals, elaborating upon the already highly stylized narrative of competitive partnership between Shagin and himself. Yet in *The End of the Mitki* Shinkarev also deepens the thematic of the two men as contrastive players within the same play by presenting them as capable thespians who periodically alternate in performing any number of seemingly distinct roles, be they of singer and musician, poet and muse, or the Commedia dell'arte figures of the mournful and passive Pierrot on the one hand and the caustic and cruel Harlequin on the other. In both volumes, "Shinkarev" is no less a character and creation than Shagin himself, and the two figures taken together come to represent an almost dialectical union of opposites (*coniunctio oppositorum*) within the movement of the Mitki. Even the grotesque body of Shagin—a stand-in for the representation of Russia as "moist mother earth" (*mat' syra zemlia*), or a feminized metaphor of nation as an uncomely crone—becomes a commodity, perhaps precisely at the moment that it ceases to exist as a self-aware performance. As we see in *The End of the Mitki*, Shinkarev cannot escape his doubling with Shagin and in fact mirrors his *bête noir* most precisely in those moments when he calls him on his attempts to arrogate to himself the role of leader:

> The personage named Vladimir Shinkarev ended up having to respond, with no little agitation and bile, to all of Dmitri Shagin's actions, exposing the motives behind these acts—thereby himself coming into a possession of a heightened sense of righteousness, from which, in my real life, I hope to free myself. . . .
>
> And how can it be otherwise? Here's an analogy, in which I dare to draw comparisons between Dante and myself. In his lectures on the *Divine Comedy*, Borges writes that among the characters that Dante brings in is one "Dante," who wanders in Hell, at every step experiencing fear and shrinking back from something. Shouldn't we pause and think, says Borges, that Dante is exceedingly deceitful, and that the perpetual dread of "Dante" is nothing more than a vehicle for describing Hell?
>
> Similarly, by describing the history of the group the Mitki, I am compelled to embellish what happened with an attitude of *ressentiment*. And at no point does Christian humility overlap with [requirements of] artistic necessity.[66]

It is not lost on Shinkarev himself that he has become a living demonstration of the vices of vanity and rapaciousness that he ascribes to Shagin. A crucial turn of phrase here is "artistic necessity," or exigency (*khudozhestvennaia neobkhodimost'*). The formation of a public identity is no less a matter of art than the fashioning of a literary narrative, or the composition by a visual artist. *The End of the Mitki* is a Bildungsroman about coming of age as an artist in the full sense of the word: What is such a person now, if not one who crafts artifacts and actions and who becomes an almost diabolically accomplished magus of image in a variety of mediums? One of these mediums is, in fact, comprised of forms of the media: journalism (of which there are several lengthy excerpts in the text) and self-advertisement through social media.

In both that book and his earlier volume about the movement, Shinkarev writes with an awareness of the drama of group discord as making for good copy, particularly when it crosses over from one media and genre platform into another. In a distinctly Groysian and Lyotardian postmodern vein of regarding social practices as ritualized genres and exquisite artifices in their own right, we may understand *Mitki* and *The End of the Mitki* as a commentary, in narrative form, about the paradox of the nonconformist group. Such a group resists aesthetic and political orthodoxies while grappling with its own all-too centripetal impulses toward corporate identity. The formation of an ideology that makes a corporate identity possible does not evaporate but in fact pollutes the environment in which individuals struggle to maintain autonomy within a flexible and noncompulsory relationality that is improvisational and open to the unexpected.

As Shinkarev demonstrates in his portrait of an apparently oppositional pair whose identities both affect and reflect off each other, it is in performance that we can jettison the frozen self-images that saddle us. Those frozen images, however, can enact their own amusing melodrama, and many Russian readers would readily hear in Shinkarev's two books about the Mitki echoes of Gogol's 1834 "The Story of How Ivan Ivanovich Fought with Ivan Nikiforovich," about the acrimonious falling-out of two close friends over ownership of a rifle. Even the body types of the two characters in Gogol's story—one corpulent and the other lithe—correspond to those of Shagin and Shinkarev. *The End of the Mitki* demonstrates the principle of the dynamic artistic text outlined by the semiotician Yuri Lotman, as possessing the features of both binary and asymmetrical systems. Dissenting from Bakhtin's contention about the democratic possibilities of dialogue, Lotman emphasizes the power imbalance that tends to occur within any verbal exchange, which inevitably turns on the dichotomy of speaker and listener.[67] Certainly we see the dynamics of that struggle for power within the interaction that Shinkarev portrays, of his relations with Shagin. In the end, however, no two individuals—no matter how incandescent their personalities and conflict—can eclipse the social movement to which they claim to belong. *The End of the Mitki* is a document of a spiritually fatal partnership. At the same time, it is a text about rise and fall that does not spare the first-person narrator, amply reflecting what Bakhtin describes as the single novelistic voice that is thoroughly caught up in the world of polyphonic and counterpoint-driven relations that it chronicles. *The End of the Mitki* is not only the eulogy of a movement: it is the conclusion of a novel with manifold authorship that needs to be understood in performative terms, as an enactment of what Judith Butler calls the "concerted bodily action" among people—of "gathering, gesturing, standing still"—that defines the very notion of human assembly.[68]

# 2

## "Who Is This Heroic Man?"

### David Bowie and the Mitki's Queering of Masculinity

Every person has, let's say, several different hypostases. I wake up in the morning and recall: damn [*yoly-paly*], am I or am I not an artist? I'll arrogantly scorn everything else, and go ahead and paint a painting. Or I think to myself: am I or am I not a husband, and I'll set out for the market to buy some potatoes. The hypostases get into an argument with each other, and one of them will happen to wake up and say—"Father, or not a father?!" "Poet, or not a poet?!" "Citizen, or not a citizen?!"

VLADIMIR SHINKAREV, *The End of the Mitki* (2010)

We can beat them, forever and ever
Oh, we can be heroes, just for one day

DAVID BOWIE, "Heroes" (1977)

The Mitki exhibited an awareness of gender identity as a conundrum the moment that they burst onto the stage of Leningrad's artistically and politically diverse youth movements. Readers first encountered writing by and about the Mitki in underground Russian literary publications, or samizdat. Although the term's most immediate meaning is "self-published," it invokes a series of secondary associations that give us a clearer understanding of what it meant to create and consume a samizdat publication, and to hold it in one's hands. Among other things, the word samizdat suggests a weighty institutional parallel to official publishing houses such as Gosizdat (Government Publication) and Voyenizdat (Military Publication), thereby framing itself as an estimable contender for the attention of readers. Contemplating his recollections of being a consumer of samizdat in the sixties, the expatriate poet and scholar Lev Losev has also suggested that the term may have been used in a jokey association with "Samtrest," the name of the Georgian wine-producing organization.[1] Among other things, the consumption of samizdat texts is a self-consciously performative act that draws our attention to the socially transformative effects of heightened affect and taboo-breaking disinhibition. During her final testimony at the Pussy Riot trial in the Supreme Court of the City of Moscow on August 8, 2012—and in a statement that referred as much to her own public actions as a punk feminist performance artist as to the media manipulation of the Putin administration—Nadezhda Tolokonnikova asserted that "the art of creating the image of an era" is not a competition and knows neither winners nor losers.[2] Writers who were involved in eighties-era samizdat created an alternate set of self-images that reveled in the increasingly glaring cognitive dissonances—many of them centered on the patently imperial Soviet ambitions in Afghanistan—that characterized the period. Somehow, this lack of an ideological center seemed completely apt as a counterweight to the increasingly hollow bromides and brittle Leninist formulations of the Soviet state in its economic and ideological stagnation. The varied oppositional pedigree of samizdat—as well as the versatile and nuanced methods of transmitting ideas and distributing texts in the "underground," and the vividly somatic dimension of consuming samizdat, which establishes a notional bridge of intimacy among members of its audience—is ideally suited to the questioning of gender roles that Judith Butler locates within the discursive mode of "improvisational possibility."[3]

Within this realm of performative experimentation—so characteristic of the milieu out of which the Mitki arose—we can recognize not just the blurring of gender lines but also the suggestion, in the parallel that Shinkarev draws to the enigmatic intimacy of Vladimir and Estragon in *Waiting for Godot*, of a markedly warm mutual regard among men that goes beyond mere organizational comity. The presentation of Dmitri Shagin as a maternal figure who presides over a community activates a series of other associations, such as the possible metaphor of him as a *matushka*, the wife of a Russian Orthodox priest. In such an instant, Shinkarev would be the custodian and high priest of the movement's sacred text of the 1984–97 edition of *Mitki*, and by extension Shagin's husband. The representation of multivalent role-playing suggests a performance of homosociality that makes all relations within the movement seem strange, or nontraditional.

The entrance of David Bowie as a character in the group's mythology is unexpected only if we fail to recognize the thematizing of this homosociality in their collective work. In one of his appendixes for *Mitki*, Shinkarev characterizes Bowie as an example of a poised and impeccably dressed hipster, with globetrotting tastes. "What I mean by the [label] the 'Real David Bowie' is not the actual singer David Bowie, but a mythical *mitkovian* one: an intellectual, a positivist-conceptualist, and a cosmopolitan with an orientation to the West—in other words, a clever person in the most pejorative sense of the word."[4] Yet Shinkarev seems to contradict or problematize this assertion in a recent interview, where he states that "David Bowie seemed to the Mitki to be a significant phenomenon and, therefore, a competitor." As Shinkarev explains, "The kind, relaxed, inconsistent and sloppy Mitki [*sic*] man [is] an earthy being" who contrasts with "the serpentine grace of the sparkling David Bowie." He goes on to say that, "Of course these are antagonists, though I don't know what Bowie himself thought."[5] In other words, this contrapuntal image of Bowie potentially stands outside of the actual singer's pioneering gender ambiguity in his work up to *Alladin Sane* and his prescient dissection of the cult of celebrity in the deceptively frothy pop songwriting of his 1972 album *The Rise and Fall of Ziggy Stardust and the Spiders from Mars.* Those who are aware of the Mitki's own mythology about the unlikely union of temperamental, cultural, and physical opposites represented by Shinkarev and Shagin, discussed in the last chapter, would notice the fact that Shinkarev in this statement establishes a parallel between himself and Bowie that problematizes the opposition of values that he otherwise asserts. Certainly, Shinkarev's critique of Shagin's attempt to serve as the leader of the Mitki (documented in the previous chapter) has more than a little in common with Bowie's characterization of the temptations of celebrities to occupy positions of spiritual authority, as in the case of the delusional American rock star Vince Taylor, who served as a model for Bowie's Ziggy Stardust. In this chapter, we will consider the Mitki's assimilation of the cultural and sexual "otherness" of Bowie and his legacy, and their forging of it into an instrument for dissecting their own understanding of masculinity.

We begin our journey to the Mitki's rendezvous with the imagined West of Bowie in what would seem an unlikely place: in the reading spaces of the seventies- and eighties-era Leningrad underground. Taking a cue from Butler's understanding of fantasy and experiential play as workshops for reconfiguring norms,[6] we are already poised to regard participation in samizdat as a "queer" act, as a form of symbolic polymorphous closeness which, as Eve Kosofsky Sedgwick describes in her book *Between Men: English Literature and Male Homosocial Desire*, signifies a threshold to a "revolutionary fulfillment of desire."[7] We need to imagine the reading of a samizdat journal as it must have been for many citizens in the Soviet Union on the eve of glasnost and perestroika: as a tactile, dizzying, and even sensual experience, heightened by the frisson of political risk and evocative (as Losev suggests) of intoxication as well as the anticipation of physical intimacy or harm. Shinkarev's *Mitki* and gossipy commentaries about the movement, such as the art historian Luka Kuznetsov's *Oppanki—Indeed!*, were serialized throughout 1985 and 1986 in, among other illegal venues, the crudely typographed journal *Krasnyi shchedrinets*. In the case of *Mitki*, pages of blurry gray mimeographed text alternated with Aleksandr Florensky's photocopied illustrations of the comical situations of life within the subculture. Florensky drew in a deliberately amateurish style suggestive of a quick sketch version of a political cartoon, with human figures emerging from the page in the sloping outlines of ill-fitting clothes; he depicted the urban human comedy of the Mitki in lines of variable thickness and broad swaths of black, as if the rotund and androgynous figures were equally the product of a leaky pen and a moment of giddy improvisation.

Shinkarev initially circulated his book without illustrations among his circle of friends, which included in its number Shagin and the Florenskys. As the scholar Ann Komaromi has pointed out, "a certain amount of ambiguity or 'play' between the physical form and the ideal content, between the signifier and the signified" is crucial to understanding the diverse range of the responses to samizdat texts.[8] Among readers, authors, and typesetters, some of these responses were spontaneous or unplanned; others were anticipated or elicited with targeted expectations. With their gravid lines, the photocopies of Florensky's images for Shinkarev's first samizdat edition of *Mitki* are meant to represent close equivalents or vivid simulacra of Florensky's actual illustrations (Figure 4). The splotchy blacks of Florensky's illustrations impress upon us the closeness, if not interchangeability, of the original art and the copy that we are holding in our hands. His artwork serves the purpose of suggesting a virtual physical link between author and audience. As we

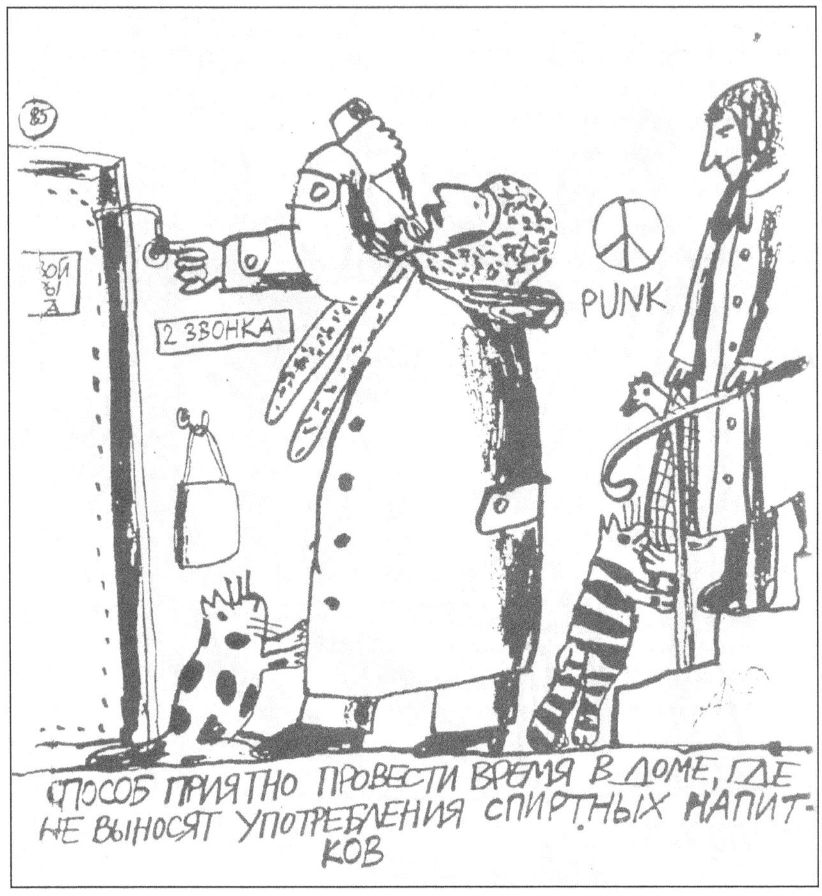


Figure 4. Aleksandr Florensky, "A way of having a good time at a place that doesn't allow the consumption of hard liquor" (Sposob priyatno provesti vremia, v dome gde ne vynosiat upotrebleniia spritnykh napitok), from Vladimir Shinkarev, *Mit'ki: Risunki Aleksandra Olegovicha Florenskogo* (1990), page 26.

cradle this text, we understand that we are very close to the experience of touching the illustrator's original ink drawings, perhaps even to the point where we imagine black splotches on our fingers and reflexively draw our hand quickly away. Certainly we picture ourselves as holding a text that is only one generation removed from the manuscript of the author, who may have manually supervised the printing of what we are holding. The serialization of *Mitki* in *Krasnyi shchedrinets* provided a simulacrum of intimate contact between writer and artist, reader and illustrator (who, before he set a seemingly unsteady pen to paper, was himself a reader of Shinkarev's text). Shinkarev's book suggested a relationship between women and men—and, perhaps most provocatively of all, among men themselves—that was analogous to the contact between paper and hand. The book was not merely an emblem for the possibilities that the Leningrad underground provided for redefining gender: it was also an examination of intimacy inscribed *within* gender, of what Sedgwick terms the "vulnerability" of internalized norms to "extreme reversals depending on the structuring of the policed desire, within a particular cultural moment [and] as an open secret."[9]

The centrality of intimacy as the result of gender dysphoria within the "brand" of the Mitki may also be understood (to paraphrase Pussy Riot's Nadezhda Tolokonnikova) as an image (*obraz*, or "icon") of the age, in this case a mirror or portrait of the ineffectuality of the muscular campaign of Soviet imperialism in Afghanistan during the eighties. Indeed, the earliest illustration among the Mitki that was perceived as politically provocative—and which gained them the outraged or laudatory attention of a much larger, and arguably national, audience in the Soviet Union—was Vasili Golubev's woodcut *The Mitki Send Brezhnev Off to Afghanistan*, which portrays men from the group outfitting the doddering Soviet leader and hapless engineer of the Soviet Afghan adventure in military fatigues before loading him onto a waiting military transport plane (Figure 5). In his print, Golubev (one of the earliest members of the Mitki) seems to suggest that Brezhnev should have directly experienced the consequences of the disastrous imperialist policies that he authored. Even in the heady reformist atmosphere of Mikhail Gorbachev's policy of glasnost in 1987, Golubev's print was shocking for its incendiary suggestion that a Soviet leader may justifiably be sent to his death.

This understanding of the Mitki as opponents of authoritarian masculinism and agents for the dismantling of gender norms was also recognized among their contemporaries in the Leningrad underground. In Luka Kuznetsov's short four-act play *Oppanki—Indeed!* (which was published in an issue of *Krasnyi shchedrinets* that also contained an installment of the "scripture" of the youth movement that it sets out to interpret), five different "Olenka" Florenskys (numbered 1 through 4, and 666) share the stage with Shagin, Florensky, Shinkarev, and two other members of the Mitki, as if to highlight the importance of gender balance within the world of unofficial Soviet culture. The play reaches a

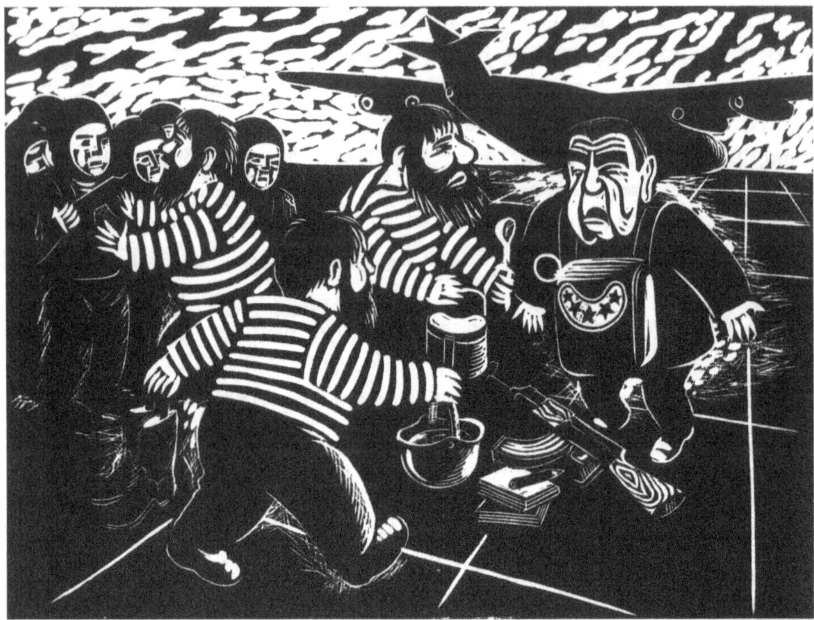

Figure 5. Vasili Golubev, *The Mitki Send Brezhnev Off to Afghanistan (Mitki otpravliaiut Brezhneva v Afganistan)* (1987). Woodcut, 192 × 267 mm. (collection of the artist)

crescendo of character-deformational burlesque when Shinkarev takes on the role of a woman.[10] Within the play, we see an awareness of the mercurial nature of desire (for various male and female others) as a marker for self-definition that is not fully coterminous with sexuality, and as the realm of indeterminate human intimacy that Leo Bersani terms "unbound affect."[11] A present-day reader of Kuznetsov's play would be reminded of Judith Butler's more recent explications of the ways in which the category of gender owes it perdurability to its protean character: gender becomes transmogrified, yet never disappears. Which brings us to the question: in the world that the Mitki document as both a social happening and the histrionic acting-out of a utopian meditation, what does it mean to be a desiring woman or man?

Before we answer this question about desire and gender, we need to reckon with the issue of what being a man means for the Mitki. Many Russian commentators have perceived the Mitki to be socially conservative, an understanding to which the group has sometimes responded with ironic and disarming equivocation. Already at the beginning of his book *Mitki*, Shinkarev admits to the thorniness of his group's gender politics, albeit with self-deprecating nuance: "The theoretical Mityok is an eminently moral individual, possessed of a worldview that gravitates to the formula of 'Orthodoxy, Autocracy and Nationality,' although in practice he is so frivolous, that he may seem to be bereft of many moral principles."[12] Like almost everything programmatic in the work of the Mitki, this statement is couched in provisional terms that partially dissolve the etched outlines of the asserted credo. In fact, the political values of the far-right and left blur and merge in the artistic production of the Mitki. The Mitki seek to topple totems of male authority, even as they are worshipfully transfixed by them; they initially seek to save their estimable if frail role models in the last days of empire by having them ride on their shoulders, like Anchises on Aeneas during the sack of Troy. Yet what we see in almost all the Mitki's fiction, poetry, music, and painting is that this empathy for the human vulnerability of entitled power networks quickly passes, as the artists attempt to cast down the paternalistic idols that they initially hold up. The Mitki are interested in ironic engagement and dialogue—a multidirectional relation—with authority, and in this respect their work echoes Mikhail Bakhtin's dictum in his work from the twenties (published for the first time in 1986, at the mid-point of Shinkarev's writing of his samizdat installments of *Mitki*) that selflessness represents an active ethical orientation and is incompatible with effacing one's identity by a prodigious outside force: "Passive empathizing, being possessed, losing oneself—these have nothing in common with the answerable act/deed of self-abstracting and self-renunciation. In self-renunciation I actualize with utmost activeness and in full the uniqueness of my place in Being."[13] In 1988, during the Mitki's first wave of notoriety, the Soviet political scientist (and supporter of Gorbachev's policies of glasnost and perestroika) Lev Karpinski wrote that Stalinism can only be understood as a unidirectional model of power, proceeding exclusively from top to bottom (*sverkhu vniz*).[14] It should therefore not surprise us that in the diverse artistic production of the Mitki, sudden descents are as much experiences of the spectacular failure of authority as they are of principled rebellion.

One consequence of the refusal to surrender one's identity is the willingness to entertain the possibility of multiple selves, and to reject the paradigm of agency that envisions heroism as a manifestation of phallic aggression. Writing about the experiential ambiguities of homosociality, Eve Kosofsky Sedgwick takes note of the fact that "issues of modern homo/heterosexual definition are structured . . . not by the supercession of one model and the consequent withering away of another, but instead by the relations enabled by the unrationalized coexistence of different models."[15] Certainly the proliferation of the "Olenkas" that we see in Kuznetsov's play suggests the synchronic sprawl of multiple and perhaps inchoate identities that Sedgwick describes, albeit without specific reference to sexual orientation. The Mitki's absurdist play-acting and writing includes a fascination with androgyny and cross-dressing as forms of youthful rebellion, pointing up Soviet-era Russian masculinity as a social construct with possibly toxic ramifications. Following the work of the Mitki, we need to contemplate the practice of "queering" in a more expansive sense, as understood from within the Russian context by critics such as Boris Eikhenbaum: as a tool for defamiliarizing the paradigm of normativity. Along the way, we will also encounter the Mitki's elevation of this practice from the status of a critical tool to an actual performance of sexualized ways of being.

There are two different ways of understanding the motivations that underpin the Mitki's undertaking of defamiliarizing (or "queering") the category of gender as a way of dethroning political authority that is morally bankrupt. One way is to regard the Mitki as consummate examples of artistic postmodernism. Solomon Volkov, one of the first commentators on the Mitki from the West, writes that the Mitki "are unwilling to split art into good and bad [which is] the characteristic typical of postmodernism. Everything is accompanied with a delicate smile. They take everything ironically and never seriously because they don't take themselves seriously."[16] In his 1979 essay "Answering the Question: What Is Postmodernism?," Jean-François Lyotard asserts that postmodernism is that which "denies itself the solace of good forms, the consensus of a taste which would make it possible to share collectively the nostalgia for the unattainable." "A postmodernist artist or writer," Lyotard argues, "is in the position of a philosopher: the text he writes, the work he produces are not in principle governed by preestablished rules [because] those rules and categories are what the work of art is looking for."[17] In the introduction to a catalog for a retrospective exhibit from 2001, Shinkarev writes that the Mitki are drawn to both popular and high culture and do not exclude the possibility that these two aspects of culture may parody Jungian archetypes as much as they echo them.[18] The destabilization of meaning is openly acknowledged, and even celebrated, by the Mitki, and it indeed places them within the orbit of any number of understandings of postmodernism. Lyotard writes that "the work and text [of the postmodernist artist] have the character of an *event*,"[19] a fact that explains the interest in performance art that such practitioners often share. The bizarre eclecticism of the Mitki's aesthetics, and their view of even the most clichéd or inane speech act as a work of art—what they term the *kheppening* or *stavka*, a language-based equivalent to Marcel Duchamp's "found objects"—would seem to catch them in the act of postmodernist relativizing.

Another, perhaps more analytical, appreciation would regard their work as an extended exercise in audience manipulation. The Mitki's employment of patriotic emblems and associations arguably brings them very close in their aesthetic and ideological strategies to the music, mock manifestos, and invented heraldry of the quasi-fascist—or is it quasi-socialist?—Slovenian movement of Laibach and *Neue Slowenische Kunst*. That movement (in its inception roughly contemporary with the Mitki) bombards its audience with the artistic symbols of authoritarianism in a way that is deliberately uncritical, inviting a queasy sense of complicity in the audience. As pointed out by Slavoj Žižek, the goal of the heavy metal music and violent aesthetic pronouncements of Laibach—whose most recent provocation was a 2015 performance in Pyongyang, North Korea, in honor of the seventieth anniversary of the country's sovereignty—is to bring to the audience's attention the probable fact of its own love for and instinctual acceptance of such antidemocratic images: "By means of the elusive character of desire, of the indecidability as to 'where they actually stand,' Laibach compels us to take our position and to decide upon *our* desire."[20] To a certain extent, the Mitki engage in the same strategy of ideological provocation. The eclecticism of the Mitki—the mutual irreconcilability of their various influences, proudly displayed in their texts and artwork like a row of garishly clashing medals on the lapel of a parading Russian World War II veteran on Victory Day—represents a strategy of deliberate ideological disorientation, an attempt to make the audience aware of the pat responses it possesses in subconscious reserve.

And yet, although the Mitki toy with the ultramundane language of tsarism and the hortatory speech of Stalinism, there is no clear-cut political agenda in their work—at least not fully in the way that Žižek has in mind—nor is their view of Soviet ideological artifacts uncritical. They are curiously uninterested in concrete political and economic questions and therefore cannot be bracketed with proponents of Russia's current far right. At this point, it is useful to contemplate anew the name of the movement, which could be translated as "little Mityas." The word Mitki suggests that Shagin, the group's nominal leader, superimposes an image of himself onto others, replacing their individual sensibilities with his own. In his book about the movement, Shinkarev gamely admits to this effacement of the individual in the group's social dynamics, and he does so without any squirming or apparent discomfort. The self-presentation of the Mitki can be considered a parody of both the Stalinist cult of personality and the lifestyle and writings of the Brezhnev-era dissident underground. But can it actually be both?

A few odd moments in the writing and artwork of the Mitki are useful in answering this question and help determine the specific character of the Mitki's postmodernism in relation to the presentation of homosocial relations in their movement. Their Soviet nonconformist provenance notwithstanding, a great deal of the Mitki's work lingers with seeming nostalgia on St. Petersburg as a symbol of imperial power. The quasi-militarism of the Mitki's subculture colors a wide range of their art and writing and is evident in the preponderance of blue and white in their paintings (often composed in alternating bands or stripes suggestive of naval emblems) and in declarations of regimented solidarity in the face of the personal hardships of social isolation and alcoholism. Their interpretations of old Soviet and prerevolutionary songs about the naval might of Peter the Great's city on the Neva stand as ironic counterweights to the movement's fascination with the myth of the dashing criminal black marketeer and their aversion to violence and coercion, reflected in the deliberately child-like art of Shagin and in the group's pacifist motto "the Mitki do not want to defeat anyone!" ("Mit'ki ne khotiat nikogo pobedit'!"), which to the Russian ear sounds like a negated version of a post-war Soviet slogan. That the Mitki succeed at all in bringing about this effect is due in large part to the fact that they make their own self-examination a subject in their work. As if to underscore their identity as a group based in St. Petersburg, the Mitki use the relatively egalitarian ideals of the Russian naval officers' corps, as established by Peter the Great in the early 1720s, as a touchstone for their anti-hierarchical social principles. In a famous statement about his new navy, Peter underscored the importance of the accountability of superiors and the necessity for a common set of governing principles for both officers and sailors.[21] The "Code of the Officer of the Navy," drafted in 1863, is an elaboration of these principles, asserting the symbolic primacy of the sailors at the expense of the officers.[22] The code ceded many disciplinary matters concerning individual sailors to the adjudication of the group rather than the commanding officers and prohibited sailors from informing on one another to their superiors.[23]

The idealistic fascination with the prerevolutionary Russian navy during the Soviet period was perhaps most eloquently expressed by Joseph Brodsky in his autobiographical essay "In a Room and a Half": "It is my profound conviction that apart from the literature of the last two centuries and, perhaps, the architecture of the former Russian capital, the only other thing Russia can be proud of is its Navy's history. Not because of its spectacular victories, of which there have been rather few, but because of the nobility of spirit that informed its enterprise." With possible irony, Brodsky goes on to characterize the image of the Russian navy as "less functional than decorative, informed more by a spirit of discovery than by that of imperial expansion, prone rather to a heroic gesture and self-sacrifice than to survival at all costs."[24] In his poetry, Shagin strikes the same tone of viewing the navy as a rare expression of freedom in Russian culture, a refuge from surveillance and bondage:

The quiet clip of the steamship,
Anchors aweigh!
Farewell, o Freedom,
Hello, my Motherland . . .[25]

Here, Shagin's enthusiasm about life at sea contains an unexpectedly lukewarm sentiment about the return to Russia. The maritime motif in the work of the Mitki tends to serve as a dampener rather than amplifier of traditional notions of Russian patriotism. The "spirit" of discovery that Brodsky alludes to seems here to be more of the otherwise unexamined self than it is of places that are located far beyond Russian borders.

Such moments of astringent paradox in the Mitki's perception of themselves—and of Russian culture as a whole—is especially evident in moments when they are accompanied with illustrations, as in the first non-samizdat edition of Shinkarev's *Mitki*, published in 1990. In a segment titled "About the Epic in the Work of the Mitki," Shinkarev's narrator tells a joke he claims is a refutation of Jean Paul's assertion of the irreconcilability of the epic and comic.[26] But what could possibly provide the bridge between the epic and comic? The scene takes place on the high seas. A woman falls from a ship into the water. "Woman overboard!" cries the captain. An American dives into the water in an attempt to save her. Even though he is an international breaststroke champion, he drowns before swimming even ten meters. A Frenchman dives. Even though he is an international diving champion, he drowns before swimming even five meters. Then a Russian man comes up from the boiler room of the ship. Even though he is afraid of water and can't swim at all, he jumps overboard anyway . . . and drowns immediately.[27] In *Mitkimaier*, the 1993 Monty Pythonesque cartoon about the Mitki, the St. Petersburg-based animation studio Troitsky Bridge worked closely with Olga and Aleksandr Florensky and Viktor Tikhomirov in bringing the group's subculture to cinematic life. The attempts to save the woman are observed by a Candide-like wealthy American named Mayer, who learns about Russia through his contact with the Mitki. Mayer (who is partially based on George von Lengerke Meyer, the American ambassador to Russia from 1905 to 1907) is on his way to Russia for the first time. A long segment of the film is devoted to providing additional narrative detail to the setting of the joke, and it clearly bears the mark of Olga Florensky's style of combining Matisse-inflected compositions of overlapping body outlines with collages of photographs and floating orthographical fragments. In the film, each swimmer is heralded by a jerky montage of stereotypical images about his nation, with glimpses of Abraham Lincoln, the Marlboro Man, Cyrano de Bergerac, Charles Aznavour, Nicholas II, and Lenin. The punchline is a deflation because the expectation suggested by the structure of such jokes is that the Russian, with his eccentric and nonlinear way of thinking and living, will unexpectedly triumph where others have failed. "Who is this heroic man?" Mr. Mayer asks about the Russian. "He is a real Mityok!" he is answered. Yet the Russian (whose appearance in the film is modeled after Dmitri Shagin) fails as well, and his failure seems especially foolish and pointless given his inability to swim.

By ending in tragedy rather than an amusing reversal, the joke itself is a failure, like a limerick without a rhyme in its last couplet.[28] The Russian's instinct for heroism seems to be stronger than his sense of self-preservation. A Russian reader and viewer would also take note of the distinct thematic echoes of this anecdote to "Iz-za ostrova na sterzhen'" ("Out from Behind the Island, and into the Stream"), the famous pseudo-folksong about the seventeenth-century peasant rebel leader Stenka Razin. In the song, Razin rides in a boat together with his wife, a captured Persian princess, and his fellow rebels. Hearing the grumbling of his men that "he exchanged us for a woman! It took only one night for him to spend with her, / And in the morning, he became a woman [*nautro baboi stal*]," the drunk (*khmel'noi*) Razin picks up his wife and hurls her into the river. Bearing this subtext in mind, we see more clearly that Shinkarev is keen to demonstrate how both men and women may be sacrificed on the altar of a martial understanding of manhood.

Shagin wrote his own version of Shinkarev's anecdote about the drowning woman in 1997 as liner notes for the third of the Mitki CDs, *Mitkovian Songs* (*Mit'kovskie pesni*). He presents a different solution to Shinkarev's anecdote. A woman on a boat piloted by the Mitki falls into the sea. "Who will save [her]?" Right on the deck is David Bowie, who flings himself into a boat equipped with all the latest western nautical technology. He starts the motor but . . . it sputters and stops. All that new-fangled technology gone to waste! Suddenly, out of the boiler room, and dressed in grease-stained clothing, comes the Mityok. "Where's our sister [*sestrionka*]?" he asks. With a yell of "*Oppan'ki!*" (in Mitki slang), he throws himself into the water. But we know that the Mityok can't swim! What will happen to him? Miraculously, he runs on the surface of the water and saves the woman and the now-sinking David Bowie. How was he able to walk on water? The captain wipes a tear from his face and Bowie throws his electronic devices (*shmudaki*) into the sea. As the Mityok miraculously saves both the woman and Bowie from drowning, Shagin affectionately refers to the pop star with quasi-feminine suffixes, as "Devidushka Bauyushka."[29] The association of Bowie—at the early point of his protean career the premier figure of androgynous glam-rock—with the West reflects an ambivalence toward precisely that mixing of gender roles that the Mitki characterize in themselves at other points of their work, with the comic inability of the Mityok to take effective action, which is now ascribed to a figure from the West. David Bowie and the woman are chivalrously rescued by a "real" man who has a mystical connection to the sea and who takes on the role of a Christ figure to the amazed response of his apostle peers.

Later in this chapter we will return to Shagin's envisioning of Bowie as a figure of cultural and sexual indeterminacy. For the time being, we need to focus on the peculiar ambiguity of this scene of rescue on the larger canvas of Shagin's work as an artist and writer of light verse. The image of the drowning person is curiously resonant for Shagin. In his 1984 poem "Ikarushka" ("Little Icarus"), Shagin describes the tragic Icarus, whose wings of wax melted during his flight from Crete with his father Daedalus, as "forgotten by all his brothers. / And only his white legs [*belye nozhki*] stick out of the green waters."[30] As we noted in the previous chapter, Shagin's source material here is painterly as well as literary: his poem is partly a translation of W. H. Auden's "Musée des Beaux Arts," an ekphrastic meditation of Brueghel the Elder's famous representation of the fall of Icarus amidst a scene of indifferent toiling peasants.[31] In 1991, Shagin produces a *lubok*-influenced drawing titled *Korabliushechka* (*The Little Boat*) that is a variation of this scene from

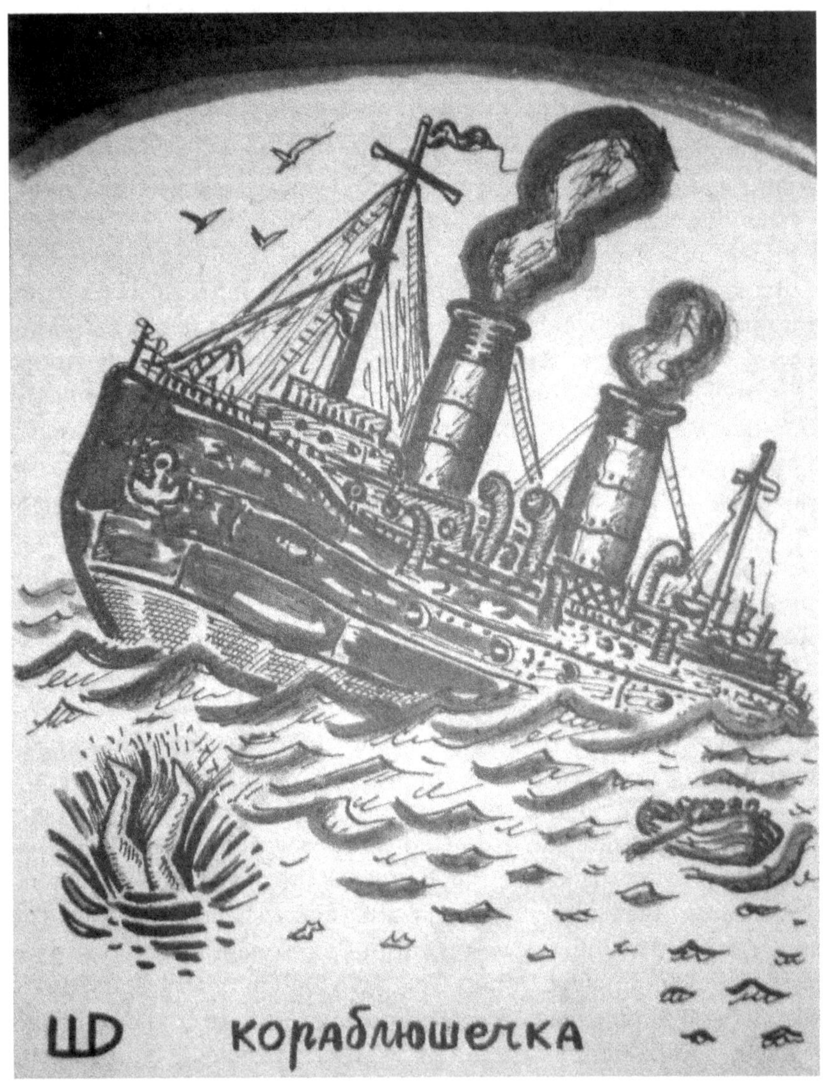


Figure 6. Dmitri Shagin, *The Little Boat (Korabliushechka)* (1991). Lithograph, 250 × 195 mm. (InterArt Gallery)

Brueghel's painting, with the crucial difference that in this instance someone has taken notice of the drowning person and has sent out a rescue boat (Figure 6).[32] The Mitki attempt to bring about an equilibrium between the ponderousness of combative male ambition and the lightness of the dandy's quasi-feminine grace, envisioning a Russian masculinity in the form of a new Icarus who escapes his tragic fate. A few years later, this figure of the drowning boy with the effeminately "white legs"—already tagged as a symbolic marker for the Mitki's failure at physical valor of any kind—was transformed into the image of the drowning woman, whom the Mityok is ultimately able to save, at least in Shagin's version. Shagin adds an element of homoeroticism to the contemplation of the canvas in Auden's poem, which is noticeably detached and lacking in overt empathy. To the nominal leader of the Mitki, members of the group are at least as much feminine as they are masculine.

Grasping the ethical aspects of this anecdote requires us to consider its stylistic and narrative characteristics. Shinkarev shrewdly uses the joke as a way of suggesting that the Mitki are interested in the creation of hybridized styles, reasserting a central feature of both their aesthetics and world view. In the previous chapter, we argued that all Shinkarev's work about the Mitki—the 1984–97 edition of *Mitki*, together with its additional chapters that appeared in the nineties, and the 2010 publication of *The End of the Mitki*—can be understood as a continuous novelistic narrative, if not Bildungsroman, that culminates in the partial redemption of one Mityok, Shinkarev himself, from the ravages of alcoholism and the temptations of callow vanity. Certainly, the pedantic, faux-scholarly tone of the early *Mitki* may be inspired by Nabokov's *Pale Fire*, itself a novel disguised as one of any number of other literary genres. But on an ontological level the dichotomy that interests Shinkarev and the Mitki most of all is not that of the serious and humorous, but of the male and the female. The anecdote about the failed rescue of the woman is especially expressive of the Mitki's enterprise of ideological self-demolition. The causal link between chivalry and the Russian sailor's de facto suicide—the most absolute form of self-mortification—is telling: to save a woman, the Mityok must risk ceasing to be a man.

Failure in its various forms—of the selfless gesture, of mythologized masculinity, of humor in a world scarred by tragedy, and perhaps even of heroism in general—is very much at the center of the Mitki's enterprise of demystifying ideological pieties. In a 1993 appendix to *Mitki* titled "Some News for Fortunate Alcoholics," Shinkarev points to the figure of the Mityok as a useful example of Russian self-examination, a "contemplation of national traits [that are] either bad or good," depending on one's point of view and attitude toward the serious social problem of alcoholism in Russia.[33] Among other things, the Mitki attempt to grapple with and redefine notions of heroism and national identity within the border zone between two eras with differing cultural ideals.

It should go without saying that heroic behavior leaves a powerful afterglow, even if its concrete results are disappointing. Certainly, the self-created and willed argot or slang of the Mitki, much of which was spoken among them fleetingly at best and was mostly Shinkarev's invention, is an example of existential self-assertion. A few words and morphological peculiarities from Mitki slang have entered into wider usage in nonnormative Russian, such as the overuse of the vaguely feminine diminutive suffix *-ushka* with a large number of masculine and feminine nouns and names of favorite artists (*veteranushka* [veteran], *parkushka pobedushki* [Victory Park], *Viskontiushka* [Luchino Visconti], *Van Gogushka* [Van Gogh]), verbs such as *ottiagivat'sia* ("to chill out, to get drunk") and nonsensical, occasionally euphemistic expletives such as *dyk, yoly-paly,* and *oppan'ki.* The art historian Tatiana Shekhter has taken particular note of the Leningrad underground's aggressive striving toward an aestheticized definition of itself, with its discourse reflecting an improvisionally rebarbative sensibility that went against the grain of everyday logic and etiquette.[34] An amusing example of the Mitki's use of argot as an anarchic conversation-stopper is provided by Shinkarev in the form of a fictitious phone conversation between Dmitri Shagin and his friend Aleksandr Florensky, husband of the artist Olga Florensky.[35] Shagin riffs obsessively and nonsensically with the various diminutive and nickname forms of people they know, with escalating levels of childish endearment, and much to Florensky's annoyance. "Shurka? . . . Shurochek? . . . Shurenochek?" Shagin asks tentatively. Florensky tells Shagin that "Kuzia" (the artist Andrei Kuznetsov) is sitting with him. Shagin, "with an ineffable tenderness towards Kuzia, whom he hardly knows," muses aloud: "Kuzia! . . . Kuziunchik . . . Kuzyarushka is sitting with you. . . . So you're chilling with Kuzen'ka are you?" Florensky becomes annoyed as Shagin arbitrarily changes the subject, calling him "brother" (*bratok*) in an intimate way and badgering him with questions about his wife, Olga, whom he cloyingly refers to as "Olenka," and "my little sister" (*sestrionka*). As Florensky angrily hangs up, Dmitri Shagin is reported to be "deeply satisfied with the conversation."[36] The entire imagined stymied conversation is best understood through the lens of Shekhter's observation that "the playful, theatricalized component of the underground's form of emotionality unfolded from [both] the foundation of the outsider's psychology and the [general] social frustration that represented the backdrop of life within the unofficial world."[37] The Mitki strive to disrupt the clockwork operation of conventional niceties, and in this regard they have a great deal in common with the American Beat writers, and Ken Kesey's Merry Pranksters in particular. The Mitki's cult of gentle subversiveness, expressed in playful communicative sabotage, is also undoubtedly inspired by the famously nonsensical utterances of Russian "Holy Fools," and there is arguably much in their visual and literary work that resonates with religious and iconographic practices of pre-Petrine Russian culture.

But there is more than verbal anarchism at work in Shagin's reference to Olga Florensky as his "[little] sister" (*sestrionka*). As the semi-fictional dialogue above illustrates, the argot of the Mitki enacts not so much a deformation of gender as it does a defamiliarization of it: as a result, we become newly aware of the ways in which gender is driven by desire, as well as by affect and cultural norms. The 1992 animated film *Mitkimaier*, whose artwork was done largely by Olga and Aleksandr Florensky, contains a chaotic abundance of different typefaces, cases and alphabets (as in the floating caption of the word "pheasant" in the bestiary segment: "фазаN") and words in Russian, English, and French, amusingly rendered in both alphabets, often within the same word and with childish spelling mistakes. In several moments of the film, the Florenskys restored the prerevolutionary "hard sign" (ъ) that was attached to words ending in an unpalatized consonant ("tiger": тигръ). In her essay about the poetics of orthography, typeface, and script, Olga Florensky uses the term "maiden [*devichii*] script" to refer to the child-like reliance on block letters, describing it as the most "interesting, pure, and vulnerable [*nezashchishchennyi*: literally, undefended] variant of daily script."[38] In other words, unregulated or untutored writing represents innocence and vulnerability. Olga Florensky's statement serves as another reminder that the Mitki are interested in exploring the feminization of male identity.

The responses of various members within the group to these meditations upon the interpenetration of gender archetypes within a single person are often fearlessly probing and self-analytical. Acknowledging what he calls the "anti-feminist" trappings of the Mitki as a movement,

Shinkarev archly takes note of the following "curious nuance," which may absolve the group of accusations of gender inequality: "the highest 'little sister' title (after terms such as 'my one and only,' 'my favorite,' and 'only') is . . . brother! [*bratushka*]." Shinkarev points out that female fellow travelers of the Mitki are called maidens (*devki*) whereas women who are full-fledged members are "little sisters" (*sestrionki*), the latter for "reasons unknown" usually carrying the name "Olenka."[39] Aleksandr Florensky's illustration for this segment of Shinkarev's book amusingly renders this transformation into terms of a thoroughgoing intershuffling of sexual traits across the gender divide (Figure 7).[40] Transgender change swiftly makes its way among these men and women, with maidens becoming hirsute "little sisters" and the Mityok Filippov ("Fil") finding himself dressed like a woman and sporting a beard where there had been a mere stubble in the preceding panel. The dresses of the "little sisters" in turn conform to the masculine sartorial identity of the Mitki, the striped patterns of their dresses echoing the design of sailors' shirts. In these images, Florensky portrays the Mitki conception of community as being as sisterly as it is fraternal; his pointing up of the vestigial traces of earlier gender identity in cross-dressing brings to mind Susan Sontag's famous observation about camp aesthetics, that attractiveness and sharply chiseled images of sexuality are often enhanced by the juxtaposition of both sets of gender markers within a single person.[41] No wonder that Shinkarev has Shagin addressing Florensky as "Shura," rather than by the more common nickname of Sasha for Aleksandr: Shura is a possible affectionate form for both Aleksandr and Aleksandra. According to various writings of the group, the logical consequence of such gender-bending is that the Mitki are "absolutely asexual," as reflected in Vladimir Shinkarev's and Aleksandr Florensky's illustrations of a situation (not described in any of the writings of the Mitki) of three Mitki sprawled in a drunken slumber in front of a television monitor showing a pornographic video, and ironically titled *The Mitki's Viewing of an Erotic Film*.[42] It is here that the meticulously maintained postmodernist stance of the Mitki falters, and where we get a sense of an acute anxiety with the multiplicity of possible meanings, identities, and alter egos. The Mitki desire androgyny yet fear it. Can a man be both emasculated and heroic?

But one detail from Florensky's illustration deserves additional commentary, and for the light it sheds on the sheer peculiarity of the subculture of the Mitki as presented in Shinkarev's book. The word for "woman" written next to the figure of Filippov in drag is deliberately misspelled. As Shinkarev explains in a parodically scholarly chapter

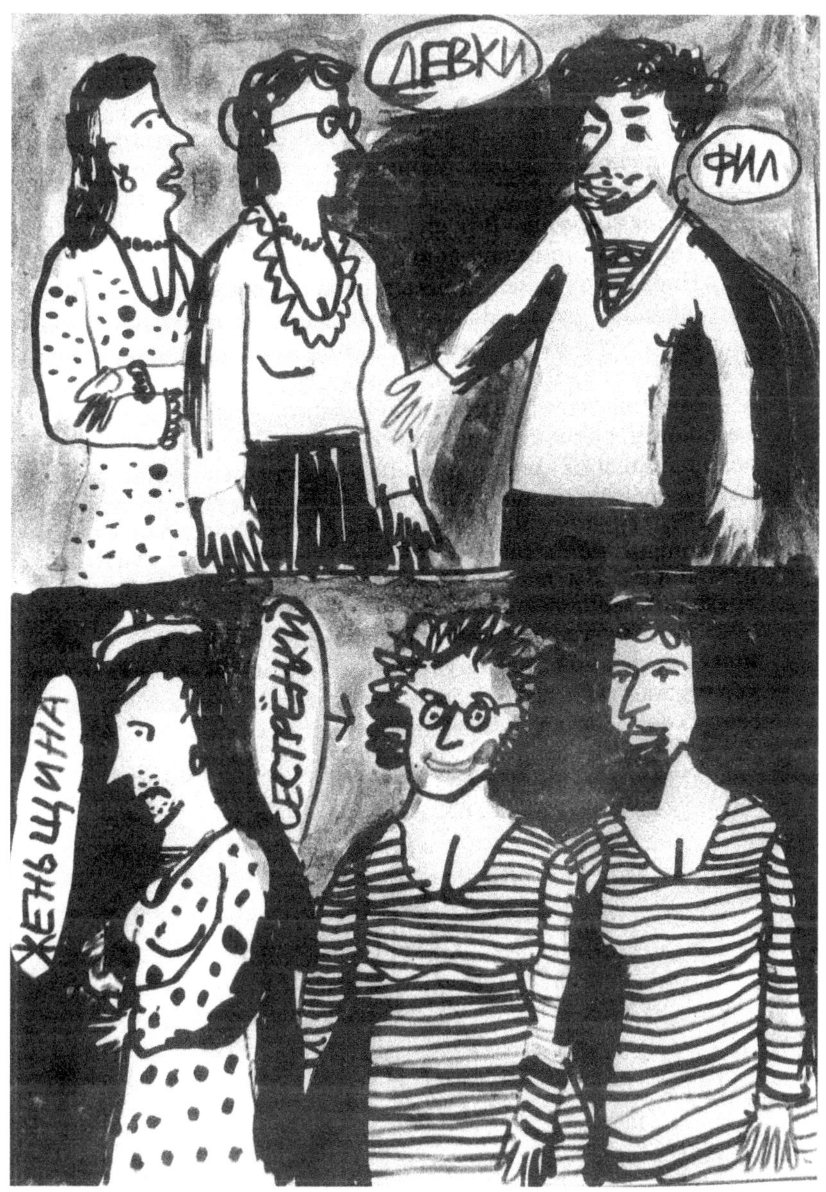


Figure 7. Aleksandr Florensky, *Little Brothers and Little Sisters* (Bratushki i sestrionki), from Vladimir Shinkarev, *Mit'ki: Risunki Aleksandra Olegovicha Florenskogo* (1990), page 85.

titled "A Report on the Article by A. Filippov 'The Mitki and Little Sisters,'" Filippov does not know the word for "woman," which is why he spells it incorrectly, with a Russian soft sign (ь) that signals the palatalization of the preceding consonant: not *zhenshchina* (женщина), but *zhen'shchina* (женьщина). Here Shinkarev also evokes a socio-linguistic fact: during the seventies and eighties, the palatalization of hard nasal consonants was an often-mocked affectation of highly educated Leningraders. Yet there is more: Shinkarev's orthographic tinkering with the word is also highly suggestive of a certain kind of onomastic gender bending. At this moment of the text, the Russian ear stumbles and pauses against the unexpectedly palatalized or "softened" nasal consonant. The insertion of the soft sign (ь) in the middle of the word makes the first syllable sound like the colloquial vocative of the name Zhenya ("Zhen' [Жень]!"), the endearing form for either Evgeni ("Eugene") or Evgeniya ("Eugenia"). In a later chapter, Shinkarev plays the role of movement archivist in recounting two different versions of a clearly fantasized story of how Fil brought his fiancée to Florensky's studio to introduce her to his old teacher and friend. In Fil's version, Florensky drunkenly makes a pass at her, and in Florensky's account, Fil barges in "shitfaced" (*p'ianyi v zhopu*) with two women, one of them his fiancée, whom he refers to as Olenka "for kicks" (*dlia smekha*), taunting Florensky with the name of his wife. Florensky tearfully comforts "Olenka" as Fil begins to paw the other woman. Both accounts begin with Florensky cooking himself ham and eggs and end with Fil in a rage, grabbing a knife off the table and lunging at Florensky but wounding his fiancée instead, who survives with a small scar under her eye. The details of these accounts from the movement's mythology serve to reinforce among the ranks of the Mitki the stricture against sexuality, which they regard as a disturbance of the fraternal principle guiding the group. "If a Mityok treated his little sisters like sex objects," Shinkarev writes in another chapter, "then the whole movement of the Mitki would be buried by an overflow of marriages, tragedies, beatings, etc."[43] Also curious is the fact that these narratives assume that active male sexuality inevitably leads to violence against women. In his mock exegesis of what he terms foundational "myths" about the movement, Shinkarev comments that the "ham and eggs" of this anecdote represent a "luminous image." In an apparent parody of Soviet-era structuralism, with its intelligent adaptation of Jungian gender archetypes, Shinkarev sees the meal of ham and eggs as mythically representative of the male and female principles, of which the male Mityok Florensky partakes.

The combined taboos against pedophilia and incest, applied even to this creatively figurative context, serve as a double-barreled stricture against the loss of innocence, a way of exploring the streamlined sameness and boredom of prelapsarian (i.e., pre-glasnost) Soviet life while problematizing it in the form of a postmodern memory. The androgyny of the Mitki represents a retreat into perceived innocence, a state that owes its gender ambiguity to a large extent to the still hovering shadow of the mother's recently abandoned womb. The subculture of the Mitki can be defined as a matriarchal society in search of a figure to serve as mother, and in this regard the rotund image of Dmitri Shagin symbolically serves as a kind of surrogate mother figure for the entire movement, described as the "erotic symbol of the Mitki: large, kind, and good."[44] Yet if Shagin becomes a figure invested with erotic power, we must ask ourselves the following question: in what ways can a Mityok desire him, and in what ways can that desire be reciprocated?

The clearest answer to this question lies within the realm of homosocial physical closeness among the Mitki, as represented in their illustrations, paintings, and literary texts. The closing of the distance between bodies—between mine and yours, and among all men and women within a nonhierarchical and anti-militaristic group—is at the center of the Mitki's project not just to efface and transform the experience of gendered identity, but also to render queer the idea of intimacy itself. For starters, the very idea of leadership is problematized and made absurd through the notional possibility of tactile contact with it. Shagin is a figurehead, a parodic instantiation of authority who playfully directs our attention to himself as a participant in a community of freely desiring subjects. All these people are presented as belonging to a world that is similar to the one envisioned by the *fin de siècle* Symbolist essayist Vasili Rozanov. In Rozanov's writings, frank (albeit hetero-) sexuality and propulsive desire flourish within an environment that is informed by a spirit of beneficent corporeality, and which contains no element of the will to dominate others. In Shagin's own poetry, the men among the Mitki often wake up together within the cramped quarters of the boiler rooms where they work. For them, the boiler room is an alternative realm, a safe space for the expression of tenderness among men that is clearly more than comradeship but less than open eroticism. In his verse, Shagin paints a portrait of Leningrad as a city of men at loose ends (many of them demobilized veterans, if not soldiers who have gone AWOL [*peredembeli*]), searching for intimacy with each other outside the regimented and hierarchical context of either the army or the workplace. Suggestive of the passionately platonic man and woman at the center of Dostoevsky's story "White Nights"—wandering together through an empty St. Petersburg as they engage in a spoken version of an ardent nineteenth-century exchange of letters—in Shagin's poetry men walk together in garrulous, argot-speaking pairs through a nocturnal Leningrad, taking joy in the urban sights whose desolation is mitigated by the company of another person. Amidst Shagin's poetic tableaux of eroticized relations between "two brothermen-bros" (*dva bratel'nika-bratka*), the dividing line between physical desire and love is difficult to discern. Perhaps this blurring of affect among modes of intimacy is most evident in Shagin's numerous ink drawings and prints of two men sitting close together at a table. One, *Sport Loves Those Who Are Strong*, is titled after a satirical sketch from Shinkarev's *A Papuan from Honduras*, in which two athletes, a Soviet and West German, face off in a televised drinking competition.[45] Yet this particular tableau, of the athlete Stepanov draping his arm across the shoulder of his opponent, does not take place in Shinkarev's novel.[46] It would seem that Shagin is keen to offset the antagonism of male opponents that we see in the novel by showing us the possibilities of tenderness in the aftermath of conflict.

In another emblematic image from Shagin's graphic art—later reproduced as a group photo, with Olga Florensky joining the clutch—several Mitki dance together wearing a single shirt, sewn with multiple arms.[47] In her 1990 book *Epistemology of the Closet*, Eve Kosofsky Sedgwick argues that the distance maintained between homosociality and consummated same-sex carnality validates both male privilege and the invasive presence of homophobia in everyday life.[48] In much of the work of the Mitki, male friendship is queered not so much in the sense that it becomes homoerotic, but rather in that it is rendered into a mutual regard that is sharply contrasted with the self-satisfied comity among men who occupy positions of power; no one here is interested in buttressing traditional institutions such as the military or the Communist Party. Yet in some of Shagin's verse and graphic work we do see a consideration of homoeroticism precisely in the sense that Sedgwick discusses, as an emotionally charged male solidarity that upholds a set of establishment values, while never really crossing over into relations of sexual intimacy.

Nor is Shagin the only Mityok to elaborate upon sexual ambiguity or indeterminacy. We see even stronger evidence of this transgressive play with various sexualities (including the association of femininity with lightness and flight) in the Mitki's 2006 group painting titled *Sisters, or A Woman's Lot* (*Sestry, ili zhenskaia dolia*) (Figure 8). Each artist painted one segment of the painting. A panel by Viktor Tikhomirov has a winged nude flying from a group of ogling and pawing men; Shagin's panel portrays the Soviet film actress Lydia Fedoseeva-Shukshina in a Garboesque pose wearing a sailor's shirt and a tattoo with the name "Olya," over a bird, a reference to Olga Florensky as the avatar of female identity among the Mitki (Figure 9).

Perhaps most interestingly, the center panel by Shinkarev has a naked woman dancing with her back to the viewer (Figure 10). The female figure and the bare room with a single swinging light bulb is essentially a female version of Shinkarev's painting *Dancing Alone* (*Odin tantsuet*), which was one of his signature images of empathy for social isolation and the flight from pain and suffering (Figure 11). Shinkarev has used the composition *Dancing Alone* in a variety of contexts: as the cover for an edition of his 1981 novel *Maxim and Fyodor*, as a panel allegorically representing Gregor Samsa's transformation in the comic strip devoted to Kafka's *Metamorphosis* (from his series *World Literature*), and as a representation of a Mityok in joyous solitude. What all these images foreground, however, is the clothed male figure. By unclothing this already iconic dancer when it is transformed into the comely figure of a woman—and in a group painting specifically devoted to the Mitki's treatment of gender—Shinkarev is pointing to the possibility of same-sex desire within the work of the movement.

Shinkarev's portrayal of the sexual ambiguity of this signature figure from his painted work echoes the specific features of Shagin's fascination with Icarus. Certainly the elegiac affect of Shagin's literary and visual representation of a feminized Icarus found its way into other chapters of Shinkarev's book and became something of a totem for the movement, as evident from Shinkarev's cover painting for the 1998 edition of his *Mitki* and Olga Florensky's Matisse-influenced poster for the first retrospective exhibit of their work, which took place in 1994 in Moscow and St. Petersburg.[49] Even the title of Shagin's drawing *Korabliushechka* (Little boat) is significant in terms of gender typology. "Boat" (*korabl'*) a masculine noun in Russian, has a perfectly good diminutive form with a suffix that is consistent with its grammatical gender (*korablik*), but as Shinkarev notes in his Mitki book, the masculine diminutive form *korablik* is "banal," and leaves a "bitter taste."[50] Olga Florensky seeks the

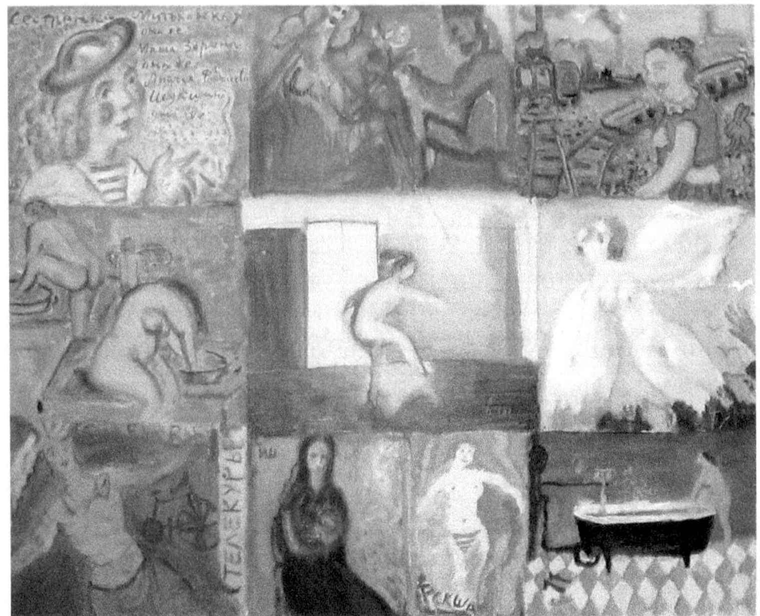

Figure 8. Group painting by the Mitki, *Sisters, or A Woman's Lot* (Sestry, ili zhenskaia dolia) (2006). *From upper left to lower right*: panels by Dmitri Shagin, Andrei Kuznetsov, Andrei Filippov, Tatiana Filippova, Vladimir Shinkarev, Viktor Tikhomirov, Aleksandr Goryaev, Yoanna Shagina, and Irina Vasilieva. Oil, 80 × 100 cm. (Mitki Art Center, St. Petersburg, Russia)

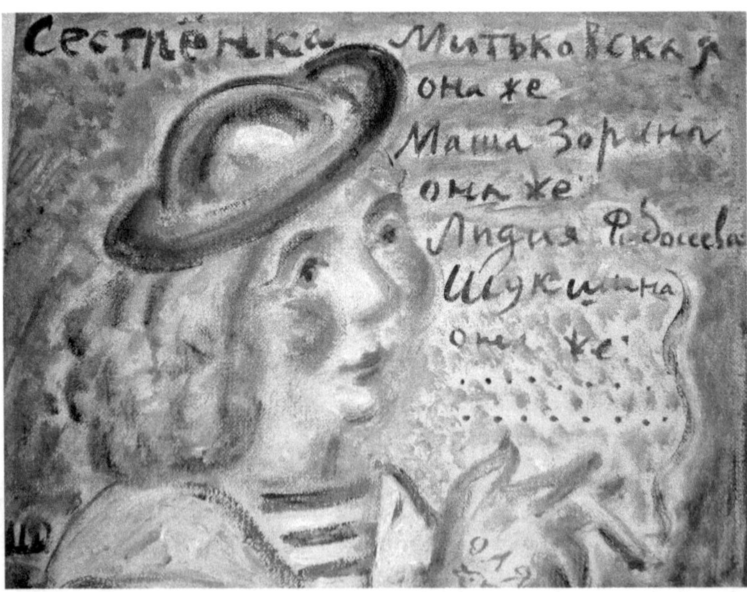


Figure 9. Detail from *Sisters, or A Woman's Lot* (2006), panel by Dmitri Shagin.

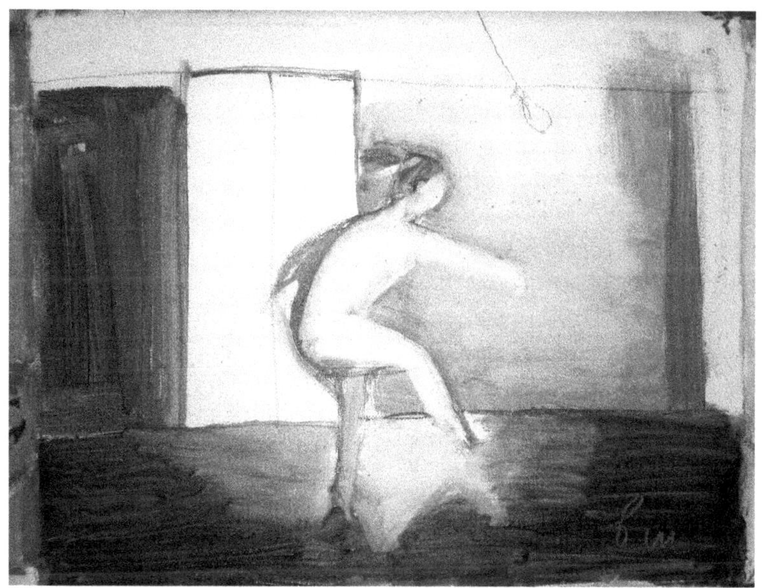

Figure 10. Detail from *Sisters, or A Woman's Lot* (2006), panel by Vladimir Shinkarev.

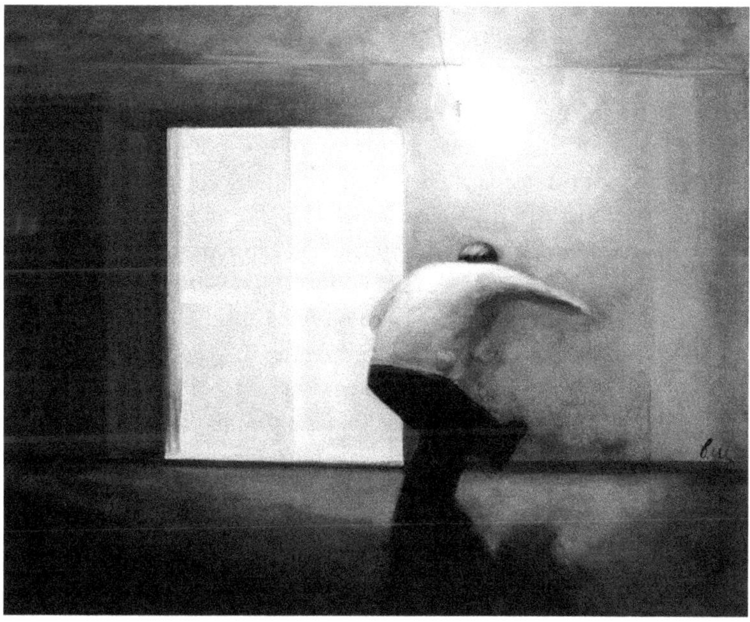

Figure 11. Vladimir Shinkarev, *Dancing Alone (Odin tantsuet)* (1998). Oil, 80 × 100 cm. (Bruno Bishofberger Gallery, Zurich, Switzerland)

same alternatives to desiccated gender typology in her illustration for the letter И from the group project *The Mitki Alphabet* (Figure 12). She represents the letter with two nouns possessing the suffix *-ushka*, a diminutive much beloved by the Mitki: *iskusstvovedushka* ([female] art historian) and *Ikarushka* (Little Icarus). *The Letter* И is the only letter in the series *The Mitki Alphabet* that has a man and woman joined together in the same collaged object, with Icarus's head being that of the film and art critic Mikhail Trofimenkov and the tip of one of his wings consisting of a photograph of the female art historian Olga Khrustaleva.[51] By locating a female image on an aerodynamically important part of Icarus's wing, Florensky suggests that his tragic fall may be attributed in part to an alliance with the feminine that upsets his balance. But by representing the female as an art historian, Florensky may also be commenting on the role of women as preservers of a certain kind of cultural memory, a notion that she wittily reinforces in her own capacity as the designer for the pose of this Icarus, whose contortions explicitly refer to the bent legs of Brueghel's Icarus. Olga Florensky, Shinkarev, and Shagin reconfigure Icarus as a figure compromised by dialectics, fatally burdened by an identity that is torn between sensitivity and aesthetic refinement on the one hand and the love of the grand heroic gesture on the other. The possibility of a synthesis between this thesis and that antithesis would seem slim at best.

It is for this reason that the Mitki use their work as a space from which to contemplate the experience of failure and defeat, as played out on both the personal and national scale. For them, the Russo-Japanese War plays a special role in such an examination. As Shagin himself stated in one interview for this project, "the image of the disastrous 1905 battle of Tsushima," where the Russians lost to the Japanese, is a "symbol of Russian history" containing "many riddles" and arguably representing the catalyst of both the tragic line of events that followed and the subsequent marginalization of the Russian navy as a military institution with distinctive values.[52] Shagin's comments reflect a common perception of the Russo-Japanese War's significance—as an expression of tsarist incompetence and obtuseness and as the fuse that lit the flame of the 1905 Revolution and subsequent agitations. Numerous memoirs of officers and sailors from that conflict emphasize the bravery of the sailors. The Russian fatalities at Tsushima represented pointlessly spilled blood because of the complacence and strategic unpreparedness of the superior officers and generals, who ignored reports about the technological superiority of weapons on the Japanese ships. As one commissioned

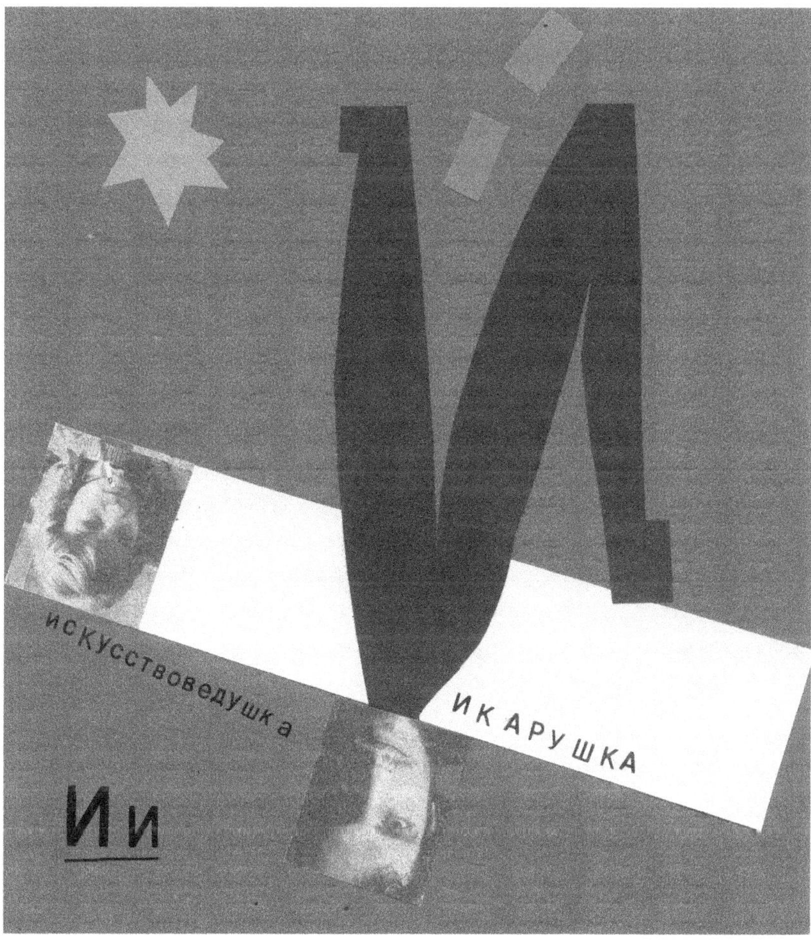


Figure 12. Olga Florensky, *The Letter И*, from *The Mitki Alphabet* (1990). Collage, 23 × 21 cm. (collection of the artist)

Russian doctor acidly wrote in his diary after contemplating some especially horrible casualties, "we don't particularly like to talk about politics."[53] The Mitki's views of heroism as a tragic waste and figures of authority as hollow men are drawn from the tragic lessons of the Russo-Japanese War. The work of the Mitki that explicitly treats the defeat of Russia in the Russo-Japanese War strikes this odd note, but with more audible dissonance because they do not shrink from acknowledging the enormity of the failure. In 1998, Mikhail Sapego, a poet and editor in chief of the Mitki publishing house Red Sailor, put together a collection of documents about Vasili Riabov, an obscure figure in the Russo-Japanese War, together with illustrations by Aleksandr Florensky. Riabov spied for Russia during that conflict and was eventually captured and executed by the Japanese. Echoing Shinkarev's statement about the Mitki's flawed selflessness ("sharing like Christians meant Mitki got it all"), in a promotional release, Riabov is described as "brave, clever," and "lov[ing] theater and his wife," but hobbled by "guilt" because he "took advantage of others."[54] Two songs that were popular at the end of the war appear on their 1996 compilation CD *Mitki Songs* (*Mit'kovskie pesni*). One of these songs, "Variag," is sung amateurishly, if spiritedly, by several members of the Mitki. The song has the bluff assertion that "our proud [battle cruiser] Variag will not surrender to the enemy, [and] no one is inclined to mercy." The other song, "The Cold Waves Splash" ("Pleshshut kholodnye volny"), is sung by the rock musician Anatoly Krupnov. In contrast with "Variag," "The Cold Waves Splash" more openly acknowledges the self-inflicted failure of the Russian fleet fighting against Japan, with one verse noting that the Variag fights "with uneven strength" and a later one acknowledging that "we ourselves exploded [the battleship] the Korean; the Variag was sunk by us." Krupnov's almost affectless baritone, modulated only by a gradual rise in volume, undercuts the potential mawkishness of the song's text, suggesting more a contemplative diagnosis of a tragedy than a traumatic reliving of it.[55]

In the next Mitki music collection, released in 1997, the dissident poet Alexei Khvostenko performs "In the Hills of Manchuria" ("Na sopkakh Man'chzhurii"). Like "The Cold Waves Splashed," the song is notable for a patriotism that does not gloss over the sobering Russian losses during the campaign from 1904 to 1905, as had many contemporary accounts. In the song, a Russian contemplates graves of the war dead, bitterly stating that "even now we can't forget the war, and burning tears still flow," and adding the defiant prophecy that "we will avenge you, / And arrange a bloody funeral feast."[56] Khvostenko sings an abbreviated version of the prerevolutionary text of the song, but without any of the pathos of its earliest recording by Ivan Koslovsky or any of its subsequent Soviet-era renditions. By singing in a tightly controlled and gravelly monotone and leaving out the final and self-lacerating verse about the unjustness of Fate and the weeping of a victimized Mother Russia, Khvostenko refuses to impart poignancy or righteous anger to even the most sanguine and melancholy moments of the text, and he communicates an odd detachment from the song's patriotic content that would probably seem inappropriate or disrespectful to some listeners.[57] The borderline irreverence evident in Khvostenko's performance, inspired by Shagin's own deliberately amateurish style of singing, reflects the Mitki's indebtedness to the Russian counterculture notion of ironic discourse, or *stiob*. That mode of discourse was most famously practiced by their friend the composer and jazz pianist Sergei Kurekhin, whose raucous theatricalized concerts titled "Pop Mechanics" represented what could be called spectacles of heightened ideological inscrutability.[58] In his performance, Khvostenko evokes a moral equivalence between both sides of strife and expresses a refusal to idealize a battle that came to be an outlet for the bloodthirstiness. As René Girard has argued, there is nothing that restores order and cohesion to a fraying community more effectively than acts of purgative violence.[59]

Yet Shinkarev is ultimately repelled by this authoritarian argument for the social utility of "othering" a nominal enemy, through real and imagined bloodlettings. Shinkarev's anecdote about the drowning Russian hero's de facto suicide recalls not just Brodsky's comment that the Russian navy is "prone rather to a heroic gesture and self-sacrifice than to survival at all costs" but also the Buddhist-influenced kamikaze strategy of the Japanese during the Second World War, most famously practiced at sea. The modulated repetition of Shagin's two-line poem "1983" is quite likely imitative of haiku structure. But it would be wrong to say that the Mitki adopt a Girardian perspective on political violence. If anything, their references to Japanese culture serve to point up the difficulties of the genuinely heroic gesture and the intermittently delusional aspects of it. In his absurdist novella *Maxim and Fyodor*, which predates the Mitki as a movement with a clearly expressed identity, Vladimir Shinkarev makes numerous references to Japanese places and literary forms. The attempts of the two socially dysfunctional main characters—who are clear ancestors of the Mitki—to take on the spiritual values of the East are no less misguided or absurd than the Mitki's efforts to portray themselves as military heroes. When Fyodor takes a gulp from a bottle of kerosene thinking that it is water, he continues to drink because "such was his mastery of Zen Buddhism that he discovered within himself the courage not to rectify his error and calmly finished the entire bottle."[60]

The role of Japanese culture as a mirror for the contemplation of the Mitki's self-images takes an unexpected turn in the group's thematic elaboration of the anecdote about the attempt to rescue the woman who has fallen overboard. In one of his pointedly doggerel verses for music, Shagin describes the Bowie who has fallen overboard together with the woman as floating in the water like a "Japanese god."[61] Bowie's sophisticated technology is referred to as *shmudaki*, a Mitki slang term for electronic devices manufactured outside of Russia that contains the unflattering word for an incompetent or emasculated man (*mudak*), which itself curiously derives from a term denoting male genitalia (*mudé*). Of course, given the lack of any physical resemblance of David Bowie to the representations of a rotund Buddha, Shagin presumably uses the presence of Bowie more as a symbolic marker than anything else. But a symbolic marker for what? One possibility is that he represents Shagin himself, who is characterized on the earliest Mitki website as the "erotic symbol" of the movement, and whose characterization (as full-figured and "kind") may be understood as an embodiment of dharma-like equanimity.[62] In this anecdote, Shagin attempts to rewrite not just Shinkarev's anecdote about the drowning woman, but Russian history as well. He tries to take away the tragic sting of the Russo-Japanese War, reconfiguring it as a parable about the confrontation between Russia and Other, masculine and feminine, that is mediated by the figure of the woman in peril and results in a reconciliation of apparent opposites or opponents, both of whom are presented as being either highly vulnerable to water or stubbornly buoyant.[63] The presence of the Other in himself is not a sign of the Mityok winning a battle—of cannibalizing the combatant in Girardian terms—but is rather representative of his a priori inner duality. History has been changed, with a new outcome in which no one is victimized and everybody is saved. The fantasy of revisiting the memory of the battle of Tsushima in a "bloody funeral feast"—as the fulfilment of revenge—has been pointedly abandoned.

The effect of this shifted interpretation of history is to draw our attention to the disparity between the ideals of masculinity and the attempted performance of them. In her series of paintings titled *Heroes of Russian Aviation*, Olga Florensky contemplates the ambiguities of heroism in ways that resonate with what Liubov Gurevich terms the appreciation for the paradoxical and absurd that characterized the Leningrad underground's appropriation of Japanese literary models. Florensky's highly elegiac representation of the prerevolutionary aviator Lev Matsievich foregrounds the tragic plummet of a hero against a nearly cloudless sky (Figure 13). The aquatic suggestiveness of the sky's vivid blue is brought to the fore by the phrase "celebration of aeronautics" next to Matsievich's

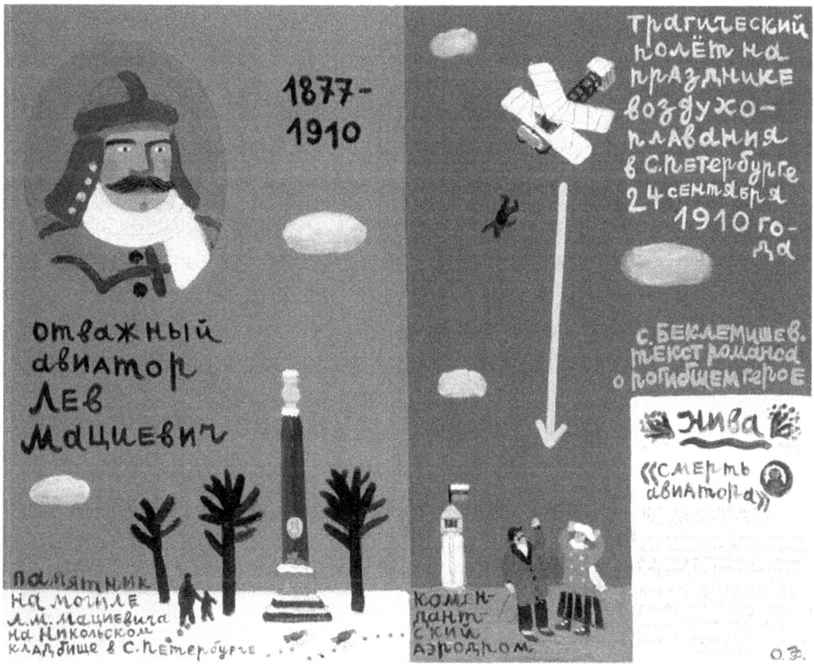


Figure 13. Olga Florensky, *The Fearless Aviator Lev Matsievich,* from the series *Heroes of Russian Aviation* (2001). Oil, 80 × 100 cm. (Collection at Tsarskoe Selo [Tsasrkosel'skaia kollektsiia], Pushkin, Russia)

tilting airplane. In Russian, as in English, "aeronautics" literally means swimming in air, although more palpably so to the Russian ear, which immediately hears the everyday noun "swimming" as the second half of the word (*vozdukho*plavanie). As if to underscore the maritime subtext in her representation of Matsievich's death, Florensky sets off the latter segment of the word with a dash.

Amidst these already busy scenes on the mythical skies and seas, we would not expect the entrance of a powerful third player in the fraught contact between Russia and its binary opposites. Yet the figure of David Bowie continues, with seeming incongruity, to trod the floorboards of this drama, long after many might think that he overstayed his welcome as a bit player. The Mitki's representation of heroic flight or escape culminating in disappointment or a tragedy that unfolds in, or over, water echoes any number of personae in Bowie's career: the heroes of "Space Oddity" and "Starman," the stranded and ultimately doomed alien protagonist of the 1976 film *The Man Who Fell to Earth* (who comes to the earth in search of water for his planet), and the man in "Heroes" who earnestly addresses his lover on the East Berlin side of the Wall, as he imagines the two of them swimming away "like dolphins." Like Bowie, the Mitki draw our attention to the fragility and elusiveness of the very concept of heroism, compromised as it is by authoritarian idealizations and gender-specific assumptions that would seem to preclude the participation of women in it. Perhaps the Mitki's behavioral affect of plangent goodness, taken together with their sexual indeterminacy, has more in common with what Shinkarev sees as Bowie's "serpentine grace" than we might otherwise think. After all, in his 2005 essay *Mitkovian Dances* Shinkarev describes the imagined choreography of the Mitki as embodying "boldness and strength, coyness, adroitness, dynamism, and grace."[64] That formulation, in tandem with the fantasy of "rescuing" Bowie and Shagin's statement elsewhere that he always wanted to become a "rock star,"[65] reminds us of the ways in which both Shinkarev and Shagin imagine themselves to be doppelgängers of the Western pop star, as well as of each other.

As noted in the last chapter, in the mid-eighties Shagin and Shinkarev became familiar with W. H. Auden's "Musée des Beaux Arts" through its inclusion in a packet of English-language poetry, distributed by the American Consulate. Another circumstance within nonconformist circles of the city, however, may have considerably enhanced the presence and resonance of Auden's poem about Breughel's painting of the fall of Icarus. The poem very likely also came to be known in the Leningrad underground through the watching of pirated tapes of *The Man Who Fell to Earth.* In the eighties in the Soviet Union, VHS players took on the status of a portals onto unseen realities, screening Western films that were not distributed in Soviet theatres. Like samizdat, the operation of *videoizdat* among its circle of users presumed a level of trust, if not intimacy. In *Mitki*, Shinkarev defines the Mitki slang term *vidak* as "videoplayer, preferably imported," explaining that its morphology is deliberately analogous to *shmudak* (audio player), which, as we have seen, contains a buried reference to male genitalia. In his illustration for the 1990 edition of Shinkarev's book, Aleksandr Florensky underscores the quasi-sexual character of such viewing, with a *vidak* connected to a television monitor showing a soft-porn film.[66] In the Soviet Union, the uneven quality of VHS tapes—which stemmed from either wear and tear or multiple copying—contributed in no small degree to the strangeness of watching them. Shinkarev pointedly draws our attention to the specific character of that experience in his 2001 paintings about Lucino Visconti's *Rocco and His Brothers* (*Rocco e i suoi fratelli*), from the series *Cinema* (*Kino*): one canvas is a ghostly image with a subtitle in English, suggesting a tape without Russian subtitle options that is frozen mid-scene, and another a digitally crisp version of the same moment.[67] The pairing of these paintings leaves little doubt about which image is unsettling and evocative, and which is sterile and soulless.

From all this, we can easily imagine how the viewing in the Soviet context of an odd film such as *The Man Who Fell to Earth* already carried the feel of biting into forbidden fruit, quite apart from its already provocative content. Among other things, that content included Bowie's full frontal nudity. In the film, a picture book combining the poem and a reproduction of the painting plays a pivotal role in evoking the melancholy fate of the alien played by David Bowie.[68] Several details of the Mitki's allusion to the poem would not be comprehensible without reference to Nicolas Roeg's film, and Bowie's mannered and enigmatic performance in it. There is nothing in Auden's poem that highlights ambiguous sexuality; nor does the text engage any notion of cultural otherness, much less any cultural program of Japonism. We find both these elements in the film, and other details that point up its role as a subtext for Shinkarev's and Shagin's writing and painting. From its dust jacket, we see that the picture book with Auden's poem and Breughel's painting are published by the company (World Enterprises) that Bowie's character owns and runs, suggesting that he, like the Mitki, is keen to use the image and text to communicate something about himself to the larger world. The mythical Mityok of Shinkarev's book, like Bowie's alien (whose laconic and often inexpressive manner leads to a series of misunderstandings), is a person whose manners run up against the socially normative values of his environment. Like Dmitri Shagin, Thomas Jerome Newton (whose name alludes to the forces of gravity that caused him to be stranded on Earth) strives for a leadership role and, later in the film, a shot as a pop star. On the lake where he crash-landed, Newton builds himself a house and outdoor deck fitted with Japanese decorative details such as Torii gates, translucent screens, and tatami mats, all of which elicit quizzical responses from outsiders such as the scientist Nathan, played by Rip Torn. Like the Mitki in their heyday, Newton is an alcoholic. Late in the film, he claims that drinking causes him to have visions of the bodies of men and women. As we shall see in the next chapter, within the mythology of the Mitki an enigmatic or ambiguous sexuality is one of several imagined consequences, or expressions, of alcohol abuse.

Yet in terms of the Mitki, perhaps the most significant aspect of the film is Bowie's seemingly affectless performance, which may in part have been inspired by the study of Kabuki theatre that he began in the late sixties under the influence of his mentor, the London dancer Lindsey Kemp.[69] An actual scene of Kabuki theatre occurs early in the film, with shots of Newton avidly watching a performance intercut with Nathan's tryst with one of his students. By all accounts, Bowie was particularly interested in the Japanese theatrical tradition of the *onnagata*, or male actors performing female roles, which he first emulated in the stage performances of *Ziggy Stardust and the Spiders from Mars*. Many people within the Leningrad underground seem to have understood correctly the performative and consummately make-believe aspects of Bowie's self-presentation. Boris Grebenshchikov's notorious stage performance in the Tblisi rock festival on March 8, 1980, of pantomiming erotic relations with other band members, was almost certainly suggested by English-language press reports (circulated among Leningrad rock circles, sometimes in retyped samizdat versions or in scrapbooks that also included transcriptions of liner notes and exquisite hand-drawn copies of album covers such as Pink Floyd's 1973 *Dark Side of the Moon*) of Bowie's stage interaction with his heterosexual lead guitarist Mick Ronson.[70]

Of all Bowie's songs, perhaps it is the 1977 "Heroes," with its portraits of East Bloc lovers imagining themselves to be king and queen as they consider a fatal escape from their living prison, that has the most in common with the Soviet-era work of the Mitki, with its attempts to break out of rigid ideological and behavioral frames of references. The building electronic drone of the song—contributed by the former King Crimson guitarist Robert Fripp,[71] whose open-ended compositions exerted a significant influence on Sergei Kurekhin's own music and stage performances, particularly his satirical "Pop-Mechanics"—together with Bowie's careful phrasing of lyrics about the despair of being caught between East and West, could not seem more resonant with the Mitki's examination of identities caught in the rigid grip of binary systems, and with their project of cultivating a deceptively light approach to tragedy. At one point of his career, Bowie compared himself to the character of Pierrot, the mournful spurned lover of Commedia dell'arte theatre, and remarked on the ways in which his cultivation of multiple personae had the effect of reconfiguring his core being: "I couldn't understand whether I was writing characters or whether the characters were writing me."[72] Such a statement seems tailor-made for the approach of gender theorists such as Judith Butler, who in her 2004 study *Undoing Gender* argues for gender as merely a provisional or initial guide to understanding the lived experience of sexuality. For Butler, gender is a concept whose reality is defined as much by performance as it is by norms. Here and in other writings, Butler insists upon the rift—both in the sense of a cognitive disjunction and an ontological gap—that invariably opens up within the spectacle of gender identity, between gender norms and people's actual performance of them.[73] As Butler explains in her 2015 book *Notes toward a Performative Theory of Assembly*, "gender norms have everything to do with how and in what way we can appear in public space, how and in what way the public and the private are distinguished, and how that distinction is instrumentalized in the service of sexual politics."[74] As Shinkarev states in his most recent book, every person should be thought of as a congeries of multiple hypostases, with the possibility of effecting a shift of balance within perceived norms. These hypostases can—and perhaps should—argue with each other. "Father, or not a father?!" "Poet, or not a poet?!" "Citizen, or not a citizen?!" And why not also: A man, or not a man?

In his first book on the Mitki, Shinkarev finds that the boiler rooms in Leningrad provide the ideal atmosphere for the flourishment of a gender-identity "sweet spot," in which frivolous flight and the grim responsibilities of manhood are placed in equipoise. Shinkarev whimsically devotes an entire chapter to the boiler rooms of buildings in Leningrad, basing his comments on his and Shagin's impressions while working in them. As the historian Viacheslav Dolinin recalls in his memoirs about dissident life in Leningrad during the seventies and first half of the eighties, the basements of buildings on the Admiralty embankment became refuges for many nonconformist poets, who were glad to work for a nominal wage in boiler rooms in exchange for being left alone by the authorities. The unsanctioned gatherings in the basements of the city included rehearsals for rock concerts, prompting the St. Petersburg-based journalist and former rock musician Vladimir Rekshan to muse that such music came from an "actual underground."[75] Boiler rooms also provided places to write, and often—as Dolinin implies, with his fond description of their warmth—to live in during harsh winters.[76] Before his arrest for dissident activism, Dolinin served as the direct supervisor for both Shagin and Shinkarev in their jobs of boiler room custodians. In describing his job of maintaining boilers, Shinkarev writes that such work requires Zen-like powers of concentration and the attainment of a spiritual "center of gravity," and indeed elsewhere in his book he hints at the countercultural influence of Buddhism on the Mitki, particularly in its Japanese form.[77]

The view that the Mitki have of St. Petersburg is highly distinct, representing an unusual—one might say even impossible—fusion of the foundational myth of St. Petersburg as an unshakable beachhead of empire with Buddhist notions regarding the transience and instability of a subject's relation to the physical universe. Joseph Brodsky hints at this mythologized view of the Russian navy when he writes of it as expressive of a "vision," of a "perfect, almost abstract order [that] was borne upon the waters of the world's oceans, as it could not be attained anywhere on Russian soil." He describes his father's naval uniform as a "pitch-black overcoat with two rows of yellow buttons," the contrast between the light and the dark suggestive of "a street within an avenue" at night. "'A street within an avenue'—that is how I thought about my father," Brodsky writes.[78] The uniform represents the autonomy of Brodsky's father within the larger regimentation of Soviet society. Heraldically, the color of the buttons also represents the yellow of the St. Andrew's cross, the older Petrine symbol of the Russian navy. Years earlier, in his "Christmas Ballad," Brodsky transforms this image of yellow against darkness into a kinetic image of the salvation promised by the Nativity and ignored by most. Brodsky's insertion of the aquatic Petrine motif into a Moscow setting points up the sterile stolidity of the Soviet capital, which is presented as a fitfully illuminated hive of alienated lives.[79]

For the Mitki, the Russian navy represents both the sacred vessel of forgotten history portrayed by Brodsky and what Japanese Buddhists have called a floating world, a mobile yet internally stable space. Such an imaginatively reconfigured world of mobility makes it possible for them to explore possible conflicts within both themselves and modern Russian culture as a whole, informed by the "spirit of discovery" that Brodsky saw in the history of the Russian navy. But the intentness with which the Mitki document the mutely accepted norms of masculinity and femininity within Russian culture also coincides with the undoing of gender that Judith Butler sees as essential to a larger project of achieving justice, the first step of which is to take note of the influence of the "geopolitical boundaries and cultural constraints on who is imagining whom."[80] Both Shagin and Shinkarev, neither of whom served in the

Soviet navy, would fantasize that their boilers were located not in the basements of apartment blocks but in the engine room of a ship. The boiler room attendant is a liminal or intermediate figure, a nodal point in the interaction between subject and object, masculine and feminine. In the anecdote about David Bowie, the Mitki attempt to answer the riddle of masculinity by finding a space to rearticulate their own transgressive desires, between the ultimately "Japanese" Bowie on the one hand and their own hypermasculine socialist heroes on the other, neither of whom they can totally reject or admire. By portraying themselves as the queerest of heroes—sailors afflicted with the "national ailment" of hydrophobia, at least as likely to fail as to succeed—the Mitki bring to our attention both the risks and creative possibilities of such an undertaking.

# 3

## Fire Water

### Alcoholism and Rehabilitation in the St. Petersburg of the Mitki

An alcoholic is a person for whom drunkenness causes problems—for himself, his family, at work, and so on. But he is not necessarily a déclassé [social] element. It can be very difficult for people to understand that they have problems.

DMITRI SHAGIN, on the Russian talk show *Obshchee delo* (June 7, 2009)

I never regretted my experience with drugs.

WILLIAM BURROUGHS, *Junky*

The paradigm of intoxication as a shared or social experience haunts many Russian descriptions of even solitary drinking. Perhaps it is not surprising, then, that the Mitki's characterizations of (and attitudes toward) alcohol consumption represent a common ground among the highly disparate writing and painting within the group. When the Mitki first became widely known in the Leningrad underground of the late eighties, the group was notorious for its seeming elevation of alcohol consumption to a cult-like status. Yet the idea of the collective is itself remarkably protean and variegated in the work of the Mitki, with shared concerns or leitmotifs receiving stylistically distinct treatments in the hands of its member artists and writers. A few Mitki have made the diversity of response a subject of their writing and painting, portraying personal vanity as an agent of chaos within the cohort idyll; even in its early days, the group's internal differences were at times reminiscent of bickering within an aging rock band. The Mitki seemed to be an internally contentious crew that was held together only by its interest in drink, which gradually became transformed into the group's core identity. Many Russian cultural commentators go so far as to assert that the Mitki's current obsolescence and general irrelevance in Putin's Russia are the consequence of their recent sobriety. It has also been argued that the Mitki's discussion of alcoholism—and more specifically the role that drinking played in the formation of their quasi-dissident subculture—represents one of the most sustained examinations of substance abuse in Russian literature, one that is more eloquent and vivid for having been launched by artists and writers who were still riding the crest of an alcoholic wave. During a 2009 televised roundtable discussion about alcoholism on Russia's Channel 1, one commentator (the actor Veniamin Smekhov) pointed to Dmitri Shagin across the studio and suggested that the legacy of alcoholism among the Mitki made it possible for them to subsume the unprepossessing "ruins of socialist realism" into an esthetic of "enchanting irony," as if to remind the audience that not everything stemming from the habitual practice of inebriation is destructive.[1] Certainly one consequence of viewing alcohol as a catalyst for a deeper understanding of the collective ideal is that collectivism itself takes on a distinctly tragic yet short-lived character: like any addictive pathology, it requires a therapeutic overcoming of trauma and dependence. In the work of the Mitki, the collective nature of Russian alcohol consumption is sublimated into a no less collective renunciation of it. But sobriety represents much more than sublimation, the process that Freud regarded as the channeling and semi-tragic attenuation of desire that comes with the civilizing project. More than anything, for the Mitki sobriety reconfigures artistic activity and is characterized by a distinct shift of emphasis from linguistic to visual creativity.

The beginnings of the Mitki can be dated to 1985, during the *longueurs* of a bus trip that the artists took from Estonia to Leningrad. The name purportedly emerged as the result of a misunderstanding during verbal badinage, and in this regard the "christening" of the Mitki is powerfully—and, quite possibly pointedly—suggestive of the stories about the situational or improvisational coining of absurd or nonsensical names of any number of rock ensembles in the West (Jefferson Airplane, Led Zeppelin, and the Kinks, among many others) and in Russia itself

(Akvarium, Zvuki Mu, Dina Arbenina's Nochnye snaipery [Nocturnal Snipers]). There is a sense that these personal accounts, whether true or not, comprise an important part of what Shinkarev himself in *Mitki* terms the "group mythology": the secondary sources outside of the primary work of the movement (the latter taking the form of literary texts, music, and/or painting) that serve as interpretive tools or filters, or as a Hadith clarifying its canonical texts. One could go so far as to say that these rumors and apocrypha result in a symbiosis between primary and secondary texts: who is to say what constitutes the group's core achievement and what serves as the mere peripheral anecdote? The aleatory ideal—the aesthetic that glorifies the accidental, the slipshod, or the jerry-built—is relevant to the group identity of the Mitki in another way as well. In one of Aleksandr Florensky's drawings for the 1990 publication of *Mitki* (the only edition of Shinkarev's book published in the Soviet Union), a "Russian" Mozart has a balalaika slug across his chest, accompanied by a caption with a migraine-inducing confusion of alphabets (MOZAPT).[2] All of Florensky's drawings in the 1990 edition (which he in fact drew during the time that Shinkarev was still writing appendixes for his book, and which also appeared in the mimeographed samizdat copies) suggest the simulation of a rushed or untutored artist, someone who picks up a black magic marker in a moment of mild intoxication. So what if Mozart wears a Russian winter cap with earflaps—just as the Mitki do—atop an eighteenth-century peruke? Who cares if the caption "Mozart was Russian" is badly smudged? Who wouldn't mash up a few details after a few drinks?

Other illustrations in the series suggest more explicitly that inebriation facilitates a mix or fusion of East and West, and perhaps even a dialogue between cultures. The top caption of one illustration of a scene from *Don't Change the Meeting Place* (the Mitki's favorite Soviet television series) reads "A Scene from a well-known American mini-series"; the bottom caption has Captain Zheglov saying to Hunchback (in Cyrillic-transcribed English) "Meik may dey!"[3] Popular culture already represents a shared or global fusion of material; it also could represent the essentially socialist principle of the abolition of private property—of what is mine being also yours. The artifacts of the media are dissolved and blended in the use of alcohol, that great leveler and vehicle for unfettered socializing (*obshchenie*); furthermore, such mixing and fusion of radically different elements—from the déclassé to high culture—is also reminiscent of the nineteenth-century Slavophile notion of Russian collective consciousness (*sobornost'*). In the cell-like world of the Leningrad underground, alcohol serves as a center of gravity of Mitki, as its internal glue.

Much of what has been written about Shinkarev's *Mitki* has situated it as a foundational text, as a bible of the group. Although Shagin insists that Shinkarev did not so much create as document the Mitki as a movement, even he acknowledges the importance of this text for putting the group before the eye of the "underground" community in Leningrad. Yet alcoholism and its behavioral correlative of burlesque addlepatedness and raucous social disorder was very much a part of the public perception of the Mitki, even prior to Shinkarev's completion of the book. Only a year after the first four chapters of Shinkarev's *Mitki* appeared in the samizdat journal *Krasnyi Shchedrinets*, in 1986 the same journal published the art historian Luka Kuznetsov's satirical four-act play about the group. Kuznetsov titled his play *Oppanki—Indeed!* in a pun on the Easter-time rejoinder "Indeed He [Christ] is risen!" that reflects an awareness of the Mitki's satirical project of exposing cults of personality. Kuznetsov liberally draws on details from Shinkarev's book about members of the group, who in his play speak in a presciently hip-hop-like obsessive sampling of portentous statements from their favorite films. As discussed in chapter 2 of this book, *Oppanki—Indeed!* is a short four-act play that has Shagin, Florensky, Shinkarev, Filippov, and Kuznetsov himself (who at the time was a Leningrad-based art historian) as characters, together with five different "Olenka" Florenskys. The postmodernist collaging of statements from the group's rank and file serves as a piquant counterpoint to the highly cultured voice of Shinkarev. Kuznetsov's satire portrays the triumph of the Mitki, with Shagin declaring that "there are many of us in every kilometer—here and the world over!" At the end of the play, the rowdy bickering reaches a crescendo of alcohol-induced disinhibition and acting out, with Shinkarev declaiming the lines of an earnest wife of a railway officer from a Soviet film and Shagin flopping in despair on a couch after he realizes that he drank the entire supply of beer in the apartment: "on [his] face there registers surprise, followed by grief." Shagin has the last word in the play. After hearing the notes of the Mitki march and the procession of "brothers and little sisters" fade away, Shagin grouses that he has gained weight: "my armor top has gotten too short . . . *Dyk* . . ."[4]

The focus on beer consumption in Kuznetsov's play, as a practice that entails a set of pacifist associations that run up against any number of views about group or national solidarity, is a specific reference to contemporary realities. Beer was much easier to obtain during the era of Gorbachev's "dry law," and for many Russians it became a surrogate for vodka. Furthermore, within the culture of Russian alcohol consumption, the associations with beer are distinct from those with vodka. Apparently, not all states of inebriation are created equal: each has its own specific poetics, and even spirituality. The status of the Mitki as those who, in the late Soviet era, enjoyed different forms of alcohol and attempted to adapt to new strictures is evident in Aleksandr Florensky's cover illustration of the 1990 edition of Shinkarev's book, which has one member of the group swigging from a beer can and another from a bottle of what might be vodka or wine. As the journalist Aleksandr Levintov notes in his witty book-length essay *Drinking and Drunkenness*, an examination of alcohol consumption in Russia and Ukraine since the end of the Second World War, vodka (a word that in Russian is feminine in gender) is something of a fickle mistress: it is "the universal substance of love and friendship, ineluctably leading to impotence, spite, fights, and wars." We're better off, he writes, relying on beer and wine, for then everything in the world will be "calmer." After all, wine is the drink of seduction, and beer is "full of peace-loving female hormones, which unfortunately contribute to weight gain and overall chunkiness."[5]

The restriction on hard liquor from 1985 to 1987 had certainly wrought a fundamental change upon the entire country. During that period, the overall mortality rate fell by 12 percent among men and by 7 percent among women. Among men, death resulting from demonstrably "alcohol-specific causes" dropped by 56 percent, coinciding with a decline in per capita consumption of 14.2 liters of pure alcohol in 1984 to 10.7 liters in 1987.[6] It is therefore not surprising that beer became ascendant as a more expedient and healthy channel for imbibing, as a state-sanctioned "safety-valve" for those living in quasi-prohibition. The fact that the quality production of beer in Russia has been historically associated more closely with St. Petersburg than with Moscow reinforces the sense of the Mitki as carriers of a distinct local identity during a time of incipient national collapse.[7] Yet the state manipulation of the alcohol market in the late eighties also reflects an awareness of the Foucauldian status of alcohol as a tool of social control, a dynamic that several specialists on Russian alcoholism have termed the "alcoholization" of Russian society. As the St. Petersburg-based sociologist Iosif Gurvich notes, from the time of the state regulation of taverns in the middle of the seventeenth century up to the present day, the Russian state has held to a certain "ideal of alcohol," consisting of a shrewd modulation of access to liquor: the selling of liquor was a state-run business during most of the tsarist era and the entire the Soviet one, and "the people's cheerfulness was useful to the government."[8]

There is a significant association within the work of the Mitki of alcohol-related full-bodiedness with a peace-loving disposition. This fanciful picture may in part be a response to the stylized meditations on the physically calamitous consequences of drunkenness in Russian literature. Eli Hetko has insightfully written about the relation of the legacy of Daniil Kharms for the painting and writing of the Mitki. The hilariously irreverent yet unsettling short prose sketches of Kharms from the twenties often have earnest individuals who find themselves in slapstick routines that unexpectedly lead to accidental—and at times deliberate—injury or death. Kharms's inclusion of highly canonical Russian authors such as Pushkin as characters in his stories of random physical confrontations only heighten their effect of dethroning elevated shibboleths of ambition and national self-regard.[9] By referring elsewhere in his first book to the movement of the Mitki as "a catalogue of the main national traits (arguably, good or bad),"[10] Shinkarev draws an implicit connection between his treatment of aspects of the Russian character and Kharms's indictment of the quotidian upheavals of the twenties. As Hetko points out, at least some of the mishaps in Kharms stories can be understood as alcohol-induced.[11] The Mitki's perception of alcoholism is as informed by literary representations as it is by tragic lived reality. The Mitki's representation of alcoholism as a full-bodied "feminine" phenomenon is openly and rather amusingly presented to the reader and viewer as an artificial and dubious construct. What, then, would be the value of indulging in a mythology about addiction?

It turns out that the dramatization of false beliefs about alcoholism serves a double purpose, of drawing attention to the actual nature of the addiction and alerting us to the habit-forming character of those beliefs themselves. Making his way through folklore and dubious general received wisdom, Levintov characterizes the consumption of beer as undercutting masculinity, not so much because it actively feminizes men but because it infantilizes them. In one of his paintings from 2008 (based on an ink drawing from the early nineties, and reproduced on the cover of the 2010 anthology of Shinkarev's writing about the Mitki),[12] Shinkarev portrays two Mitki sitting in a sandbox with what looks suspiciously like an old-fashioned milk jug (a common fixture of the Soviet period) filled with beer. Outside the box and nearby, two children sit playing on the ground and another swings on a swing set. All three children have their arms exuberantly outstretched in a manner identical to the pose struck by the larger Mitki figure. The vertical composition of the painting frames the human tableau with a rainbow on the top, and a punning caption on the bottom reads, "Rainbow Arch, don't drink our beer!" (*Raduga-duga, ne pei nashe pivo*) (Figure 14). The "rainbow arch" functions as a kind of superego: with other forms of alcohol having been taken away, beer becomes the last refuge for alcohol consumption. In several of his monochrome (and often conceptually somber) prints and drawings, Shagin clearly expresses an awareness of this larger agenda, which covers both the Gorbachevian restrictions and the earlier saturation of the country with alcohol in times of widespread political upheaval and a depleted treasury. In one drawing, Shagin stands at the end of a long line leading up to a kiosk marked with a "Beer" sign (Figure 15).[13]

The kiosk stands in front of an unmarked fence, beyond which looms a factory chimney. The entire scene suggests the setting of a prison camp, with inmates standing in line for food. Genuine "cheerfulness" and joy have no place in this setting. Another of Shagin's drawings, captioned "They Stand Silently," has two downcast men in front of a boarded-up beer kiosk.[14] The iconograph of the "X" mark, denoting a restriction or abolition of a substance or product, is evident elsewhere in Shagin's work. In his self-portrait as a recovered alcoholic, both his posture and the boarded-up *kvas* kiosk behind him recall the St. Andrew Cross, the emblem of the Russian navy since its founding by Peter the Great. Taken together, these images suggest that weaning anyone from alcohol necessarily takes on an incremental form, moving from potent spirits to fermented beverages of descending alcoholic content and culminating in the consumption of *kvas*, a drink with negligible alcohol content and a flavor that is reminiscent of darker beers. In this self-portrait, Shagin carries in his pocket a copy of a book about the "Twelve Steps" and stands triumphantly before the viewer, with St. Isaac's cathedral in the distant background and, closer to the foreground, a boarded-up *kvas* kiosk.[15] The entire tableau suggests a completion of the recovery process and liberation from the ponderous chains of dependence. In his 1987 painting *Brothers on the Bridge* (*Bratki na mostu*), two men walk with their arms around each other past what this is an active beer kiosk and across a bridge (Figure 16). The men are oblivious to the figure of Icarus,

Figure 14. *Top right*: Vladimir Shinkarev, "Rainbow Arch, don't drink our beer!" (Raduga-duga, ne pei nashe pivo) (2008) Oil, 55 × 70 cm. (collection of the artist)

Figure 15. *Bottom right*: Dmitri Shagin, "Beer," from *Bezzavetnye geroi* (1998), page 31.

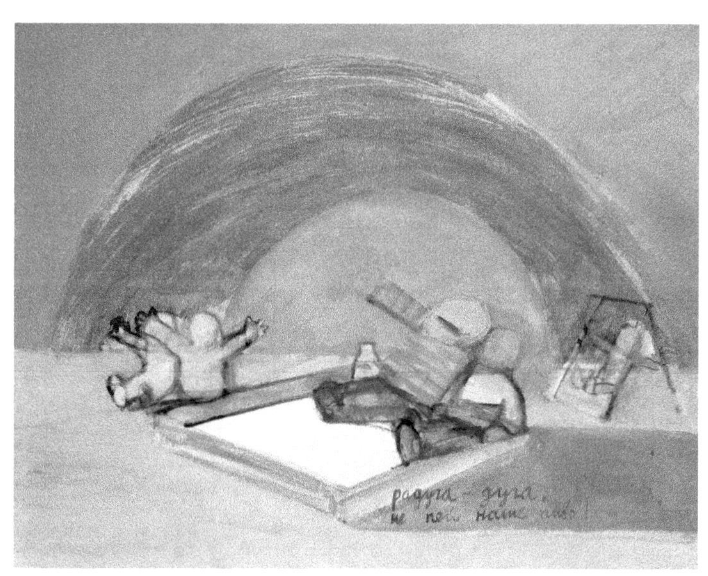
радуга-дуга,

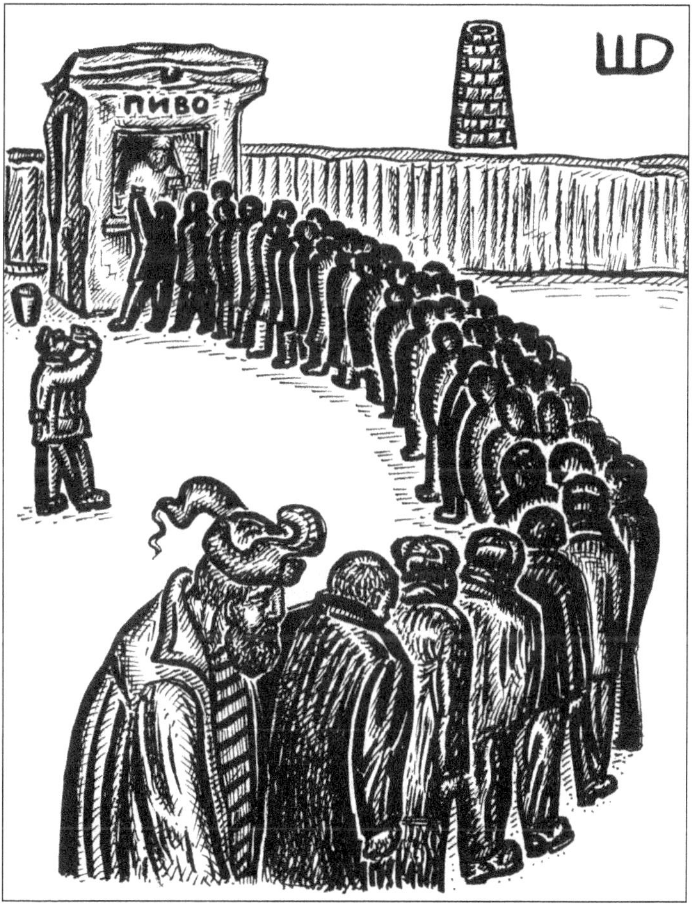

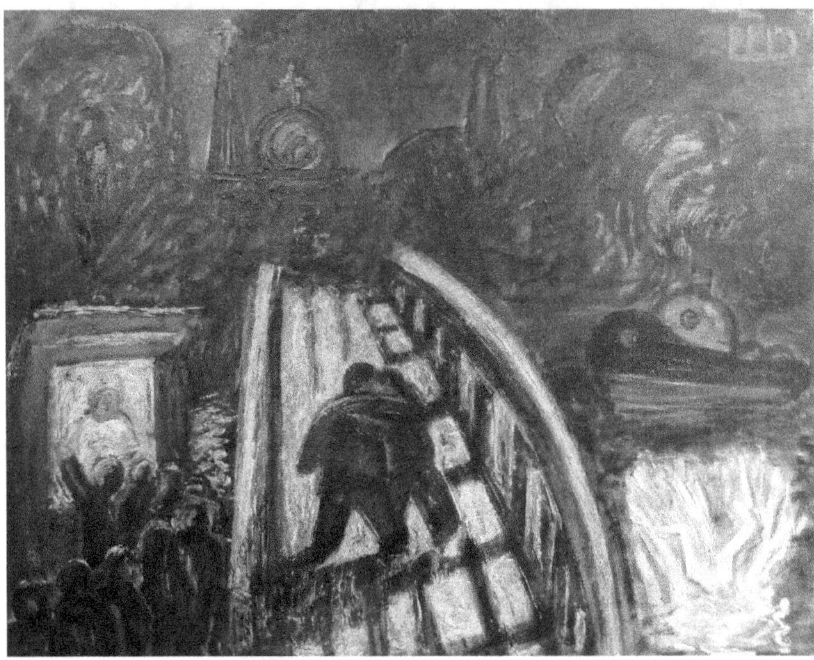

Figure 16. Dmitri Shagin, *Brothers on the Bridge* (*Bratki na mostu*). (1987) Oil, 73 × 93 cm. (InterArt Gallery)

who has just fallen into the canal, whose liquid demise in this instance may refer to their possible fate as alcoholics.[16] In these images, Shagin underscores what we might call an addiction to sobriety, as a form of heightened connection with others that paradoxically draws its power from the sociality among alcoholics. While alcoholism is represented here as a spurious or false medium of healthy group consciousness, there is no getting around the fact that Shagin represents it as the paradoxical prototype for the sociality that he describes in the twelve-step program. The recovering alcoholic's search for potent surrogates for alcohol—whether they take the form of kindred yet alcohol-free liquids such as *kvas* or anodyne national narratives about drunkenness—is indefatigable.

Suggestions of this unexpected confluence between states of inebriation, principled sobriety, and diegetic imaginaries are evident in Shinkarev's work as well. A parsing of Shinkarev's considerable literary and artistic productivity from the eighties to the present day enables us to come to a nuanced assessment of his views on alcoholism: among other things, they are remarkable for having evolved very little. One is left, in fact, with the impression that his period of sobriety that began with his 1993 stay in the rehabilitation center in Ashley, Maryland, did not in the slightest alter the representations of alcoholism in his writing and painting. As early as 1988, in the anecdote from *Mitki* titled "A Sexual Trauma (Told from the Perspective of D. Shagin)," Shinkarev describes a fictionalized Shagin's partial abstention from drink during the period of the group's "mythic" alcoholism. Shagin wakes up in a child's bed to the haranguing of his grandmother, who holds up a pair of women's underwear she had found in the bed; she also mentions that he had been holding an unfinished bottle of Russian Cahors wine, which his wife took in anger and finished herself.

To make sense of the shaming of alcoholics in this anecdote, we need to examine the relation between sexuality, guilt, and addiction in the collective work of the Mitki. One of Shagin's earliest autobiographical sketches has a segment titled "First Love" that is clearly written with the intention of providing a psychosexual explanation for the Mitki's attitude toward gender:

> In kindergarten Mitya came to love a girl by the name of Olenka. When nap time came, Mitya would lie in the bed with Olenka and tell her various and sundry fairy tales, and they played with dolls and suede teddy bears. But one day their teacher came upon them. She dragged Mitya from Olenka's bed and took off his underpants and proceeded to parade him before all the class groups of the kindergarten, saying "Here, children! Look at this shameless one!"[17]

Mitya finds himself in an idyll that begins as an example of nascent sexuality among the young, with children sharing the same bed, but then devolves into the boy's identification with stereotypically girlish forms of play, ending in a public shaming through exposure of the boy's genitals. The narrative is ambiguous about the actual source of the teacher's outrage—is she angry because they shared the same bed or because he behaved like a girl? Certainly, the particular form of this humiliation suggests that the "shameless one" was on the verge of doing something with his sexuality; on the other hand, the highlighting of his genitals also suggests the perceived absurdity of a child behaving like a girl while being anatomically male. Furthermore, if "little sisters" are characterized in Mitki lore as Olenkas, then sharing a bed with one broaches the possibility—or at least the thought—of sexual relations, and therefore incest. The anecdote serves as a recapitulation of trauma and also opens a window onto the intolerant Soviet mores toward fluid or ambiguous gender behavior.

Seen from this perspective, Shinkarev's 1988 chapter from *Mitki*, titled "A Sexual Trauma (Told from the Perspective of D. Shagin)," would seem to frame alcoholism as a rebellion against rigid and cruel social mores. Expanding on this segment from Shagin's autobiographical writing, Shinkarev's anecdote—a kind of waking dream—has Shagin waking up and finding women's underwear in his bed. In his own drawing of this scene, Shagin is lying in a baby's crib, fully dressed in his winter clothes and sailor's shirt.[18] In Florensky's drawing for the 1990 edition of the book, his grandmother dangles the incriminating women's underwear over his head and attempts to shame him as both a father and a man. "I'm going to tell your wife and kids!" she threatens. "Maybe they're my wife's," he lamely suggests. "No! Not hers!" the grandmother yells. Attempting to change the subject, he asks her to bring him a bottle. "[Your wife] already drank it," she answers.[19] In her gloss on this text on the Mitki's earliest website, the journalist Natalia Shuliakhovskaia writes: "Thus ends the tragic story about a sexual trauma. . . . There was something mysterious in the story: guests came and drank but whose underwear it was . . . nobody knows."[20] If a Mityok is asexual and sleeps in a bed too small for even one adult, let alone two, there may be only one answer to this riddle: the women's underwear had not been left by a sexual partner but had been worn at some point by the Mityok himself. The wife acts out her disgust at his sloth and cross-dressing through drink and her abandonment of him.

In this anecdote, Shinkarev and Shagin call into question the ideals of their own group, acknowledging the imperfections in their neo-Tolstoyan and quasi-Shaker utopia of sexual abstinence and the impossibility of being both passive and heroic at the same time. The grotesquely accusing grandmother represents the Stalinist narrow-mindedness and prudery of the older generation (what Shinkarev calls, in a parody of Jungian terminology, "the magnification of negative personality types in the figure of the mother"),[21] which cannot tolerate the Mitki's way of life. The dream's narrative is an enactment or performance of infantilization; it opens a site from which the audience can critique the phony paternalism of the Soviet state. Strangely, the otherwise judgmental grandmother does not accuse Shagin of infidelity. Also conspicuously absent from this anecdote is any suggestion that Shagin is suffering from a hangover: he responds in a quick-witted (if clearly embarrassed) manner to his grandmother's sharp questioning and engages in some consummate play-acting as a way of parrying her comments.[22] Here we arrive at the realization of the Mitki's contradictory ethic of drinking: alcoholism is both a rejection of false morality and an act in which the ideal of "sharing like a Christian" (as articulated in the first chapter of Shinkarev's book, written in 1984) has elements of selfishness that in fact clash with Christian ideals. Shinkarev's and Shagin's interlocking narratives about alcoholism need to be understood as works of imagination that see addiction in metaphorical terms, as an act of cultural rebellion during the final years of the Soviet Union. Writing in 1995—two years after Shinkarev gave up drinking—the art historian Liubov Gurevich insightfully argued for the centrality of alcoholism in Shinkarev's work, as a counterintuitive form of spiritual discipline akin to the practice of Buddhism:

> At the end of the day, a person will be stumped by the fact that the practice of Zen is a part of a culture which is, in itself, the product of that very same [tradition of] Zen.
>
> In our culture, is there an analogue to the practice of Zen? How can we, here, immerse ourselves in an experience that is intense and highly focused, akin to sitting at the bottom of a well?
>
> What is the one thing that liberates us from all distracting circumstances, obligations, and vicissitudes?
>
> Shinkarev replies: alcoholism.
>
> Alcoholism fulfills all demands.
>
> And this is no parody, although a certain comic effect does arise from the intersection [of these ideas]. The fact of the matter is that [Shinkarev] takes alcoholism seriously and, I would venture to say, quite positively.[23]

Needless to say, what is entirely distinct from the mythology that Gurevich shrewdly dissects is the emotional and clinical reality of alcoholism. Nevertheless, both aspects of addiction—as a cultural phenomenon and a physiological pathology—are abundantly represented in their work.

What makes the Mitki's treatment of alcoholism interesting is their keen awareness of—and playful engagement with—the cultural dimensions of even therapeutic discourses. In this respect, the post-rehabilitation salvific ideas of the Mitki evoke early Protestant inspirational literature, most noticeably the work of John Bunyan. For both Shinkarev and Shagin, alcoholism is an expression of the democracy of sin. We wallow in a state of unctuous imperfection, only to move out of what Bunyan calls (in an aquatically suggestive turn of phrase) adulthood's "slough of despond." For all that—and in a dramatic departure from the historically Protestant frame of reference—the sense of group alcoholism as a blessed state never completely leaves the writings and paintings of the Mitki from the late eighties to the early nineties. The Mitki's affection for Kagor wine is particularly telling in this regard as many Russians associate it with communion wine. Considerably sweeter and heavier than its French counterpart from the Cahors region, Kagor is often diluted with water when administered in the Orthodox Church. Even in his 1993 post-rehab essay and appendix to *Mitki*, titled "The [Good] News for Happy Alcoholics" (*Vest' schastlivym alkogolikam*), Shinkarev writes that the "drunkenness of the Mitki" was possibly the final expression of the "warm" humanity of alcoholism within Russian culture. With some ambivalence, Shinkarev characterizes the "topic of alcoholism" as both "mystical and [deeply] wounding [*raniashchaia*]."[24] If suffering or wounding has a spiritual dimension, then alcoholism becomes an expression not of a discarded past, but of a continued state of being. For the Mitki, the statement "I am an alcoholic" is both the classic turning point within the twelve-step process of recovery and an idiosyncratic assertion of alcoholism as a simulacrum of spirituality.

Perhaps not surprisingly, the vows of sobriety that many of Mitki took during the mid-nineties coincided with the gradual dissolution of the group and the sense that it had solidified very much into a relic of Gorbachev's "dry law" and the paradox-riddled transition to a post-Communist Russia. The turning point in the history of the Mitki is arguably not the collapse of the Soviet Union in 1991, but rather the trips of Shagin, Shinkarev, Viktor Tikhomirov, and the Florenskys to the United States in 1993. At various points during their trips that year, the alcoholic-dependent members of this group visited the rehabilitation center in Ashley, Maryland, founded by the philanthropist Louis Bentley and managed by the Catholic priest Joseph C. Martin. After familiarizing themselves with the principles behind the therapy, Shagin, Shinkarev, and Aleksandr Florensky have asserted the continuing relevance of the Mitki's legacy regardless of the ready availability of alcohol and their own new lives of sobriety. In a neo-Hegelian vein, Shagin has argued that sobriety is a natural extension, and progression, of the Mitki worldview, ensuring the movement's continuing relevance and robustness. As he explained in a 2004 interview, "it's quite true that alcoholics resemble each other regardless of geographical affiliations and details." Going on to describe this social ideal as one whose strength is never threatened by the group's internal diversity, he added, "We're all different people. . . . That's how God made us, but as alcoholics we resemble each other, like native brothers. And, in fact, we are brothers. There, in Alcoholics Anonymous, there are no barriers, we're all workers [*rabotniki*], from business consultants to plumbers [*vodoprovodchikov*]"; furthermore, AA gives the sufferer an appreciation of the "miracle of healing" and a sense of "joy at finding one's brothers." Shagin argued that Alcoholics Anonymous has a great deal in common with the "philosophy of the Mitki": like the Mitki, the organization is a sodality that cultivates "kindness, friendship, and mutual assistance." This, he explains, is a "'mitkovian' program, with the exception of [the presence of] port wine."[25] As Trysh Travis points out in her recent cultural history of AA, "the organization's decentralized and somewhat anarchic structure [is a] defining characteristic that has carried over into the broader recovery movement," whose groups are "structured rhizomatically, growing laterally, with new groups proliferating at will."[26] From this point of view, what Shagin terms the "joy at finding one's brothers" (which he expresses in a pithy and somewhat archaic turn of phrase as *radost' bratraniia*) emerges both as the ideal correspondent to the egalitarian principles of AA and as a corrective to authoritarian models in general, be they Russian or non-Russian. Yet in a significant slip of the tongue, here Shagin also seems to acknowledge the continuing centrality of alcohol to the movement of the Mitki in the moment that its members foreswear it: even in their sobriety, the Mitki are shaped in the most fundamental of ways by their experience with dependency. But in the context of the Mitki, what exactly is recovery or rehabilitation? The Russian term *reabilitizatsiia* is resonant in a way that is more acutely political than its English counterpart because it calls to mind the Soviet practice of restoring reputations, careers, and legacies after extended periods of suppression and undeserved scorn. Under these circumstances, we wonder what might be gained—or recovered—on the road to sobriety.

To answer this question, we need to return to the Mitki's highly metaphoric characterization of alcohol. Shagin's singling out of plumbing as one of the representative professions whose practitioners are afflicted with alcoholism is peculiar, as if to underscore the aquatic basis of the illness. But what is the actual link between water management systems and alcohol consumption? In his introductory essay to the Mitki's Moscow 1997 exhibit titled the group's first "post-rehab" installation (sponsored, with deliberate irony, by Kremlyovskaya Vodka), the cultural critic Vladimir Yakimovich fancifully describes the differing cultural attitudes toward alcoholism in Moscow and St. Petersburg, noting in particular the symbolic significance of the liquidity of alcohol as the property that explains its greater appeal for some substance abusers.[27] Yakimovich elaborates on this conceit by emphasizing the literary nature of Petersburg dipsomania. He envisions the consumption of alcohol in the social settings of the "Hero-City" as an impromptu speaking out to like-minded disaffected others, a practice of improvisational expostulation that leads to unexpected bursts of literary creativity. In this view, speaking and drinking—while proceeding in opposite directions through the mouth—become cognate or related activities. Expanding on Yakimovich's cultural speculations, we may conceive of the Leningrad/St. Petersburg form of alcoholism as a variation on Mikhail Bakhtin's conception of the satirical Rabelaisian image of the gaping mouth as an omnivorous womb—as an organ that ingests dead cultural artifacts only to give them a second and transformed life (or rebirth) in the form of laughter.[28]

As we have seen in the previous chapters of this study, there is certainly much about the specific humor of the Mitki that can be traced to Bakhtin's paradox of laughter as both violent and redemptive. Through Yakimovich's essay, we see more clearly that their understanding of substance abuse is also deeply informed by this conception of the perpetually unresolved dialectic—between female and male, high and low, human and animal—as an engine for the powering of creative labor. In his memoir about the role of alcohol in his life, Shagin describes scenes of spontaneous sociability, noting how in 1975 he befriended his mother's new husband, the "young and brilliant photographer" Boris Smelov. "We began to drink at his shoots, sometimes falling asleep on benches and in attics. I began to take part in the openings of the exhibits of 'unofficial' artists; it was very cheerful, we drank and read verses."[29] Yakimovich argues that alcohol for the Petersburg *intelligent* represents a return path to the amniotic sack, a conduit to the nurturing water of the natural world. We might also note that the link between labile fluidity and garrulous orality is reflected in the Mitki's love of argot terms such as *bormotushka* for a bottle of wine—which suggests an equivalence between flowing liquid and speech (from *bormotat'*, "to mumble")—and *bukhat'* for drinking, derived from the onomatopoetic noun *bukh*, for a sudden loud noise. One drinks directly from the bottle by grabbing it "by its throat" (*gorlom, gorlushkoi*), or drinking from its throat (*iz gorla*), as if giving it a drawn-out kiss.[30] The word *sobutil'nik* itself (fellow tippler, "co-bottler") is probably formed by analogy with the Russian word for "interlocutor," *sobesednik*. In a tacit acknowledgment of the aquatic subtext of the Mitki's subculture, Shagin in a 2002 interview stated: "I love water in all its forms. It's on that account that Piter [St. Petersburg] is so dear to me. There one has a great deal of water. Every year [after the winter], when river passage is allowed again, I cruise on a launch along the Neva and the Bay of Finland. From the water, you can look differently at the city and at life in general."[31] Although Shagin in this statement is not specifically associating the love of water with alcohol consumption, his portrayal of St. Petersburg as a liquid muse—a seemingly impossible figure of an urban Nereid—is telling.

In *Selfless Heroes*, his 1998 autobiographical account about his humbling transformation into a recovering alcoholic, Shagin reexamines his lifelong propensity for excessive consumption of food and drink, returning to his personal narrative about family politics and gender roles. One of his first recollections was the small apartment he lived in with his parents on Mayakovsky Street, with its windows looking out onto a courtyard with a well (*dvor kolodets*). "Friends came to my father," he writes, "artists and writers." He then notes that his favorite toy was a syringe. What seems an abrupt shift of focus from the setting of his upbringing to an unusual toy in fact obscures a connection between the two. He goes on to recall an argument between his parents that resulted in his mother "[throwing] a syringe with an ampoule of morphine out the window. Then my father was put in prison. I was three years old. My mother and I would bring him parcels in the Priazhka jail. I remember the face of my father behind the bars, and him waving to me." Vladimir Shagin's substance-abuse problems influence Dmitri's choice in forms of play, suggesting a link between addiction and the bohemian lifestyle of the elder Shagin and his friends. Substance dependency begins as a form of entertainment, in which conversing and drinking emerge as parallel forms of intoxication. "Guests often came to visit us, and I took part in their dinner conversations and drank dry wine from the age of ten. Sometimes I would become intoxicated and experienced a euphoria."[32] Among adults such as Shagin's father, whose life was marked by political and material difficulties, such indulgence segues into self-medication for emotional problems.

In Shagin's account, the images of the courtyard well and the syringe complement each other, as conduits of fluid. The fact that Shagin remembers his mother throwing her husband's syringe out the window, and in the direction of the courtyard well, only reinforces the subtext of liquidity, which emerges as a persistent mythic marker of alcoholism in the work of the Mitki. Interestingly, Natalia (née Neizel) Shagina's chastisement of her husband is presented as a prelude to his incarceration ("then my father was put in prison"), with the suggestion of the operation of a Soviet superego on the level of the nuclear family. From the perspective of a young child, the punishment of the father serves as a rebuke to the son, for whom the syringe also represented a form of entertainment, and who was presumably no longer allowed to play with one because of the father's growing substance dependency. One might regard the boy's playing with the father's instrument of sedation and addiction, and bringing it back into the space of their apartment, as an example of both identification with his father and of subconscious Oedipal aggression. The fact that the Russian word for syringe (*shprits*) is German in origin only points up the boy's transgressive affect, as he symbolically takes on the role of an enemy to his family. As we shall soon see, the memory of the Leningrad blockade looms large in Shagin's recollection of his upbringing. In the same segment of the memoir, Shagin draws attention to the opposition between himself and his father by contrasting their forms of addiction: "[in high school] I would smoke pot on and off, but couldn't stand the thought of injections—it just wasn't my thing [*ne moe*]."[33] In his autobiographical writing, it is certainly odd that Shagin's alcohol addiction provides him with an imagined opportunity to separate himself from the specific dependency problems that his father experienced. In the end, he is of course only exchanging one form of dependency for another. Over the course of his autobiography, Shagin becomes more cognizant of the lure of alcohol as a vehicle for rebelling against the established order. Yet alcoholism as a reaction against restriction, a response typical during Gorbachev's "dry law," becomes for him, in the end, an unsatisfying form of rebellion.

Within this family romance, women play other roles as well, some that directly contradict the image of them as deniers of the enjoyment of controlled substances. Interestingly, Shagin attributes his propensity for gluttony and bibulousness to the child-rearing philosophy of his grandmother, and to the Leningrad blockade. In some instances, women are also regarded as enablers of dependency, in their capacity as those who often prepare and present food and drink:

> From childhood, I had an unhealthy gravitation to food and drink. [As a child] I was unable to fall asleep without drinking a liter bottle of milk.

My grandmother lived through the horrors of the blockade, the death of her parents and a young daughter from hunger. She constantly fed me, murmuring, "Eat, Mitya, eat, and then there won't be any hunger." Grandmother would pick me up from kindergarten and feed me to bursting, asking that I not reveal our little secret to my mother.[34]

The result of this secrecy was that "at home [he] would have to eat yet another full meal," and that he grew up "very fat." The grandmother and mother represent competing images of female identity, one as an indulgent provider and the other (in a depiction that echoes the punitive images of the teacher and grandmother in the anecdotes discussed earlier) as a strict regulator of bodily regimens. The stepfather takes on a role of facilitator of permissiveness and indulgence that runs parallel to that of the grandmother:

When I was six years old, my mother got married a second time, to a paleobotanist who was a researcher. I remember one of my first heroic victories. Mother made a large duck. As we sat down with stepfather at the table, I asked, "is it all for me"? Stepfather joked, "yes, it's all for you." And I, without speaking a word and to the amazement of the entire family, silently ate the entire duck.[35]

The stepfather's intercession has the effect of thawing out the rigid tensions with the disciplinary regime within a family fractured by mental illness and dependence. Yet this green light to self-indulgence is not without its own negative consequences. We are made to understand that the competing and often highly contradictory models of adult behavior confuse the young Shagin and his peers.

In his sardonic autobiographical account, prodigious alcohol consumption becomes for Shagin a sign of adult masculinity when he reaches the threshold of puberty. "It was in the pioneer camp in Yukki that I drank for the first time as an adult. We were no older than thirteen. The three of us bought two bottles of red port wine and drank it up behind the fence, feeling that we were real men." This sort of activity, as it turns out, represented the norm in any number of institutions in which Shagin spent his youth and is perhaps best described in a critical article in the newspaper *Leningradskaya Pravda* in 1987, concerning the alcoholic lifestyle of the Mitki and other bohemian youths in the city at the beginning of Gorbachev's dry law. The piece also contains the first reference to the movement in the official Soviet press.[36] Poetry by the Mitki and their quasi-dissident fellow-travelers contain surprisingly detailed and realistic accounts of everyday alcohol consumption among the young intelligentsia during the Soviet period. The Russian-Jewish poet Oleg Grigoriev slyly revamped nursery rhymes into compressed (yet grittily realistic) sketches of adult inebriated misbehavior. The work of Grigoriev (who died from alcohol-related causes in 1992) crucially shaped the metrical and narrative structures of the Mitki's verse more than any other literary source and was an important body of memoir writing outside the official Soviet publications about substance abuse in Leningrad during the Brezhnev and Gorbachev years. More recently, the writer Evgenii Lesin recalls student life in Leningrad in 1983 as characterized by rushing back to the institute after shopping with "a bottle [of strong port]" in his knapsack.[37]

Against this backdrop of material privation and stinging frustration, the female mother-substitute takes shape as a facilitator—or as rehabilitation terminology would have it, as an enabler—of excess. The image of the Feminine as a force that relieves tension and resolves inner contradictions is an important one for the Mitki. In the end, alcoholism becomes for them an emblem of successful stress management in the face of personal and collective traumas, as a palliative against the paralyzing fear of scarcity, giving the illusion of the "abundant" resources trumpeted by the Soviet press. In this context of a nexus between women and alcohol, the augmentative merging of all Mitki women (i.e., those who enable them in their dipsomania) with the figure of the Mitki poet and artist Olga Florensky reveals an obsession with the Feminine that recalls the pre-Christian East Slavic notion of the "Moist Mother Earth" (*mat' syra zemlia*) and the goddess Mokosh (lit., the "wet" one) from the pagan Slavic pantheon. Women in the movement serve as priestesses or vestal virgins in the Mitki mythology of alcoholic afflatus. How can female Mitki simultaneously play the roles of muse and confrère, mother and brother?

Before we answer that question, we need to reconsider the ways in which the virtues of alcohol in the Mitki's early writing are consistently refracted through the lens of sexual politics, discussed in the previous chapter. The figure of Olga Florensky serves a kind of resident symbol of the female gender, a fact that poses the possibility of a competitive relationship between herself and Shagin, as authority figures within the movement. Shinkarev describes the transformation of "maidens" into "little sisters" or "Olenkas" as requiring the passing of a test in which they make it possible for the male Mityok to "chill-out."[38] The initial subservience of this function is leavened by Shinkarev's emphasis on the collaborative nature of the interaction between men and women in the context of the Mitki, exemplified by both standing together in line for the purchase of liquor.

It is here, in the moment of contemplating the prospect of an asexual *kollektiv*, that the spiritual implications of alcoholism enter the worldview of the Mitki. For the Mitki, alcohol represents a vehicle for artistic inspiration and fraternization. Yet this interaction emerges as distinctly asymmetrical because women, who are simply not portrayed as drinkers in the work of the Mitki, function as little more than enablers of alcoholic men. For the Mitki, sex is the apple of discord within the garden, the force that renders unfeasible "brotherly" relations between men and women. We also see, in the writing of Shinkarev and Shagin, an implicit acknowledgment of the imperfections within the gender comity in their group, traceable to the use of women as the providers of money for alcohol. In an unexpected feminist mode, the two men acknowledge the incompatibility between exploitation and a healthy eroticism. As Shuliakhovskaia explains in her droll commentary, modeled on the tone and content of Shinkarev's book, the Mitki avoid "eroticism" for two reasons. First, they would otherwise not be able to survive (*inache prosto ne vyzhit'*) because of the jealousy and violence that would result from such urges, shattering the already tense equilibrium of disparate personalities within the group. The popular image of the rock group on the cusp of post-pubescence and adulthood is never far from the Mitki's personal mythmaking, and in this regard one recalls Yoko Ono's statement about the beginning of her liaison with John Lennon: "I sort of went to bed with this guy that I liked, and suddenly the next morning I see these three guys standing there with resentful eyes."[39] Secondly, abstinence and androgyny are essential for creative purposes: one needs to direct the libido to something more useful, such as painting.[40] Alcohol here plays a special role as an anti-aphrodisiac—as a path to a highly sublimated eroticism—and as a surrogate for physical intimacy by evocatively simulating the exchange of bodily fluids. In one sketch, Shagin describes a woman throwing herself at Shinkarev, who grabs a bottle of vodka and drinks himself unconscious. "What can one do with him, a drunken man?"[41] Shagin wonders sensibly. Shagin prefaces this anecdote with a quasi-Freudian comparison of the Mitki's use of alcohol to St. Sergius of Radonezh's self-mortification by cutting off his own hand, with alcohol becoming an instrument for self-castration. The bottle—like the needle—becomes a vehicle for a certain control or possession of one's own body, freeing it from the strictures of the superego. In this instance, indulgence comes to represent (in a highly counterintuitive way) a pathway for renunciation. At the same time, Shagin also insists that the Mitki's eroticism is directly connected to alcohol.[42] But what exactly does this special eroticism consist of?

The role of alcohol as a perceived medium for both creative activity and sublimated sexuality is crucial here, as is also evident in Shinkarev's work. In a 2008 essay, he recounts drinking mineral water at a party where everybody else was drinking vodka. By accident he picks up someone else's glass and in shock tastes vodka. Deciding not to create the embarrassing spectacle of spitting it out in the presence of everyone, he quickly walks to the bathroom. Time seems to slow down and then stop for a blissful moment as "each molecule of alcohol, penetrating me, brought a radiant and purifying wave of joy, health and talent . . . everything that I had lost over a period of nine years of sobriety. You fool—how much time was squandered for absolutely nothing!" Spitting out the liquor, Shinkarev muses that the perception that "alcoholics are unproductive and incapable of work" is belied by "the collected works of Faulkner and of many other alcoholics."[43] He underscores the role of alcohol as a de Quinceyan controlled substance enabling artistic activity, and as a building block in the Mitki's group narrative. Shinkarev also hints at the sexual nature of the Mitki's alcoholism, and its mythic underpinnings as a search for the Eternal Feminine, when he writes in his book *Mitki* about the movement that the male Mityok's libido is transferred to the "beaded little purses" (*bisernye koshelechki*) of the women who buy them liquor.[44] Even the act of purchasing alcohol is eroticized, the peculiar fixation on the texture of the purses ("beaded") suggesting a surrogate for the sex organs of the "little sisters." The cumulative effect of all these mixed signals about the much-vaunted gender equality among the Mitki renders their group identity into a form of extended performance art.

Several considerations from the work of the Mitki contextualize the unsavory social parasitism of some of Shinkarev's anecdotes. As Shinkarev himself explains, alcoholism represents a total form of freedom only in the sense that its obliteration of boundaries approximates states of infantilism and self-annihilation. In one chapter of his 1985 *Mitki*, significantly titled "He Drank since Morning, and Was Free for the Entire Day," Shinkarev notes that drunkenness is a "total defense" because when "you drink, there is no need to fulfill destiny, and therefore there is no need to defend oneself"; in fact, there is "nothing left to defend."[45] To the Russian ear, Shinkarev's lexical choices here are highly suggestive. The particular verb he uses here, "to defend" (*oboroniat'*), is primarily military or strategic in its connotation and pointedly cannot be used to describe a verbal defense or even personal physical parrying; the phrase "to fulfill destiny" is parallel to Soviet-era verbal formulae about fulfilling or overfulfilling projects of a planned economy, or bringing to fruition a stage within the historical dialectic. Alcohol becomes, in effect, an instrument of resistance against normative Soviet values and a substance for attaining a sense of agency and integration with a system of values that is higher than nation or country. Noting with approval Jung's characterization of alcoholism as a "quest for wholeness," Shinkarev goes on in his sketch "Alcohol" to assert that for the "genuine alcoholic [this thirst] is the equivalent of a spiritual thirst, one with which the greatest luminaries [of culture] burned."

Striking a similar note of defiance in his assessment of the movement during the late eighties, on the "Alcoholism" round table of the Channel 1 talk show televised on June 7, 2009, Shagin notes that drinking for the Mitki and many other Soviet citizens was a response to the "Gorbachevian terror" of the dry law, and that the stricture (*zapret*) against alcohol served as a pretext for indulging in it.[46] Both Shinkarev and Shagin seem to suggest that in an authoritarian society, drunkenness becomes a state in which spontaneous things happen, counter to the demands of the planned economy and a Foucauldian order. As Andrei Bitov—a St. Petersburg writer deeply sympathetic of the Mitki—once put it, "order is a horrible thing: a prison camp is order."[47] In such a context, drunkenness becomes not only a gesture of rebellion, but also a means for cultivating a form of interiority that gives the illusion of autonomy, of not defining oneself exclusively in opposition to authority. In his 1994 *lubok* (chapbook) *A Few Episodes from the Period of My Epic Drinking*, Aleksandr Florensky incisively portrays this shift from the absolute nature of the Mitki's Soviet-era alcoholism to their no less categorical embrace of sobriety. Florensky's ink drawings are captioned by droll comments that are accompanied by English translations by Dmitri Priyatkin, in what the reader suspects is a gesture of accommodation and gratitude toward the Anglophone culture that cured him of his illness. The illustrations highlight various forms of alcohol-driven sociability and misbehavior, with the implication that their flashes of fellowship and political resistance are only simulacra of the real thing. In one, a soused Florensky in the year 1985 "knocks at the door of the police room at the Moscow Central Station, thinking that [his] passport, driver's license and money are in there"; in another, the artist and a friend turn their backs on a political demonstration in order to devote themselves to drink, flattering themselves with the conceit that "on August 19, 1991, during the *putsch*, me and my friends lurked in ambush near the Mariinsky Palace, ready to stop the tanks in case they appear." A distinct leitmotif in this series of drawings is the notion of alcohol as a retardant in adult emotional development. The inability to drive a car, or ride a bike or horse, figures prominently in their failed attempts at adult autonomy and control over their circumstances: the drawings with the captions "driving a car with Svet Ostrov in Narva, while pissing drunk [*buduchi vypimshi*] and nearly innocent of any driving skills" and "made three unsuccessful attempts to mount a horse, while traveling across Svanetia in Georgia, while my wife is being harassed by a Georgian" are only two examples of reduced transportational and masculine prowess in the series.[48]

In these captions, we see reminders of the seductive liquidity of alcohol, and a correlation between alcoholism and protracted childhood. The quicksilver property of liquor is consistently presented in relation to the painstaking retention of fluids or its opposite, incontinence: bottles are hidden in toilet tanks, moonshine is siphoned from stills, and the artist lolls drunkenly on the toilet as a gushing tub faucet threatens to flood the bathroom. Once again, we are in the territory of viewing alcoholism from a Bakhtinian perspective, as a symbolic manifestation of the cycle of ingestion and excretion, order and chaos. The female Mityok emerges as a mediator between the starkly opposing states brought on by inebriation, by serving as an example of someone whose childlike attitude represents a pacific sociability that is distinct from the agitated one of the male alcoholic. Yet a troubling question arises here: does the female Mityok's attitude represent first and foremost a mature Christian ethic of forgiveness, the behavior of another infantilized adult, or (as discussed earlier) the act of an exploited woman? Thus, in one picture, seeing her husband drunk one morning, the artist's wife Olga Florensky "wanted to punish me, but finding a toy hippopotamus in my pocket, was touched and mellowed out [*sic*]" (Figure 17).[49] Florensky's series of drawings ends with a portrait of calm sobriety with two friends in the Maryland rehab center in 1994. Curiously, in this picture he and his friends are sitting in front of a groaning board of food with a single carton of juice, but no glasses for drinking.[50] Without the false consciousness of pseudo-collectivism maintained by the communal model of Russian drinking, the cost of sobriety appears to consist of individuation and adulthood, and the recognition and acceptance of scarcity. In

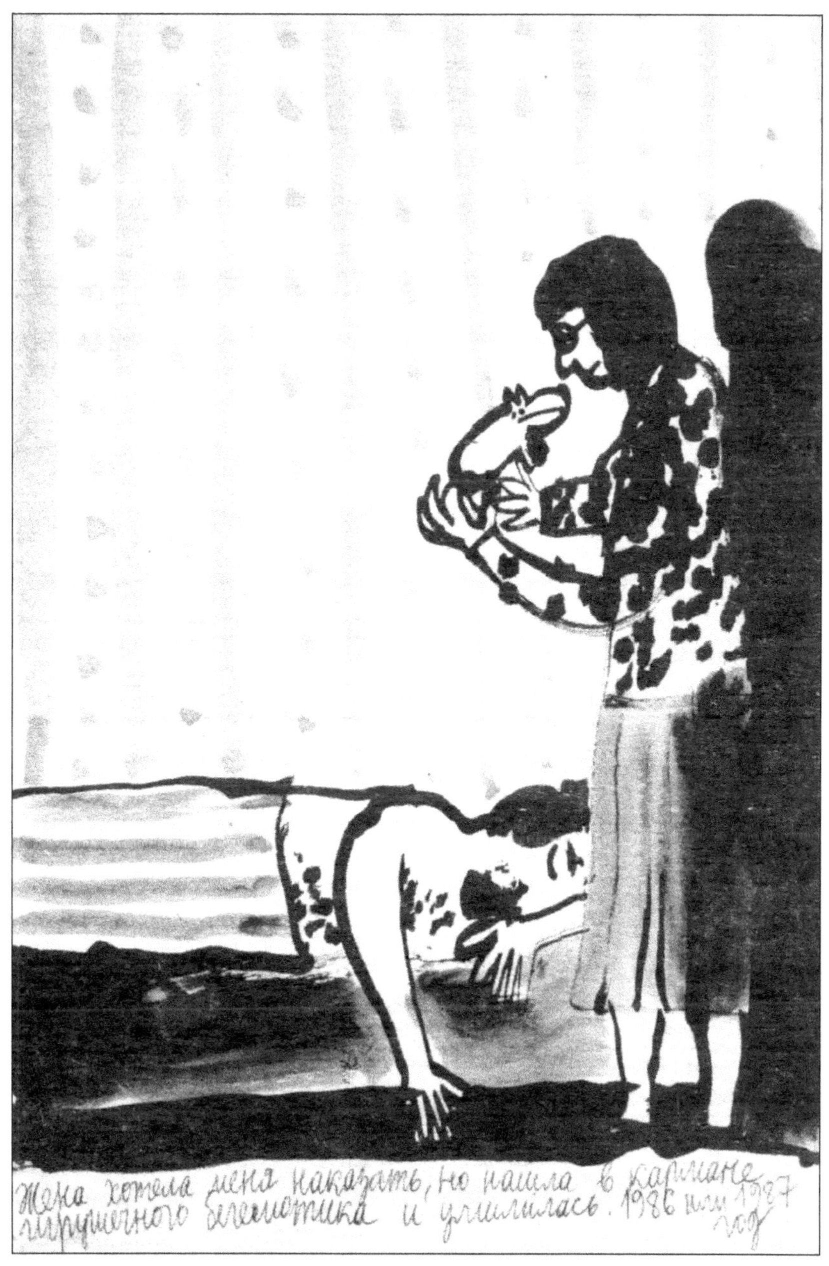


Figure 17. Aleksandr Florensky, "My wife wanted to punish me, but finding a toy hippopotamus in my pocket, was touched and mellowed out [*sic*]" (Zhena khotela menia nakazat', no nashla v karmane igrushechnogo begemotika, i umililas') (1994), from *A Few Episodes from the Period of My Epic Drinking*, page 33.

effect, the child turns away the mother's breast, understanding the radical Otherness of the world that surrounds it.

In his confessional autobiography *Selfless Heroes*, Shagin also portrays his stay at the same rehabilitation center as a process of weaning himself from liquids in general. At one point in his account, he paraphrases a lecture by the recovering alcoholic Father Martin as emphasizing that the seductiveness of alcohol stems in part from its fluid properties, by its ability to fully occupy the space of any entity or receptacle: "A liquid is a substance that takes on the forms of the vessels in which it is located. Although alcohol does not have form, it nonetheless dictates [*diktuet*] our conduct."[51] Alcohol functions as a substance that rebukes moral austerity, by negating the emptying out or *kenosis* of the ego that monastic orders demand. The general flavorless and water-like translucence of vodka in particular is expressive of this protean quality. As Levintov notes, vodka appeals to all classes and callings within Russian society, from tsars to presidents, from the homeless to the most competent office workers in the marriage bureau. Vodka also "gravitates to the diversity" of the groaning board, "providing nuance and highlighting the specific flavors of each appetizer."[52] The image of alcohol as a dictator of the individual's quotidian space is one that finds uncommon resonance among contemporary Russians. In the hands of the Mitki and many other Russian bloggers and cultural consumers, vodka becomes a metaphor for the loss of freedom and the dependence on authoritarian modes of thought. Like all addictions, that dependence has its considerable attractions. One could say of vodka what Gordon Gekko famously stated about greed in Oliver Stone's *Wall Street*: it is good and right because it "cuts through and simplifies." As Shinkarev himself has put it even in his post-recovery phase, "vodka—what a compelling and steadfast word!"[53]

At the end of his own stay in Ashley, Shagin describes painting a picture as a gift to the rehab center, a canvas with a stark juxtaposition of the center's church interior with the sea beyond the window.[54] This image, suggestive of a surrealist painting, clarifies Shagin's enigmatic statement about loving "Piter" (St. Petersburg) on account of his love of water "in all its forms." Shagin suggests that the recovering alcoholic is engaged in a lifelong endeavor of distancing himself from liquid without being able to abandon it completely. This effort yields the positive result of obtaining "from the [vantage point of the] water [*s vody*]" a "different"—i.e., more abstracted—view of "the city and life in general." Shagin seems to be saying that the love for this city is like liquor for the alcoholic, a desire that never truly leaves. In a moment of self-discipline, Shagin refuses to flee to the source of liquid—to run out, as he does in his childhood memory, to the courtyard well where his father's syringe was tossed—choosing instead to visualize the source of temptation in its most vivid colors. In his *Civilization and Its Discontents*, Freud coins the pejorative term "oceanic feeling" to denote an ego's inability to separate from the mother's breast, a state that can linger into adulthood as a solipsistic world view or—as in Freud's recounting of his friend Romain Rolland's sensations of being invisibly linked to the physical universe—as a crypto-pantheistic understanding of an ineffable interconnectedness among persons and things. Yet Shagin turns out not to be an apologist for apperception, as was Rolland in Freud's account. Shagin in fact submits what Freud calls "clear and sharp demarcations" between himself and the substance surrounding St. Petersburg. He portrays himself as a well-adjusted Tantalus, who has learned to feast with his eyes rather than his mouth on the diminishing perspective of liquid, and it is perhaps significant in this regard that since their sobriety the Mitki have turned more to the visual arts than to literary activity.

In an acknowledgment of these cognitive effects of alcohol, the Mitki in their recent work draw attention to the consequences of being "under the influence": the eye swims while the tongue is loosened. In Shinkarev's piece "Alcohol," the link between visuality and sobriety on the one hand, and inebriation and rhetorical and literary creativity on the other, emerges with force in the recovery phase of the Mitki's work: after all, the artists whom Shinkarev adduces as flourishing under the influence are all writers. As Aleksandr Florensky noted in one of the interviews conducted for this study, he knew that his alcoholism became a problem when a Swiss friend visiting his studio said that there was "something different there . . . what is it? . . . I don't smell any paint!"[55] The Mitki's ultimate rejection of alcohol may be regarded as an attempt to canonize their reputations as primarily visual rather than literary artists, and to burnish the street cred of their name brand during a time where the cultural role of alcohol had evolved into something very different from the forbidden fruit of the late eighties. In his recent study of the success of various treatment programs for alcoholism in Russia, Eugene Raikhel notes that the Mitki "served as objects of identification for prospective [Russian] AA members who viewed themselves as members of the cultural intelligentsia, and others who perhaps questioned the respectability of the program" because of the perception of it as a "cult" originating in the West. One might also add that this negative impression of AA was probably exacerbated by the increase in Baptist missionary activity in Russia during the nineties, which reminded some Russians of the historical roots of AA in American Protestant sobriety movements. What emerges here as most important is the matter of choice among modes of expression, and the perceived impossibility of achieving a synesthetic union between different artistic media. We are made to understand that the alcohol-driven attempt to achieve a fusion of music, the visual image or sign and language (as expressed in Aleksandr Florensky's whimsical drawing of Mozart as a Mityok), and modes of stylized unconventional behavior may result in artifacts of nuanced expression. As Raikhel puts it, there was no little irony in the fact that the Mitki, who had "earned [their] fame through something like punk aesthetic," ultimately become a "source of respectability" among Russians seeking to treat their dependence upon alcohol: "like many other artists, [they] had reformulated and commodified their aesthetic," with the result that "their drunken past provid[ed] a patina of respectability to their new sober image."[56]

At this point in our discussion, we need to return to the peculiar symmetry in the work of the Mitki between the states of inebriation and strict sobriety. In interviews and his own writing after his abandonment of drinking, Shagin elaborates on the links between sobriety, Eastern Orthodox spirituality, and the aquatic mythology of the city in ways that draw unexpected parallels between the diametrically opposed states of alcohol indulgence and abstinence. In a 2007 interview with a newspaper of the Russian Orthodox Church, Shagin replied to a question about St. Petersburg as a source of inspiration for his writing and painting by stating that Peter the Great "correctly" chose the place for the new capital, by locating it on water.[57] He goes on to say that "for me it's especially significant that the chapel of St. Kseniya the Blessed is located on Vasiliev Island": she and St. John of Kronstadt "lived in the city, and protect it." It should be pointed out here that both Shagin and Shinkarev live on Vasiliev Island—which had a reputation as a seedbed for highly educated circles of dissident Soviet-era circles—and that Kronstadt is another island in the archipelago of the metropolitan region, one that was famous for a 1921 revolt of army and navy officers against the increasingly undemocratic policies of the Soviet regime. Water, and the pockets of dry land embedded within it, are associated with a certain independence from the literal and figurative mainstream. In the same interview Shagin describes the essence of creativity as "bringing joy to people" and adds that "God speaks to us through [other] people."

Shagin draws a structural parallel between the sociability of intense alcohol consumption and the comity that emerges from abstinence in twelve-step groups. Shagin himself seems to be unaware of this analogy, as it emerges in curious forms from various corners of his work. In his intellectual and creative evolution, he now attaches significance to his baptism into the Russian Orthodox Church at the age of sixteen and uses terms that complement the characterization of his later sobriety: "After many years, it occurred to me that if I hadn't been baptized then, I would not have survived [and that] my life without that would have been more tragic." The state of sobriety, and other forms of purification, can only occur through the process of *bratanie*, a term that is best understood in English as "enbrotherment." *Bratanie* requires that the individual's ego be broken down in the solvent of a form of sociability. From this perspective, alcoholism represents an *attempt* at personal salvation—a groping for true consciousness in a benighted society—albeit a certainly misguided one. Both inebriation and sobriety serve in equal force as catalysts for the aesthetic impulse. In a significant departure from Freudian notions of individuation, the Mityok's dispatching of his own "oceanic feeling" serves to enhance androgynous fellowship, as suggested by the parallel that Shagin draws between the feminine and masculine nouns "Piter" and *voda* (water), both objects of the Mityok's affection that serve in the capacity of stepparents. Like political rehabilitations during the Soviet era, the Mitki's rehabilitation from alcoholism perpetually retains the memory of a past that is (as Aleksandr Florensky puts it) no less "epic" than it is inglorious.

The larger question that emerges from this discussion is this: How can the Mitki portray sobriety in elegiac or regretful terms while also drawing attention to alcoholism as an expression of stunted growth and compromised personal autonomy? Perhaps we should ask more pointedly, why portray alcoholism as having any positive value? Is the attitude of the post-alcoholic Mityok essentially what William Blake famously said about Milton's toward the nominal villain of *Paradise Lost*: that he was of the Devil's party without knowing it?

In answering these questions, we need to examine a range of the Mitki's references to alcohol consumption. Again, where in other areas of the Mitki's writing and painting (concerning gender dimorphism, sexual politics, and attitudes toward developments in the contemporary art world in the West) we see a range of different and often clashing opinions, the treatments of alcoholism emerge as remarkably of one piece, as if each member of the movement—even now in 2018, in its retrospective phase—functions as a member of a carefully orchestrated ensemble playing the same composition. The topic of alcohol becomes, in effect, the only truly collective text of the Mitki, the one area where their aesthetics and ethics of mutual assistance and anti-hierarchical social configuration become most vividly manifest. The grudging acknowledgment of the enhancing influence of alcohol on the experience that feeds into artistic creation may be considered the first note in this shared melody. In one of the interviews for this study, Aleksandr Florensky admits that in the eighties he was often moved to paint by the sensations he experienced during inebriation because "all feelings are intensified" in the state of alcoholic intoxication.[58] Yet he also noted in the same conversation that he never fully absorbed the holdings in the city's galleries and museums until he became sober. "So, you don't drink anymore? Well, do some more artwork, read some books you haven't read before, go to some museums." The "post-alcoholic" work of the Mitki brings to mind yet another of William Blake's memorable formulations, this time about the "road of excess" unexpectedly leading to the "palace of wisdom." Like the Mitki, Blake was a writer who was acutely aware of the tension and occasional incommensurability between the painted image and the written word. Until their shared experience of sobriety in 1993, the Mitki portrayed alcoholism in terms that were primarily literary.

After the visits of Shagin, the Florenskys, Shinkarev, and Tikhomirov to the United States that year, the Mitki represented alcoholism primarily in drawings and paintings rather than in writing, as if sobriety resulted in a kind of muting of the literary voice. The link between the deeper appreciation of visuality in all its forms—looking, reading, and observing—and the cessation of drinking emerges as a distinctive feature in the recent work of the Mitki. The reasons for this overall shift in modes of representation—and its exact relation to sobriety—are still unclear, and certainly need to be investigated further. At this point, we may speculate, however, that the group model of rehabilitation that is central to the twelve-step program may have contributed to an internal dialogue among the Mitki, resulting in the emphasis of topics and terms within the group's overall discourse. As Trysh Travis explains in her study of the recovery movement in the United States, the adherents of twelve-step programs "number in the millions; it is a diverse and multifaceted cultural formation, with an intellectual history and an evolving aesthetic."[59] Perhaps for some alcoholics the culture of talk and dialogue that is central to the recovery movement leads to a certain fatigue in literary contemplations of the problem, with the shift to a different mode of expression not associated with the process of recovery becoming a welcome relief. From that point of view—and regardless of the current dispute between Shagin and Shinkarev about who truly represents the custodian of the movement's legacy—the Mitki may be considered more collectivist in spirit now than in the period of their Soviet-era and alcohol-fueled "glorious youth" (*slavnaia molodost'*).

And it is for that reason that, oddly, they no longer exist as a group: cooperatives do not flourish among undifferentiated or isomorphous identities or agents of labor. The building of the Mitki as a brand for sobriety was admirable, and in many ways effective in publicizing the options for rehabilitation within the borders of the Russian Federation. Shagin's meeting in 2001 with Eric Clapton—at the House of Hope in Perekiulia, near the border with Finland—brought both international and national attention to what continues to be the only nonprofit rehabilitation center in the country. Yet the newly tightened focus of this "mission" resulted in an inevitable flattening of the playful ambiguity within the Mitki's cultural production. In one fell swoop, the Mitki became defined by their relation to a specific social problem and ceased to be a plurality of voices responding to a range of issues. As Judith Butler points out, "the point is not to regard the body merely as an instrument for making a political claim, but to let this [particular] body, the plurality of bodies, become the precondition of all further political claims."[60] In his 2008 *The End of the Mitki,* Shinkarev writes that "sobriety shook the Mitki to the core and turned them on their head."[61] In the next chapter, we will see how the legacy of rhetorical polyphony remains intact in the prolific ongoing activity of Olga and Aleksandr Florensky.

# 4

## Mosaic Authorship

### A Coproduction of Olga and Aleksandr Florensky

The more I think about the role of effigies in the life of man, the more I find myself leaning toward the following idea: can it be that he doesn't have to kill, in satisfying his despotic creative urges? Or, as one friend put it—a Russian born in Germany, with an uncertain grasp of the language of his ancestors—that he does not have to *enmortify* [*primershchvliat'*] animals? Let the ARTIFICIAL ANIMAL be utterly artificial—may it go with God, in all its violations of anatomy and truth!

OLGA FLORENSKY, from the statement about her exhibit *Taxidermy* (1999)

Cursed be anyone who makes a sculptured or molten image, abhorred by the LORD, a craftman's handiwork, and sets it up in secret.

Deuteronomy 27:15

In 2000 Andrei Bitov, the St. Petersburg novelist and early promoter of the Mitki, made a statement about the creative team of Olga and Aleksandr Florensky that was as baffling as it was provocative. In his preface to the Florenskys' *Movement in the Direction of a Book*, Bitov wrote that the book was the "result of incest" because Olga and Aleksandr, "belonging as they do to the legendary Mitki . . . are—in their capacity as 'little brother' and 'little sister'—sundered from each other as husband and wife." We can imagine that Bitov was attempting to provide a key for an audience not familiar with the wide-ranging genre profile of the

Florenskys' essays, artwork, and poetry over a period of almost a quarter of a century, by linking it to the Mitki's social ideals of ascetic Tolstoyan amity and provisional gender equality. Bitov sought to underscore the radical character of the values within the group, in its refusal to hew to any number of lazily normative assumptions about relations between the sexes. He seems to be telling us that the cultural mainstream assesses the renunciation of carnal relations as being no less egregious and disruptive of the social order than the actual commission of taboo sexual acts. Creative collaboration, in this conceit, would seem to exclude the experience of physical intimacy.

Bitov's act of rhetorical épatage is as revealing of popular conceptions of the Mitki as it is of his own considerable insight into the group. For one thing, he assumes no line of separation between the Mitki and the Florenskys, which some would see as giving insufficient credit to the distinctiveness and aesthetic autonomy of the latters' work. Perhaps more importantly, what we begin to sense here are the limits of language—in Russian, and here, in English—in characterizing the affective or experiential aspects of creative collaboration. In Shinkarev's accounts of the Mitki, the Florenskys play vivid secondary roles in the unfolding drama of relations between himself and Dmitri Shagin, whom I have termed the "glimmer twins" of the movement. Bitov's metaphor of incest intuits the centrality of intimacy in the work of the Florenskys. Yet I would go further, and argue that the Florenskys are in fact the figures among the Mitki who are most emblematic of it as a social and creative movement.

Unlike the output of Shinkarev, Shagin, and Tikhomirov, their work actively demonstrates—as opposed to merely positing or suggesting—the ways in which a collective may consist of only two people, without tipping over into what Hannah Arendt anxiously characterizes as the "totalitarianism for two."[1] In contrast with Shagin and Shinkarev, the Florenskys do not position themselves as custodians of a movement. Writing about *Russian Trophy*, the Florenskys' multimedia installation of recreated and fancifully imagined military heraldry, the Russian Museum's curator of contemporary art, Aleksandr Borovsky, argued that the Florenskys strive to bring to our attention an "unconscious that is collective, [yet] not rooted in any historical situation."[2] We should extend this insight, by adding that they are also keen to draw back the curtain that conceals an unconscious that is collective, yet paradoxically not defined by any group. Bitov's characterization of the Florenskys' working methods is a sharp and attention-grabbing quip, a conversation-starting conceit; in this gambit of provoking a response, he perhaps involuntarily identifies a key operational principle within their production. In the work of the Florenskys, the collective unconscious is brought to the fore through the intimacy of two, which subsequently serves as a generative template of larger affiliations. The production of O & A Florensky consists of close interaction among at least three distinct artists: the individual artists Olga and Aleksandr, and their collaborative identity, represented by the brand name "O & A Florensky." From within the interstices of this triad, other personae replicate: Olga and Aleksandr respond weightily and almost histrionically to each other's separate projects *Taxidermy* and *Modest Architecture*, and "O & A Florensky" in its installation of *Movement in the Direction of the IYE* makes a deliberate addition to the mythology of the Mitki. The Florenskys' work is an especially eloquent demonstration of Yuri Lotman's argument about the developmental character of binary oppositions within a text or subculture: a binary entity should be understood as a multiplicity, "insofar as each of its constituent languages is subjected, in their turn, to a [process of] fragmentation."[3] In the work of the Florenskys, no artifact is produced without the intention that it converses with other objects, or even people. Collective authorship that bypasses these dyads is doomed to failure and to the undermining of every democratically articulated agent that attempts to engage with it.

From the perspective of this differentiation in their output, it seems highly appropriate and productive to use the Florenskys' own practices of self-naming as an entry point for the interpretation of their work on its own terms and as a portal for exploring its significance as an annex built onto the sprawling complex of the Mitki's textual and visual artifacts. These two people have multiple identities, none of which is nullified by the performance of a close working relationship that we see and hear so vividly in their work. We know these two artists as alumni of the Mitki, and we also know them under several different names: as Olga, Olya, Aleksandr, Sasha, and O & A Florensky. I will refer to them individually by the full forms of their given names and collectively by the glyph of their "company" name.

The work of both Olga and Aleksandr foregrounds a fascination with different writing systems and modes of visual representation, as if to remind us of the fundamental unity of writing and painting that is expressed in the Russian verb *pisát'*. As it appears both in Russian and in English in the work of the two artists, there is more to this glyph than a commercial symbol. The onomastics of Russian demand that the surname be morphologically plural if it is carried by more than one person: *O & A Florenskie* ("O & A Florenskys"); usage in English dictates that a couple's Christian names be followed by the surname in the singular: "O & A Florensky." Almost everywhere we look in the work of the Florenskys, we feel the impact of their effort to sensitize us to the artistry of writing as visual symbol and spoken word. A range of different writing systems appear, or are simulated, in their work—Georgian, Roman, Hebrew, and Cyrillic in its Russian, Church Slavonic, Montenegrin, and Ukrainian—and often in the same composition. Many of these orthographic juxtapositions appear in the drawings and paintings that document their travels outside the Russian Federation. The two artists' closeness to each other within the same workspace and in their travels abroad—and to native and foreign audiences—is the very subject of Olga and Aleksandr's creative output.

The intersection of "O & A" with the various languages that use the Roman alphabet, and with the various forms of Cyrillic (both Slavic and Central Asian), draws our attention to the particular importance or centrality of those letters in understanding both the Florenskys' and the Mitki. The letter referring to Olga's name is of special significance. Olga and Aleksandr represent themselves as *O* and *A*, the two most prominent vocalic phonemes in the Russian language. As a phoneme whose pronunciation is affected by the absence or presence of stress, *O*—the female element within the Florensky collective, image, or brand—is especially evocative, alternating as it does with the sounds [o], [a], and [ə]; in contrast, *A* in Russian only alternates with [ə] when it is unstressed. By containing both [o] and [a], the *O* here does indeed emerge as the first and foremost—the alpha—of this pair. The sense of "O & A Florensky" (or, as it would be transcribed from the Russian, "O & A Florenskie") as a mashup of identity is thrown into even sharper relief by the fact that the plural form may refer to two women, two men, siblings, or a group of people with unspecified gender status. In this play with the ambiguities of meaning that these vowels possess in the Russian language, the Florenskys are drawing on aspects of the Mitki's self-representation. As we discussed in the second chapter of this book, Shagin hints at a view of the group as a family consisting of one sister and many brothers, and indeed Shinkarev describes male Mitki as "brothers" (*bratushki*) and female members as *sestrionki*.

In real life, Olga seems to abet this overall impression of gender hybridity, often appearing in group photographs of the Mitki and in the portrait photographs of her shows (such as the *Moveable Bestiary* exhibit, upon which she and Aleksandr Florensky collaborated)[4] with a pageboy haircut and unisex clothing.[5] The figure of Olga within the Mitki functions as a kind of female deity or totem, suggested by Shagin's obsessive statement "I have only one little sister—Olenka" (Odna u menia sestrionka—Olen'ka). The Russian letter *O* in both its stressed and unstressed variants (the former pronounced as *o* and the latter as *a* or the "shwa" sound) seems to have for the Mitki a kind of sacral association or incantational power, as in their use of exclamations such as the drug-user's slang expression *obsad* (literally, [we're] surrounded!; oddly an expression of approval or praise),[6] *oppan'ki* (from their own slang, presumably a Slavicized variant of "opa!") and, most unusual of them all, the woman's name "Oksana," which has some additional significance that we will discuss shortly. Thus, in Shagin's story about the Mityok sailor saving the woman, the hero yells out *oppan'ki* before walking on water to fetch the drowning woman.[7] The letter serves as an orthographic glyph pointing to a world where customary social and physical laws are suspended, and it also reasserts the Mitki's connection to the feminine. In Glagolitic, the original Cyrillic alphabet designed by St. Cyril in the ninth century, the presence of circles in orthographic forms probably denoted unity, integrality, and divine perfection. The letter also represents a bridge between different cultures, a point of orthographic and phonetic intersection between the Roman, Cyrillic, and Greek alphabets, and Russian and Ukrainian variants of Cyrillic. The play between different writing systems fascinates many members of the movement,[8] and the printed variants of its name (митьки, мітьки, the block Roman typeface of the earlier name of their publishing concern MITKILIBRIS) point not just to a bridge with the West but also to the Russian past in the form of prerevolutionary orthography.

Both Florenskys continue the conversation that the Mitki began in the eighties about gender roles, by drawing our attention to the frequent arrogance underlying gestures of seemingly selfless heroism. By thematizing the commercial aspect of their own work, in which advertising images become subjects of recreation (as in Olga's series "Signboards 2010–13," where handmade examples of what she terms examples of "quotidian script" [*bytovoi shrift*] undergo yet another level of nonstandardized stylization) the Florenskys acknowledge marketing as an aesthetic of intersubjective group production. In their post-Mitki work, Olga and Aleksandr Florensky—both individually and as a team—have explored the deeper implications of the Mitki's collectivist idyll, reaching conclusions that are more self-aware and boldly analytical for excavating and dismantling the artifice and role-playing that are embedded within the seemingly jerry-rigged and inconsequential walls of alternative workspaces. Among other things, the Florenskys place the interpenetration of female and male identities (which had been daringly broached at the peripheries of the work produced by various members of the Mitki collective in the eighties and nineties) squarely at the center of their post-Mitki creations.

For all this, Olga and Aleksandr's treatment of gendered categories diverges from those of their fellow Mitki in their heyday, in matters of both emphasis and style. The cooperative of "O & A Florensky" draws attention to the fluidity of gender and individual agency in ways that Shagin, Shinkarev, and Tikhomirov do not dare to contemplate. In Shinkarev's work, the Mitki engage in a pantomime of solidarity, drawing our attention to the grotesqueness of group homogeneity. Olga writes in the preface to her 1998 exhibit *Taxidermy* (the first part of an installation that was followed by Aleksandr's *Modest Architecture* and their collaboration *A Moveable Bestiary*), "perhaps, for the sake of their despotic creative ambitions [people] do not need to kill" other creatures, and would be more fully satisfied by doing symbolic violence to artificial totems of them.[9] Twelve years later, in *The End of the Mitki*, Shinkarev would write that the group was not founded by anyone, but came about as a spontaneous formation of artists who wanted to share their works more freely with fellow artists.[10] Both sides of the Mitki—the appreciation of the loose yet colloidal association in which each artist is separate yet buoyed by the strong gravitational presence of colleagues, and the use of ritualized play as a stratagem for short-circuiting exploitive authoritarian practices—are evident in the work of the Florenskys.

Since the publication of Shinkarev's *The End of the Mitki* in 2010, the Florenskys have been no less interested than Tikhomirov and Shinkarev in shifting their creative output from the legacy of the group. Olga and Aleksandr have recently taken up a range of new projects that seem to bear no relation to the Mitki, or which at least seem disengaged from the pointedly literary informatics of the work that they produced during the late eighties and throughout the nineties. Many of these more recent projects seek to posit a dynamic and ever-changing relation between images and writing systems; others serve as visual diaries, often taking the form of travelogues. Yet while these new paintings, drawings, and

Matisse-inflected collages make no actual reference to the Mitki or the enigma of how artistic collectives and their collaborations manage to function and flourish, the Florenskys arguably have continued to refine aspects of the conceptualist agenda of the group's output.

Among other things, the new works by the Florenskys make us aware of the norms of female and male as conceptualist in themselves, as categories of artifice; the pieces also foreground the process of dialogue that needs to take place between language and the visual sign, a process of cognitive accessibility that serves as a model for the project of collaboration. In these post-Mitki projects, painting and drawing emerge as media that etch records of the experienced moment, drawing our attention to an overlooked relation between the act of representing something—bringing together details into the portrait of a very specific object, person, or scene—and its collaborative backstory, which in the case of the Florenskys is the chronicle of a shared life. In its scrupulous record-keeping of group production, much of the Florenskys' recent work recalls what Victor Tupitsyn has called "Communal (Post)Modernism," a hybrid concept of collective intersubjectivity that conflates Jean Baudrillard's notion about the "ecstasy of miscommunication" with the Moscow conceptualist artist Andrei Monastyrsky's interest in creative spaces that emerge as "zone[s] of non-differentiation."[11] The communal aspect of the Florenskys' post-Mitki output of drawing and painting is enhanced by settings as varied as galleries and the social media pages of Facebook and vKontakte, where the artists foreground conversation between themselves as members of a creative team and visitors to those sites.

In certain respects, Olga and Aleksandr's recent projects represent a return to the signature aesthetics of the Mitki, especially evident in their organization of images into book-like series and their focus on truncated narratives as the most eloquent representations of the stymied melodrama of the absurd. Their work in 2014 and 2015 is also startling for its focus on contemporary political realia. Olga Florensky's collages from the series *Moby Dick* draw special attention to the pictorially emblematic nature of certain scenes from Melville's novel, while unexpectedly reaching out to other contexts that would seem unrelated to the book. The artist's signature (О Ф) is present in collages that are already cluttered with expository details, such as the arrows indicating the movement of the whales and the boats that pursue them; in other and more spare pictures from the series, the letters are palpably absent in compositions that would seem to demand the inclusion of orthography to

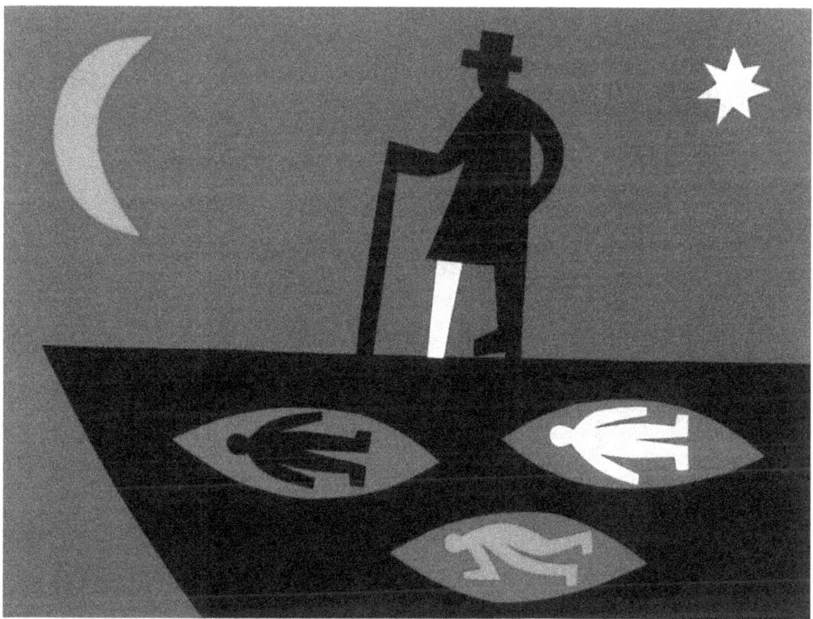

Figure 18. Olga Florensky, *Night on the Pequod*, from the series *Moby Dick* (2014). Colored paper collage, 20 × 30 cm. (collection of the artist)

balance out the minimalist arrangement of forms, as in the portrayal of Ahab on vigil, standing over a hold filled with the corpse-like bodies of sailors (Figure 18, *Night on the Pequod*). The measurements of each drawing (20 × 30 centimeters) suggest a horizontally positioned page of printed text, like a flip book of oversized postcards. The unusual choice of scenes from the novel, often of *longueurs* during the quest for the white whale, such as *Cape Cod Promontory* ("Mys Keip Kod"), and static character portraits, such as *The Harpoonist Queequeg*, suggests that this is not so much a visual retelling of the novel (as is patently the case with Rockwell Kent's illustrations for his famous twentieth-century edition) as it is a guidebook to one person's experience of reading it. The series of images is highly eccentric in its incompleteness yet vividly expressive of an illustrator's spontaneous emotional response to Melville's narrative. No wonder the artist signals that she occasionally loses awareness of herself, at certain key moments (such as in *Stubbs' Sperm Whale*) leaving out her initials. Olga Florensky wants us to understand—to follow—the stages in her act of reading *Moby Dick*. Her collages take the form of images that represent a series of cumulative responses to

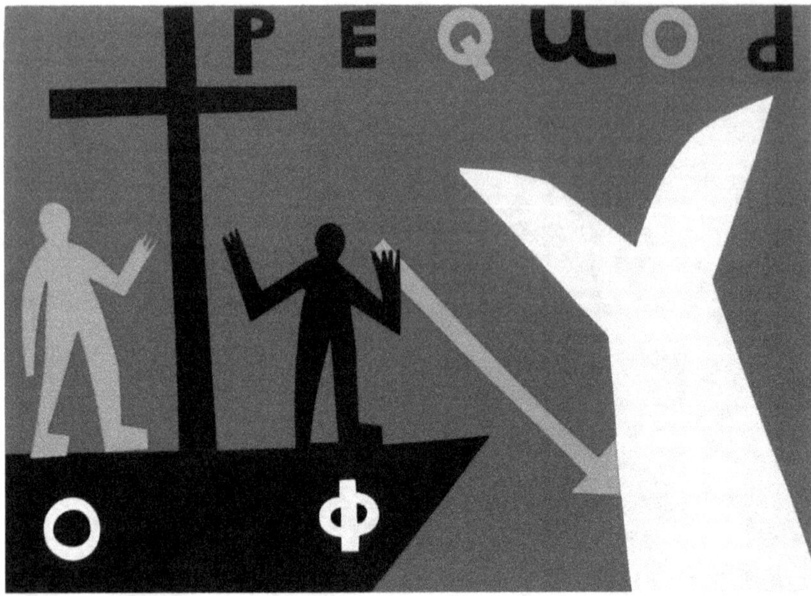


Figure 19. Olga Florensky, *The Pequod Whale Boat*, from the series *Moby Dick* (2014). Colored paper collage, 20 × 30 cm. (collection of the artist)

thematic patterns rather than representations of turning points in the drama of Ishmael's participation in Ahab's obsessive hunt.

Along the way, the quirkiness of the artist's own feelings about the unfolding drama becomes more evident. A collage with the neutral title *The Pequod Whale Boat* (Figure 19) has two human figures, one cut out from black paper and the other from red (possibly signifying Queequeg and Ishmael), standing under a cruciform mast while looking at the tail of a sperm whale rising at a steep angle out of the water. A red arrow that improbably covers the entire distance between the whale and one of the raised hands of the black figure suggests the anticipation of harpooning—a mental traversing of imaginative space—rather than the expressionist portrayal of an actual spearing of prey. Such diagrammatic compositions would seem to evoke a fear of the white whale that is ever-present in the minds of the Pequod's crew, who (like Ahab) find themselves obsessed with the prospect of encounters and visualize possible scenarios of victory or defeat. Certainly, the crucifix of the mast hovering over the sailors raises the fatal possibilities of such an encounter.

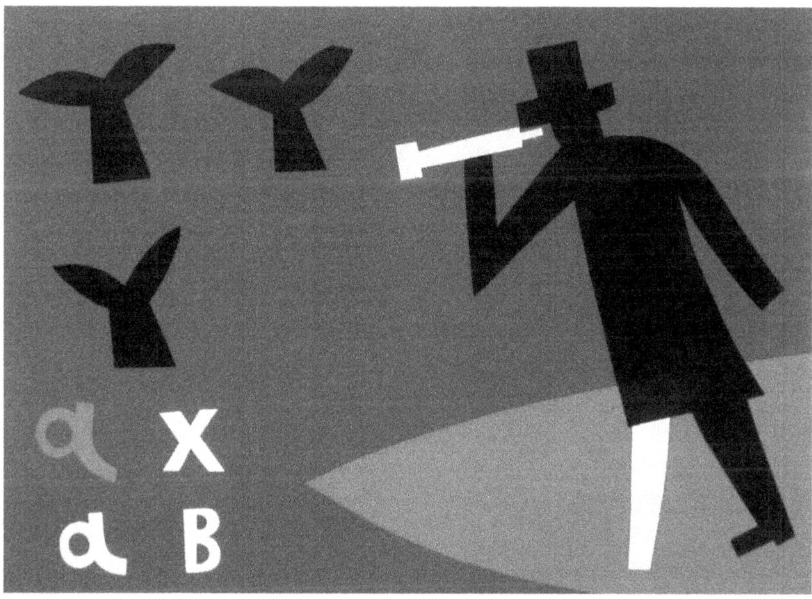


Figure 20. Olga Florensky, *Captain Ahab on the Whale Boat*, from the series *Moby Dick* (2014). Colored paper collage, 20 × 30 cm. (collection of the artist)

In another collage, titled *Captain Ahab on the Whale Boat* (Figure 20), the name of the character floats in a square formation in the lower right-hand corner of the composition, with the first two letters stacked over the remaining ones. The first line of the Russian name for Ahab (*Akhav*) hints both at the attentive surprise of the character's spotting of three tails rising out of the water: *A kh* (Oh!); the right vertical column of letters forms *Kh* / *V*, which is very familiar to the Russian eye as an abbreviation for the Easter greeting *Khristos Voskrese* (Christ is Risen!). The insertion of an allusion to a signature phrase of religious devotion in the Orthodox Church calls our attention to other aspects of the composition, which otherwise bear no direct relation to Russian cultural realia. The predominant color scheme of white, blue, and red recalls the three horizontal bands of the Russian national flag and suggests a link between the destructive obsession of Ahab and what some have regarded as the reckless course of the current Russian president. Like Shinkarev in *Mitki* and *The End of the Mitki*, Olga identifies disaster at sea as a *locus classicus* for a consideration of failed Russian heroism. In the second of these books, Shinkarev traces a growing tendency in the trips the group made outside of the Soviet Union and Russia in 1989 and 1991, seeing them as catalysts for the false consciousness of the Mitki as a brand name. For citizens of a moribund empire and declining world power, traversing the globe may lead to a narrowing of horizons and misunderstanding of leadership as arrogation—as a form of Ahab-like monomania—rather than an enhancement of empathy. In *The End of the Mitki*, Shinkarev describes in detail a pattern that emerged in the years subsequent to these trips, in which Dmitri Shagin increasingly insisted that he alone had rights to the use of the name of the group.[12] Like Shinkarev, Olga Florensky connects this paradigm of foolhardy daring with a failed leadership. Yet in her work, "failed leadership" is perhaps a tautology. What we see in the representations of power in both her *Moby Dick* series and in the collage cycle *Classic Death* (a series consisting of her versions of famous canvases devoted to suicide and dramatic death, such as Cranach's Cleopatra, David's Marat, and Repin's Ivan the Terrible and his son) is how all political power culminates in self-immolation.

The allegorical signification of Olga's Melville series is playfully ambiguous and encourages alternate political readings as well. The white whale may also suggest the Russian state and Ahab a preeminently American figure suffering the narcissistic injury of wounded national pride. In two of the ten collages, she renders Ahab conspicuous by using a black cutout for his figure. In one of these his cane is an outcropping or continuation of his shape, as if his disability were a part of his core identity, fundamentally defined (or so it would seem) by blackness. Could we not also say that Ahab represents the American president at the time the collage was made, a black man struggling against the mighty behemoth of a newly puissant Russia? In at least two other ways, a Russian observer might make an associative leap between the white whale and the Russian empire. One response of viewers of Olga's work could be to see in her entire series of *Moby Dick* collages a stark dramatization of racialized notions of Russian national identity, particularly those propounded by Aleksandr Dugin, the influential ideologue of the eschatological right wing. With his belief in a contemporary Russia that strives to restore its Eurasian geopolitical identity as the inhabitant of Arktogaia, a racially white "land of the sun," Dugin identifies Russia as a bulwark against the mixing of cultures that is distinctive of the new world order of neoliberal commerce. What would be the consequences, Olga might ask, if we—as members of the *intelligentsia*, that educated Russian public with its network of Facebook friends mimicking *tusovki*,

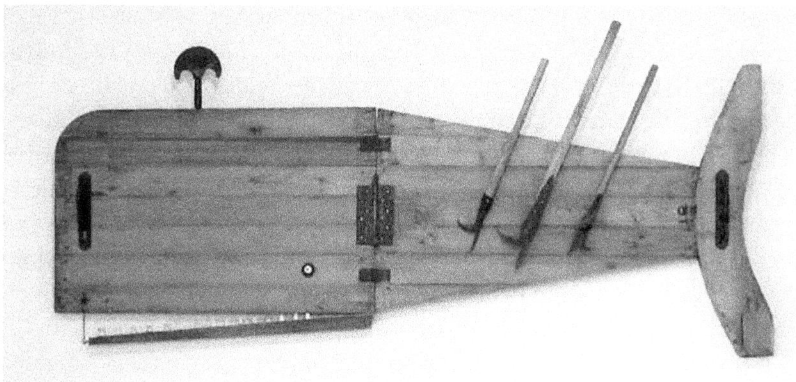

Figure 21. O & A Florensky, *Moby Dick*, from the series *The Story of Moby Dick* (May 2011). Sculpture. (Perm Art Gallery, Perm, Russia)

the unofficial gatherings that began to proliferate in the late Soviet era—were to take such views uncritically, and at face value? In the Facebook blurb for the series *The Story of Moby Dick*, Olga explains that the collages were an offshoot of a joint project about the novel that she and Aleksandr worked on during a stay in the city of Perm. She indicates that the two of them put together twelve sculptures made from pieces of "old wood and iron," all of which were devoted to "whales, whalers and boats."[13] Perm was notorious as the site of one of the harshest prisons in the GULAG. This fact must not have been lost on the Florenskys, who for their pieces made use of the kinds of materials from which this prison was made. One of those sculptures, of the white whale, consists mostly of horizontal strips of wood, with a serrated blade for a jaw (itself on a hinge, and therefore suggesting functionality) and three harpoons sticking out in parallel formation near the tail, evoking more the billowing train of a queen's dress than wounds of grievous injury (Figure 21). This is a whale, we are told, that scoffs at any attempts to kill it, and that wears its wounds as prizes. The final versions of her own compositions about Melville's novel, with their jagged shapes encroaching upon human figures, filter the artist's response to the flotsam and jetsam of a part of her nation's history through an idiosyncratic response to Melville's novel.[14]

The limited chromatic range and clashing angular shapes of Olga's *Moby Dick* collages suggest a world that is rich with gesture yet deficient in light, as if the people inhabiting it were dehumanized into outlines and ciphers that are hemmed in by hostile environments, and planted in a setting of fog-like gloom. A strong argument can be made that this series of collages by Olga represents an attempt to breach the fourth wall with her audience, by placing her viewers within the position of experiencing the claustrophobic world within her illustrations of Melville's novel. In her short statement about the series, she emphasizes the naïve or primitivist aspect of the images, connecting them to Soviet campaigns of exploration of the far North: "perhaps the strongest influences [on these collages] were the vividly composed drawings of schoolchildren from the Institute of the People of the North, done in the thirties, which are held in the Museum of the Arctic and Antarctic in St. Petersburg."[15] In our inclination to view the series as a racialized geopolitical allegory, we find ourselves mirrored in the figures trapped within this particular story, and thereby may come to understand the battle against the "white" behemoth of the Russian state as an ideological over-interpretation. Perhaps this story is really about a conflict among any number of deluded and imperfect human agents, who reach for larger meanings or justifications for their struggles and quests. The fact that the Florenskys' wooden Moby Dick is brown, and not white, certainly steers us in a direction that would seem to jettison political allegory.

Yet Olga's collage series is evocative in ways that bring us back to a political understanding of individual agency within any collective undertaking, and that sprout rhizome-like from it in a horizontal associative chain from the deeper layer of the interpretations that she deliberately provokes. Using her images in this series as an avenue for anticipating another direction of audience response, we can understand the subject and timing of the *Moby Dick* collages as an extended reference to the political allegory of Andrei Zviagintsev's contemporaneous film *Leviathan*. In that film, Zviagintsev uses motifs from the Bible and seventeenth-century Western European political theory as starting points for the extrapolation of parallel thematic lines, proceeding as much from the Book of Job (with the Almighty's chiding statement to Job that "none is so fierce that dare stir [the leviathan] up: who then is able to stand before me?" [41:10]) as it does from Thomas Hobbes's treatise about the extension of the divine right of the monarch into the principles of the modern and fundamentally secular state after the execution of Charles I in England. Zviagintsev imbues the image of the whale with the spirit of frosty indifference that both the cosmos and the political state manifest to the sundry misfortunes that befall the hero of his film. Olga Florensky worked on the series during the time that the film attracted controversy in Russia, where it was widely seen by people through torrent movie websites that illegally provided streaming; she also posted the collages of *Moby Dick* shortly after the controversy about the alleged Russophobia of *Leviathan* peaked, as if to draw attention to the confluence of ideas present in Zviagintsev's film with the tableaux of Melville's novel. Kolya, the protagonist of Zviagintsev's film, boldly challenges the behemoth of the Russian Federation; running parallel to our admiration for his fearlessness and pluck, however, is our understanding of his foolish hot-headedness and the futility, if not self-destructiveness, of such an undertaking. Kolya's challenge to the state is no less catastrophic for him and his family than Ahab's quixotic and rage-filled hunt is for the *Pequod* and its crew. While the Mitki as a group clearly no longer exist in the second decade of the twenty-first century, we see that at least some of its artists continue to pursue its project of radical demystification of political ideals, of placing us (as Slavoj Žižek puts it) in the uncomfortable position of deciding upon the nature of our own political desires.

In due course, we will return to the aesthetics of political indirection in Olga and Aleksandr's group and individual work and to the myriad ways in which it furthers and maximizes Shinkarev's treatment of the tension between the ideals of leadership on the one hand and collaborative and collective endeavor on the other. In keeping with the interweaving of projects between the two artists, let us examine a recent cluster of Aleksandr's drawing series, which both echo and complement Olga's multiple series of collages that reimagine the representational spaces within the interstices of the ossified canons of literature and painting. Perhaps the best starting point for examining this recent work is his series of drawings titled *Drawings about Jerusalem* (2012–January 2013). We can trace the genesis of this collection of drawings (which currently exists as a self-contained series solely on Aleksandr's Facebook page, in one of his photo albums) to a project that he began a little less than two years before. In 2011, Aleksandr was invited by the Russian-Israeli poet Mikhail Korol to Jerusalem, to illustrate a collection of his work with drawings of the holy city, each of which would contain a poem with a Cyrillic letter that corresponded to a poem about an overlooked site in the ancient urban landscape. Accepting the invitation, Aleksandr began working in earnest shortly after his arrival, producing a series of drawings of parts of the city that were relatively obscure and seemingly unremarkable. Having together examined and discussed several of the drawings within the finished series, both Aleksandr and Korol came to view the project as not so much a collaboration between poet and painter as an attempt to bring about an amalgam of visual image and spoken word. Korol suggested that such a union of media could at least simulate a seemingly effortless and immediate interaction between them, resulting in synesthesia that seamlessly conjoins language with visual form.

Perhaps Korol was moved to make this proposition after viewing and reading the Florenskys' *Movement in the Direction of IYE*, a joint project that created an installation of artifacts collected by a fictional ethnographer name Ivan Petrovich Barinov, who collects objects and draws images about his expedition to research the (no less fictional) people called the *IYE*. In that project, Olga and Aleksandr lampoon any number of blatantly colonialist and at times racist expeditions to the non-Slavic regions of Siberia undertaken by Russian ethnographers both before and after the Revolution (such as in the multiple forays of researchers into Yakutia), while also demonstrating, in Barinov's mock diary, a grudging respect for the strangeness of the subject matter that results from his immersion in the culture of the *IYE*. Over the course of the diary, there are suggestions that Barinov is not completely able to transcend his own cultural prejudices, and that in fact his patronizing interpretations of the *IYE* are filtered through his assumptions about rural Russian culture, with its deep roots in the institution of serfdom. Certainly, his surname "Barinov" signals his social privilege (*barin* means "lord"). The attributed Russianness of the *IYE* is signaled at several points in the texts and images, as in the appearance of prominent Russian phonemes in the name of the tribe, and in the droll, Mitki-like statements such as: "the *IYE* for the most part are taciturn, curt in their responses, jocular and whimsical. As an example, they never say straightforwardly 'dead,' but always express things in the conditional mode: 'presumably dead.'"[16]

In such moments of Olga and Aleksandr's work, we hear echoes of Shinkarev's idiosyncratic observation in his 2008 *The End of the Mitki* about the koan-like poems of the Mityok Mikhail Sapego. As Shinkarev notes, Sapego's poetry has a strongly ekphrastic component and is composed with the understanding of being declaimed in an intimate setting consisting of close friends and family, in contrast to the more histrionic and volatile performativity that informs the mood of a *tusovka* or public get-together. Such poetry serves as its own form of visualization or illustration (*samo sebe illiustratsiia*), with any number of seemingly peripheral turns of phrase serving as hot springs that shape the landscape of the text.[17] Here, the poet is truly a recessive if not spectral presence, as the poem is "illustrated" (and given substantive dramatic motivation) by a filigree within the margin of its incomplete page, or the interjection by a listener in the room.

Before resuming our discussion of Aleksandr's negotiations with the Russian-Israeli poet over the working details of this project, we need to linger on the features of *Movement in the Direction of IYE* that might have caught his attention, as a Russian-Israeli poet who wanted to create a more idiosyncratic version of his already-published guidebook to holy sites in Jerusalem. Certainly, the understanding of the multimedia character of spoken art—and the ways in which a speaker even as blinkered as the privileged Barinov never has exclusive dominion over their own words, which after all have been populated by the usages of other people—saturates the Florenskys' joint projects and would have appealed to Korol in his efforts to produce a Baedeker of the city that would be both learned and deeply affective. As Olga and Aleksandr put it in a joint statement they wrote in 2000, in the beginning of the nineties "texts of various kinds gradually began to appear in [their] work: the preface essay to the catalogue, the commentary to the exhibit, the press release, and then the texts that constituted the inextricable component of the projects, together with the objects themselves, photographs and drawings or paintings." Language itself took on concrete form, with their texts moving into the realm of the applied arts, in the form of signage and mechanical constructions. The result of this shift within their projects, toward what we may understand as a total experience of art or *Gesamtkunstwerk*, was that the boundaries between the genres practically disappeared, with the plastic arts in some instances becoming "inseparable from the verbal," as exemplified by the Florenskys' work on cartoons.[18] In the quasi-anthropological field notes that accompany *Movement in the Direction of IYE*, Olga and Aleksandr underscore a kinship between Professor Barinov's project and the Mitki:

> Is Ivan Petrovich Barinov a myth or a reality? Working with the archive, we were unable to free ourselves of the feeling that we were well acquainted with that name for quite some time. Collating several facts, dates and accounts of eyewitnesses, we suddenly understood that the earliest fragmentary information about I. P. B. came from Evegni (or simply, Zhenya) Barinov, our prematurely departed friend from the creative group the "MITKI," a self-sufficient painter, and first cousin of this researcher on their mother's side.[19]

"Evgeni (Eugene) Barinov" was in fact the name of a fictional character in Shinkarev's writing. This alter ego penned a thirteenth chapter of his *Mitki*, in which he drew attention to the hypocrisy and shallowness of the movement. Treating the recovery of this "lost" chapter as the sad testament of a dyspeptic commentator and expelled member of the group, Shinkarev in his own mock-commentary underscores Evgeni Barinov's "inferiority complex and misanthropy of a beginning artist [who is] incapable of understanding the naturally occurring subordination within the movement."[20] In their *Movement in the Direction of IYE*, the Florenskys could not resist amplifying Shinkarev's conceit of the texts of others as found objects, even during the time that the Mitki were already entering into their retrospective phase. In both instances, the statement of another is treated with a light condescension that only points up the mirroring between the author of the discovered text and the first real audience, or editor, of it. Who is to say that the character of the audience is not as revealing and important as that of the original author? The first-person plural of the Florenskys' text is both a reflection of the dual authorship of the text that appears in the preface ("From the Authors") and, in an evocation of the formal conventions of nineteenth-century European scholarship, a reference to the single "researcher" (*issledovatel'*) who is distantly related to the subject of the work at hand. And are we in any position to say with certainty who is peripheral here and who is of central importance?

In the case of the 2012 series *Drawings about Jerusalem*, Aleksandr's partnership with someone other than Olga and the former members of the Mitki did not come to fruition in the extended project that was originally planned. According to a 2015 interview that I conducted with Aleksandr, ultimately he and the poet Korol realized that they were operating within very different aesthetic frames of reference, and that his words and Aleksandr's images did not mesh in the right way or work against each other with dissonances that could be productively explored.[21] Although they did not complete their joint project, Korol nonetheless encouraged Aleksandr to continue his abecedarium series as a model for documenting other cityscapes, seeing in it an interesting outsider's perspective on a city fraught with religious and political conflict. One interesting creative dividend of the original invitation to illustrate a collection of poetry is the presence—in subsequent series devoted to Paris, New York, and Tbilisi—of text within several spaces of the drawings, as if the project's premise of the reverberation between word and image had taken on a life of its own. In contrast to his

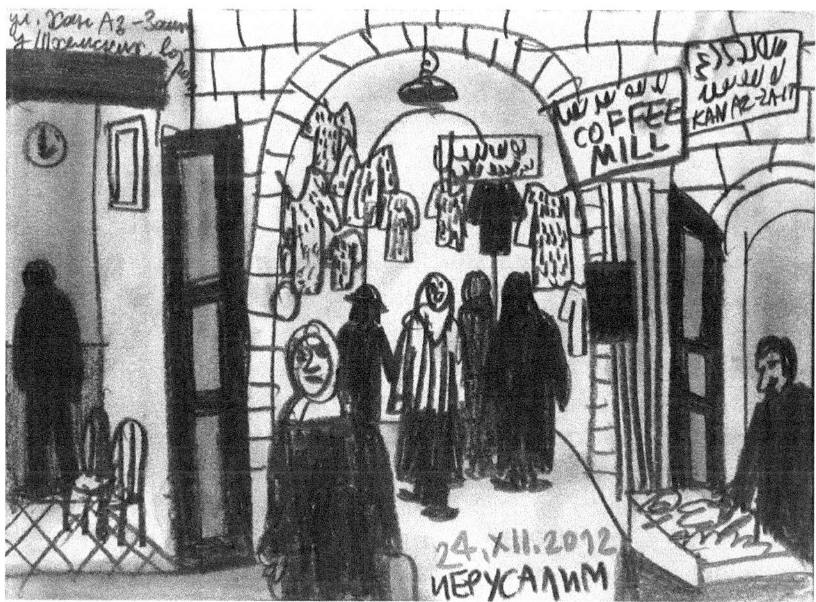


Figure 22. Aleksandr Florensky, *December 24, 2012*, from the Facebook series *Drawings about Jerusalem*. Digitally altered drawing posted on the same date listed on the drawing.

collaboration with Korol in the drawing book *A Jerusalem Abecedarium*, in his Facebook series *Drawings about Jerusalem*, Aleksandr confines his text to the presence of street signs and advertisements in the cityscapes—in Hebrew, Arabic, and English inscriptions—and to the artist's own captions, which consist of succinct identifications of location and category of structures. Most of the drawings are of markets and commercial districts. The conflation of text and image is often jarring, especially with the appearance of notices for brand names such as Adidas. The world of global capital makes itself clamorously known within the city, and Aleksandr seems to point to the disjunction between foreign and local, old and new, in his representation of different commercial zones (Figure 22). Interestingly, the last of the *Drawings about Jerusalem* is a depiction of the harbor, a tableau that hints at the city's opening-up to the outside world in a way that is very different from the incursion of commodities into it: here, the possibility of directly and physically encountering that world is positioned as a possible new beginning. But the beginning of what? The composition's lack of engagement with anything that could serve as an answer to this question is highly characteristic of all of Aleksandr's recent travelogue series, which often perversely focus on modest sites or scenes that are neglected by tourist guidebooks.

Following his series of charcoal drawings about Jerusalem, from 2012 to 2015, Aleksandr applied the same format of a logbook including image and word to journeys he made to Voronezh, different sites in Montenegro, and Copenhagen; he even produced a series titled *Petersburg ABC*, in which he applied his method of documenting the unfamiliar to sites within his native city. In several important respects, *Montenegro ABC* represents the culmination of his visual diary approach to the experience of travel. Olga and Aleksandr in fact create cycles of images about specific localities as platforms from which to contemplate an increasingly globalist and neoliberal world order, and the ways in which our agency as spectators depends on the simulation of unpolished and direct appreciations of cultural diversity.

As we have seen from our discussion of Shagin and Shinkarev as a creative team, authorship in the work of the Mitki often raises questions of identity that cross the boundaries of gender, artistic identity, and ideology, touching tentatively upon the nuances of sexual affect in the process. As Andrei Bitov underscores in one of his essays about the Mitki, these identities are not only not fixed: they are often concurrent and subject to the quirky self-fashioning of each of these individuals. "An artist is compelled to make use of his or her 'image,'" Bitov notes, "be it a Rembrandt, a Van Gogh, a Dali." While the image of the Mitki had been in the air, it was still necessary to invent it. As Bitov explains, when that image splintered, one of the Mitki's twelve apostles rendered it into language for the world at large. Bitov sees Shinkarev's 1985 *Mitki* as something that came about by chance. In Bitov's view, the book began as a private letter addressed to Dmitri Shagin ("a person with the [diminutive name] Mityok"), only to grow into the chronicle of a movement:

> Authorship is not only fame; it is also a responsibility. [As the Mitki say,] who do you think will pay me, Pushkin? In this book, Shinkarev takes responsibility for everything. Mitya Shagin will sing, Vitya Tikhomirov will shoot a film, Olya Florensky will scrupulously write verses, and [Aleksandr] Florensky will discover some new "Rabbitland" [*Zaiatslandiia*] . . . and they will all continue to paint remarkable paintings.[22]

Yet these border crossings are highly kinetic and restless, and several of them may be traversed by the same individual in very short order. As Bitov subsequently argues, no one in this group inhabits just one identity. His treatment of the Florenskys is revealing for the reason of his audible awkwardness in naming them together. Bitov uses Olga's nickname "Olya" followed by her surname (*Florenskaia*); he refers to Aleksandr just by his surname, which is made easier in Russian because of its masculine ending (*Florenskii*). Interesting here is the fact that he does not describe them as being married. What these two people share is a surname, which means that they may be siblings or cousins.

Within the Mitki's portrayal of alcohol as a spiritually grounding source with a subterranean link to femininity, Shinkarev's definition in his glossary of the movement's slang of the nonobscene expletive "Oksana!" as a "ritual exclamation during a recollection in public of one's favorite women"[23] is especially evocative and useful in parsing the sexual politics of the Florenskys' work. The Ukrainian name Oksana is a variant of the Russian Kseniya. Although there is more than one St. Kseniya in the Orthodox calendar, the Russian St. Kseniya of St. Petersburg resonates with the context of the Mitki more than any other. Born in 1731 to a family of civil servants, Kseniya married the colonel Andrei Fyodorovich Petrov, who was closely involved in the life of the Orthodox Church in the court of Elizabeth. Both Andrei and Kseniya probably knew the Empress personally. The two ably sang in the court church choir and lived in what by all accounts was a chaste and, in the telling words of a nineteenth-century commentator, "brotherly" marriage, distinguished by a heightened sense of mutually respectful companionship. Kseniya mourned her husband's sudden death from an epidemic by dressing in his clothes and insisting that everybody address her as "Andrei Fyodorovich," The day after his death she asserted that "Andrei Fyodorovich has not died. . . . The one who has passed away is Kseniya Grigorievna, and Andrei Fyodorovich is before you, he is alive and will live even longer, will live forever."[24] At his funeral she dressed in his full military uniform and refused to respond to her own name when called, regarding it as a desecration of the dead. "Leave off! Don't touch the deceased woman [*pokoinitsu*]," she yelled out. "What did she ever do to you? God forgive!"[25] Ignoring the complaints of her in-laws, she gave away the property she inherited from her husband and lived on the streets of St. Petersburg as a mendicant who gave almost everything she collected to other destitute individuals. She also became known for her gift of prophecy, which often took the form of giving advice to bereaved widows.

The continuing narrative about St. Kseniya's life informs Olga Florensky's description of her working partnership with Aleksandr as a union that is motivated by the fear of narrow self-definition.[26] As Kseniya continued to live outdoors, braving the harsh St. Petersburg winters, her husband's clothing deteriorated and she again began referring to herself in the feminine first person and feminine-form adjectives while still calling herself Andrei Fyodorovich, and friends who ran into her retained the habit of referring to her by his name.[27] Toward the end of her life, she gave up the sartorial conceit of wearing clothes exactly like his and donned a robe and scarf whose colors merely suggested his old uniform. One of the most interesting aspects of this story is the way in which Kseniya gave up her identity as a woman in exchange for that of a man and later fashioned a compromise whereby she recovered a sense of her original status as a woman, conflating it with her changed sense of self after the death of her husband. In a certain sense, the life of St. Kseniya is a story of androgyny as ethically conditional selflessness, as losing a constructed identity by identifying closely with the Other without losing a complete sense of one's self. Kseniya's act of cross-dressing represents a moment of empowerment, of negotiating among various constructed identities. Like any male heir, she does what she sees fit with her new property, and her fixation on her husband's military clothing suggests an awareness of its representational symbolism of power. But what emerges also from St. Kseniya's hagiography is the notion that the pivotal moment of Andrei's death is described by Kseniya herself as an "orphaning" of the deceased,[28] as if her relation to him had been motherly as well as brotherly, so that anything that literally happened to him somehow had an emotional parallel in herself. Andrei was resurrected in her—his mother and brother.

The association of St. Kseniya resonates in three respects with the Mitki and with the partnership of the Florenskys. In the first place, St. Kseniya represents the deliberate effacement of the self in the form of solidarity with the less fortunate and underprivileged; in a similar vein, the Mitki shun power and aggression, and they congregate with those who adhere to the same principles and lifestyle. The Mitki's attraction to the socially marginal denizens of the city echoes the details of St. Kseniya's biography, a parallel made more evident in Olga Florensky's poetry about St. Petersburg. In her verses, Florensky locates the city's spiritual center not in massive imperial buildings but in decaying courtyards, cemeteries, and flea markets frequented by the poor. In this spirit, Olga Florensky glosses her poem "Morning" ("Utro") as a description of Vladimir Square, where all sorts of "marginal individuals" (*raznye marginal'nye lichnosti*) sell junk by the fence of the famous Our Lady of Vladimir church. The poem ends with the exclamation "How easy it is to live in a harmonious spirit with others and to think that diamonds appear only in filth!" Her illustration for the poem has the Baroque church steeple dwarfed by a hand stroking a stray cat, as if to accentuate the secondary nature of the city's architectural landscape.[29] Second, the image of a female saint quite literally assuming the mantle of her husband, dressed in his uniform and dealing with her husband's legacy as she sees fit, resonates with the Mitki's own fascination with role-playing and carnivalistic inversion, and the Florenskys' spirit of internal competition that results in parallel projects, such as the recent series of landscapes of Roccasecca. The image of a world turned upside down involves cross-dressing not just for Olga Florensky, but for the male Mitki as well, who embody many characteristics that could be understood as conventionally feminine. Third, the personal eccentricity of St. Kseniya—her nonnormative verbal behavior and passionate espousal of simplicity to an almost comic extreme—is representative of the tradition of the itinerant Holy Fool that plays an important role in the Russian variant of Eastern Orthodoxy. The Mitki deliberately emulate this tradition, as in the case of Aleksandr Florensky's arch postcard series of different cities.

But there is another sense in which St. Kseniya and the Mitki occupy common ground. Kseniya is the patron saint for the city of St. Petersburg, a figure who underscores that the soul of the city lies not in its corridors of power but among its dispossessed; the Mitki as well are representative characters in a symbolism of the city that highlights a sense of alienation from privilege and prestige. In one of his poems, Roald Mandelstam (the only serious writer in the Arefiev circle and an important early influence on the Mitki) writes of St. Petersburg as a "ship, over which the waters have closed," and of its streets as a "snare" (*teneta*), addressing them with unexpected rapture as "nocturnal paths to nowhere" (*nochnye puti v nikuda*). Florensky's own poetry, with its fluttering tableaux of the lower depths of the city, owes more than a little to Roald Mandelstam's Baudelairean meditations on the sweet desolation of Leningrad, and the work of both writers may also recall the Marquis de Custine's description of St. Petersburg as a cemetery-like landscape of oppressive monuments rather than a place of habitation.[30] But Mandelstam's poetry also has masculinist overtones of Mayakovskian solipsistic valor, distinctly absent from Olga Florensky's poetry and present in the mock overtones in Shagin's and Shinkarev's writing. In his melodramatic poem "The Dark Guest" (*Mrachnyi gost'*), Mandelstam writes of his friends the "homeless, drunks, and thieves" as "the heroes of myth," describing his voice as "sonorous, piercing, and coarse" (*zychen, priam i grub*) and his songs as not fit for an audience of "ladies." The social and political atmosphere (to say nothing of the era) of the Arefiev circle were certainly more astringent and somber than that of the Mitki, as is amply manifest in the scenes of domestic violence and random street thuggery from Arefiev's own paintings. That many of his portrayals of family discord occur between husbands and wives only highlights the sense that Arefiev regarded gender relations as profoundly damaged and morally compromised. In their paintings and literary output, the Mitki attempt to transform the Arefievists' bleak vision of discord between women and men, going even so far as to redefine notions of masculinity and femininity by untethering them from traditional notions of gender-dictated social roles.

In the work of the Florenskys, nowhere do we see this interest in representing the discord between men and women in general, and toxic masculinity in particular, more clearly than in Olga's remarkable cloth appliqué collage banner *Bluebeard* (Figure 23). Olga made the collage in 1992, during the height of the Mitki's notoriety in Russia. Composed with close attention to the details of Charles Perrault's tale, Olga's Bluebeard stands poised to stab his wife, after she has discovered the dungeon with the bodies of his previous wives. The magic key that she dropped on the floor of the dungeon indelibly retains the blood of the other women, whose bodies surround her and Bluebeard like a grotesque parody of a wedding arch. Different moments of the narrative are blended into the composition, with two different representations of the key: one clean or unbloodied (and cut from the same yellow cloth as the knife that Bluebeard holds) and another that is deep red and matching the wife's breasts. The composition of her body, with its separate appliqués for her arms and breasts, remind us about the possibility of dismemberment. The wife's protective gesture over her pubis, and the phallic shape of both representations of the key (together with the color that its unsullied key shares with the knife held by Bluebeard), all powerfully draw attention to the sexual violence that is the undercurrent of Perrault's tale. The size of the banner brings the scale of the bodies uncomfortably close to real life, as if we were looking at some small distance through a window of a house where an atrocity is about to take place. The vividness of the scene banishes even the comfort of knowing that the wife's brothers will soon burst into the room to save her. Here

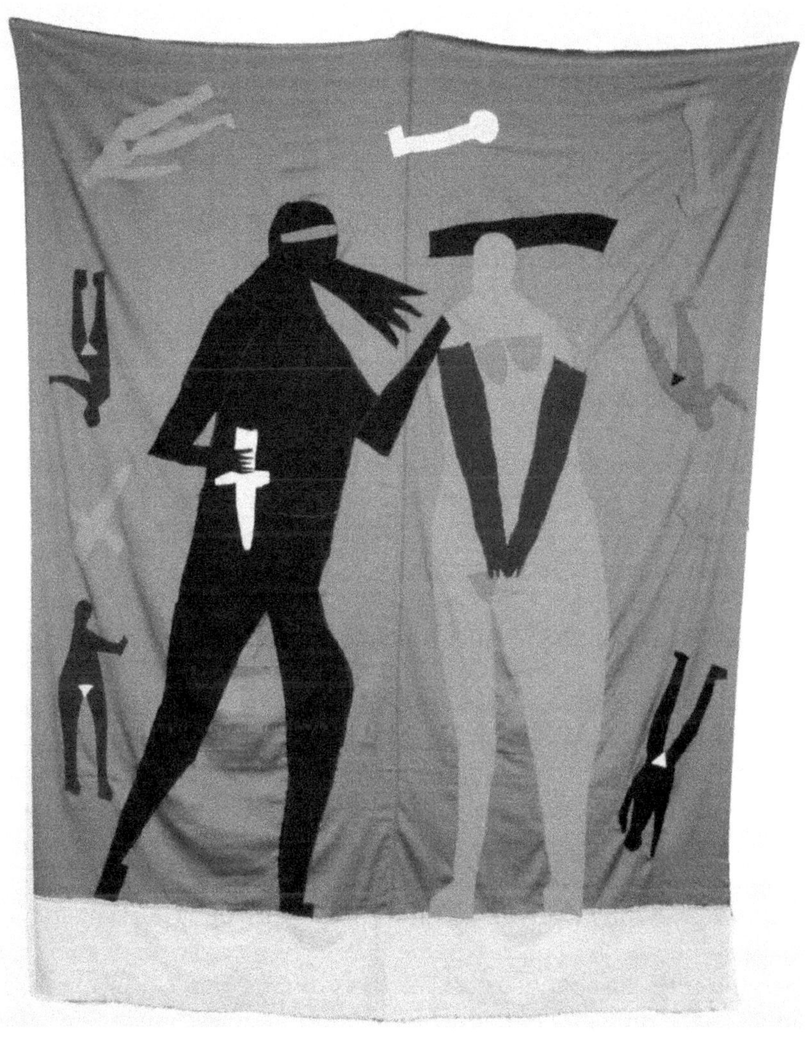

Figure 23. Olga Florensky, *Bluebeard* (1992). Cloth appliqué and collage on cloth, 214 × 175 cm. (Claude and Nina Gruen Collection of Contemporary Russian Art, in the Jane Voorhees Zimmerli Art Museum, New Brunswick, New Jersey)

we have a full-throated telling of a tale of human dysfunction that we see in Arefiev's paintings and that we hear in the poetry of Roald Mandelstam, which exerted such an influence on Olga's own verse. The signature palette of the Mitki—white and shades of light blue—are absent from this composition, as if to underscore that the image of gender-crossing openness that we find in the heyday of their work does not belong in this world of gendered violence.

Nonetheless, as we have already seen from our discussion of Shinkarev's anecdote of the drowning woman whom the Mityok is unable to save—as containing a subtext of the legend of Stenka Razin's tossing of his wife into the water in order to appease his confederates and confirm his own masculinity—the central narrative of the Mitki does acknowledge the victimization of women, to the point that they foreground the ways in which their primitivist and naïve utopia falls short of fully addressing it. This reflects a level of awareness, and self-examination about certain features of traditional culture, that is startling. The quality of union between the sexes becomes, in the work of the Mitki, a bellwether for sociality in general. In this regard, it is significant that the pose from Olga's "Bluebeard" reoccurs three years later in her and Aleksandr's woodcut "Two Friends Goethe and Schiller (Standing Together)," which they produced during a seminar that the entire group spent in Weimar. Using German transcription of the Russian titles (here, "Dwa druga Goethe & Schiller (wmeste stojat)," the Florenskys draw a parallel between the two German poets' famously prickly and competitive relations and their own working relations by using the Russian preposition "together" (*vmeste*), both in the print and in the title of their series, with the letter "b" being put to use as a Cyrillic letter instead of the German "w" in the title page: "Olga & Alexander Florenskije, bmeste." As in Shinkarev's 1985 *Mitki*, in the work of the Florenskys we encounter a group identity that includes disagreement and incompatibility as two panels within the larger centerpiece of its passional narrative. The disorienting coexistence of different alphabets impresses upon us the difficulty of finding a common language, among even the closest of partners.

From all of this, the fact of interpersonal relations—of sociality itself, of the possibility of consciousness lying athwart the dividing lines of gender and other forms of human diversity—emerges as the dominant element within an entity that is as much a consortium of ramified engagement with modes of social being as it is a commercial enterprise. What emerges from the work of the Florenskys—in their relation to each other and to their involvement with the Mitki—is an understanding of authorship as something that is necessarily the result of artists' engagement with both the larger marketplace and each other. Olga and Aleksandr acknowledge the experiment of the Mitki as a living parody of the Stalinist cult of personality (what Shinkarev would elsewhere underscore as the group's aspiration not just to love the common folk, but to be revered by them),[31] foregrounding what Boris Groys describes as the "multiple authorship" of not just the group show, but of any curated exhibit:

> The traditional, sovereign authorship of an individual artist has de facto disappeared; hence it really does not make sense to rebel against such authorship. And in fact every art exhibition exhibits something that was selected by one or more artists—from their own production and/or from the mass of ready-mades. These objects selected by the artists are then selected in turn by one or more curators, who thus also share authorial responsibility for the definitive selection. In addition, these curators are selected and financed by a commission, a foundation, or an institution; thus, these commissions, foundations and institutions also bear authorial and artistic responsibility for the end result.[32]

Since the late nineties, the work of Olga and Aleksandr has fallen into categories that resonate with the conception of multiple authorship that Groys outlines here, in terms of handiwork and degrees of collaborative undertaking. In the collective of "O & A Florensky," work that is unmistakably that of an individual artist takes on a fugitive character, as if all large projects (such as the 2006 multimedia installation *Russian Trophy*) could only be the product of the couple as a team.

This stark picture of collaboration vs. individual output is rendered somewhat ambiguous in instances when their separate work is exhibited in the same show organized by them. It is somehow fitting that memorialization, and the lingering focus on architectural ruins as markers of mortality, assume a prominent thematic place in the work that Olga and Alexander produce separately from each other, whether it be her 2014 series *Classic Death* (about the "almost erotic ecstasy" that artists allude to in their representations of the possibility of violent death)[33] or his stylized primitivist portraits of Olga and friends from St. Petersburg and Georgia (whose placid expressions and poses emanate from seemingly ageless figures) and multiple abecedaria devoted to the more obscure and forgotten structures of the major cities such as St. Petersburg, New York, Jerusalem, and Paris (2011–15).

Far from showing a world where history is being erased by the onslaught of neoliberalism and globalism, Olga and Aleksandr provide us with representations of scenes of antiquity where modernity is compelled to shout out about itself, to make itself heard among historical artifacts and architectural ensembles that still seem inhabited and thoroughly functional, much like the fanciful representations of Roman ruins that proliferate in the paintings of Hubert Robert. The Florenskys suggest that transitory states of being are more at home within the isolated production of the discrete artist than they are within the activity of a creative collective. The joint project of the Florenskys *Russian Trophy* (which consists of maquette-like models of famous buildings in St. Petersburg, using various antique machine parts) has a stolid monumentality that we don't see in their recent drawings, collages, and paintings.

And yet, even this understanding is one that both artists *share*—or in some sense have come into agreement about—and which therefore reflects a unitary understanding of the redemption of isolated agency that they seek to empower within liminal spaces. The liminal space in question is a niche, a predetermined groove or track, for the flight of the single artist from the stifling closeness of others. In its establishment of individual agency as a category that works best when it is provided with the counterpoint of collaboration that all shared studio space represents, the Florenskys' archetype of an individual creative agent brings to mind Foucault's understanding of the genealogy of a subject coming to know itself separately from the social environment that it lives in: individual autonomy is not an *a priori* reality and must be "understood simultaneously" as a cluster of "modes of action and thinking" that "provide the key to understanding a correlative constitution of the subject and object."[34] Cast as it is within the context of labor and production, the Florenskys' Foucauldian understanding of creative space for individual artists as a paradoxically dictated margin for freedom—as a carceral space with the illusion of free license—brings to mind some signature post-War Soviet conceptions of collectivism, such as Anton Makarenko's theory of a "goal-oriented complex of persons, who are organized [and] who possess the organs of the *kollektiv*" into which they are embedded, as if they were the peritoneum that holds up the working parts of the body politic. Makarenko remained an important social theorist in the field of Soviet education from the thirties until the era of perestroika and glasnost and was particularly interested in creating schools that strove to become crèches for developing collectivist sensibilities. As he saw it, people educated in such a manner would live in "relations of reasonable dependency."[35] Consciously or not, in their work the Florenskys evoke the image of artists who occupy the same space for labor, with elbows brushing up against each other at their easels and drafting tables, within the forward momentum of their contiguous professional lives. In their autobiographical writing, narrative texts for exhibits, and (in Olga's case) poetry, they sketch out a self-image that foregrounds the ideal of group authorship, while underscoring the need to expand and redefine that authorship, as something more than merely a circuit board for the grounding of individual transmitters of expressive energy.

In the body of their writing and artwork, the Florenskys move from the background of an empowering *mise-en-scène* of cohabiting artists who through their work act out the way in which they live, to the foreground of the drama of a provisionally single entity, the evolution of the "Florensky" brand. We see this in the way that Olga and Aleksandr manage their Facebook pages. Although they do not maintain a page dedicated to "O & A Florensky," the pages that they each have for themselves contain numerous cross-references to each other's work, to the work and Facebook page of their daughter, Katya, and to their shared name brand. Most important here is the sense that each page represents a virtual curated exhibit venue, with "albums" of projects that in many instances contain titles suggestive of gallery placards, such as Olga's *Fountain in Roccasecca. September 2016. Paper. Acrylic. 15 × 20 cm.*, from her album series *September in Roccasecca*, and Aleksandr's portrait (from his series album *Georgian Beauties*) titled *Eter K. Oil on Canvas* [*Kh M*], *24 × 30* [centimeters], *2015*.[36] The Florenskys' Facebook pages clearly function in lieu of personal web sites and mimic many of the features of exhibition spaces. Each album becomes an exhibit catalog—in some cases containing even short essays by the artists that serve as guides to the show—and the discussion threads to each album and posted picture serve as the equivalent of the notebooks that many galleries and exhibits provide for visitors' comments and observations. The pages emerge as timelines of change for each artist, with their joint projects placed within their individual pages, as if to emphasize that each of them bears a perspective on the name brand while also occupying a distinct stylistic and media niche that is not repeated by others within the Florensky "brand."

Much like the British artists Gilbert & George, the Florenskys use a corporate-sounding name to denote the work of coproduction. As in the case of Gilbert & George, the Florenskys believe that the work of an artistic collective requires special attention to branding, in a way that the work of the individual artist does not. Why should this be so? It may be that the very idea of collaborative work among artists is an enigma, involving as it does the possibility of subordination of one will to another, of the absorption of one artist into that of another, or of the creation of one corporate entity (the singular "O & A Florensky") into which all voices become thoroughly subsumed. In this regard, it is significant that the Florenskys' first collaborative work, *Jazz. Imitations of Matisse*, was a series of collages that treated the work of another artist's work as a found object.[37] While the entire series is labeled as a collaboration, it is quite clear that certain compositions are primarily the handiwork of one artist. It seems that a pointedly individual style in no way undercuts the performance of a partnership. While the partnership of O & A is different from Gilbert & George in the sense that their individual styles are readily recognizable, both partnerships exist in a tension with public descriptions of themselves as individualists. In answer to a question from a 2004 interview, George defined liberalism as the state in which "it's easier for the individual to blossom, where our liberties are defended, where people keep their distance from all these 'do not' signs that stop us from thinking what's never been thought before."[38] Yet how is it possible for committed individualists to flourish in a collaborative? The identical and conservatively styled suits that Gilbert & George wear for their gallery openings and in the photographs for their compositions and installations serve to further problematize this declaration of individualism, as does Olga and Aleksandr's apparent theft of each other's work.

Among several such instances of creative poaching, in their 2002 book *Movement in the Direction of a Book*, Aleksandr places his signature beside what is clearly Olga's composition of "Little Icarus" from the *Mitki Alphabet*. Similarly, Olga makes liberal use of her partner's stylized representations of prerevolutionary Russian military history in her 1994 claymation stop-action film *A Story about the Miracle of Miracles* (*Rasskaz o chude iz chudes*), a quasi-steampunk retelling of Nikolai Leskov's story "Lefty" (*Levsha*). In the works of both artists, the legacy of Russian Constructivism would seem to be especially important. The frantically inventing and physically transforming figures of Olga's film evoke Varvara Stepanova's statement from 1920 that "a person cannot live without [the witnessing or creation] of a miracle." By their very nature, a woman or man can "live a full life only when [they] invent, discover, or conduct experiments." In the landmark essay "Constructivism" that she wrote the following year, Stepanova argues that "revolutionary deconstructive activity [would] expose art in all its foundational elements" and result in decisive shifts (*sdvigi*) in the minds of "the workers of art." Such shifts would have the effect of highlighting for artists the necessity for a "new ideology in constructivism."[39] The Florenskys would seem to suggest that collaboration, by its very nature, necessarily involves acts of appropriation and recombination of elements from others—whether it be from one's own partner, or from the generous outpouring of material culture from the world at large.

Yet most recently, the Florenskys have cultivated a more internally ramified view of collective authorship. This orchestration of differentiated artistic labor has attained a particularly developed form in the Marat Guelman-curated exhibit *Florenskys in Montenegro*, at St. Petersburg's Name Gallery in March and April 2017. In his own post on the gallery's Facebook page, Guelman writes that "Sasha and Olya are [highly] inventive" in their capacity as creators of single and multiple worlds. "Sasha is a painter without quotation marks; Olya sees everything and is capable of everything. Katya is a gambler" who is also a collector of puzzles.[40] In his own response to the exhibit, the Montenegrin curator Petar Čuković asks, "What in fact can we say about the Montenegrin opuses of Aleksandr, Olga and Katya Florensky, [except to note that] we need to look at the art of all three as a single entity."[41] There is much to suggest that Guelman's and Čuković's comments are responses to the ways in which the Florenskys have represented themselves on social media. Simultaneous with the exhibit about Montenegro, Aleksandr posted on his Facebook page a series of his own work from Roccasecca, representing subjects and media that are completely different from Olga's artwork from the same town on the western coast of central Italy. Olga's images of the town are done in a style of acrylic that mimics gouache and comprises luminous scenes of the harbor and Castello Roccasecca, with the occasional inclusion of strolling figures (some of them herself) that recall the compositions painted on seventeenth- and eighteenth-century Dutch tiles; Aleksandr's work from the same area consists of minimalistic portraits in pencil and painted scenes of fog-bound boats.

In the art world, there is of course more to branding than the establishment of a signature multifaceted commodity. The branding of a group of artists also underscores the clash of seemingly opposed identitarian archetypes: in the case of Gilbert & George, a queer sensibility clashes with the primly mainstream demeanor projected by a pair of artists against a backdrop of stained glass surfaces with unapologetic representations of same-sex love from Thatcher's England to the present. In the Florenskys' case, the simulacrum of a family business—which, like Gilbert & George, is saddled with an ampersand that suggests an old-fashioned firm of certified public accountants—runs against the grain of repeated reminders of the mutual autonomy of the woman and the man who comprise the couple. In this brand name, the woman's initial comes first, resulting in a sequence of letters that suggests a reversal, or an upending of expectations: here, Alpha follows Omega. Above all, "O & A Florensky" is a conjunction of heterogeneous artisanal sensibilities, of artists experimenting in different media with an awareness of what Judith Butler, in her discussion of the socially constructed nature of gender norms, terms the usefulness of "fantasy [as] a part of the articulation of the possible."[42] Butler sees the reshuffling of gender norms as a kind of revitalization of gender as a social construct:

> The distance between gender and its naturalized instantiations is precisely the distance between the norm and its incorporations. . . . The norm only persists as a norm to the extent that it is acted out in social practice and re-idealized and reinstituted in and through the daily social rituals of bodily life. The norm has no independent ontological status, yet it cannot be easily reduced to its instantiations; it is itself (re)produced through its embodiment, through the acts that strive to approximate it, through the idealizations reproduced in and by those acts.[43]

In their current work, we see a particularly strong development of what can be understood in "O & A Florensky" as a heightened awareness of the biopolitics of collaboration and collective production within the realm of unofficial art. In a post-Soviet Russia that has, to all appearances, discarded the legal distinction of official and nonconformist art, the Florenskys endeavor to keep relevant and alive the concept of unofficial art by redefining it as a discourse that unfolds through a series of physical artifacts, as a studio space for bringing together different personae—gendered and otherwise—into a layered and scrupulously mortised foundation for a perpetually unfinished building project. During its early years of "unofficial" group exhibits and work on the samizdat publication of Shinkarev's manifesto—in its halcyon days as not just a group, but as a movement—the Mitki already foregrounded the conundrum of collectivity within a setting of creative dissidence, rendering the very idea of group work anxiety-ridden, if not dialectically fraught. Already in 1980, Olga Florensky was one of a group of four unofficial poets who called themselves the "Association of the Non-Joiners" (*Assotsiiatsiia neprimknuvshikh*). In their pithy manifesto (which was distributed in typed copy, via samizdat), she and the other three figures assert a view of poetry as a medium that becomes prophetic to the extent that it can bridge the divide between word and image. According to the manifesto, poetry can take on this function of envisioning possible ways of being and living only when it eschews the hackneyed or persistent (*ustoichivyi*) image.[44] In her poetry as well as her graphic work, Olga Florensky displays a keen interest in what may be understood as a strong Futurist variation of the Russian Acmeist movement, one in which the striving for a scrupulous "transparent clarity" within poetic language is fused with passion for improvisation. Olga's early meditations on what might be termed the multimedia potential of unshackled poetic speech—as a form of perceptual experimentation that brings together sound, color, and space—complements Butler's understanding of norms as archetypes that are no less powerful for being finished or makeshift, created or constructed.

Olga's own strongly ekphrastic poetry from the eighties, during the time of the Mitki's formation, draws our attention to an apparent project of renewing language through heightened visuality and synesthesia, at times facilitated by the narrators taking on other gendered personae and masks.[45] In her satirical and profanity-laced 1992 poem about the Mitki, "Rap Royale" (whose title comically also suggests "Piano [*roial'*] Rap," a hip-hop poem accompanied by, or clamorously banged out on, an upright piano), Olga foregrounds the ill-mannered egoism of individuals within the group, pointing to the presence of attitudes that would seem not to sit well with its ideals of genderless comity.[46] With its strong Tsvetaevan inflections—especially manifest in the use of the truncated line, which hints alternately at a stymied or discordantly triumphant assertion of the self—Olga's poetry adopts a playfully experiential attitude toward gender categories that excavates what Sibelan Forrester, in writing about Tsvetaeva's work, identifies as the reflex of viewing one's creative production as an example of presumption. As Forrester puts it, the female poet acknowledges her exclusion "by gender from legitimate participation in the poetic tradition" by playing the role of pretender to the throne of the canon.[47] The beginning and final strophes of Tsvetaeva's poem "Two" (*Dvoe*, 1924) starkly illustrates gender as socially constructed, as an artifact of language that is fixed within a narrative or mythology, with the poet enjoining the listener to "speak the sound" of the Homeric names of Helen and Achilles as resonantly as possible (*zvuk nazovi sozvuchnei*). "You will see that the world sound is built on consonance, in defiance of chaos," with the growing realization that the two are a "split pair" (*razroznennaia para*), tossed aside from each other.

Drawing on Tsvetaeva's project of forging a range of personae among women and across the gender divide (with an interest in the mythopoeic narratives and histrionic rhetorical gambits of contemporary male poets such as Mayakovsky and Khlebnikov), Olga is interested in using sound—what Tsvetaeva refers in her poem to metonymically as the pluck of the zither, the vibration of the reciting voice—as a laboratory for constructing new modalities. Bearing in mind this cultivation of multiple possible identities within a single space of production, it is no wonder that "O & A Florensky," in the statement for the 2015 installation *Internal Space*, describe the goal of their multi-media exhibit as a "free reconstruction of the accessible library study of curiosities, that was widely in existences at the end of the 19th century in St. Petersburg."[48] The building of an imaginary space entails an awareness of the ways in which forms of consciousness may begin with an awareness of the subject's vulnerability, with what Olga (in the statement of her *Taxidermy* exhibit) calls the "maniacal passion [of humanity] to perfect God's creation," by creating dummies whose vivid forms broach the ticklish subject of the shabbiness of the living and real. Here, we find ourselves contemplating anew the insights of feminist critics such as Sandra Bartky, who in 1990 wrote that "feminist consciousness is [one] of *victimization* [author's emphasis]."[49] The identities that we possess and the consciousness that we have of them are fundamentally rooted in our awareness of them as objects, as targets of a privileged audience.

In the work of the Florenskys, we see no treatment as eloquent about the nuances of collaboration—and of the possibilities for artists' victimization by their own hands or by those of others—than the ensemble of texts and images that they provided for an illustrated edition of the poetry of Oleg Grigoriev. As their contemporary the painter Oleg Frontinski insightfully notes, Grigoriev's poetry was remarkable for straddling a shadowy terrain in epigrammatic verse, between poetry that both children and adults could enjoy and poetry that is overshadowed by the theme of the "socialist Absurd and alcoholic heroism."[50] One of Aleksandr's illustrations for the collection draws as much on his perception of the influence of Grigoriev's astringent and misanthropic verse on the subculture of the Mitki (particularly on Shagin's "Icarus" cycle) as upon the poem itself:

Мазохисту на лавке
Втыкали дети булавки.
Не от тоски, не от шалости,
А тыкали от жалости.

[Some kids stuck needles into a masochist lying on a table. They did it not out of despair or mischief, but out of pity.][51]

The apparent deflation or mitigation of the children's sadistic use of pins is itself mitigated by the buried pun of *zhalo* ("stinger") in the word *zhalost'* ("pity"), a play on words that suggests a yoking of cruelty and mercy that never becomes fully resolved or attenuated.

Aleksandr illustrates this poem with a deliberately crude, *lubok*-like ink drawing that has a young naval cadet as one of the children doing the adult masochist's bidding, hinting that the iconic figure of the Mitki—the sailor—in fact has a naïve notion of what it means to help others (Figure 24). It is far easier to linger on the promoted image of the Mitki, as a group extolling the joys of physically demonstrative fellowship and pacifism, than to take note of the violent absurdism that underlies much of their work. We hear the cadences of Grigoriev's bemused ruminations for children about sudden mortality in the following stand-alone couplet from the Leningrad underground of the late seventies and early eighties, which Shinkarev quotes elsewhere in his work:

Шла машина грузовая-
Эх! Да задавила Николая.

[A transport truck goes by—Whoa! It ran over Nikolai!][52]

In Grigoriev's children's poetry, we find a kind of violent bestiary combined with social satire that anticipates by at least thirty years the English poet Frieda Hughes's *grand guignol* verses for children. But what is the purpose of foregrounding such catastrophes?

Although there may be no single answer to this question, we do see one possible explanation in the work that Olga and Aleksandr have produced in relation to this poem. In a short memoir that appears in the appendix for the same edition of Grigoriev's work, Olga recalls how she and her five-year old daughter, Katya, once ran into Grigoriev.

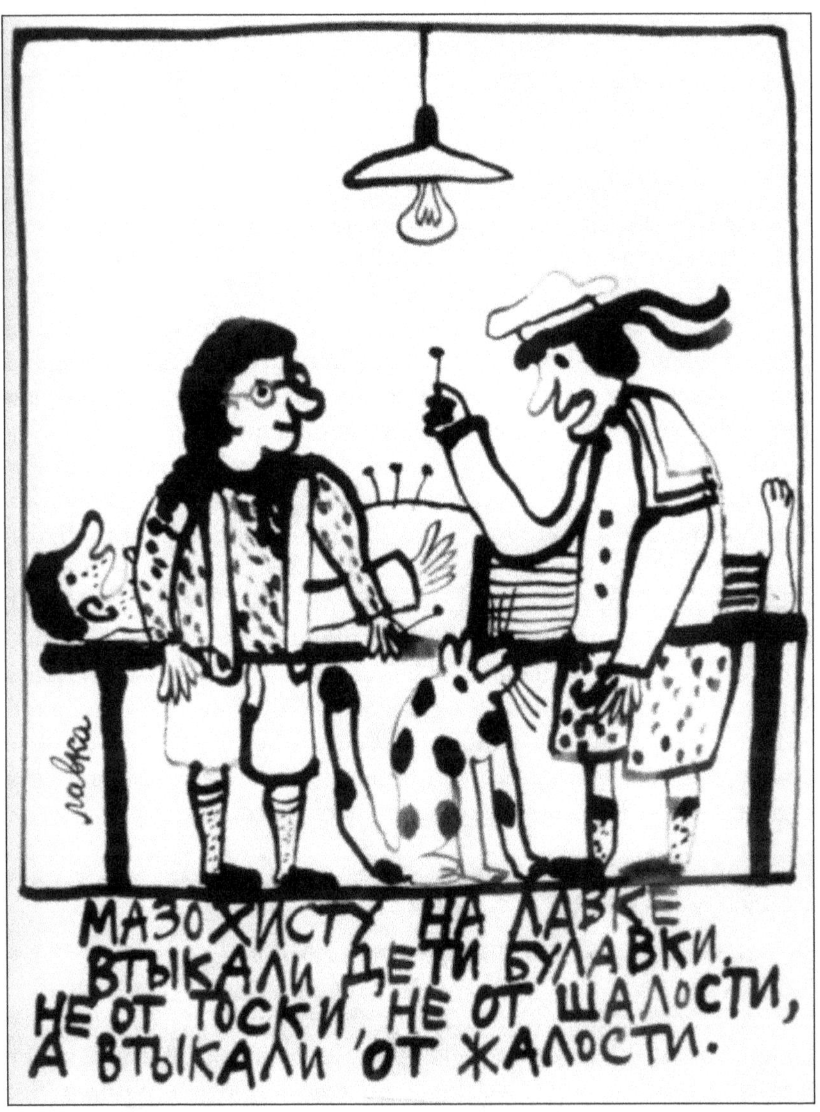


Figure 24. Aleksandr Florensky, "Some kids stuck needles into a masochist lying on a table. They did it not out of despair or mischief, but out of pity" (Mazokhistu na lavke vtykali deti ne ot toski, ne ot shalosti, a ot zhalosti), from Oleg Grigoriev, *Vinokhranitel'. Stikhotvoreniia* (2008), page 317.

Noting how her daughter already knew much of Grigoriev's poetry by heart—none of which had been published outside of samizdat—Olga says "Katya, say hello. This is Oleg Grigoriev, who wrote the poem 'Children threw logs at each other.'" Katya responds by jumping on him, and hanging from the frail man like a dead weight. "I was afraid that she would cause him to collapse. I tried to extricate her from him, explaining that great men shouldn't lift such weights. Oleg stood motionlessly and smiled apprehensively, as Katya with a grimace recited aloud to him 'Some kids stuck needles into a masochist lying on a table. . . .'"[53] In Olga's recollection and Aleksandr's illustration, we sense the potential for terror within the consciousness of a group as tightly knit as the Mitki. If everyone is close within a subculture—to the extent that even members' children know its lore by heart—then people within it have as much power to do harm to each other as to do good. The paradigm that the Florenskys seem to recommend instead, in a gesture of reproof against impulses toward thoroughgoing collectivism among the Mitki, is one where each person operates according to the paradox of what might be termed a relational autonomy. Perhaps that is precisely what the partnership of "O & A Florensky" models itself upon. Such a model may be what makes for a functional creative marriage and family, whether it be the Florenskys themselves or the "Glimmer Twins" of Shagin and Shinkarev.

In many ways, the particular understanding of an artistic collective that we find in the work of the Florenskys—as a fragile cluster of nonisomorphic cells, a network of elements that are diversified by their identities as agents or facilitators of particular processes or functions—represents an expansion of the Mitki's aesthetics of the collective action that devolves from the assumption of homogeneity into the reality of an absurdist, ad hoc performance of disaggregate group work that imbeds itself within a larger, and distinctly hostile, world of spectatorship. The writers among the Mitki—Tikhomirov, Shinkarev, Mikhail Sapego and Olga Florensky herself—tend to regard group work as a kind of labor that goes against the grain of human nature, and the accomplishment of projects produced by absorptive collectives as a subvariety of both the miraculous and the horrific.

Writing in 2011, Tikhomirov identified naïveté as the primary national character trait of Russians, connecting it with the legacy of the peasantry under autocracy and rightly underscoring its morally neutral identity: it is no less easy for "a naïve person to take away the life of another person" than it is for him or her to retain "the traits of a small child—namely, those that are angelic or divine."[54] In his prickly 2008 memoir *The End of the Mitki*, Shinkarev takes note of the foul atmosphere of cynicism and uncharitable hypercompetitiveness that often informed the work of postmodernist artistic collectives in the late eighties and early nineties.[55] The work of the Florenskys reminds us of the rich possibilities of what could be paradoxically termed a charitable hypercompetitiveness, of a scenario that takes an almost manic ramification and remerging of consciousness as its subject. Bearing in mind the usefulness of Groys's conception of "multiple authorship"—along with Bitov's reading of the Mitki in general and the Florenskys in particular—as examples of intimate (perhaps even "incestuous") collectives that are ramified by their internal diversity, perhaps we need to apply to the Florenskys' work a model of relational autonomy that is otherwise missing in many characterizations of group identity as being, in the words of Deleuze and Guattari in *Anti-Oedipus: Capitalism and Schizophrenia*, appalling examples of depersonalization in which "group fantasy is plugged into and machined on the socius," which ultimately defiles those who indulge in the fantasy.[56] The art historian Liubov Gurevich coined the term "mosaicness" (*mozaichnost'*) to describe an esthetic of alienation through a theatricalized eclecticism, which she argues is the hallmark of the nonconformist art and samizdat writing of the Leningrad underground. Gurevich's formulation helps us to hear the satire that dare not speak its name, making us understand how a vivid yet meretricious surface conceals a network of critical glosses about contemporary reality. Within the mosaic principle, simplicity can be conjoined with refinement, and autonomy with interaction, resulting in a gravitation toward the "absurd and the paradoxical." In the writing and graphic work of Vladimir Shinkarev, Gurevich writes, we see how "Zen Buddhism chime[s] in response to the aesthetic of the avant-garde," reflecting a "fusion of the absurd and primitivism which, as it turns out, is a special flower of the second culture of our city."[57]

What we see in the work of Olga and Aleksandr is a demonstration of precisely this form of fractured authorship, expanded to include the practices of dialogue among artists in a group and their aesthetic and commercial exchanges with the marketplace. More than anything produced by the Mitki in their decade-long heyday from the middle of the eighties to the nineties, Olga, Aleksandr, and their daughter, Katya (a highly talented artist in her own right, whom both Olga and Aleksandr have argued is both *post*-postmodernist and more *mitkovian* than many of the original members of the group), draw our attention to the *topos* of the group endeavor as being successful only insofar as it contains moments of dysfunction, of partial disharmony or fractional misalignment within its mode of operation. Among all the Mitki, it is their work that represents the most sustained examination of the dynamics of fractured or "mosaic" group authorship. Seen from this perspective, we can regard the achievements of the Florenskys as having the character of a rediscovered narrative about the Mitki, an overlooked statement of Mosaic Law that clarifies the underlying ideals of the movement. The work of the Florenskys asks us to believe in the palpable material reality of the multiple cultural—and, in some cases, roadside—signs that they display to us. Like those who believe that the highly diverse first five books of the Bible were written by Moses, we are disinclined to think that any of their works—either collaboratively or individually produced—could have been created by anyone but them in their roles as different hypostases of the same author.

# 5

# Satire, Sex, and Chance

## The Creative Diary of Viktor Tikhomirov

The typical man [among the Mitki] is situated both over and beyond sex. Many things interest him intensely, from where he could get a drink to the particularities of non-classical perspective; but sexual activity will never interest him. Yet he is not an ascetic, and may even be a pronounced hedonist. The point is that sexual relations are located somewhere just beyond the periphery of his purview, and don't enter into the top ten hits of pleasures. For him, the best way of whiling away the time with another person is: "Can we have a chat?"

Art critic ANNA MATVEEVA, "No One Knows About Sex" (2013)

[The painter Natalia] Goncharova chases the machine out of herself, like bad blood. Once I see my fear, I am no longer afraid of it. Goncharova has a family relation with nature. . . . If Goncharova is at war with the machine as an instrument of enslavement, she is in a coalition with the one that is enslaved by nature.

MARINA TSVETAEVA (1929)

Viktor Tikhomirov is an artisan who capably operates within several very different media platforms. He is a painter of canvases that draw on Russian folklore and the satirical narrative (as opposed to the graphic stylistic) tradition of the popular woodcut print or *lubok*; he is also an idiosyncratic filmmaker in the lush synesthetic and deeply serious vein of Tarkovsky and Sokurov (the latter is a close friend and the subject of one of his documentaries). In his political cartoons for the newspaper *Business St. Petersburg* (*Delovoi Peterburg*), he relies on the graphic conventions of the *lubok* that he scorns in his paintings, employing sharp outlines and vivid primary colors to communicate the exhibitionistic fatuousness or hypocrisy of civic institutions and the unworthy public actors and benefactors who claim to represent their interests. Tikhomirov's essays, blogs, and occasional op-ed style pieces for *Business St. Petersburg* and other local newspapers are, as the poet Viktor Krivulin remarks in an essay on his prose, written in the style of an engaging monologue spoken by an inquisitive urban *gorodskoi gulyaka* (flâneur), entertaining us with coruscating observations about the live-action *commedia dell'arte* that is the post-Soviet city of St. Petersburg.[1] Within each of these media, moreover, Tikhomirov employs a startling range of emotional registers, engaging in a form of brinksmanship that compels his audience to constantly reevaluate their expectations of his work, forcing any number of questions. What is Tikhomirov's central identity as a creative worker who is proficient in any number of media platforms and traditional visual media? And is there a common denominator among the dizzying range of the subject matters that he represents in word and image? The answer seems to be that he is a portraitist of social chaos, which may be alternately—or even simultaneously—funny, glum, tragic, hopeful, and filled with metaphysical yearning and pain. Interestingly, these affects in his work do not cancel each other out. Tikhomirov's production is nothing if not protean and dynamic. As Shinkarev notes in his assessment of Tikhomirov's overall achievement, one intuits the presence within it of a "concentrated" joy, "as essential as a daily dose of vitamins." Shinkarev explains that the spirit of exaltation in the very pictorial representation of things is dissolved into, and subtly laced throughout, the often unruly—if not physical violent—conflicts that Tikhomirov portrays.[2]

Krivulin, Tikhomirov, and the Mitki—along with experimental poets such as Elena Shvarts—were prominent figures in the largest literary movement without a name during the seventies and eighties in Leningrad. We may regard them as literary archeologists seeking to rediscover the Atlantis of Russian Absurdism in the work of the OBERIU or "Union of Real Art," previously sighted during the unsettled and ideologically eclectic era of the New Economic Policy (NEP, 1921–28). Even within this landscape of literary rehabilitation, however, Tikhomirov occupies a very specific niche. More than any other member of the Mitki, with his prodigious creative output Tikhomirov brings us into close contact with the contemplation of the absurdist aspects of performativity in relation to eroticism and sexual identity. Tikhomirov is particularly interested in the aleatory aspects of sexual affect and performativity. As he puts it in "Up with Impotence!" (*Daesh' impotentsiiu!*), a droll blog essay he wrote in early 2016 and posted on his Facebook page, the absence of conventionally performative sexuality is noticeable in two classes of seemingly highly dissimilar groups of people. Tikhomirov takes note of the curious fact that "all revolutionary figures were impotent, and as a result achieved their goals" and that impotence is also powerfully present among "people [possessed] with imagination."[3] In his writing and visual work, Tikhomirov casts a light on the largely undocumented relation between external action and cultivated imaginaries that exists within sexual affect. Here we find no element of the surrogacy, fateful substitution, or channeling that Freud alluded to in his outlining of sublimation in *Civilization and Its Discontents*. Tikhomirov does not subscribe to the notion that harnessing or channeling sexuality contributes to creative or political productivity. He sees the identities of the creative worker and the political firebrand as complementary, if not cut from the same cloth, because of the way that they rely on methods of improvisatory responsiveness to chance events. This responsiveness is, by its very nature, sexual, expressing a love for—and cultivation of—connection that is simultaneously affective, performative, and relational to people and things. In Tikhomirov's work, chance is both a matchmaker for lovers and a catalyst for the formations of communities and movements, echoing Gilles Deleuze's understanding of *amor fati* as the love of many that only masquerades as the adoration of the single outcome or result: "for there is only a single combination of chance as such, a single way of combining all the parts of chance, a way which is like the unity of multiplicity."[4] The intersection of sexuality and chance serves, in Tikhomirov's imaginative universe, as the site where coalitions are formed, and liaisons take place.

Yet another, and more disquieting, observation that emerges from Tikhomirov's work is that chance is also the matchmaker from hell: it is both the go-between for lovers and the enabling emissary between tyrants and the communities that they oppress. Bearing in mind this caveat about the consequences of a seemingly elastic erotics of connection within the social realm that Tikhomirov portrays, we see considerable common ground between his imaginative universe and the guardedly sanguine theory of conditional or simulacrum-like freedom that Svetlana Boym describes in her 2010 book *Another Freedom: The Alternative History of an Idea*. Correlating Hannah Arendt's notion of passionate love as the "totalitarianism for two" with observations in

Kierkegaard and Dostoevsky about the contingency of identity within even freely chosen spheres of affection, Boym takes note of the ways in which "the love relationship becomes a minidemocracy [*sic*], an enlightened despotism, a theocracy a tyranny, anarchy . . . put[ting] an end to the individual autonomy of the two lovers and shrink[ing] their world." Love may also have the ambiguous result of "carv[ing] out a new unpredictable 'third space' that is never the sum of the two," producing instead an "adventurous hyperbolic mathematics of knots, curves, folds, parallel lines and lives that can only occasionally cross."[5] Within the random eruptions of sexual attraction and group formation in the political sphere, Tikhomirov takes note of the impulse toward mutual subjugation that lies at the base of most social relations. The experience of the leaderless youth group or movement—caught within the parentheses, to paraphrase Sylvia Plath, of adult insight on the one hand and prepubescent blindness on the other—then becomes the ideal within what may be regarded as the narrativized ethical system that Tikhomirov constructs over the range of his work.

For many people, this researcher included, any viewing or reading of Viktor Tikhomirov's production begins with a visit to the sprawling attic apartment where he does most of his work. In St. Petersburg, his studio is located a stone's throw from the Church of the Savior on Spilled Blood, the Byzantine Revival structure built on the spot where Alexander II was assassinated in 1881. The bomb that the group the People's Will tossed under the royal carriage also, in effect, broke the ground for the construction of a church that pioneered the fusion of the patchwork design of St. Basil's cathedral in Moscow with reinterpretations of Byzantine architectural design and Romanesque decoration, which became fashionable in the building of new churches in the years leading up to the Revolution. As if to draw attention to the explosive historical charge of the neighborhood, Tikhomirov often includes Savior on the Blood in his paintings and films, usually as seen from the one window in his studio that faces in its direction. Yet perhaps we are getting ahead of ourselves by taking up the invitation that certain of Tikhomirov's paintings seem to offer up, that we embark on a mental journey—projecting ourselves outward—from the actual space of his studio. Tikhomirov wants you to enter into these tableaux, on the condition that you consider, as Svetlana Boym would put it, the possibilities of the tangents and normally divergent "knots, curves, folds [and] parallel lines" that their representations of sociality cast out at their viewers.

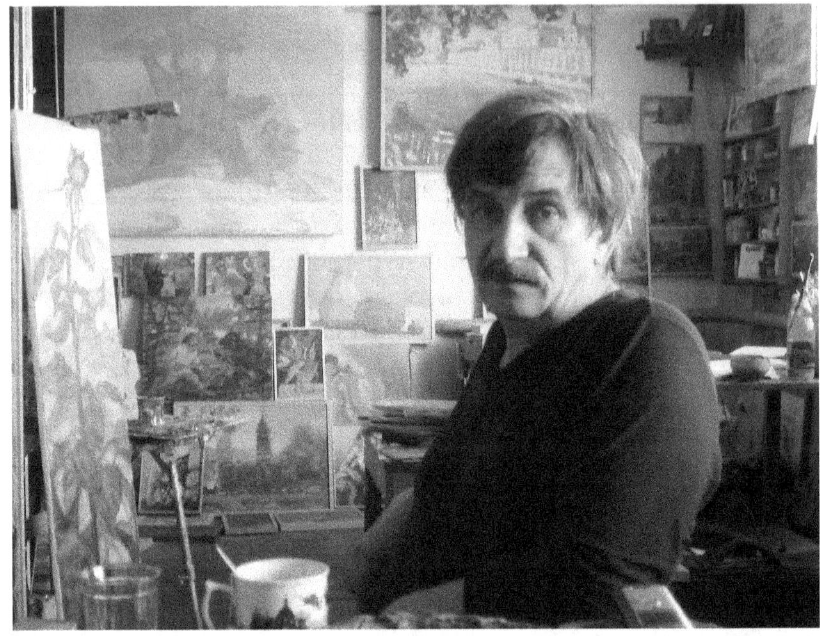

Figure 25. Photo of Viktor Tikhomirov in his studio in 2009. (Alexandar Mihailovic)

What do you see when you first step into Tikhomirov's workspace? Several things vie for your attention: the incandescent polychromaticism of paintings that take up every available inch of wall space and obstruct the floor with vertical stacks that lean against easels, bookcases, and chairs; the sheets of political illustrations draped across tables, with their images of vibrant pastels infusing traditional Russian folkloric motifs into galvanized portrayals of the corruption roiling within local institutions; and the strong presence of the book culture of a movement, with volumes by Tikhomirov and his friends left open on battered side tables, under pillows, and often underfoot—bear traps lying in wait for the unwary visitor. The diversity and chockablock, overflowing living archive of Tikhomirov's production both startles and welcomes (Figure 25). Within the space of his studio, you get the sense that Tikhomirov takes sociality itself as the major subject matter of his work, that the exchanges of opinion, the ebb and flow of his business, and the questions from journalists, colleagues, and friends who drop by—all gain ready entrance into the daily log of his painting, writing, and cinematic portraits. Such sociality is abundantly evident in Tikhomirov's generosity in sharing his studio time with visitors, who become unwitting participants—if not collaborators—in his project, like the residents of the Polish *shtetl* who become the models for figures in the frescoes of Gospel stories in the Catholic church of Isaac Babel's story "Pan Apolek." Tikhomirov continues to paint, write, and edit while visitors as varied as fellow artists, actors, businesspeople (most notably, the St. Petersburg-based construction magnate Vyacheslav Zarenkov, who funded Tikhomirov's 2017 documentary *Andrei Kuraev: Direct Speech* (*Andrei Kuraev. Priamaia rech'*) and who is himself a painter and librettist), and alumni of the now largely inactive Mitki pass through the open door of his work space. Certainly, the narratives of Tikhomirov's films are cluttered with agitated human canvases, of characters simultaneously talking to and past each other. His 2014 film *Chapaev Chapaev* restlessly glides from one scrimmage to another, of Whites and Reds caught on the field of battle during the Russian Civil War, and of women and men misunderstanding each other in the attempts to navigate among the barrier islands of their performed identities as artists, officers, scientists, lovers, and engineers.

In the world of Tikhomirov's creation, artifice and practical know-how are brought back into the foundational coalition playfully imagined by Walter Benjamin in his famous essay about Nikolai Leskov, and by Vladimir Nabokov, who underscored a technology of art in much of his critical writing, as in his assertion that "the boundary line between the work of fiction and the work of science . . . is not as clear as is generally believed."[6] Nabokov in turn drew many of his notions about the applied science of the artistic method from Oscar Wilde, who in one of his most important essays about the self-sufficiency of aesthetic value wrote that "nature is so uncomfortable," with grass being "hard and lumpy and damp, and full of dreadful black insects . . . why, even [William] Morris' poorest workman could make you a more comfortable chair than the whole of Nature can" ("The Decay of Lying").[7] We also find in Tikhomirov's work an ever-present consciousness of the artist's craft as expressed in settings that are intensely collaborative and infused with a garrulous amicability, which, far from being characterized as a distraction, is highly efficacious for the completion of the task at hand. In his essay "Russian Design," from the mid-1990s, Tikhomirov writes approvingly of artists who fix all their old tools themselves, and who never accumulate old technologies that can't be rehabilitated by their own hands: "There's no point in concealing the sins [*chtoby grekha tait'*], humanity will surround itself with mountains of garbage. . . . It would be fantastic to create a market where any new designer technology would be perceived as horrific, and where putting the brakes on technological progress would be considered a noble act."[8] In the same essay, Tikhomirov goes on to say that Greenpeace is, among voluntary political associations, perhaps best positioned to contribute to such an endeavor, and he speculates that in its membership it may become more of a Russian youth movement because of the spirit of practical sustainability that animated the best of the Russian artists' studios.

The virtue of technological simplicity and the understanding of resistance to the cult of the new as being an inextricable element of youth movements are ethical premises that lie at the center of Tikhomirov's work. His production, like his studio, is cluttered without being disordered. Every artifact or implement that we see there is something that is put to good use, whether it be for video production or painting or for the critical discussion among visitors, whose commentary enters his subsequent work, much like brush strokes that are periodically added to the leaning canvases that litter his studio. In his 2002 short documentary *Chapaev, Furmanov, Mit'ki*, conversations between himself, Shinkarev, and Shagin in his studio, about the parallels between the Mitki and the famous literary and cinematic representations of the legendary—if largely enigmatic—Soviet hero Chapaev from the Russian civil war, take on a new form twelve years later, as thematic frames for Tikhomirov's novel and film adaptation *Chapaev Chapaev*, about the exquisite constructedness of Soviet patriotic mythology. The closed nature of the world of Tikhomirov's studio is crucial here: tight boundaries and looming surfaces are, after all, what make the criss-crossings—some random, others planned—resonant as well as evocative. In a similar mining of conversations in this workspace, the loaf of bread that the priest Andrei Kuraev breaks open in his visit to Tikhomirov becomes both a still life and a scene in the documentary that Tikhomirov made about Kuraev.[9] In the still life, on view both in Tikhomirov's studio now and in the film, the roughly halved loaf of bread (itself a clear biblical symbol for fellowship) is positioned next to an onion just picked from the garden (Figure 26). The composition may allude to Grushenka's anecdote in Dostoevsky's *Brothers Karamazov*, about the failed attempt of a sinner to escape the fires of hell by grabbing onto the stem of the onion that she gave, in the sole act of kindness from her life, to a starving woman. A small mound of salt tops the bread, in the traditional Russian practice of ceremoniously expressing warm hospitality (*khlebosol'stvo*; literally, bread and salt) to an honored guest. The salt is oddly undisturbed by the wrenching open of the loaf, which shimmers with

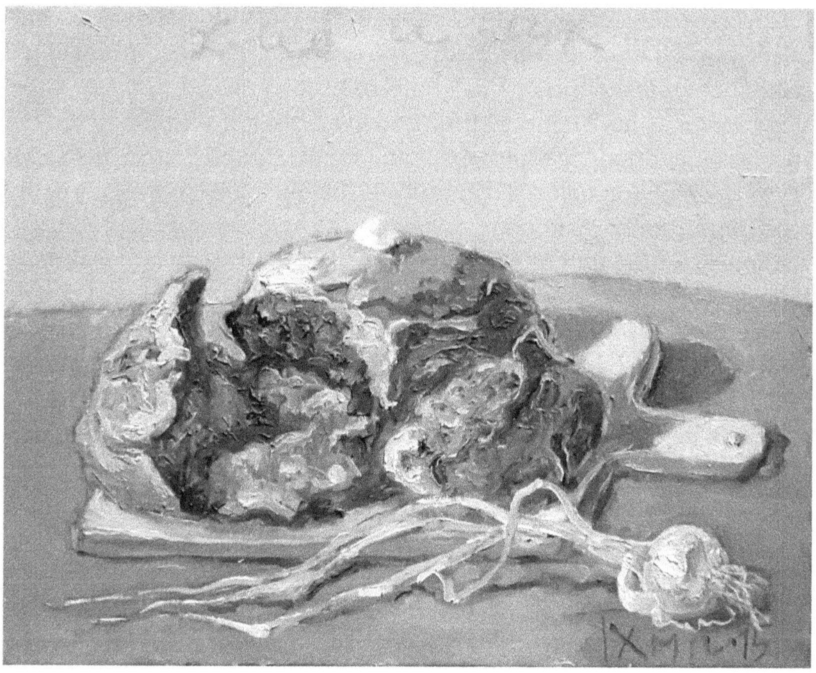

Figure 26. Viktor Tikhomirov, *Bread and Onion* (2015). Oil, 40 × 50 cm. (collection of the artist)

iridescent tones that are more reminiscent of a freshly cut melon than a baked good. The painting breathes with anticipation of a contact with others that will have a woke physical directness about it, and which will be free of the trappings of electronic communication. It seems very fitting that the original title of the canvas was *The Loaf of Bread Broken by Deacon A. Kuraev, While Speaking with the Artist* (*Karavai, kotoryi razlomil d'iakon Kuraev, beseduia s khudozhnikom*).

Within the film, the gesture that this painting foregrounds takes on weighty portent. Kuraev's breaking of bread begins and ends Tikhomirov's 2017 film, which is interesting for his references to the director's own diverse work as an artist. The camera lingers on the canvases during the interviews with Kuraev. At different points of his conversations with the priest, the director switches seamlessly from the video to audio recordings of them, played to listeners such as Vladimir Shinkarev and the rock musician and songwriter Yuri Shevchuk in their own studios. In one interview, which is intercut with scenes from Kuraev's large public lectures about the complex character of human fellowship—and the necessary acceptance of expressions of male vulnerability in a culture that might not tolerate them—the priest warns Tikhomirov of the risk inherent in an author's creations of his own world (*sozdanie avtorskogo mira*), as leading to a stifling social isolation. Kuraev hints that such a danger may be especially acute for Tikhomirov, with his proficiency in multiple fields. Tikhomirov's diverse work represents a network of mutually reinforcing references, a chamber of different modes of representation that reflect and amplify each other. In all his films—but especially in his documentary about Kuraev—the paintings seem to clamor to become actors unto themselves. Several canvases, such as Tikhmirov's 2009 painting *Nestor Makhno Throws a Woman Overboard*—which is not shown in the film about Kuraev, and which fancifully conflates the history of the anarchist from the Russian civil war (1919–22) with the apocryphal account of Stenka Razin's drowning of his wife—would seem to be mocking pitches for the overwrought historical mash-ups by directors such as Nikita Mikhalkov (Figure 27). The word for woman in the painting is spelled in the Mitki way, with a palatized *n* (*zhen'shchina*, discussed in chapter 2). Tikhomirov here re-engages the subtext of the drunken (*khmel'noi*) Stenka Razin's sacrifice of a female figure for the sake of homosociality, which is the subtext of Shinkarev's anecdote of the failure to save the woman who falls overboard (*za bortom*). Bearing in mind our earlier discussion of how the typical Mityok emerges as a doppelgänger of both David Bowie and the drowning woman, we realize that Tikhomirov uses this canvas as a screen for presenting misogyny to us on a grotesque scale, and for projecting self-images that signally lack self-awareness. With his cross eyes, tightly closed red lips, and formless clothing, this gargantuan Makhno—who is surrounded by feral looking men with wide-open eyes and blood-red, sharp-toothed mouths—is more an unthinking masthead for others than he is a man. So much for Makhno—or Razin—becoming a real man, as a result of throwing his wife overboard. Tikhomirov's attitudes toward this morally ambiguous totem of twentieth-century Russian political culture is both bemused and wary. There is certainly not a whiff of hero worship here.

Traversing the busy space of Tikhomirov's studio and passing an eye over his books and paintings such as these—which seem like performers in their own right—you are reminded that fixed roles, identities, and norms are nothing but faded labels that become dislodged over the course of time, like miniature placards in dusty museum exhibits. Certainly, such roles lose their fixity over any performance of them. The

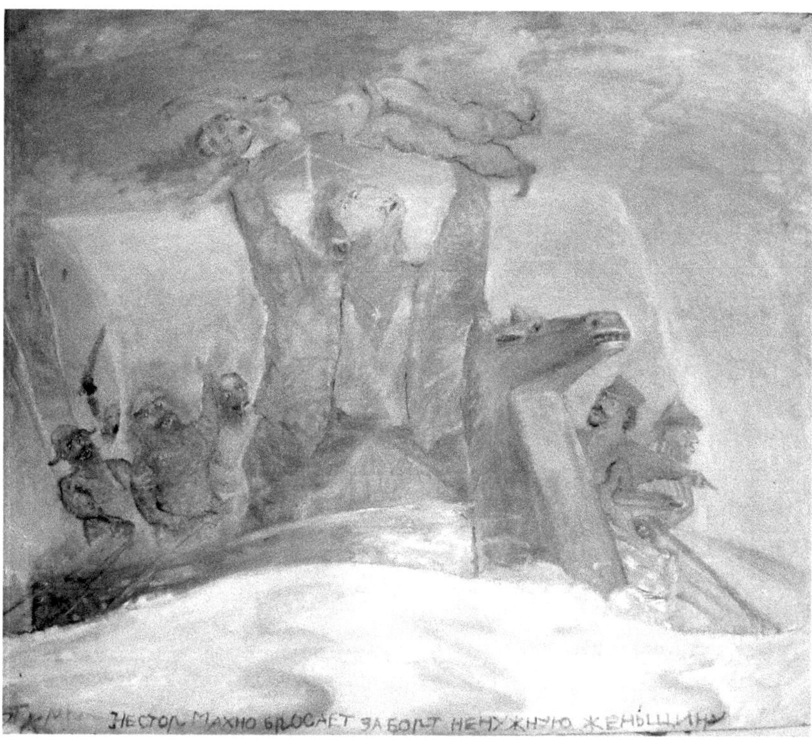

Figure 27. Viktor Tikhomirov, *Nestor Makhno Throws an Unneeded Woman Overboard* (2009). Oil, 120 × 160 cm. (collection of the artist)

social conservatism of some of Tikhomirov's views—which he voices most often in interviews—stands in striking juxtaposition to the deliberately oblique treatment of normative archetypes across the ekphrastic landscape of his filmmaking, painting, drawing, and fiction. Tikhomirov repeatedly draws attention to the slippage between a social role and its instantiation among people, between what Judith Butler calls the "inherited discourse of the metaphysics of substance" and the actual performance of what his audience might assume to be the normative message of such discourse.[10] Joining together the method of a cinematographer with the cool sharpshooting of a sniper, Tikhomirov prompts us to consider the possibility that the provocation to "Action!" (*motor*) lies at the center of all representations of frenetic social interaction within an urban setting. A vividly lived experience passes from view precisely when we attempt to affix a label upon it. Among other things, Tikhomirov's cinema is a self-conscious obituary for superannuated norms, which are always outpaced by action and a keen understanding of improvised performativity as an antidote for unchecked mythmaking. For Tikhomirov, filmmaking plays a particularly important role in waging war upon political belief systems that retrofit themselves onto experiences that do not correspond to their facile assumptions. Watching films such as *Grass and Water*, *Sokurov*, and *Chapaev Chapaev*, we realize that Tikhomirov, like the other members of the Mitki, is engaging in a project of rendering prosaic—and therefore demystifying—the political sublime of Soviet-era leadership cults. We also become aware of the double meaning of the Russian term *kadr* in the narratives of his films, as both a frame or still within a sequence of moving images (Fr. *cadre*: "setting," "frame"), and as an activist or revolutionary cell or group—a militia-like cadre—that is intent upon the demolition of an existing order of things. But the question that emerges most insistently from Tikhomirov's writing and visual production is this: What are the specific orthodoxies that merit dismantling?

To answer that question, we need to describe in some detail the different forms of social aggregation that Tikhomirov portrays. A typical production of Viktor Tikhomirov reminds us that sociality is the assertion of a communal interconnectedness, reminiscent perhaps of the notion of "conciliarism" or *sobornost'* that the nineteenth-century Slavophile philosopher Alexei Khomyakov developed to describe the operation of Russian consciousness as a cellular tissue of believers that augments itself from an collocation of disparate individuals. Such a network eventually consolidates itself into a power grid of reciprocated desire, evolving into a single collective intelligence that possesses what the French sociologist and early theorist of cyberspace Pierre Lévy terms an "open-ended dynamic of voice composition and message negotiation."[11] A consideration of Lévy's view of the democratic possibilities of political collectives on the Internet—which he formulated during the mid-nineties, during the time that the Mitki experienced what may be understood as their second renaissance, as a group contemplating the passing of autocracy from Russian forms of governance and the uncertain promise of democratic reforms—can illuminate a great deal about Tikhomirov's understanding of the stubborn legacy of the Stalinist cult of personality and the gravitational pull that it continues to exert upon conceptualizations of community. Lévy makes some crucial distinctions about the fundamentally beneficent character of collectivism, and these distinctions are completely consistent with the principles of morally self-correcting values that Khomyakov and other Slavophiles (such as

Nikolai Fyodorov) see as emerging from communal consciousness. As Lévy writes, "collective intelligence has no relationship to the stupidity of crowd behavior":

> Panic, collective enthusiasm, etc., are the result of the epidemic propagation of emotions and representation among masses of isolated individuals. The people in a crowd that is in a grip of panic or wild joy are not thinking collectively. True [*sic*] they communicate, but in the minimal sense reflected by the passive and immediate conduction of simple messages, violent sentiments and reflex actions. The overall effect of individual actions is completely lost on the individuals who constitute the crowd. It is claimed that the only way to make a community less erratic is through transcendence (hierarchy, authority, representation, tradition, etc.). But this is false.

In his art work and his films and prose, Tikhomirov draws our attention to what happens when an audience responds passively to cultural prompts: it slides precipitously along the well-worn grooves of authoritarian thinking, with dire consequences to itself as well as to those whom it scapegoats as its enemies. Tikhomirov's thinking here resonates with Lévy's discussion of the Janus-faced coin of collective intelligence, as facing either in the direction of a dynamic multilog of speakers or a coalesced mob that acts out in frenzied rage. His utopianism about cyberspace notwithstanding, Lévy is quite cognizant of the myriad attractions of communal violence and scapegoating. He explains that such pseudocollectivism can be eschewed if certain "technical and organizational mechanisms" are put into place, the function of which is "to expose the dynamics of the collective to everyone involved" in it, thereby making it possible for them to "modify and evaluate" the community to which they belong. "Intelligent communities are the direct antithesis of the incoherence and brutal immediacy of crowd behavior," which does nothing more than "channel the community into a rigid structure."[12] Yet as we can see, the ideas of structure, order and curatorial oversight are present everywhere in Lévy's own characterization of the charismatically interactive community that he describes.

Tikhomirov seems to have been aware of the moral ambiguities of the kinds of virtual communities offered up by the Internet in the mid-nineties and theorized by early evangelists for digital culture such as Lévy, during the time of Boris Yeltsin's personal decline and the ascent of an unapologetically revanchist leadership that scorned the promise of democratic participation in regional representative institutions, such as the lower house of parliament or Duma. Writing in 1997 about the Mitki's staging of a New Year's human pyramid of themselves, with those on top holding sparklers, Tikhomirov comments that while the "idea of collectivism—of the subordination of one's own ambitions to the group ideal—is one of the most *mitkovian*," its instantiation among "creative personalities" is "practically impossible." He explains that "the natural ambitiousness, capriciousness, and tendency towards pessimism—as well as the panic fits [among members of the collective]—render the experiments of collectivism into victories," rather than a manifestation of processual communal negotiation of shared ideals.[13] Writing these words at the end of 1997, Tikhomirov must have been aware of their resonances with the rise of a leadership that emphasized not the subordination of every person to the one ideal, but of everyone to the one person.

Of special importance in this statement is Tikhomirov's peculiar focus on the *esprit de corps* of the military, at the expense of any actual mission or campaign. In his 1992 film *Grass and Water* (*Trava i voda*), Tikhomirov portrays a teenage boy's coming of age in the coeducational setting of a summer Pioneer's camp during the early sixties. Many of the camp's routines—the morning reveilles, the line inspections, and the call and response of the camp counsellors and their wards—emerge as benign versions of an actual military organization, with the counsellors in many instances being scarcely older or more experienced than their charges. In both the film and the short story that serves as its basis, Tikhomirov underscores the attraction of a collective that has no leader—a view that is all the more suggestive in a film that is set during the time of Khrushchev's "Thaw," with its endeavor to dismantle the authoritarian Stalinist cult of personality. Young men and women freely compete amongst themselves, engage in harmless badinage and blunted verbal barbs, and flirt. The protagonist of the film, with his everyman-like surname of Ivanov, in fascination witnesses both a nighttime tryst of two of his counsellors and the profane, alcohol-soaked gathering of his father with his fellow veterans from the war. Both acts of witnessing are invested with a powerful sense of taboo, as if sexuality and the traumatic effects of wartime violence were somehow linked, and in equal measure anathema to the genuine fellowship of the Pioneer camp, with its members poised on the crepuscular cusp of puberty that separates childhood from adulthood. Ivanov's father and his friends drown their memories of violence in liquor and self-anesthetizing physical feats of one-upmanship. One man, Nikita (played to powerful effect by Dmitri Shagin), pulls a thick metal nail from the floorboard under the table where they are drinking and proceeds to wrap it around his finger like a vine; in response, Ivanov's father takes a horseshoe from his box of sundry carpenter's tools and bends it open into a shape resembling the Roman letter "W." As Nikita mournfully leaves the apartment on crutches, we see that he is missing a leg. In the film, the boy for the first time becomes a witness to both the effects of wartime trauma and adult intimacy. We are made to understand that both forms of physicality put an end to the fundamentally kind-hearted camaraderie that we see elsewhere in the film. Tikhomirov's casting of Shagin as a wounded war veteran who feels the need to replay victory through an attempt at physical supremacy is both a shrewd commentary about the fleeting nature of the essentially egalitarian collectivism embodied by the Mitki and an elaboration of his observation elsewhere in his essayistic prose about the irreconcilability of such fellowship even with the ideal of its group striving toward victory.

Tikhomirov's mindfulness about the political ambiguity of the collective ideal is evident in any number of his works. In his series of aphoristic anecdotes "Legends of the Revolution" (which are clearly composed in the genre of the absurdist writer Daniil Kharms's prose sketches, with their unflattering or surprisingly humanized portraits of cultural idols such as Pushkin), Tikhomirov offers an incisive thumbnail sketch of the actual relations between the corporate, unindividuated masses and their leader:

> Lenin loved to clamber out on the top of his armored limousine (or onto his balcony) and look out onto the masses. And those masses were dark and backward, with no way of getting past their crudeness [*khot' kol v golove teshi*; literally, however much you played around with trying to crack open that head]. And here Il'ich tutored them from that height, about the how and the what. . . . And they all would go "Hurrah!" or "Down with it!"—using those words, and no others. They were given newspapers and radios, and would respond the same. There was just no way of getting them to do actual work. Lenin even began to take sick from this, and went to Gorki and called out to Stalin:
>
> "Koba, do me the courtesy of teaching them yourself—give it a shot [*poseki*]!"
>
> "Oh, I'll give it a shot alright [*poseku*], Volodya—no worries!" answered the leader, engagingly baring his brown teeth in a smile.[14]

The masses that we find in this anecdote can only respond in a primitive way to Lenin's prompts—with formulaic praise or blame, or rote repetition—and are incapable of creating anything real, or of doing work. Gone is the ideological opposition between Stalin and Lenin, which even in Russia today continues to be played out in different ways—often, as in some of the Putin government's recent pronouncements about twentieth-century Russian history, with Lenin rather than Stalin emerging as the muddy source of Soviet totalitarianism. Quite to the contrary of any notion of Lenin and Stalin as being ideological antipodes, here the two men work in close consultation with one another; in fact, they seem to be assuming the responsibilities of dual leadership, with Stalin pulling the strings of power in Lenin's estate of Gorki outside of Moscow. Stalin's wolfish grin at the prospect of meting out rough discipline to the masses takes on additional meaning with his repetition of Lenin's request "to take a shot at it," using the verb *posech'*. The implied meaning of this verb in the given context is not its primary definition ("to cut" or "slice"). Here, the speakers invoke one of the verb's more specialized secondary meanings from Russian criminal argot: to take aim with a gun, or to metaphorically make a successful attempt at something, seizing a moment. In Tikhomirov's retelling, Lenin and Stalin are both thugs, and accordingly speak the same highly marked slang. Tikhomirov is keen to draw our attention to the lure of ecstatic violence that lies at the heart of the absorptive and assimilationist (rather than dynamically agglutinative and recombinant) form of collective consciousness that Lévy describes as the counterpoint to the mass psychology of politicized hysteria.

Yet the predator/prey dynamic that Tikhomirov points to in this sketch also opens up an understanding of the wolves of the world as possessed of a sadism that is oddly jocular and self-abasing, affording us a partial glimpse into the physical ravages of aging that are suggested by Stalin's possibly rotting teeth and Lenin's gormless and neurasthenic response to the obduracy of the masses. Here we are in the territory of other postmodernist writers and filmmakers from the so-called last Soviet generation, most notably Vladimir Sorokin and Aleksandr Sokurov, who portray figures of political leadership as either hapless invalids or grotesquely caricatured solipsistic thugs. The libidinous Stalin of Sorokin's scabrous and pornographic 2004 novella *Blue Lard*, and Sokurov's portrayal in the 2001 film *Taurus* of Lenin as an addlepated Chekhovian landowner in his final decline, share striking similarities with Tikhomirov's irreverent treatment of Soviet leaders in *Legends about the Revolution*. With its exuberantly roving satirical lens and focus on episodes of unconstrained goodness and fellow feeling, Tikhomirov's fiction and cinema would seem to have little in common with the moral austerity of Sokurov's films. As we shall see later, however, the two artists share an understanding of the ways in which political power and sexualized affect often converge.

Perhaps most importantly, Tikhomirov underscores the brutality of political leaders not so much by drawing our attention to their moral flaws, but by comparing them to their counterparts in the animal world. One predator/prey dichotomy plays a particularly prominent role in Tikhomirov's political satire. Operating very much within the Russian literary and folkloristic frame of reference, Tikhomirov follows Mikhail Bakhtin's characterization of satire as a genre that foregrounds unresolved paradoxes, one that juxtaposes seemingly contrary figures or sets of values. Bakhtin sees the blurring of lines between the animal and human worlds as being particularly important in satire, which he describes as turning conventionally understood power dynamics on their head by rendering the scoundrel into the fool and vice versa.[15] In a drawing from 2006 in pen and ink with watercolors, titled *Overcoming the Wolf* (*Preodolenie volka*), which was exhibited in the Dream Museum of Sigmund Freud—possibly the oddest exhibition space in St. Petersburg—Tikhomirov shows an anxious wolf holding up a hand mirror with the reflection of himself as a hare;[16] another illustration, from his cycle *Legends about the Revolution*, has a scowling and walleyed Lenin, sitting in a boat of dead rabbits and holding one up with the boastful statement "without a single shot" (*bez edinogo vystrela*), accompanied by the caption of "Hobbies" (*uvlecheniia*) at the bottom of the illustration.[17]

In another of the *Legends about the Revolution*, a youthful Lenin and Stalin find themselves pursued by a pack of wolves as they flee by sled from a tsarist prison, with Lenin behaving like a dissembling trickster and addressing them in friendly manner, as if they were a faithful dog and two Muslim men from Central Asia: "Sharik [Rover]?! Dzhul'bars?! Mukhtar?!" Scorning Lenin's play-acting, Stalin removes his mitten and shoots one of the wolves in the eye, and the rest of the pack peel off in fear. "The Revolution, they say [*mol*], can't be carried out by wearing mittens," he sententiously intones.[18] The kinship between predators and the leadership of both the Soviet Union and the current Russian

Federation is a persistent leitmotif in the satirical bestiary of Tikhomirov's writing and artwork, with the rabbit and the wolf—rather than the sheep and the wolf—as an idiosyncratic pairing of antipodal forces.

In his artwork and prose, Tikhomirov constructs a narrative landscape where prerevolutionary ways of thinking and modes of representation—most notably the tradition of the satirical and political illustration of the *lubki*—routinely mingle in anachronistic abandon with figures from different Soviet periods, the "wild nineties" and the resurgent nationalism of the aughts and the teens of this century. In a political cartoon from October 2015 for the newspaper *Business St. Petersburg* (*Delovoi Peterburg*), Tikhomirov pointedly goes against the grain of the idiom "a wolf in sheep's clothing" (*volk v ovech'ei shkure*) by having a wolf (representing here the governor of the republic of Komi in the Russian Federation, accused of embezzlement and involvement in an organized crime group) wearing a rabbit's skin (Figure 28). In a striking departure from traditional folkloric iconography, Tikhomirov's symbolic imaginary frames the rabbit and the wolf as being only superficially opposed to each other: the rabbit merely uses different and more camouflaged materials for the construction of his supremacy over others. In the cartoon, Tikhomirov blurs this ethical line with the words inscribed on the rabbit's hide, on which the governor boasts of his probity ("I'm like all of you—one for all, and all for one!"). On the rabbit's ears, however, we see the baffling non-word *zaya*. At first, we read this as the word for rabbit, *zayats*, missing the final letter in what we assume is the conceit of hasty and spidery penmanship. But the phrases proclaiming innocence on other parts of the skin foreground the first-person singular pronoun *ya*, giving us a key to understanding this incomplete word, seemingly written in haste: we need to read it as *za ya*, meaning (ungrammatically) "for myself." Tikhomirov consistently shows that the putative victims may be no less shrewd and capable of surreptitious cruelty than the wolves of the world, who are in turn often as vulnerable as their prey. The fact that the newspaper *Business St. Petersburg* (where Tikhomirov holds a regular post as a satirical illustrator) is printed on pink paper contributes to the impression that these cartoons (originally done in ink, tempera, and watercolor) are blooming from the noisome substratum of the Putin-era business world, where crime, politics, and commerce freely intermingle.

We come closer to understanding the specific character of Tikhomirov's views about political power in Russia by examining his treatment of the duality of totalitarian leaders and their flock as locked in a

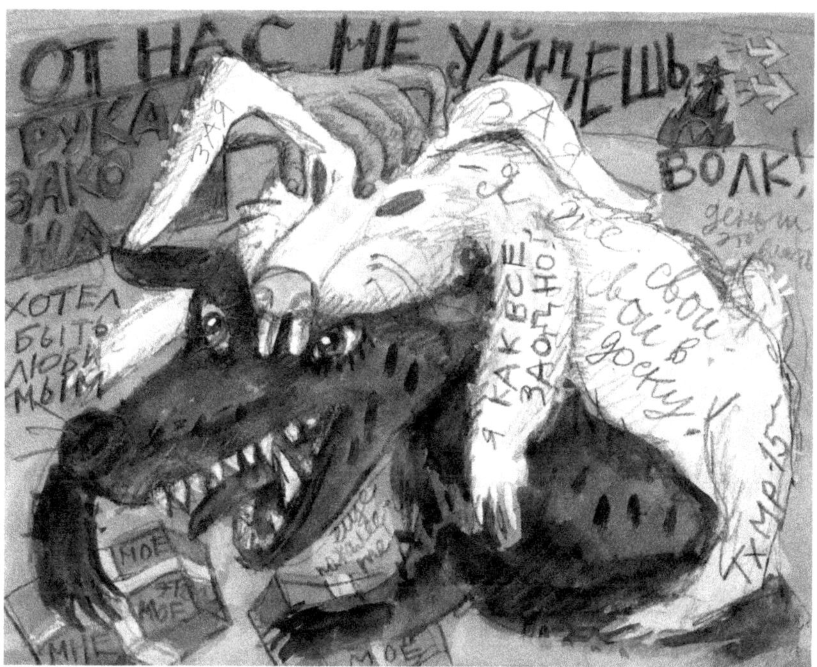


Figure 28. Viktor Tikhomirov, "Wolf, you won't get away from us!" (Ot nas ne uidesh', volk!) (October 2015), political cartoon for *Business St. Petersburg*. Colored drawing.

dynamic of mirroring and mutual amplification of exploitive violence. We should not, however, go too far in emphasizing his view of these archetypes as reducible to analogies that are disguised by masks, which advertise a heraldic dichotomy (much like the contrastive pairing of comedy and tragedy) that are at odds with their deeper affinities and complementarity. Tikhomirov is intent upon demonstrating that wolf and sheep do indeed represent a dichotomy, but not in the usual understanding of victimizer and victim. In a sense, he is after game that is even bigger than the Soviet leadership, or the persistence of its legacy into the present day. Crucial here is Tikhomirov's understanding of a populace that is caught up in a borderline libidinous fascination with authority figures, who themselves are oddly asexual. Such a relationship can only be characterized as dysfunctional, inasmuch as it finds itself locked into a forward momentum that the nonreciprocation of desire does nothing to brake. As in much of world folklore—particularly in West African culture and in rural African American storytelling, exemplified by the figure of B'rer Rabbit—in Russian folklore the figure of the rabbit is an often shrewd and unscrupulous trickster, a comic performer who uses his thespian skills to hoodwink his natural predators. He is also often sexualized, as evinced in incantatory proverbs from the folklore associated with Russian agricultural practice, such as the one in which the winter grain, in need of cooling to offset decay, pleads with the newly fallen snow to mount it like a rabbit: "Oh, white bunny rabbit, come closer and lie on me—while this may be hard for thee, how nice it is for me!"[19]

Or perhaps Tikhomirov's work reminds us that human connection, no matter how slight and circumscribed (whether it involves two people or two thousand) succeeds only to the extent that it is embedded in a larger community, much as the Islamic conception of the *umma* or community of believers becomes a model for all other, smaller scale types of relationships. As Tikhomirov reminds us in his feuilletons about the thuggish crudity of Lenin and the tattered and tainted social contract of Soviet society in periods as seemingly disparate as the early twenties (which he portrays in his picaresque novella *Gold On the Wind* [*Zoloto na vetru*], a quirky blend of garrulous voice-over social commentary and fairy-tale narrative) and the political and economic stagnation of the seventies and early eighties, this shared spirit or ethic of comity within informal associations of individuals inevitably makes itself felt among a wide range of relationships that exist outside of its interstices. In a significant departure from assumptions about group cohesion encouraging hostility to the outside world, Tikhomirov is keen upon portraying empathy for outsiders as a product of sociality within a distinct community.

By far the most prolific member of the Mitki, Tikhomirov uses the media platforms of satirical prose, film, and painting as laboratories for the cultivation of insights about the hidden corners of Russian cultural and political identity in the third decade after the collapse of the Soviet Union. Tikhomirov's attitude toward the Soviet legacy is ambiguous. In a highly representative statement in one of his interviews for this book, he stated that that Soviet films were good for demonstrating that justice can be victorious.[20] Tikhomirov sees his art of visual representation as having a primarily satirical function, as being modally positioned at a jauntily oblique angle against the unruly daily life of a nation burdened with a recent history of multiple collapses and crises. His project is not revolutionary or radical. He is more interested in the granular experience of living with any number of orthodoxies and negotiating among them. What personae and masks can we give ourselves, in negotiating a movement between the unfolding drama between the encroaching spectacle of globalism on the one hand, and the shopworn yet essentially stable conceptions of personal identity on the other? Tikhomirov makes the savoring of visuality in all its forms—of seeing, critical reading, and close observation—the major subject of his work, and the perceptual adjunct to the sociality that occupies the spaces of both his studio and his creative products. Visual representation emerges in Tikhomirov's work as something very close to what Susan Sontag argues is the essence of camp: it is a solvent of high seriousness, a tonic against the sanctimony and self-regard that are as capable of unfolding within a nation as within a person. Why should we think that a country can be any less guilty of vanity than an individual? Tikhomirov's highly varied creative productions are an extended paean to sobriety and to the cessation of dependence on meretricious ideals. As one of the most versatile members of the Mitki, Tikhomirov achieves a higher synthesis of the group's concerns about the perils of collective delusions and self-indulgence. Tikhomirov uses the multimedia platform of his work to communicate an idiosyncratic understanding of autocracy, as a social and institutional practice representing a form of substance abuse.

In his film *Chapaev Chapaev*, Tikhomirov presents us with a novel understanding of the hero of both the Vasiliev brothers' 1929 *Chapaev* (notable for being an early Russian sound film) and of the cultural typology of the Russian civil war itself. How can we disentangle our understanding of the war hero from the film that mythologized him? In this regard, it is notable that Tikhomirov presents us with a Chapaev who appreciates his legendary status more than he should. This Chapaev is a Bolshevik celebrity in the making, and on the make. He is an ideological contradiction in terms, a figure who fights for collectivist values while advancing a self-image that includes among its selling points a pungent vanity and obnoxious self-regard. Much like Ostap Bender—that other, and seemingly antipodal, hustler and con-artist anti-hero of the twenties—Tikhomirov's Chapaev is a press agent for himself—a "grand strategist" (*velikii kombinator*), in the phrase of Bender's creators, the satirists Ilf and Petrov—who looks to celebrity during a time when money has begun to lose its value. This Chapaev is frivolous and narcissistic; he is interested solely in the production of his own persona, which emerges as a negative-image version of Walter Benjamin's notion of the flâneur, here transposed from the contemplation of an actual urban space, with its overflowing possibilities for archiving impressions, to the sparsely furnished space of an aspiring dandy, who has scant interest in his social environment. In this film, Chapaev's view of himself as no one's fool is precisely what results in him becoming one. In sharp contrast to the Vasiliev brothers' Chapaev—whose language seems primitive and direct in a way that contrasts sharply with the rhetorical poeticisms of the White officers who fight him, and with the stark bureaucratic locutions of the commissar sent to educate him—this Chapaev is a cultural worker engaged in the creation of specular commodities. Early in Tikhomirov's film, Chapaev decides to be the director of his own film. He is particularly enamored of himself as a man of words: as he ludicrously intones at one point of the film "I am a Poet!" (*Ya—Poet!*).

As we have seen, one of Tikhomirov's narrative objectives is to address the potential for entropy and decline. Approaching the problem in a way that is different from some of his contemporaries, he refuses to attribute cultural dissolution to political reforms or system change. As he tells us, the forces that precipitate failure and self-destruction are always here, and there is no point in attributing them to policies such as perestroika, glasnost, or the fitful attempts during the early nineties to decentralize the Russian state. In this sense, Tikhomirov, like his Russian contemporary the filmmaker Alexei Balabanov, seems to hew to a conservative understanding of evil, viewing the potential for its eruption as being largely independent of any set of social or economic circumstances. Tikhomirov attempts to demonstrate the ways in which appeals to simplicity and nostalgia are fraught with pitfalls. For one thing, the actual practice of simplicity quickly jettisons nostalgia, seeing in it a state of alienation from the experience of immersion in the present.

Yet simplicity grinds and strips the gears of modernity as well. In its emphasis on routine as a thinner for the coagulated networks of electronically mediated social relations, simplicity rejects both the longing for the past—which contains, after all, the affective consensus of imagined communities—and the utopian perspectives of social relations that are optimized for what Vladimir Shinkarev terms the "aesthetic enchantment" of money.[21] In a wide range of respects, Tikhomirov and Shinkarev emerge as a particularly important pairing of conceptualists within the Mitki. As Shinkarev explains, money is the one force that rebels against humanity, insofar as it declares the end of history with the triumph of a neoliberal project that sees all realms of creative labor as fueling the engine of commerce, even in situations where nothing is being specifically bought or sold. No matter—all forms of human congress are mere grist for the mill that pulps relations into base material for the leavening of a market product. In his critique of the capitalist utopianism that is implicit in Francis Fukuyama's celebrated notion from the early nineties of the "end of history" (formulated in part from observations of the collapse of the governments of the East Bloc), Shinkarev in his 2010 book *The End of the Mitki* explains that the aesthetic enchantment of money is an event that can happen only once in regard to a particular product. As he puts it, we painters and sculptors need to seek out and find that place "where there is no money, to isolate and protect [*uberech'*] from money at the very least a parcel [*klochok*] of reality."[22] Filling some of the gaps in Shinkarev's reasoning, we find ourselves contemplating the instrumentalization of all human relations, as a series of actions that are orchestrated in the manner of an assembly line, into the production of a commodity. From this realization, we come to an understanding of all solitary and communal activities within creative labor as being nothing more than preambles to a transcendent singularity. What, then, is simplicity? Shinkarev invokes the concept, without using the actual term, in his characterization of artistic labor as a series of random gestures that are fundamentally autonomous, with each of them having a value separate from their contribution to the making of an artifact. For both Shinkarev and Tikhomirov, seeing, reading, and communicating with others either in oral or written form are fundamentally primitive acts, taking place within a social network that Svetlana Boym, in an expanded reference to Hannah Arendt, characterizes as "experiments in thinking" or "passionate thinking." These are shared activities, yet in a rather special sense: they are communal and have nothing to do with the "totalitarianism of two" that lies at the center of romantic or erotic love.

It is at this point that we newly encounter the puritanism of the Mitki and come to a clearer understanding both of its significance as a structural principle in their worldview and of Tikhomirov's multilayered portrayal of sexuality as a morally neutral and therefore explosive force, which is no less violent than the impulses that drive mass hysteria and authoritarian political systems. Like others among the Mitki, Tikhomirov regards sexuality as a divisive force. Sexuality offers up the prospect of the two as a surrogate for collectivism or communality, for what fin de siècle aphorist and religious philosopher Vasili Rozanov (arguably, like Lev Tolstoy, an important influence on the Mitki from the prerevolutionary era) describes as consciousness of justice (*spravedlivost'*) that flourishes among women and men who abjure their sexual selves.[23] It is this conscious choice of shutting down sexuality that opens up our understanding of freedom, as a state of being that is, in Boym's terms, a "liminal adventure in unpredictability." In the universe of Tikhomirov's work, sex is much like any number of controlled substances: a medium that offers the prospect of transcendence while rarely actually providing it. Like the cult of simplicity that lies at the center of what may be characterized as the ideology of the Mitki, sexuality represents a constellation of beliefs that are as much the crystallization of cultural constructs as they are the outgrowth of untidy experience. The fact that the Mitki view sexuality as an artificial conceit in no way mitigates its capability for creative destruction. Cultural constructs are no less able to wreak havoc for being artificial and biopolitically manufactured. The idealizations of simplicity and Tolstoyan countervitalism that we find in the work of the Mitki in general, and in Tikhomirov's multigenre production in particular, are fraught with the power to dismantle and destroy.

In many of Tikhomirov's canvases, female sexuality holds a special power to disrupt and reassemble the world, surpassing that of men. In the 2007 collaborative canvas titled *Sisters, or A Woman's Lot*, which has panels by nine different Mitki depicting aspects of gendered existence as perceived by different members of the group (including three women artists), Tikhomirov paints a voluptuously female angel flying from the grasping hands of bearded men with lupine snarls that recall his characterization of Stalin from his cycle *Legends about the Revolution* (Figure 29). Here, because the predators do not have a specifically political character, the wolf-like figures possess an affect of sexuality that is not overtly represented in Tikhomirov's portrayal of political leaders. As Bakhtin argues, the job of satire is to offer up a corrective to the world by drawing attention to the slippage between actual people and their literary instantiations. Wolves and their prey therefore inevitably represent possibilities of identities rather than any specific identity. What interests Tikhomirov is not so much the idealist understanding of satire, famously expressed by Schiller as the fitful glimpsing of a higher reality through the thicket of an imperfect one, but rather the Bakhtinian idea of satire as a form of representation that is genuinely capable of transforming the world. In his panel of this painting, Tikhomirov provides us with an instructive portal onto the grotesque spectacle of predatory sexuality.

At the very least, *Chapaev Chapaev* offers up options for the creative dismantling of social and gender roles. One of the main characters in the film is a patriotic woman named Matryona who dresses as a man, calling herself Petka ("Pete"), to join the side of the Reds in the civil

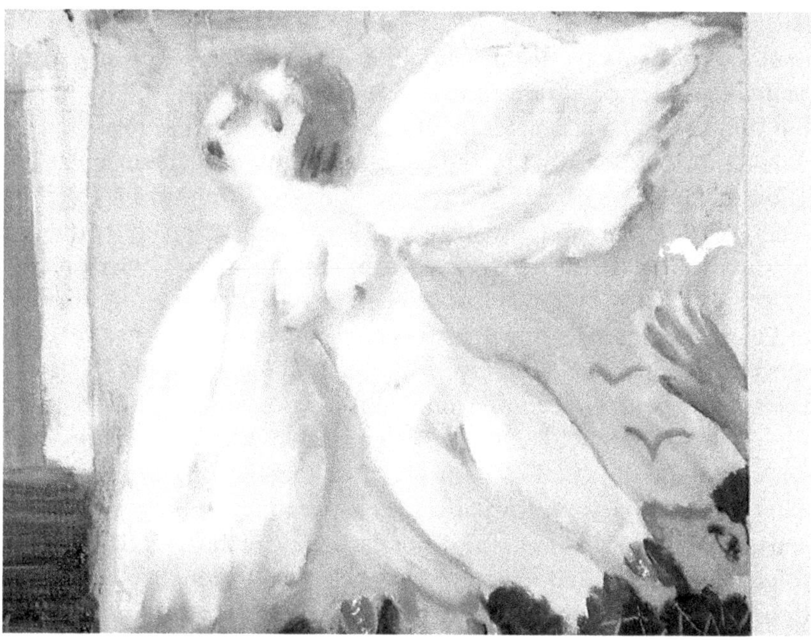

Figure 29. Detail from *Sisters, or A Woman's Lot* (2006), panel by Viktor Tikhomirov.

war. As the critic Lilya Nemchenko notes in her perceptive review of *Chapaev Chapaev* for *Kinokultura: New Russian Cinema*, "the majority of the film's protagonists 'tries on' several roles, as if trying on a costume," and that also goes for the actor Semen Semyonovich Voron, who plays the role of Chapaev in Tikhomirov's reimagined filming of the protagonist within the Vasiliev brothers' *Chapaev*. As Nemchenko points out, Voron "is an erotomaniac, a narcissus [*sic*], a demagogue and a coward" who falls very much into the mold of the Soviet-era "trickster" as characterized by Mark Lipovetsky, as a figure representing the creatively hybridic attributes of "ambivalence, liminality," a love of the flamboyantly performed "artistic gesture," and a "link to the sacral" that emerges from his asocial épatage. And why shouldn't a clown be allowed to be as outrageous as possible?

Many aspects of Tikhomirov's film reinforce this notion, including several that Nemchenko does not discuss in her otherwise thorough analysis. The name "Voron" ("raven") draws attention to the predatory nature of the character playing Chapaev and links him to the ravens in Russian folk poetry and music, feeding on dead or dying heroes who have fallen in battle. By casting "Chapaev" less as a revolutionary figure than as a particularly fulsome and nihilistic anarchist—evocative of the *hajduk*-like Nestor Makhno, who fought against both the Reds and the Whites, or the character of Sidorov in Isaac Babel's story "Italian Sunshine," whose only ideological attachment is to violence itself—Tikhomirov engages in a dethroning of Soviet-era heroic ideals that seems, as Nemchenko shrewdly notes, long "overdue" given the quarter century that has already passed since the collapse of the Soviet Union.

Yet Tikhomirov's film is less an elegy than it is a stark reevaluation of a genre and its codes, much in the same manner that violent American films such as Sam Peckinpah's *Wild Bunch* (1969) and Ralph Nelson's *Soldier Blue* (1970) were for the John Ford–era Westerns produced under the so-called Hollywood studio system. The overall jocular and slapstick comedic tone of Tikhomirov's film, together with its histrionically melodramatic performances and sporadic yet glaring and self-conscious anachronisms in the historical setting of the twenties (such as references to the Nazis as enemies of the Soviet Union, and characters dancing to Bill Haley's "Rock Around the Clock") cast a shadow onto the mythic aura of the Russian civil war as a foundational moral struggle for the future of the fledgling nation. The role of Voron/Chapaev is played by Ivan Okhlobystin, an actor, former Russian Orthodox priest, and independent candidate for the presidency of the Russian Federation in 2011. In 2013, Okhlobystin placed himself in the center of political controversy with a series of militantly homophobic comments in apparent support of the anti-LGBTQ laws recently drafted by the lower house of parliament. At one public speaking engagement in Novosibirsk from that year, in response to the question "what is your attitude to homosexuals and [the LGBTQ Pride] parades?" Okhlobystin shot back that he would like to "stuff them alive into an oven." Continuing to speak over raucous applause, he said that the acceptance of same-sex love was nothing more than "gay fascism" and that as "a [religious] believer," he could not regard it neutrally or as anything other than an "active danger to [his] children."[24] Although production on *Chapaev Chapaev* was well under way when Okhlobystin made these appalling comments, prior to his casting in the film he was well-known for his starkly authoritarian and reactionary views, which included (among other things) advocacy of the Russian monarchy in its more autocratic and nonconstitutional incarnations.

Certain details in the film, particularly in relation to its source material in the 2010 novel of the same title, point to Tikhomirov's use of

Okhlobystin's public persona as a template for Voron/Chapaev's self-aware thespian exhibitionism and ideological truculence. In one nighttime scene at the bivouac of Chapaev's division, Matryona/Petka repells the sexual advances of a fellow soldier named Vasiliev, who believes her to be a man. Walking in on this attempted assault, with his saber Chapaev slashes Vasiliev neatly—and nonlethally—down the middle of his body (Figure 30). Witnessing this punishment from his cot, the division's commissar for political education idiosyncratically rephrases and misattributes the prohibition against same-sex love in Leviticus 20:13: "Karl Marx, for example, teaches us what? 'Men who lie with each other as with a woman—both commit a vile act, and let both be given over to death!'"[25] Later in the film, Vasiliev wakes up in the military hospital, catatonically removes the bandages from himself, and signs the medical report not with his own name but with those of the "Vasiliev Brothers," who would eventually make the classic 1934 film *Chapaev* (Figure 31). In both his novel and the screen adaptation, it is curious that the trauma visited upon the homosexual Vasiliev results in him taking on a schizoid character, exchanging sexuality for the identity of artists.

There is more, however, to this episode in the narrative of both the novel and film. Vasiliev's sexuality is repressed by having him split in two, and it is this mitochondrial cell division that transforms him into a cinematic artist. All the same, we viewers and readers are disturbed by the affectless manner of the traumatized Vasiliev, who now seems to take on a wide range of human responses only through his labor as a film director. We get the sense that Tikhomirov is representing here a distinct genealogy of human faculties, a narrative about the convoluted relation of sexuality to creativity. Okhlobystin's Voron/Chapaev and the homosexual Vasiliev become parents to the zygote that emerges as the Vasiliev twins, with Vasiliev (coded as "female" by virtue of his sexual orientation) being fertilized by the phallic sabre of the virile Chapaev. The presence of the publicly homophobic Okhlobystin in the role of Voron/Chapaev—and Tikhomirov's problematization of the "normative" violence of even male heterosexuality—draw our attention to the ambiguity of desire, with violent homophobia in *Chapaev Chapaev* existing as a mask for unconscious same-sex desires. Both in the novel and the film, Tikhomirov makes us aware of this ambiguity, with Chapaev's scream after slicing Vasiliev: "I'll do away [*razvedu*] with your pederasty in the division!" The turn of phrase is quite peculiar here, given that the verb (inf. *razvesti*) is so manifold in its secondary

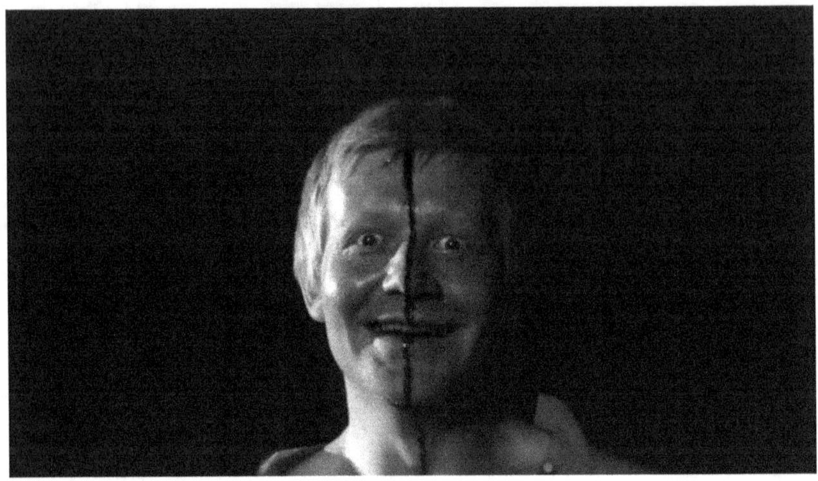

Figure 30. The "split" Vasiliev, still from Tikhomirov's *Chapaev Chapaev*.

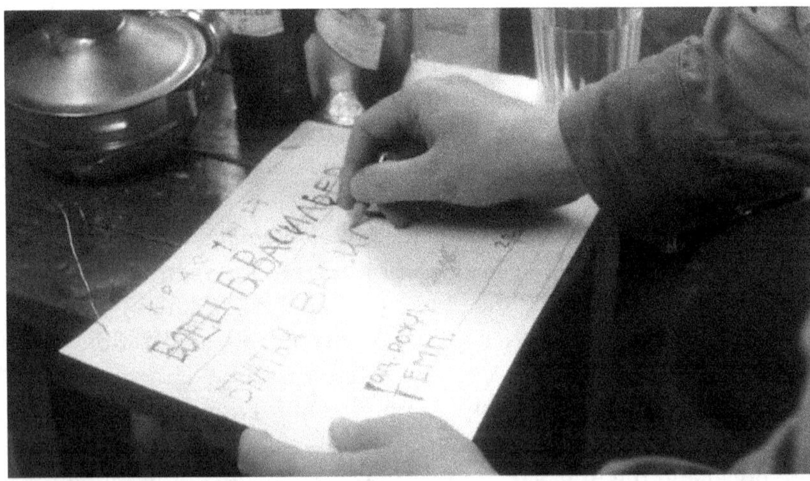

Figure 31. The Red Army soldier Vasiliev refers to himself in writing as the "Vasiliev Brothers," still from Tikhomirov's *Chapaev Chapaev*.

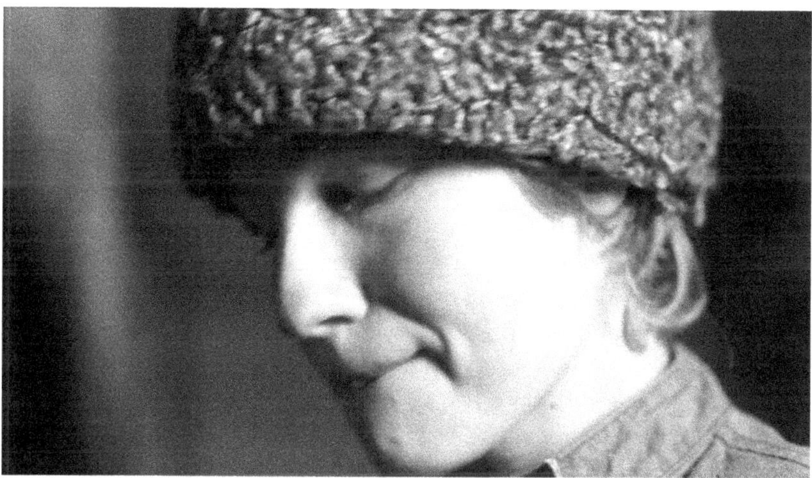

Figure 32. Matryona/Petka, still from Tikhomirov's *Chapaev Chapaev*.

meanings, suggesting "cultivate" and "spread" as much as it does "dissolve" or "nullify." Is Chapaev unwittingly promulgating or expressing "pederasty" with this violent act? Much in the same manner that Eve Kosofsky Sedgwick argues that same-sexual desire in Melville's *Billy Budd* ultimately dissolves the binary opposition of the knowledge/unawareness of homosexual impulses within an all-male setting, so does Tikhomirov suggest that it is impossible for men to abjure their need for sexual contact when they are among themselves. Indeed, shortly after his punitive wounding of Vasiliev, Chapaev himself plies Matryona/Petka with cloying and inappropriate compliments, telling her that she "smells fresh." Like Vasiliev, Chapaev does not know that Petka is a woman (Figure 32). In the version of this scene from the novel, we are told that "recently, the commander slept more and more with private Petka under the same coat, on the floor," and on this occasion he asks her/him to sidle up to his back, exclaiming with barely concealed erotic affect "how I love to sack out [*drykhnut'*] with you!" Viewing this entwined pair from a bunk, the recently enlisted volunteer Anna—who is the only recognized woman in the division—gazes lustfully at Matryona's/Petka's "comely [*prigozhee*] face [and] trembling eyelashes," musing "oh, if I were a man, I too would be able to invite him under [my] overcoat, and to embrace him hotly."[26] Tikhomirov employs the plot device of the concealment and misrecognition of gender identity as a way of drawing attention to the presence of same-sex desire among both men and women, configuring the affective love triangle of Petko/ Chapaev/Anna in a manner that is reminiscent of the one of Viola/ Orsino/Olivia in Shakespeare's *Twelfth Night*.

Any viewer of *Chapaev Chapaev* who is also conversant with the novel will also, of course, be struck by Tikhomirov's decision to downplay in the film version the homoerotic aspects of the book on which it is based. Perhaps Tikhomirov was thinking about the 2013 law that criminalizes representing or portraying forms of LGBTQ affection. Nonetheless, in both the film and the novel the portrayal of same-sex affection—whether it be openly sexual or, in Sedgwick's terminology, "homosocial"—is surprisingly nonjudgmental. Tikhomirov's representation of same-sex love in *Chapaev Chapaev* is very much of one piece with his portrayal of active heterosexuality: both cleave to a force that is potentially destructive of any coherent sense of self. In 1992 in the Mitki newspaper, Tikhomirov wrote about the fledgling gay rights movement in the newly post-Soviet Russian Federation in a manner that suggests his ambivalence about all overdetermined understandings of sexual identity:

> Homosexuals—and what a lengthy name it is!—are also sympathetic. . . . It goes without saying that these unfortunates [*etikh bedolag*] should not be subjected to abuse [*travle*], and that to call them by shortened words is not worth the trouble. But can it be that this is what things are all about? I have no wish to venture into an intellectual consideration of this theme. As a man, [the idea of homosexuality] is traumatizing to me. A significant number of "uncertain" [*neustoichivykh*] men might find themselves going astray, because this theme is nothing less than a gambling with death [*rod igry v smert'*]. . . . And as far as humanity is concerned, if anything will save it, it won't be homosexuality or necrophilia, but something else that is a bit more banal.[27]

Tikhomirov wrote this essay during the public discussion about the possibility of repealing the anti-homosexuality law that had been grandfathered into the criminal code of the Russian Federation after the collapse of the Soviet Union the previous year; within a scant ten months of Tikhomirov's essay, on April 29, 1993, President Yeltsin would sign the bill eliminating that law. While Tikhomirov's understanding here of homosexuality as a form of necrophilia and self-destruction has clear antecedents in the international hysteria over the

AIDS pandemic and older Russian homophobic writing (particularly Rozanov's fanciful essay "Moonlight People" ["Liudi lunnogo sveta"]), we may also regard his response as both an expression of his general sexual ethics and the aesthetics of the Mitki and other St. Petersburg artistic movements, particularly Evgeni Yufit's association of Necrorealist artists. As Alexei Yurchak points out,

> The necrorealists' [*sic*] references to the zone between life and death, between sanity and insanity, between healthy citizens and decomposing bodies was a refusal not only of the authoritative discourse's boundary between bare life and political life, but of the whole discursive regime in which the boundary was drawn. The Mitki's practices achieved the same. They looked like good Soviet citizens who obeyed the law and were content with everything; however, in fact they downgraded themselves to the level of bare life.[28]

Tikhomirov's characterization of male homosexuality can be understood as an assessment of it as a practice that has epistemic dimensions, posing the question about the exact location of the boundary separating life from death. Arguably, such an assessment of one form of sexuality has much in common with the Leningrad Necrorealists' aesthetics of semantic and existential indeterminacy. One of their public performance pieces from the mid-eighties involved the simulation of homosexual rape near suburban railroad tracks, with men "wearing sailors' jackets, with pants pulled down to their ankles and heads swathed in bloody bandages." As Yurchak writes, "the bizarre sight in the middle of a deserted countryside must have left engine drivers bewildered and confused," as it resulted in "the trains react[ing] with loud hoots, while moving away at a high speed."[29] In his statement above, Tikhomirov may be elaborating upon the Necrorealists' provocative rhetorical framing of homosexuality as an aspect of life within military organizations such as the navy. Without minimizing or underestimating Tikhomirov's hostility to what he regards as a personal choice of lifestyle, we can also interpret his reservations about homosexuality as an expression of his view about sexuality in general, as an outcome of an accident—or, as he puts here, as an instance of gambling (*igra*, "game") with the forces of chance. Given the reluctance of many gay men and women in Russia at that time to view their sexuality as an all-encompassing identity—and Tikhomirov's own history of warm relations with queer artists, singers, and filmmakers in Russia, particularly Timur

Novikov—his question "can it be that this is what things are all about?" can be understood as a query about the wisdom of regarding sexuality as a desideratum for any thoroughgoing self-definition.

To be sure, Tikhomirov's interest in the utopian possibilities of divesting social roles of their traditionally associated gender markers—or of switching those markers among men and women, reversing the polarity of cultural constructs that ordinarily rule over their lives—is very much a goal of the Mitki as a movement. Tikhomirov views himself both as a member of a group and as embodiment of one; he is both an alumnus of the Mitki and a one-person artisanal trust of film director, painter, and writer. As we have seen in earlier chapters, asexuality emerges as a model for a communal ethos in the work of the Mitki. The American critical theorists Lauren Berlant and Lee Edelman have recently argued for the exploration of a "sex without optimism," one that jettisons the redemptive narrative of carnal joy or the idea of physical intimacy as a reprieve or relief from social anomie and unhappiness. Yet as Berlant points out, personal or cultural practices that bear no relation to sexuality do not necessarily evacuate or exclude it. She notes that "relief, play, interruption, glitchiness . . . can provide a space of interest" within which "other rhythms" and "forms of encounter with and within sexuality can be forged."[30] In many ways, Berlant's articulation of this idea of what we may term the liminality of asexuality in cultural practices has many affinities with the understanding of sexuality that we see in the work of the Mitki. We see examples of love informed by sexual intimacy in the Florenskys' graphic work (both in the representation of themselves as an artistic partnership and in the patent sexual agency of some of the figures in their drawings, paintings, and sculptures) and even in the distinctive mix of gallows humor and fairy-tale lyricism of the world that Shinkarev sketches out in his prose, where erotic love is portrayed as a powerfully affective—if at times distant—ideal for the physical closeness and warm amity among the Mitki.

This network of associations is most evident in Tikhomirov's most recent major project, his 2017 novel *Eugene Telegin and Others*. An ambitious updating of Pushkin's novel in verse *Eugene Onegin* to the setting of youth cultures in seventies-era Leningrad, *Eugene Telegin and Others* portrays the Soviet state as sclerotic and largely irrelevant to the ways in which people go about their daily business. Tikhomirov's novel contains no true believers or patriots, only disenchanted former conservatives (such as Eugene's dying uncle, who destroys his Leninist and Stalinist memorabilia after reading Solzhenitsyn) and young people who don't give a toss about the values of the Pioneers and the Komsomol. Here, as in other places in Tikhomirov's work, human goodness and comity emerge unprompted by the administrative state, which is helpless in stemming the tide of youth movements that are intent upon creating their own mythologies. "Even the interference of the General Secretary [of the Communist Party] himself," we are told, was ineffectual in eradicating the interest in Western rock music.[31] Pushkin's early nineteenth-century bored aristocrat is transformed into a compulsive reader of antiquarian editions and an avid listener of the Beatles, Rolling Stones, and Jethro Tull. Unlike Pushkin's Onegin, Tikhomirov's Telegin experiences a specific kind of boredom: he is only bored by Soviet cultural normativity, which he opposes partially as a gesture of rebellion against his divorced parents. At his deceased uncle's dacha, he listens to recordings on his "Chaika" reel-to-reel tape player and spends time with a young nonconformist artist with the droll name of Vladimir Lenin—Tikhomirov's version of Pushkin's Lensky. A yawning gap in class exists between Telegin (whose parents are well-travelled and belong to the Soviet elite), on the one hand, and Vladimir and the sisters Tatiana and Olga on the other.

Most relevant to our discussion here is the midpoint of the novel, where Tikhomirov stages Vladimir's jealous fit over Eugene's flirtation with Olga at a lakeside dance party with music provided by Telegin's tape player. The effect of the music upon the young people is both erotic and utterly commanding, filling the listeners with a "harsh rhythm" (*zhestkii ritm*) that contributes to Vladimir's jealous rage:

> Blood pounded in his temples and ears like hot mallets. The spectacle of the bent knees [of the dancers] had become intolerable, as if they were anonymous, and all one. All of a sudden, such movements and body contacts seemed to him in the highest degree indecent, and worse than the most shameless embraces and kisses. All these dances immediately struck Volodya as outrageous and vile.[32]

Tikhomirov frames this moment as the thoughts of someone who has an epiphany about the nature of such music, precisely at the instant that he is most under its influence. Tikhomirov conflates the moments of the break in the friendship with the death of Eugene's friend, who here—in contrast to Pushkin's novel—dies not at Eugene's hands, but as the result of his own violent fit of rage. With a log in his raised hand, he charges at Eugene, who turns away from him. Vladimir falls headlong into the rocky shallows of the lake, and is fatally concussed. Earlier in the novel, the narrator makes statements about the buried eroticism of music that distinctly recall Tolstoy's story "The Kreutzer Sonata": "from the very moment" of hearing this new kind of music, Eugene had the sense of living a "new, other kind of life." "And he wasn't the only one who felt this—it was true for his [entire] generation as well."[33]

The author's attitude toward rock music is ambivalent. Much of the music in the novel emerges as a healthy version of *stiob*, the Russian rhetorical practice of folding theatricalized mockery into statements and patterns of behavior that are at the expense of an anxious mainstream. As the early Russian rock critic Aleksandr Zhitinski observes about the Leningrad music scene, it was easy for some to see in *stiob* something criminal, which in fact was noting of the sort. "The concept of *stiob* is profound and ramified"; it was "one form of defending oneself from 'adults' or, to be more precise, fools." Zhitinski sees the rhetorical stance of *stiob*—which was highly representative of the rock circles in the city before the collapse of the Soviet Union—as built on a "subtle imperturbable irony, and on a desire to jeer at those fools."[34] Yet Zhitinski also stresses that *stiob* may have nothing to do with blasphemy or enacted disrespect and in some instances could simply be an effort to add some whimsy and lightness to a difficult life. In *Eugene Telegin and Others*, Tikhomirov communicates the full range of the puckish humor and open, unceremonious camaraderie among the musician characters.

Nonetheless while Tikhomirov admires the way that this youth cultue rebukes the stuffiness and hypocrisy of the older generation of Soviets and inserts social values into spaces vacated by those of a stagnating administrative state and official cultural order, he is appalled by its encouragement of what another character in the novel, a spectacle-wearing rabbit (Tikhomirov's nod to magical realism, as well as to Russian folk fables) calls the "oppressive passions" of human beings.[35] The fact that the main agent of violence in the novel is someone with the name Vladimir Lenin makes complete sense within the scheme of sexualized violence that Tikhomirov establishes in his varied work as a whole.

*Eugene Telegin and Others* and Tikhomirov's parable-like anecdotes about Lenin and Stalin's crypto-lecherous rapacity serve to remind the reader that the appreciation of the autonomy and identity of others is as much a political act as it is moral one. In his 2004 documentary *Sokurov*, Tikhomirov devotes special attention to Sokurov's statements about sexuality. Tikhomirov begins this segment of the film with a statement by the Necrorealist artist Yufit, who asks him "you like women, right?" Sokurov, Yufit goes on to say, "has killed all of that within himself" (*a on eto vse v sebe ubil*). Tikhomirov follows Yufit's elliptical comments with an ominous clip of a charging mastiff, and Sokurov's discussion of sexuality as destructive of one half of every person. Sokurov states in the film that men are particularly vulnerable to what he calls the upheaval or "perturbed tragedy" (*smiatennaia tragediia*) of sexual experience, which inevitably results in a failure to understand the beloved as a separate person.[36] Tikhomirov consistently portrays sexual experience as a wobbly fulcrum, equally capable of representing a wondrous balance of social impulses or a calamitous upturning of them. As different as they are as artists, there is no question that Tikhomirov's understanding of the suggestibility (*vnushaemost'*) of consumers of culture has clear affinities with Sokurov's complex puritanism. In the world of Tikhomirov's cinema, prose, and graphic work, sexuality is often more related to terror and violence rather than to love; it certainly has no bearing upon kindness, generosity, or communal good will, and in fact, it seems more closely allied, as already shown, to the mass hysteria that buoys closed societies. In his paintings, Russian folktales such as the story of Masha and the Bear—which are normally more resistant to Freudian interpretations than their counterparts in European folklore—are sexualized to an extent that suggests more the work by an Expressionist steeped in Krafft-Ebing than the naïve fauvism that characterizes the paintings of the other Mitki artists. Both homosexuality and heterosexuality result in a trauma to the self and threaten the links to that most natural of fellowships: the sense of shared humanity.

Certainly, in Tikhomirov's paintings the warning about the harm that powerful or thuggish men can do to women is ever-present. We may say about Tikhomirov's creative diary what Marina Tsvetaeva said about the rural primitivism of Natalia Goncharova's paintings: that it draws attention to the ways in which raw instinct, within certain media and modes of expression, may run roughshod over the modern social contract and common decency. In Tsvetaeva's view, Goncharova could forgive nature anything, and viewed its incandescent power with grim fascination, if not awe; within Tikhomirov's work, cinema can play a special role in demystifying false idols, which painting and even literature is incapable of doing. Why is film—and documentary filmmaking in particular—so useful for his new enlightenment project? In partial response to this question, one might observe that the representatives of high culture whom Tikhomirov chooses as the subjects of his films (Kuraev, Sokurov, the classical pianist Polina Osetinskaia, and the Nabokov specialist Boris Averin) are all keen to communicate their values and experiences to a socially wide range of others, and that they are committed to what they see as the promise of a democratic culture. Yet to fully answer this final question about Tikhomirov's work, we may want to bear in mind the semiotician Yuri Lotman's assertion, from early in his career, about the ways in which a language-based description of an object may have a transformative affect upon it: "One and the same system can find itself in a state of both ossification and plasticity. Moreover, the very act of description can switch the second of these two back into the first."[37] Once again, we are back in the interactive world of the Mitki, where the mechanism of collaboration becomes the engine for a certain kind of purification of language and image, and where the simplicity and almost Cartesian self-consciousness about the content of one's beliefs may solidify into a useful tool for sculpting it.

In this regard, the attention that Tikhomirov devotes in his films to the craft and skill of the interview process, particularly as it unfolds in the space of the studio where he paints, is especially important. In films such as *Andrei Kuraev: Direct Speech*, Tikhomirov documents how people learn to listen and respond. The creative diary of Tikhomirov's work—which he thematizes as emerging from his studio and personal exhibition space, with its peculiar mixture of commerce, misunderstanding, and unforced amity—serves as something of a rebuttal to the nineteenth-century thinker Nikolai Fyodorov's portrayal of the Russian city as an "agglomeration of unbrotherly relations" (*sovokupnost' nebratskikh otnoshenii*), and the Russian museum—an institution that, in Fedorov's view, had strong urban roots—as a "passive," mortuary-like repository of artifacts.[38] Tikhomirov brings urban community and exhibition space into an unexpected relation with each other, demonstrating how, in Lévy's words, "The intelligent city not only listens to its environment but also to itself and its internal variety."[39] Given the recent direction of Tikhomirov's work, one wonders if his creative diary will someday become the subject of a film. Such a film, about urban sociality itself, could serve as a counterexample to what Shinkarev, in one of his essays about St. Petersburg, describes as the maleficent "contemporary reality [*sovremennost'*] that eats into the body of the city."[40]

# Conclusion

## Icarus Rising, or The Mitki against Twenty-First-Century Russia

I would like to speak about the idea of correction. . . . Yet again I find myself convinced that [the only] possible genuine education for Russia would be one in which it educates itself.

NADEZHDA TOLOKONNIKOVA, at the inquest against Pussy Riot for the crime of insulting the feelings of religious believers (Mordovian Supreme, July 2013)[1]

I would like to serve as loam
For future circumspect days;
So that a decent young person
Would grow from my soil;

For a fine young person
Who scorns the dime of others
assessing things with maddening clarity—
Declaring "I love you!," come what may.

DMITRI PRIGOV, from his collection *The Organs of Power* (*Organy vlasti*)[2]

From its beginnings, the Mitki have represented a movement that prided itself on not being a child of its times. This noncorrespondence with the prevailing ethic of a particular setting and period raises many questions about the character of the status quo against which they set themselves. Just what is the dominant order of the day, whose strictures drive people to establish counterexamples? Such a question is more fraught and tricky than one might think. The great antinomian model of many youth groups that have responded in different ways to the booms and cracks of shifting geopolitical alliances, such as the Suez Canal crisis of 1956–57, the end of the Cold War, the collapse of the Soviet Union, and protest movements that erupted on Tiananmen and Tahrir Squares, posed questions that were as much about self-definition as they were about their emerging formulation of aversion to entrenched political orthodoxies. It is easy enough to say what we don't like, and what we can't abide in the social environment that we inhabit; it is quite something else to say what we stand for, in a manner that comprehends our identity as transcending mere reaction. Our political identity takes shape the moment that we rebel against a specific order of things—or, at the very least, at the instant that we are pushed to reject a particular normative modality. This antinomian turn often results as a response to one of two rather different sets of circumstances: a particularly egregious event or legislative measure (such as the Tsar's guard shooting on an unarmed crowd on "Bloody Sunday" in 1905 or the Whiskey Rebellion in the United States in 1791) or a political conflagration sparked by a circumstance that initially seemed trivial or external to the simmering malaise (such as the precipitation of the Easter Rebellion in Ireland by Germany's build-up to the first World War). Yet this entire way of conceptualizing the emergence of youth and protest movements suggests that rebellion comes from an uncharted space, as if from nowhere. There seems to be no political or aesthetic identity that does not come from reaction. The event that seems to have triggered the Mitki's formation was the disastrous Soviet campaign in Afghanistan. In his poem "1983," Shagin writes, "How good everything was then!" describing the mood of the year that preceded both the Soviet incursion into Afghanistan and the beginning of their movement. The first visual representation of the Mitki in their own work was Vasili Golubev's 1987 woodcut *The Mitki Send Brezhnev Off to Afghanistan* (Figure 5). As we noted earlier, this image expresses a powerful impulse toward disestablishment of a certain political order. We must never forget that a political turn of events certainly helped to catalyze the movement, even though it may not have wholly defined it.

So, as a group of artists the Mitki do share a genealogy of protest. But does this mean that their legacy, in the divergent avenues of their creative labor, has matured into a model for possibilities of resistance? We recognize protest movements by their pronouncements, which invariably hold up a double-sided mirror, with one side reflecting the problematic world that they live in and the other their performative response to it. Although images play a powerful role in the dissemination of protest, language is often the dominant tool for its projection into the larger world, as viral slogans such as "Black Lives Matter" and "Occupy Wall Street" demonstrate. In a 2006 interview for this project, Viktor Tikhomirov, like many members of the Mitki, underscored the importance of distinguishing between the Mitki as a youth movement from the late eighties and early nineties and as a circle of artists working in various visual media. Here again, we find ourselves confronting the dichotomy of image and word—or, at the very least, the dominance of the former over the latter—in the formation of a counterculture.

Younger artists who have been said to "join" the Mitki in more recent times (based essentially on the fact that their work was included in shows with older members of the group) have largely supported the validity of this distinction. When asked about the legacy and group identity of the Mitki, the young painter and printmaker Irina Vasilieva unpacks a narrative of contrasts that have nothing to do with politics and everything to do with technique and style. "Dmitri Shagin is a remarkable landscape artist [*peizazhist*]," she argues, explaining to me that the particular interest of his achievement lies in his treatment of urban scenes through the lens of an impressionist artist who is steeped in rural subjects.[3] Weighing this discerning assessment, we ask ourselves: What can a movement slogan such as "the Mitki don't want to defeat anyone!" tell us about the consummate crafting of a graphic image and its branding upon our mind's eye? And speaking of branding (in another sense), what does the "brand" of the Mitki, now primarily cultivated by Shagin and the eighties-era Leningrad rock alumnus Vladimir Rekshan, in the performances of their inoffensively nostalgic—if low-wattage—spoken word and musical ensemble "Rekshagina," have to do with the essentially solitary experience of looking at an image, which antimovement art critics (such as Jed Perl in New York, and Lyubov Gurevich in St. Petersburg) emphasize as the sine qua non of appreciation? In a provisional answer to the second of these questions, we may say: not a great deal. Bearing in mind that reading is also a form of looking, we may expand this view to encompass the assessment of literary texts, tipping our hat to Vladimir Nabokov's caustic observation that there is "[no] masterpiece the appreciation of which would be enhanced in any degree or manner by the knowledge that it belonged to this or that school," and that "conversely [there are] any number of third-rate works that are kept artificially alive" by being assigned "to this or that 'movement.'"[4]

In his most recent memoir about the Leningrad of the seventies and eighties, Rekshan appropriately emphasizes the fluid and makeshift character of its underground music and art scene, particularly in comparison with its counterparts in Moscow. Rekshan attributes the loose and less manifesto-driven nature of youth movements in Leningrad to the prominence of café Saigon on Nevsky Prospect. As the Leningrad historian Yulia Valieva points out, a wide range of groups met at the Saigon, where the ethic was raucously dialogic, almost as a matter of principle.[5] Coteries and far-flung "unofficial" networks would routinely find themselves in close contact there, drawn into freewheeling conversations that resulted in a porous structure of countercultural labor in and around the city. Flamboyant individual musicians and artists such as Sergei Kurekhin, the experimental keyboard player and one-time member of the Leningrad-based rock ensemble Akvarium, tended to nestle themselves within ad hoc associations or cooperatives rather than polemical movements. Some groups, such as the Cooperative of Experimental Representational Art (TEII) and Timur Novikov's New Academy of Fine Arts, gave themselves bureaucratic-sounding monikers, in order either to satirize Soviet orthodoxies or camouflage their own nonprescriptive and open-ended creative undertakings. Things were more a matter of style and unruly aesthetic diversity than of any revolutionary impetus. As Rekshan notes, given that artistic Bohemia "is a relative concept," we should not be surprised that so much of unofficial music and art in Leningrad ended up in an "enormous cemetery of unrealized expectations."[6] Seen from this perspective, the Mitki seem to have a tenuous status as a youth movement, a fact that may throw into some jeopardy any understanding we may have of them as a dynamically indeterminate group of visual artists. The perception of them as a youth movement seems to rest primarily on Shinkarev's texts, where such characterizations of the Mitki are too droll to sustain the impetus of an actual social groundswell. At a particularly argumentative point of *The End of the Mitki*, his 2010 obituary for the movement, Shinkarev goes so far as to associate the group's original formation principally not with Dmitri Shagin or a youth-oriented worldview, but with the idea of a catch-all cooperative of nonconformist artists, where the name becomes a bland acronym meaning "Youth Initiative: Work, Culture, Art" (*Molodezhnaia Initsiiativa: Tvorchestvo, Kul'tura, Iskusstvo* [*MITKI*]).[7] For a workable legacy of a youth movement, such conceptual offshoots are meager wings indeed for flying into any future of progressive action.

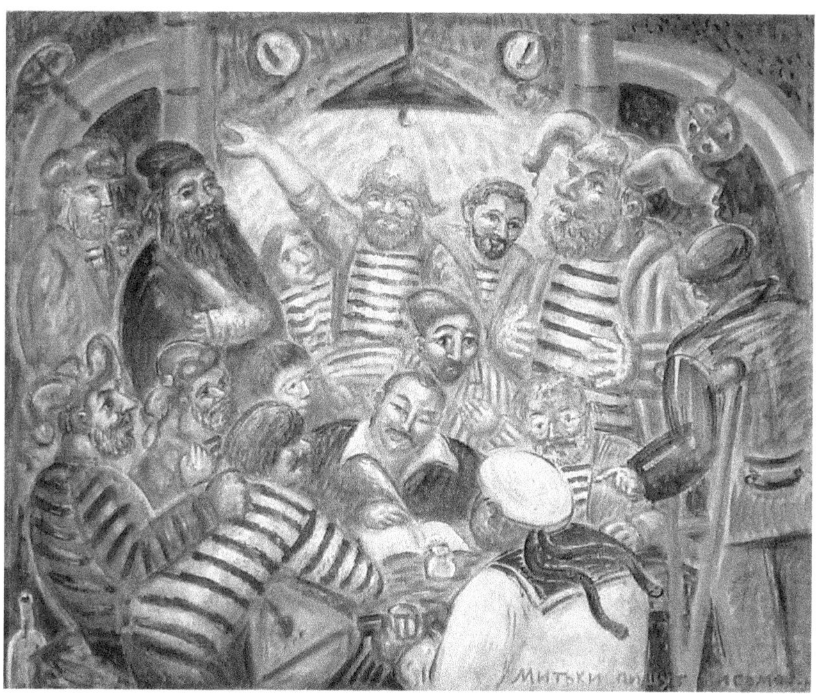


Figure 33. Dmitri Shagin, *The Mitki Write a Letter [to the Oligarchs]* (2006). Oil, 80 × 60 cm. (Mitki Art Center, St. Petersburg, Russia)

This is not to say that the Mitki have camouflaged their distinct markings as an offshoot of the Soviet-era underground, or that they have jettisoned the reflex for public protest. In 2004, Shagin and a few other members of the group made a public spectacle of their opposition to price hikes on food. Shinkarev's Bakhtinian characterization of the Mitki's mythos of the boiler room, as a grappling with the perspective of other voices, appears to reach a culmination of expression in Dmitri Shagin's painting from that year, *The Mitki Write a Letter to the Oligarchs* (Figure 33). Responding to the doubling of the price of bread in the remaining state-owned food stores in St. Petersburg, Shagin based his image on Ilya Repin's famous 1891 painting *The Zaporozhian Cossacks Write a Letter to the Turkish Sultan*. Repin pictorialized the Cossacks' profane rebuttal to Mohammed IV's order that they submit to Ottoman rule. In their 1663 letter, the Cossacks subject the Sultan to a litany of profane abuse, in florid dialect declaring him to be a castrated tomcat, Devil's secretary, and Armenian swine. They conclude the letter with the injunction that the Sultan kiss their backsides.

Shagin organized an exhibit that consisted solely of his painting and his version of the letter, which he wrote in a hilarious mix of Cossack dialect and Mitki slang. At the opening of the 2004 exhibit, Shagin gave a dramatic public reading of the text, displaying it on a strip of white cardboard that points up the humble material means of the group. His letter is a protest against wealthy entrepreneurs who contribute to the dramatic new class differences within Russia. Shagin relies on much of the same bestiary imagery from the seventeenth-century letter, intensifying the scatological and xenophobic elements present in the original and rising to a level of far-fetched invective and ironic self-characterization suggestive of an American poetry slam. The oligarchs are now castrated Alpine goats, Babylonian cooks, Americanoid villains, the bungholes of stallions, and fools who are incapable of herding swine even on a Soviet collective farm. Shagin signs the letter as the Cossack leader (ataman) of the Mitki, "together with all of his factory bunnies [*fabzaichata*]."

In the painting, Shagin underscores the internal diversity of the Mitki within Shinkarev's boiler room, and he has stated in radio and Internet interviews that he wanted to present the Mitki anew, not as a cultish movement of the fringe but as a populist "cross-section of our society." Gone is the strict sartorial conformism of the group as presented in earlier paintings and photo opportunities. The movement chronicler and scribe Vladimir Shinkarev writes the letter, and immediately to his right and left are the artists Aleksandr and Olga Florensky. Aleksandr is wearing a modified sans-culotte cap and Olga a red sweater instead of a sailor's striped shirt. Standing behind her is the Orthodox priest and painter Ivan Sotnikov, also refusing to wear Mitki clothing, and standing above Shinkarev is Mikhail Sapego, poet and editor in chief of the Mitki publishing house Red Sailor. Sapego is known for his unapologetically pro-Soviet views, and here fittingly wears a red jacket and a peaked cap with a star, a style famously worn by Bolshevik troops during the Civil War that followed the Revolution. Shagin himself takes the place of Repin's laughing corpulent Cossack, the earflaps of his winter hat improbably flying like the bells of a fool's cap as he tilts his head upward. The center of the painting's composition is defined as much by color as it is by the positioning of the figures and their contours. Shagin repeats the triangular configuration around which Repin structures his painting, but he anchors it more clearly in the presence of specific figures (Sapego and the two Florenskys). All wear incendiary red to point up their commitment to revolution and their link to the boiler as crucible of transformation, which becomes the source of "danger" and the implement for the greater good that Shinkarev describes in his book. Shagin underscores this connection between the boiler and social change by having Sapego's peaked hat point directly to the boiler's pressure gauge, and by creating a carnivalesque image of himself as a jester figure who is physically larger than anyone else in the room. In portraying himself as a clown staring above the heads of his comrades, Shagin seems to be taking a page from Mikhail Bakhtin, who noted that "carnival laughter points itself upwards, striving for the change of powers and truths, a change of world views."[8]

It is possible that this reentry of the Mitki into the public eye earned them some negative attention. On April 6, 2005, in St. Petersburg, a scandal enveloped the small world of nonconformist art and came to represent the clash between the new, proudly mercantile spirit of Putin's Russia and the aesthetic values of the former Soviet artistic underground. Two private security guards armed with sledgehammers and crowbars came to the Mitki's studio and gallery space on Pravda Street. The guards, hired by the nameless individuals who were suing to privatize the space in order to build an upscale apartment, broke down the front door and burst into the exhibit room. Hearing the commotion, the few artists who were working in their studios ran out and struggled with the intruders, who yelled "Down with the Mitki, the antidemocrats!" throwing down paintings from one of the walls. The intruders fled as soon as the police arrived. Valentina Matvienko, the mayor of St. Petersburg, was moved to make a public statement supporting the group's continued use of the studio space, and the municipal court provisionally ruled on April 21 in favor of extending their lease. Understanding that no publicity is bad publicity, Shagin was quick to use the spotlight of public attention for renewed self-promotion, and for several weeks after the break-in staged a series of press conferences that drew attention to the increasingly harsh real-estate environment in the major Russian cities. At issue was the fact that half of the floor space had been designated as an apartment decades earlier, and yet the Mitki's contract stipulated that it was to be used exclusively as a workspace. With no residential owner at hand, the entire property could technically be put on the market for developers. Unfortunately, even the mayor was unable to stave off the powerful real-estate interests in St. Petersburg, and in the end the Mitki had to give up the space in an out-of-court settlement, in exchange for a museum space in another part of the city.

Shagin's campaign against eminent domain evoked many memories for people of his generation. Leningrad dissidents often saw their autonomy in terms of escaping claustrophobic living and working spaces, and to this day many residents of St. Petersburg continue to live in communal apartments for financial reasons. Writing in a Kafkaesque vein, one Leningrad dissident described the world of conventional life as a room with "two doors, through which pass people, beasts, and things" with a dehumanizing lack of differentiation.[9] The boiler room attendant occupies an underground and possibly oppositional space, unseen by conventional eyes, and yet he provides an essential service for others. Shinkarev likens his production of heat to a farmer reaping a harvest. Although the "sacred space" of the boiler room resembles a monastery more than it does a production line, it does not demand a vow of celibacy, and the attendant can even invite women there. Not having "the opportunity to [interact with others] in the usual way," the boiler room attendant "develops within himself the possibility of interaction on a higher level, through art." A dialogue in fact takes place between the underground and conventional daily life, even though the latter does not publicly recognize its engagement with voices of opposition. The Mitki's literary work reflects an obsession with habitational space, whose potential for fostering creativity exists in inverse proportion to its comfort level and livability.

Shinkarev's assertion that the boiler room has "an atmosphere of healthy anxiety and a certain danger that sharpens all feelings and potentials"[10] should be seen as an expression of the Leningrad artistic underground's metaphoric and sometimes literal search for alternate fields of creative work and self-definition. Dmitri Shagin's father, the important underground painter Vladimir Shagin, was homeless by choice for a period of at least two years in the early sixties. With a like-minded artist friend (the Russian-Jewish Alexandar Arefiev), he scrounged up an existence by collecting empty bottles and living in abandoned workshops and tool sheds; at times they found themselves living in the covered areas located in the city's cemeteries. Like many dissidents, Vladimir Shagin was eventually incarcerated in a psychiatric hospital, where he was subjected to a regime of semi-experimental and excruciating medical treatment. Undoubtedly drawing on his family experience with homelessness and marginalization, Shagin used the 2008 protest against the group's eviction as an occasion for drawing renewed attention to the unjustness of eminent domain in the major Russian cities.

The lawsuit and the attack on their studio space, which took place five years after Shagin's exhibit of the painting, brought the Mitki more palpably into the political present, resulting in the end of their way of life as quasi-squatters. They were co-opted by Matvienko, a close ally of

Vladimir Putin, who in a Faustian bargain presented them with a city-funded museum property that was more handsome but equipped with insufficient studio space. In light of these and other events, there is much about Shagin's 2006 painting that now seems inadequate as a critique of injustice. Shagin's fauvist and sentimentalized presentation of bloated figures—at best, a disingenuous cross-pollination of Soviet and prerevolutionary clichés about Cossacks as loveable anarchists, on the one hand, and idealizations of defiant military nationalism, on the other—falls flat in a Russia overshadowed by morally difficult campaigns in Ukraine and Syria, and dominated by armed forces that routinely brutalize their conscripts and refuse to give an account of their practices to the public. Shagin has subsequently abandoned his public critique of the real-estate industry in Russia, the group's considerable loss of studio space notwithstanding. For *The Arefiev Circle and the Mitki* exhibit, in which he most recently showed his work (February 2–18, 2017, Vellum Gallery in Moscow), Shagin changed the title of the painting from *The Mitki Write a Letter to the Oligarchs* to *The Mitki Write a Letter*, thereby robbing it of its content as a critique of plutocracy. All of this points to the discursive limits of rhetorical nostalgia as a tool of social protest and the need for a post-ironic dissidence that is radically different from the satirical indirection of oppositional models during the last five years of the Soviet Union. Lost in the shuffle of their move from Pravda Street was the predicament of Vladimir Tikhomirov, brother of Viktor and a painter of limited financial means who was living "illegally" in the studio, and who was evicted.

There was much about the loss of this space, in symbolic as well as material terms, that effectively brought the Mitki to an end both as a youth movement and as a school of artists possessed of a distinctive style and aesthetic orientation. The patent decline of the Mitki as an artistic movement since the mid-1990s makes the show-stopping conceit of Shinkarev's 2010 publication of *The End of the Mitki* seem almost superfluous. In 2015, Shagin painted a large canvas titled *Seizure of the Mitki's Studio* (Figure 34). The effectiveness of the painting can be attributed in part to the portrayal of the incident in comic strip panels, an artistic choice that works well with the depiction of himself and his adversaries as possessing rotund, cartoon-like anatomies that seem to push against the tight boundaries of their spaces. Shagin's thematically jocular treatment of what happened was probably made easier by the passage of nine years. By all accounts the incident was genuinely frightening for the people present in the gallery, notwithstanding the perpetrators' comical

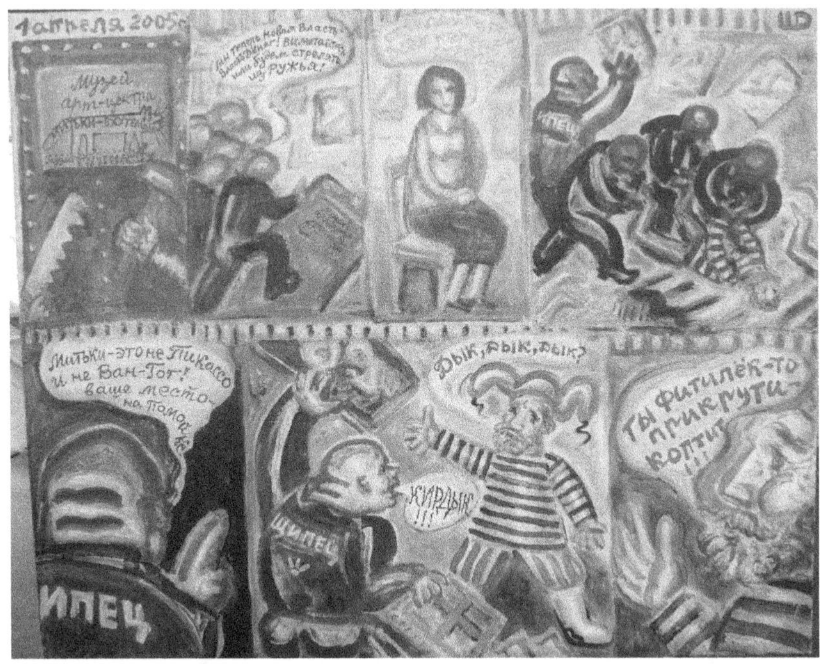


Figure 34. Dmitri Shagin, *Seizure of the Mitki's Studio* (2015). *Translations from upper left to lower right*: (1) "Mitki Art Center" (2) "We're the new power now! Money is power! Clear off, or we'll shoot you with our rifles!" (3) "Go ahead and shoot us, you scum. You can't shoot all of us!" (4) [Attack by thugs, led by one nicknamed "Muzzle" (*shchipets*).] (5) "The Mitki aren't Picasso or Van Gogh! You belong in the garbage dump." (6) "You're finished!" "*Dyk, dyk, dyk!*" (7) "Turn down the wick—it's smoking!" Oil, 80 × 100 cm. (Mitki Art Center, St. Petersburg, Russia)

bellowing of slogans. We see that the Mitki are passing into the category of legend, even within Shagin's own work.

Yet if we view the collective textual and visual work of the Mitki as an expression of a style of cultural being, we see more clearly its continuing implications as a rhetorically sophisticated art of protest. As Nicholas Mirzoeff argues in his wide-ranging scholarship of the emergence of a culture of visuality, the ascendance of digital art would seem to bridge the chasm between word and image, creating a market that is democratic both in its distribution and accessibility of encounter, and in the articulation of a "message" that manages to be both language-based and saliently visual. The Mitki anticipated the calibration of word and image on the square or marketplace of nonconformist literature and art, in a manner that also resonates with the possibilities for agentive consumption that Mirzoeff conjectures in his outlining of visual subjectivity as the point of intersection between "visibility" and "social power."[11] The materiality and risk-taking of the work of the Mitki during the final years of the Soviet Union manifest an awareness of the appreciation of vivid human connection, if not intimacy, among those reading and viewing their work. The risk often took the form of obtaining access to typed manuscripts and visiting apartment exhibits where, in the words of E. M. Orlov, the Director in 2006 of the St. Petersburg Museum of Non-Conformist Art, the "home, apartment, or room could either become a window to infinity or a limitation, a finite space, a dead end."[12] In her scholarship about Soviet-era "unofficial" culture, Ann Komaromi convincingly argues that in samizdat the dividing line between politically dissident and the aesthetic (primarily) literary publications and subcultures was often quite blurred. As she explains, "through their playful subversive projects," artists, fiction writers, and poets often "showed as much interest in preserving culture and defending the author as those serious political dissidents who protested the trial of dissident authors with demonstrations and letters."[13] If nothing else, movements of political opposition teach us that protest takes many forms, which cross boundaries of both medium and genre.

The playfully recombinant and readily generative character of the Mitki slang, with its tendency for the viral-trending reiteration of a sentence in the interrogative mode, is something that could be seen and heard in many street protests in Russia at least until the "Mink Revolution" of 2011–12. In Shinkarev's novella *A Papuan from Honduras*, a binge-watching alcoholic who is unwinding after his work at a factory all of a sudden sees an interview from Paris in which Jean-Paul Sartre behaves and speaks in the deformed lingo and gurgling bass of Dmitri Shagin: "Like [*Dyk*], I ask you, did you prepare for the intervieweree thing [*intervʼiueshchke-to*]?"[14] As early as the late eighties, the practice of deftly unsaddling warhorses of high seriousness, by juxtaposing them with a language that sought to fully verbalize the principles of a resurgent Dadaism, was already firmly in place within the larger circle of people who fraternized with the Mitki. Shinkarev's *A Papuan from Honduras* is a largely third-person narrative that consists almost entirely of accounts of scenes from different movies that the protagonist, Valera Marus (a channel-surfing Oblomov), watches from his cot. The novel is also peculiar for its linking of alcoholism with binging on pop culture. Strangely—and very much in keeping with the Mitki's idiosyncratic glorification of indiscriminate consumption—these activities are regarded as potentially oppositional. The subtitle of the novel, which Shinkarev wrote in 1987 in the boiler room where he worked, is "A Delirium [*Bred*] in Two Parts." At the end of the book, the omniscient narrator makes himself known with the unexpected announcement that the novel "is not a delirium at all, but rather a form of resistance [*soprotivlenie*]—not always successful, and at times seguing into a pandering [*patakanie*] that contributes to an ever-growing encompassing nonsense."[15]

There is much about Shinkarev's supine protagonist that is indebted to the character of Thomas Jerome Newton that David Bowie plays in Nicolas Roeg's *The Man Who Fell to Earth*, a film that plays a key if unacknowledged role in the Mitki's group mythology. Newton, an alien from a planet whose water supply has dried up, can't tear himself away from watching multiple television screens while knocking back alcohol and shouting at the televised images to "leave my mind alone!" Like Shinkarev's protagonists, these practices of overindulgence also confirm Newton/Bowie's outsider status. Asked later in the film by his girlfriend Mary Lou how he can drink so much without ever getting sick, and what happens to him when he drinks, Newton answers, "Because I see things." "What things?" she asks. With a sly smile, he answers, "The bodies of women and men." The ability to see and understand—and to emulate and mime—may come from the practice of excess, whether it be through drink (which was, as we have seen, something of a political gesture during the time of Gorbachev's "dry law") or the avid absorption of the representational possibilities that popular culture offers. Those possibilities include tableaux of unfettered intimacy, both within and across categories of gender and class. One could say of the graphic art and writing of the Mitki what Andrei Sinyavsky once quipped about Nikolai Gogol's story "The Viy": that is a piece of make-believe which foregrounds an almost sexual lust (*vozhdelenie*) to discover things that are hidden out of sight.[16] The iconoclastic Sergei Kurekhin is an example of a musical and performance artist and equal opportunity prankster who fooled television audiences, mainstream journalists, and members of both the Russian liberal intelligentsia and the far right (most notably Aleksandr Dugin) with his earnest musical and mock-political performances.[17] As early as 1984, in the first installment of *Mitki*, Shinkarev refers to Kurekhin as a "buddy-buddy" (*koreshok-koreshok*) of the movement. More recently, and possibly referencing the example of Bowie's public persona, Viktor Tikhomirov characterized Kurekhin's "Pop-Mechanics" concerts as manifesting a palpably alien consciousness (*inoplanetnoe soznanie*).[18] The Mitki's project of resistance consists in part of the disorienting character of their mock-intoxicated mimicry and their willingness to cross affective boundaries into otherwise uncharted spaces of sociality during the years immediately preceding and following the collapse of the Soviet Union.

The treatment of neutral televised statements, as edifices to be ripped apart and reassembled ungrammatically or non-normatively—and to comic effect, often in tandem with amusingly primitive visual images, typefaces, and scrawled phrases, reminiscent of a French Situationist or Punk poster—was often evident in picket signs from the Mink Revolution, and is evocatively similar both to the example above from *A Papuan from Honduras*, and to the group's Dadaist practice of using seemingly nonsensical lines from late Soviet-era film serials as a basis for their slang. A series of demonstrations in and around Moscow from the second half of 2011 featured signs parodying the vapid televised statement of a pro-Putin woman from Ivanovo, who opined that the fact that "we've begun to dress more better [*bolee luchshe* (*sic*)]" is surely a testament to the strong leadership of Russia United. Among opposition groups, the fatuous statement by "Sveta from Ivanovo" went viral in social media postings and picket signs in public demonstrations, resulting in a chain of parodies of her ungrammatical statement: "We've begun to get together / vote [deliberately misspelled as избиратца] / make picket signs more better!"[19] Many of these signs—and those of other protests from the time—draw on the mixed-media conventions of the Mitki's early editions and paintings, distinctive for juxtaposing roughly outlined, faux-primitive images (drawn or cut in the spirit of sketches and collages by Shinkarev and Olga and Aleksandr Florensky) with the visually distorted and malapropistic texts. The humble materials of the cultural signs (in both senses, as placards and symbols) at these demonstrations dovetail with the Mitki's overall undertaking, of creating audiences that become potential constituencies—and therefore partners—in a movement defined by a sprawling horizontal, rather than hierarchical, structure. Nothing could be further from the Putinist conception of the democratization of the state as a process of verticalization that has proceeded with particular momentum since 2007, representing a consolidation of the office of the Presidency at the expense of the independent elected officials from the regions of the Russian Federation that fall outside of the major urban areas.[20] During some of the same demonstrations, it was therefore hardly surprising that the noun *gorizontal'* was coined, used in posters such as one that read "The Horizontal of Our Linked Arms Are Stronger Than the Vertical of

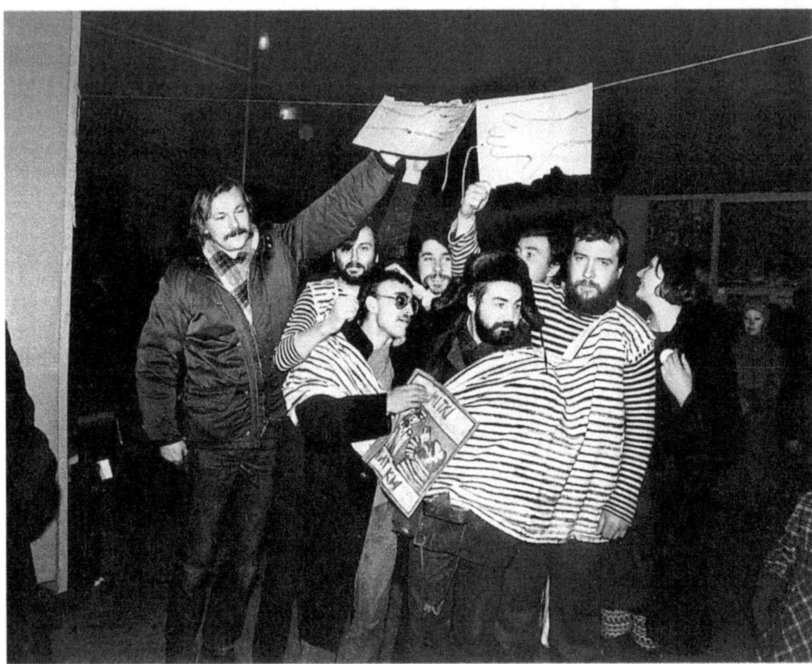

Figure 35. The Mitki at the Gavan art opening, with the New Academicians, taken by Viktor Nemtinov in January 1987.

Power."[21] In this view, true democracy is necessarily unscripted, and never taxonomized into a chain of political being that gains in coherence to the extent that it is removed from the public square of actual human bodies. In the opening for the January 1987 exhibit that they shared with Timur Novikov's New Academicians, the Mitki wrapped themselves in an outsized sailor's shirt and lifted aloft a poster of hands that were poised to shake (Figure 35); two and a half years later, multiethnic residents of the Baltic republics of the Soviet Union formed a human chain of linked arms across their borders, as a demonstration of shared political identity.[22] The linking of bodies that we find in the lore of the Mitki during its decade-long heyday, from the middle of the eighties to the middle of the nineties, teaches us a great deal about the necessity of both goodwill and physical disinhibition for the formation of just communities.

The linking of arms, the lingering embraces—in which, as Shinkarev puts it in his early chapters of *Mitki,* one person stands hugging the other, with "closed eyes, as if falling into a meditation"[23]—is essential for coming to grips with what the protagonist of Ralph Ellison's *Invisible Man* describes as a style of speaking "on the lower frequencies": connecting with those who are fundamentally (and perhaps even oppositionally) different from you.[24] With its multiple African American and Russian points of reference (to, among other texts, Richard Wright's *Native Son* and that most polemically anti-Petersburg of novels, Dostoevsky's *Notes from the Underground*), *Invisible Man* is steeped in an understanding of what we may term political intimacy. Movements of protest play a crucial role in Ellison's novel, as expressions of what could be understood as an eroticized solidarity. While the Soviet-era methods of underground textual transmission and the viewing of "unofficial" art had a bracing tactility and physical directness that has been largely evacuated from present-day forms of interface with the digital marketplace, they did possess an understanding of contact with other, alien agents (who are otherwise at a remove) as having a galvanic, and explosive, character. This artifact—text, painting, print, drawing—comes to me directly from the hands—from the bodies—of other people, and as I view or read it I am close to touching them. In collaboration with the Mityok Aleksandr Florensky for an illustrated edition of Pushkin's *Eugene Onegin*, the Moscow-based conceptualist poet Dmitri Prigov wrote that "the stormy and selfless underground [in the Soviet Union] cultivated an intimate relationship" to the unorthodox texts that it recopied and promulgated from one set of hands to another. Prigov describes this undertaking as one that recalls "the monastic-humble copying of a sacred text," an activity that contributed to the compilation of a larger "sacred text of Russian culture."[25] The samizdat text took the form of a typewritten manuscript printed on tissue papers that were placed between multiple carbon pages; even as a copy, it retained Walter Benjamin's understanding of the "aura of the original" that was otherwise lost in the process of reproduction. The samizdat text was both a physical object commanding attention and a metonym for the mortality and material evanescence of the person responsible for it. Writing about the premature death of his fellow Leningrad-based writer Lev Vasiliev, Viktor Krivulin mused that "[Vasiliev's] physical being had thinned to transparency—the parchment transparency of a typewriter sheet with an unreadable copy of a poetic text."[26]

As Alexei Yurchak observes, the specific image of corporeality that we see in the work of the Mitki is profoundly non-normative: steeped in a lifestyle of bare or minimal existence, the *mitkovian* body is unhealthy and moribund and therefore, like the actors in the performance art of the Necrorealist Evgeni Yufit, deeply at odds with the heroic ideals that dominated the Soviet public and informational spaces. Yurchak argues that the Mitki's "manner of addressing others as 'little brothers' and 'little sisters'" may be understood as an attempt to reconfigure kinship relations, where the notion of "one's own" (*svoí*) is amplified to the point where the boundary between "family ties" and "pure friendship" has been rejected in favor of a "deep involvement" in the lives of others. Yurchak takes special note of the group's rejection of "the traditional role of masculine men" and their performance of "a grotesque lack of masculine heroism and physical sex appeal."[27]

There is much about the collective work of the Mitki that seeks to subject normativity to a cool critical eye. At one point in the 1984–85 chapters of *Mitki*, Shinkarev communicates the almost *grand guignol* polymorphousness of the movement's corporeal identity by providing a recipe for its ideal meal. A Mityok would buy "three kilos of head cheese, (costing about thirty kopecks per kilo), four bread baguettes, two packs of margarine for giving that feeling of satiety [and carefully mix] all these ingredients in a dish, simmering them and pouring them out into a ten-liter jar." We are told that a single member of the group could subsist on this concoction for a month.[28] What can one do with such a revoltingly omnivorous body, and where does it belong? We have seen that there is much about the work of the Mitki that attempts to reposition affective boundaries, by integrating queerness into forms of seemingly nonsexualized intimacy. In the work of Shagin and Tikhomirov, we see that same-sex desire is recognized, without ever being acted upon. Yet does this nonconsummation represent a purging or anathematizing of desire? Writing about homophobic responses to AIDS during the nineties, in her landmark *Epistemology of the Closet*, Eve Kosofsky Sedgwick takes note of "the profundity with which the omnicidal impulse is entangled with the modern problem of the homosexual," who is in fact a figure with the "potential of representation within the universal."[29] The practices of group and individual bodies that we see in the texts and images of the Mitki ask us to reconsider "normality" and to expand our understanding of different ways of being. Without specifically endorsing Pussy Riot's pro-LGBTQ views, Shagin's support of the group's activities does indicate an openness to human difference that is otherwise completely absent from other vocal Russian Orthodox believers who opposed the harsh measures of their arrest while chiding the protestors for their nonnormative acceptance of different forms of sexual orientation. The movement's understanding of different modalities of sexuality as something that, to use Sedgwick's phrase, has the "potential of representation within the universal" could not be more provocative in a country whose government has sought to criminalize homosexuality since 2011.

All the same, the Mitki's work yokes social conservatism to an erotics of friendship and movement solidarity, creating a dissonance that is audible to the point that it can be said to openly invite commentary. We may come closer to understanding the game acceptance of this self-contradiction if we examine it through the lens of postmodernist praxis. In an interview with Gerald Pirog, the Moscow Collective Actions Group artist Igor Makarevich takes issue with the use of the term "postmodernism" to describe contemporary Russian art. According to Makarevich, postmodernism is only possible in a country that has experienced a bureaucratization of art, "when it has shrunk to the limits of its possibilities [and] spreads out into hundreds of smaller zones" through which "only a specialist or critic" can become oriented.[30] While acknowledging Makarevich's bracing common sense of finding the label of "postmodern" to be overused in assessments of contemporary Russian art, we may also reapply his understanding of the concept as a labyrinth of multiplicities to the ambiguities of the Mitki's production. Boris Groys, one of the most rigorous and eloquent theorists of Russian postmodernism, has recently argued that ideologically ambiguous objects—works that bundle widely divergent aesthetic taxonomies (e.g., being at the same time "documentary and fictional" or, as in the case of Gerhard Richter's painting, "abstract and realistic")—unexpectedly carry the greatest promise for a political art. Groys calls these works "paradox-objects":

> A contemporary artwork is as good as it is paradoxical—as it is capable of embodying the most radical self-contradiction, as it is capable of contributing to establishing and maintaining the perfect balance of power between thesis and antithesis. In this sense, even the most radically one-sided artworks can be regarded as good if they help to redress the distorted balance of power in the field as a whole.[31]

Bearing in mind Groys's understanding of artistic postmodernism as a form of art that goes against the grain—by virtue of its cultivation of ambivalent congeries of different subcultures—or as Makarevich calls them, "zones"—we find ourselves asking a provocative question. In a movement that prides itself on satirical ambiguity and performativity, do we even need to resolve such contradictions? The status of the Mitki's legacy as a powerfully unresolved paradox is, in fact, precisely what brings their writing and graphic work into the ambit of the performative aspects of contemporary art. In their visual and textual documentation of human gravitations within the solar system of a subculture that transmits information about itself to the larger galaxy of underground audiences, the Mitki embodied a predigital version of the flash mob and social media page. Writing about the ways in which the immediacy of community can be molded into digital practices, Judith Bessant argues that "new media can work to integrate, to *orient participants toward each other* in ways that talk in terms of a [new] generation [author's emphasis]" of agentive actors. Bessant also points out that this syncretic understanding of digital media is abundantly in evidence in Pussy Riot's 2012 "Punk Prayer" in Moscow, which "symbolically reclaimed the site [of the rebuilt Church of Christ the Savior] not only for protest but for worship."[32]

The Mitki have always understood their stylized performativity—and the means that they use for disseminating the news of it—as an ensemble of strategies for symbolically recuperating physicality and corporeality, in saving a political world that otherwise dwells on mortifying ideological abstractions. And perhaps corporeality is the consummate—and most political—of the artifacts that Groys labels as "paradox objects." This is undoubtedly what Olga Florensky had in mind in the catalogue essay that she wrote for her 2015 exhibit *Classic Death*: "Letters, numbers and symbols were put together at times in the most paradoxical of ways," an impression that she facilitated by having "flat objects not on the walls, but in the air, to underscore the free essence of the fabric"[33] (or, as the Russian word "fabric" [*tkan'*] would also have it, to underscore the free essence of bodily tissue). Perhaps this image of the necessary freedom of the flesh—the recognition of the irreducible realism of the body and the precincts that it creates for itself—is what Andrei Bitov had in mind when he described the postmodernism of the Mitki as "life-affirming." He also may have been pushing back against the conclusion that many people drew about the movement, that its use of the figure of Icarus as a mascot signaled an ideologically lethal passivity and fatalism. These statements by Florensky and Bitov (who in some ways may be regarded as an honorary Mityok, if not a fellow traveler of the movement) complement recent attempts in North American critical theory to rehabilitate postmodernism from the militant flatness and affectless vacuity that is often attributed to it, in favor of an appreciation of texture and depth that may productively emerge from the dissonant juxtapositions of cultural objects.[34] Surely this is what Bitov has in mind when he characterizes the Mitki's postmodernism as a lived-in art installation where a can of shaving cream is reverently positioned on a shelf as if it were an icon, pea jackets are described as the perfect form of clothing, and lines from kitschy songs in Soviet-era movies are declared to be as good as the poetry of Pushkin and Lermontov.[35] Or, as Olga Florensky, puts it, "flat" works of art become bodies inhabiting our space, jostling with us in a bid for equality as we contemplate them.

Perhaps nowhere do we see more clearly these principles of empathy, as facilitated by an initial repulsion to the bodies of others, than in Shinkarev's entry for an exhibit of fanciful, and deliberately unrealizable, installation proposals titled "Written Painting" that took place in the Anna Akhmatova Museum in the fall of 2004:

The Installation "A Cat Overate and Lies amongst the Flowers"

On a carpet with the dimensions 8 by 8 meters [we see] densely planted plastic and cloth flowers and foliage—sunflowers, burdock, dandelions, forget-me-nots, and cow parsnip—all 8–10 times larger than their natural size. In the middle, in a pose of extreme exhaustion, lies a cat 2.2 meters high, and knitted from 40 well-worn black sheep hides. The wide-open eyes of the cat gaze onto the viewer with reproach and despair. The sides and back of the cat regularly expand with the help of a piston, which raises and widens the plastic hemisphere [of the cat's body]. At the instant of the exhalation of the mechanism within the cat's body, you can hear a heavy wheeze bordering on a gurgle and cough. The sound of the breath, like the cat itself, is 8–10 times larger than its natural scale. Butterflies and dragonflies hover in the air, hanging from the ceiling, and are 8–10 times larger than their natural size. The insects, flowers, and wool of the cat wobble slightly from the action of the ventilator.

The installation fills viewers with a painful empathy (8–10 times its natural scale) for the unfortunate animal, arousing in them an aesthetic sensation 8–10 times larger than its natural scale, and causing them to fall into melancholy thought.[36]

Shinkarev's proposed installation emerges as a grotesquely three-dimensional and kinetic version of a primitivist painting and partially corresponds to a few of his canvases that contain scenes of rapacious animals, represented in a naïve style. Empathy—for the forty hapless ewes sacrificed for the installation, for the gluttonous yet clearly artificial cat, and for the queasiness of the viewer—is everywhere in this description. Also present, however, is what Liubov Gurevich characterizes as the Mitki's fey and ironic humor and the thematizing of excess as a lever for activating moral insight.[37] No less important is the patent influence of Olga and Aleksandr Florensky's mechanical installations, which serve here as a demonstration of the emergent connection with others that is the beating heart of this proposal. In *The End of the Mitki*, Shinkarev counts the Florenskys among a group of engaged nonconformist artists in the mid-1980s that was the immediate forerunner of the Mitki. As he points out, the earlier group lacked a common aesthetic, or any conceit of hierarchy; it thankfully did not categorize its members according to the "leaders/followers" dichotomy (*vedushchie—vedomye*).[38] Among the Mitki, the principles of democratic horizontality and open-ended fellowship—and of the abjuring of leadership—reverberates throughout the work of Shinkarev and the Florenskys in particular.

The Mitki play the role of what the historian Paul Avrich, in his path-breaking study of the quashed 1921 rebellion of sailors at Kronstadt, describes as "libertarian socialists." The sailors at Kronstadt (the neighboring naval base to Petrograd/St. Petersburg) attempted to purge the modes of oppression that wormed their way into "the inner world of the toilers."[39] The Mitki shadow-box behind the illuminated screen of the Russian navy's storied history, alternately blending and clashing with its scenes of the Russo-Japanese War, the exploits of the battleships *Potemkin* and *Aurora*, and the Kronstadt uprising. They have always played with the image of themselves as both defenders of, and rebels against, the empire. The multimedia installation of the Mitki—their nonconformism, the primitivist embrace of the fleshly and prosaic over the high-flown within their artwork, writing, and filmmaking, and the melodramatic spectacle of their influence upon one another—takes the defamiliarization of conventionality as its moral goal. As we have seen, they mythologized alcohol as one substance for bringing about this desirable alienation. No less important for them, however, was the role of disgust as an avenue for altered perception. In a 1914 essay on Chekhov, the Formalist critic Boris Eikhenbaum describes the unflinching contact with everything that was "lowly, tawdry, and awful" as the force that occasionally propelled the stories into the realm of dreams. Eikhenbaum writes that the disgust engendered from such contact was the "alcohol of choice for Chekhov's art."[40] Addressing the high school students engaged in the most recent wave of protests across the Russian Federation, the political scientist, blogger, and government critic Georgy Satarov—in a now-famous Facebook post from June 13, 2017, titled "Russia Has a Future"—wrote that one must be a political actor both during demonstrations (*mitingi*) and in the intervals between them. It is during the doldrums of political and social movement, Satarov writes, that we should take the opportunity to "fantasize further" (*dal'she fantaziruite sami*).[41] Group activity is not simply a schedule of sporadic meetings: it is a way of being. Bearing in mind Satarov's injunction to the largely leaderless yet powerfully grassroots and often playfully irreverent character of the current youth protest in Russia—and substituting "corporeal" or "bodily" for Eikhenbaum's "lowly, tawdry, and awful" as the formula for cultivation of a productive ambivalence—we come very close to grasping the ways in which the Mitki's poetics of a total art of physical democratic creativity may serve as an analogy to, if not an example of, new forms of resistance.

# Appendix

## Vladimir Shinkarev, "In Praise of the Boiler Room"

Excerpt from Vladimir Shinkarev's *Mitki* (*Sobstvenno literatura*, 326–27, 329–30) translated by Alexandar Mihailovic.

What does a man experience, emigrating to the world of boiler rooms?

To be honest, the first look evokes vertigo and fear, the atmosphere of a movie thriller—it is no accident that the gripping conclusions of many American films take place in boiler rooms, as in the film *Commando*. A chock-full three-story building, where time doesn't advance . . . the twenty-four hour shift is too long for you to look forward to it ending. Beautiful suprematist crisscrossing of pipes and knobs of radiators; the cubes of the boilers, and the colorful flags of threatening posters. "Check the level of water in the boiler!" "Check gas pressure in the system!" "In the event of a gas odor, apply cleaning solvent to valves and pipe joints, and find the location of the leak!" (All of these warnings, incidentally, are far from idle . . .) The patent animism of the space frightens you: the jumble and dance of the spirals of steam and hot and frigid air, and the variety of sounds—a few coming from incomprehensible sources, from evident poltergeists.

More than half of the light bulbs in this fortress have been taken out by service personnel for their own use, and the illumination is spotty, as blinding tongues of steam give way to pitch darkness, and specks of fire dance farther off. The automated safety device glows, and the ripple on the water inside the accumulator tank shimmers. . . .

A man who has no center of gravity within himself, who has a need for a constant stream of external impressions, finds it hard to be in a boiler room. Schopenhauer had special contempt for such people, who incessantly entertain themselves during times of compulsory waiting by drumming on the table with their fingers, rocking their leg, or whistling a tune.

The boiler room gives its attendant a priceless trait: the ability to sit still. In general, I would advise a person not to flee solitude, even when it is compulsory. In all likelihood, creative abilities develop from solitude. A person is required to interact all the time with other people and with God; when he does not have the opportunity to socialize in the usual way, he develops within himself the possibility of interaction on a higher level, through art.

But that's not the only boon of the boiler room. The atmosphere of healthy anxiety, and a certain danger, sharpen all emotions and potentials. This atmosphere is closer to a monastery than to a production line. Yet "monastery" is too strong: here there is no vow of celibacy, and women are invited.

In the American magazine for mercenaries *Soldier of Fortune*, a veteran of the Vietnam war shares an observation that surprised even him. Nowhere do you experience the sex act as keenly and rapturously as in war time, in an atmosphere of anxiety and danger. Better yet—right on the field of battle. Do I really need to explain why I mention this?

But all this is rather secondary, in comparison with the most important fact that I can confirm: the boiler room is the promised land of creative activity, the paradise of the literary artist. While I can't vow that every line I wrote was written in a boiler room, it certainly does seem that way to me.

# Notes

## Introduction

1. For more on the subculture of theatricalized apartment exhibit openings, see Sergei Kovalsky, "Apartment Underground Russian Avant-Garde Art," in Schlatter and Maitre, *The Space of Freedom*, especially pages 15–24.

2. Volkov, *St. Petersburg: A Cultural History*, 530.

3. Evdokimov, "Piterskie podpol'shchiki," in his *Zapiski lzhesvidetelia*, 418–19.

4. Shinkarev, *Sobstvenno literatura*, 238.

5. Ibid., 236.

6. Florenskaia, "Dukh ego byl tverd i chist," in O & A Florenskie, *Dvizhenie v storonu knigi*, 96.

7. In one memoir essay, the Leningrad-based underground art curator (and later director of the St. Petersburg Museum of Non-Conformist Art) Sergei Kovalsky describes in vivid terms the pacifism of the Leningrad underground, using Shevchuk's line as a point of reference: "What really did it for me was a song that sounded like a requiem for freedom, sung by Martha Kubishina, the exiled Czech singer. The song was broadcast on all the radio stations except the Soviet ones and the emotions it conveyed were so strong and sincere that they made me believe in the 'injustice of good' (as Yuriy [*sic*] Shevchuk of the rock group DDT later sang) which the Soviet soldiers had brought about" (in Schlatter and Maitre, *The Space of Freedom*, 17).

8. Shinkarev, *Sobstvenno literatura*, 320. A longer translation of this chapter in Shinkarev's *Mitki* can be found in the Appendix to this book ("In Praise of the Boiler Room").

9. Florenskaia, "Podval'naia skazka," in O & A Florenskie, *Dvizhenie v storonu knigi*, 108–10.

10. See, for example, Marek Bartelik's discussion of the difficulties in finding a "school" for Moscow Conceptualism, in his "The Banner without a Slogan:

Definitions and Sources of Moscow Conceptualism," in Rosenfeld, *Moscow Conceptualism in Context*, 2–23 (esp. 11).

11. Groys, "A Style and a Half: Socialist Realism between Modernism and Postmodernism," 82; Lyotard, *The Postmodern Condition*, 37–41.

12. Remnick, "Letter from Moscow: Post-Imperial Blues," 82.

13. Gessen, "Retrofitting Totalitarianism."

14. Bersani and Phillips, *Intimacies*. For an interesting overview of Bersani and Phillips' book, see Roth, "Leo."

15. Gurevich, "Prel'stitel' (popytka kritiki)," 291–311.

16. Chemiakin, *Chemiakin*, 1:134–43.

17. Smelov, *Boris Smelov: Retrospective*, 237, 436.

18. Sinyavsky, *V teni Gogolia*, 352.

19. "Prezentatsiia issledovaniia Vladimira Shinkareva 'Konets mit'kov'."

20. Quoted from Davis's speech "Leadership in the 21st Century," delivered at Williams College on April 12, 2014. For more details, see Gillian Jones, "Political Activist Angela Davis Breaking Down Barriers," *Berkshire Eagle* (April 14, 2014), www.berkshireeagle.com/stories/political-activist-angela-davis-breaking-down-barriers,377136; and Kirsten Lee, "Angela Davis Examines Leadership and Intellectual Activism," *Williams Record* (April 16, 2014), http://williamsrecord.com/2014/04/16/angela-davis-examines-leadership-and-intellectual-activism/. See also Davis's discussion about the necessity for eschewing "the traditional, black charismatic leader" in her essay "The Truth Telling Project: Violence in America," 85.

21. Lifshitz, "Pro Domo Sua," *Novoe literaturnoe obozrenie* 88 (2007), http://nlobooks.ru/sites/default/files/old/nlobooks.ru/rus/magazines/nlo/196/722/726/index.html.

22. See Tatiana Likhanova's two articles about the break between Shinkarev and Shagin: "Mityok-Raskol'nikoff [*sic*]" (March 24, 2008) and "Konets mit'kov" (November 15, 2010).

23. Debord, *The Society of the Spectacle*, 17.

24. NAMEGALLERY, Facebook, April 16, 2017, www.facebook.com/NAMEGALLERY/.

25. Interview with Vladimir Shinkarev, conducted in St. Petersburg, Russia (March 13, 2005).

26. Quoted from C. J. Chivers, "With Lenin's Ideas Dead, Russia Weighs What To Do with His Body," *New York Times* (October 5, 2005), A6.

27. Solomon, *The Irony Tower*, 129–30.

28. www.youtube.com/watch?v=-tkQgTgTmDM.

29. Pivovarov, *Vliublennyi agent*, 61–62.

30. Tikhomirov, *Evgenii Telegin*, 266–67.

31. Jameson, "Postmodernism and Consumerist Society," 115–17.

32. Quoted in the artist biography "Irina Vasil'ieva: Kul'tproekt": http://kultproekt.ru/hudojniki/99105062015103613668/.

33. "В акциях, где использован элемент "лежание в яме" в его конкретном виде, для зрителей так до конца и не ясно, есть ли на пустом поле "исчезнувший" участник или его там нет." www.conceptualism-moscow.org/files/7tom.pdf.

34. Shinkarev, *Mit'kovskie pliaski*, 24.

35. Shinkarev, *Maksim i Fedor. Papuas iz Gondurasa. Domashnii ezh. Mit'ki*, 265.
36. Monastyrskii, *Slovar' terminov moskovskoi kontseptual'noi shkoly*, 13–14.
37. Shinkarev, *Sobstvenno literatura*, 314–16.
38. "Mrachnye Kartiny," Facebook page of Vladimir Shinkarev, www.facebook.com/vladimir.shinkarev/media_set?set=a.187182634721410.33791.100002890249623&type=1 (accessed March 3, 2012).
39. Lipovetsky, *Charms of Cynical Reason*, 69–70.
40. Evdokimov, *Zapiski lzhesvidetelia*, 407–8.

## Chapter 1. Glimmer Twins of the Leningrad Underground

1. Shinkarev, *Sobstvenno literatura*, 281.
2. Ibid., 251.
3. Shinkarev, *Sobstvenno literatura*, 229; Shinkarev, *Mit'ki. Materialy k istorii dvizheniia. Konets mit'kov*, 263.
4. Shinkarev, *Sobstvenno literatura*, 258.
5. The character of Anton Goremyka comes from an eponymous short story by the nineteenth-century fiction writer Dmitri Grigorovich.
6. Shagin's comment to a German researcher in 2002 about the importance of humor for the Mitki in addressing the challenges of poverty and privation are especially expressive of the deliberately naïve images in his paintings, although they can also apply to much of Shinkarev's work as well: "Wir haben dem Leben gegenüber eine humorvolle Haltung" (Hamel, *Puschkinkult in weißen Nächten*, 100). As we shall see, there is a great deal of mutual influence at work among the Mitki.
7. In her German anthology of Russian poems and essays about the city, Judith Peltz discusses the notion of St. Petersburg as a giant stage set, noted even in the nineteenth century by commentators such as the Marquis de Custine (*Poetischer Sankt Petersburg-Führer*, 16).
8. Elman, *Uptight with the Stones*, 40.
9. Richards, *Life*, 104–5.
10. Shinkarev, *Mit'ki. Materialy k istorii dvizheniia. Konets mit'kov*, 14, 77.
11. "Dmitri Shagin: Dlia kartiny Repina nastupila temnaia polosa."
12. Shinkarev, *Mit'ki. Materialy k istorii dvizheniia. Konets mit'kov*, 270.
13. Likhanova, "Mityok-Raskol'nikoff [*sic*]."
14. Jameson, "Postmodernism and Consumerist Society," 125.
15. Shinkarev, *Mit'ki. Materialy k istorii dvizheniia. Konets mit'kov*, 250.
16. Sontag, "Notes on Camp," 521.
17. Shinkarev, *Sobstvenno literatura*, 246.
18. Ibid., 365
19. Shinkarev, *Mit'ki. Materialy k istorii dvizheniia. Konets mit'kov*, 253.
20. Ibid., 254.
21. Ibid., 400.
22. Shinkarev, *Sobstvenno literatura*, 228.
23. Ibid., 236.
24. Shinkarev, *Mit'ki. Materialy k istorii dvizheniia. Konets mit'kov*, 304.
25. Baudrillard, *Simulacra and Simulation*, 152.

26. Shagin, *Dyk!*, 48.
27. Shinkarev, *Sobstvenno literatura*, 252.
28. Ibid., 280.
29. Shinkarev, *Mit'ki. Materialy k istorii dvizheniia. Konets mit'kov*, 37–38.
30. Groys, "A Style and a Half: Socialist Realism between Modernism and Postmodernism," 82.
31. Shinkarev, *Mit'ki. Materialy k istorii dvizheniia. Konets mit'kov*, 289.
32. Ibid., 254–55.
33. Nemerov, "The Flight of Form," 797.
34. Shinkarev, *Mit'ki. Materialy k istorii dvizheniia. Konets mit'kov*, 295.
35. Ibid., 398–99.
36. Shklovsky, "Iskusstvo kak priem," 137.
37. Ibid., 144.
38. Beckett, *Waiting for Godot*, 37.
39. For a telling account of the tense creative relations between Grebenshchikov and Kurekhin, see Kan, *Kurekhin. Shpiker o kapitane* (238–39), and Kushnir, *Sergei Kurekhin. Bezumnaia mekhanika russkogo roka* (184–86).
40. Gordon, *Reading Godot*, 13, 87, 90.
41. Ibid., 145.
42. Shinkarev, *Maksim i Fedor. Papuas iz Gondurasa. Domashnii ezh. Mit'ki*, 348.
43. Shinkarev, *Sobstvenno literatura*, 385.
44. Shinkarev, *Mit'ki. Materialy k istorii dvizheniia. Konets mit'kov*, 303.
45. Shinkarev, *Sobstvenno literatura*, 227.
46. Woodhead, *How the Beatles Rocked the Kremlin*, 108.
47. Zhitinskii, *Puteshestvie rok-diletanta. Muzykal-nyi roman*, 195. The translation comes from Steinholt, "You Can't Rid a Song of Its Words," 100.
48. Zhitinskii, *Puteshestvie rok-diletanta. Muzykal-nyi roman*, 196; Steinholt, "You Can't Rid a Song of Its Words," 100.
49. Shinkarev, *Sobstvenno literatura*, 279–80.
50. Andrei Bitov, "'Nichego' Vladimira Shinkareva," in Sapego, *Mit'ki*, 14.
51. Shagin, *Dyk!*, 26–27.
52. Shinkarev, *Sobstvenno literatura*, 280.
53. Barthes, *Image-Music-Text*, 160.
54. Ibid., 44.
55. Bakhtin, *Problems of Dostoevsky's Poetics*, 70.
56. Ibid., 21–22.
57. Sedgwick, *Epistemology of the Closet*, 192.
58. Shinkarev, *Mit'ki. Materialy k istorii dvizheniia. Konets mit'kov*, 325.
59. Shinkarev, *Sobstvenno literatura*, 258.
60. Shinkarev, *Mit'ki. Materialy k istorii dvizheniia. Konets mit'kov*, 265–66.
61. Gurevich, "Prel'stitel' (popytka kritiki)," 296.
62. Bakhtin, *Sobranie sochinenii*, Tom 4 (2), 104.
63. Shinkarev, *Mit'ki. Materialy k istorii dvizheniia. Konets mit'kov*, 297.
64. Roudinesco, *Jacques Lacan: An Outline of a Life and History of a System of Thought*, 279.
65. Lacan, "The Mirror Stage as Formative of the *I* Function as Revealed in Psychoanalytic Experience," 76.

66. Ibid., 421.
67. Lotman, *Vnutri mysliashchikh mirov*, 221–22.
68. Butler, *Notes Toward a Performative Theory of Assembly*, 48.

## Chapter 2. "Who Is This Heroic Man?"

1. Komaromi, "The Material Existence of Soviet Samizdat," 605.
2. Quoted from Gessen's *Words Will Break Cement: The Passion of Pussy Riot*. The full Russian text of Tolokonnikova's testimony can be found at: www.novayagazeta.ru/society/53903.html (accessed July 10, 2014).
3. Butler, *Undoing Gender*, 15.
4. This statement appears in the 1996 edition of Shinkarev's *Mitki*. Vladimir Shinkarev, *Maksim i Fedor. Papuas iz Gondurasa. Domashnii ezh. Mit'ki*, 293–94. The absence from other editions of this section, titled "The Final System of the World Order, or How to Achieve the Ideal in Two Days," is made more noticeable because of the inclusion of a section titled "The Second Improved Final System of the World Order" in all editions of the work, immediately following the location of the omitted section. In his second droll digression about his Weltanschauung, Shinkarev begins with the statement "being completely satisfied with my first final system of the world order, I am nevertheless compelled to submit a second one, which, however, does not in any way supersede the first" (ibid., 297). Shinkarev's reasons for omitting this section are not clear. In an interview conducted by the author of this study, Shinkarev enigmatically stated that his animosity toward the symbolic figure of David Bowie stems from the latter representing "the spirit of advertisement" (*dukh reklamy*) (St. Petersburg, October 30, 2004). One can note that Bowie's famed sartorial showiness contrasts sharply with the deliberate plainness and monotony of the Mitki's quasimilitaristic wardrobe, and that the purging of external distinguishing characteristics is incompatible with the protean fashion statements of dandyism. As we shall see, these differences coexist with a deeper affinity with Bowie, thematized within the work of the group.
5. Hetko, "We Could Be Antiheroes."
6. For more on Butler's linking of fantasy to improvisational modes of being, see *Undoing Gender*, 215–17.
7. Sedgwick, *Between Men: English Literature and Male Homosocial Desire*. See especially chapter 7 ("Homophobia, Misogyny and Capital: *Our Mutual Friend*").
8. Komaromi, "The Material Existence of Soviet Samizdat," 618.
9. Sedgwick, *Epistemology of the Closet*, 101.
10. Kuznetsov, "Voistinu oppan'ki!"
11. Bersani and Phillips, *Intimacies*, 67.
12. Shinkarev, *Sobstvenno literatura*, 223.
13. Bakhtin, *Toward a Philosophy of the Act*, 16.
14. Karpinski, "Pochemu stalinizm ne skhodit so stseny?," 650.
15. Sedgwick, *Epistemology of the Closet*, 47.
16. Volkov, *St. Petersburg: A Cultural History*, 249.
17. Lyotard, "Answering the Question: What Is Postmodernism?," published as an appendix to *The Postmodern Condition: A Report on Knowledge*, 81.

18. Shinkarev, untitled preface to *Mit'ki-Arkhitipy*, 2. Shinkarev's piece was reprinted in the exhibit catalog *Krasnaia strela. Sankt-Peterburg-Moskva. Vystavka k 300-letiiu Severnoi stolitsy*, 1.

19. Lyotard, "Answering the Question: What Is Postmodernism?," 81. The notion of the postmodernist as the architect of an event is not to be confused with Lyotard's term "performativity," which describes a social system's positivist maximalization of information transmission, which strives to replace the teacher or artist with nonhuman resources such as computers (48–53).

20. Žižek, "Why Are Laibach and NSK Not Fascists?," 287.

21. "As with the officers, so with the enlisted men." Quoted in Masiagin and Iakimov, *Ofitsery baltiiskogo flota*, 17.

22. Ibid., 164.

23. Ibid., 21–22, 164–65.

24. Brodsky, *Less Than One*, 466.

25. "Daite khodu parokhodu," Shagin, *Dyk!*, 32. The translation is mine.

26. Shinkarev, *Sovbstvenno literatura*, 244.

27. Ibid., 245–56.

28. *Mit'ki ne khotiat nikogo pobedit', ili Mit'kimaier*. As Alexei Yurchak points out in his sociological dissection of this anecdote, "the unexpectedness is a part of the Mitki aesthetics. . . . [The Russian] fails to win not because he is not good enough but because the very discourse of winning and losing is alien to his discourse" (240). Yurchak makes the overall point in his discussion of the Mitki that the Mityok represents classically Russian traits as defined in folklore, especially as embodied by the figure of "Ivan-Durachok" (Ivan the Fool).

29. Liner notes, *Mit'kovskie pesni. Na more tanki grokhotali*. The text was also published as "Spasenie sestrionki" ("The Rescue of a Little Sister") in *Mit'ki. Pro zaek*, 99–100.

30. Shagin, *Dyk!*, 48.

31. Shinkarev discusses Shagin's fascination with Brueghel's painting and gives an amusing mock exegesis of the poem in his *Mitki* (*Sobstvenno literatura*, 252–54).

32. Reproduced in the Shagin web page of the movement's web site (http://mitki.kulichki.com/mitki/shagin/shd8.gif).

33. Shinkarev, *Sobstvenno literatura*, 348. Written several years after the book's initial circulation in samizdat, the appendix describes Shinkarev's self-recognition as an alcoholic and his treatment in a twelve-step program in the United States.

34. Shekhter, "Andegraund kak novaia khudozhestvennaia real'nost'," in Koval'skii, *Iz padeniia v polet*, 52.

35. For a discussion of this imaginary dialogue, and its communicative sabotage, see Baranov's "Zhargon v kontekste postmodernizma" (especially 292–93), the first piece of scholarly writing about the Mitki.

36. Shinkarev, *Sobstvenno literatura*, 227–28.

37. Shekhter, "Andegraund kak novaia khudozhestvennaia real'nost'," 53.

38. Florenskaia, *Psikhologiia bytovogo shrifta*, 8, 12.

39. Ibid., 259.

40. Shinkarev, *Mit'ki. Risunki Aleksandra Olegovicha Florenskogo*, 65.

41. As Sontag puts it in her 1964 essay "Notes on Camp," "the most refined form of sexual attractiveness (as well as the most refined form of sexual pleasure) consists in going against the grain of one's sex. What is most beautiful in virile men is something feminine; what is most beautiful in feminine women is something masculine" (519).

42. Shinkarev's ink drawing is reproduced on the web page "Mit'ki i seks" of the movement's web site (http://mitki.kulichki.com/sex/). Florensky's illustration is a mixed media piece of drawing and collage, with the screen taken up by an innocuous photograph of a woman on a beach (*Kollazh v Rossii. XX vek*, 21).

43. Shinkarev, *Sobstvenno literatura*, 260.

44. "Eroticheskii simvol mit'kov: bol'shoi, dobryi, khoroshii." Shuliakhovskaia, "Mit'ki i seks."

45. In *A Papuan from Honduras* the relation between the two athletes is unrelievedly antagonistic (Shinkarev, *Sobstvenno literatura*, 201–12).

46. Dmitri Shagin, *Sport Loves Those Who Are Strong* (*Sport liubit sil'nykh*) (1991). Woodcut, 250 × 195 mm. InterArt Gallery, New York.

47. A photo taken in 1998 and printed in the St. Petersburg edition of the newspaper *Smena* (https://vk.com/photo-20482116_183123204).

48. Sedgwick, *Epistemology of the Closet*, 100.

49. Shinkarev, *Mitki* (1998). The poster is reproduced on the cover of the exhibition catalogue: *Mitki: Retrospektivnaia vystavka k 10-letiiu dvizheniia*. Florensky's first portrayal of Icarus in the medium of a collage appears in the margin of a poster for the traveling 1989 exhibit "Mitki [*sic*] in Europe" (ibid., 44).

50. Shinkarev, *Sobstvenno literatura*, 242.

51. Olga Florensky identified the individuals in the two photo portraits in an e-mail to this researcher from October 18, 2005. In the same message, she strikes a chord of gender blurring consistent with the fusion of the sexes in her Icarus collage, writing that the composition was a tribute to Khrustaleva and Trofimenkov as "brother art historians" (*bratushki-iskusstvovedushki*) in their capacity as editors of a planned *Mitki Encyclopedia*. The form *iskusstvovedushki* can be the plural of either the feminine (*iskusstvovedushka*) or masculine (*iskusstvovedushko*) form of the Mitki's fanciful diminutive for "art historian." The masculine form explicitly occurs in Shinkarev's dictionary of Mitki slang: "*Iskusstvovedushko*: An art historian, who serves the *mitki*" (*Sobstvenno literatura*, 305). The *Mitki Encyclopedia* project was ultimately abandoned. I am very grateful to the Florenskys for the access they gave me to the entire *Mit'kovskaia azbuka*.

52. Interview in St. Petersburg, April 14, 2005.

53. Kravchenko, "Cherez tri okeana (Fragment)," in *Sindrom Tsusimy. Sbornik statei*, 38. See also Pleshakov (*The Tsar's Last Armada*) about the divide between the sailors and the lower ranking officers and the admiralty on the eve of the campaign in the Pacific.

54. Sapego, *Pro razvedchika Riabova*. http://ficus.reldata.com/km/issues/pro_razvedtcika.

55. "Variag" (track 5), "Pleshshut kholodnye volny" (track 4), *Mit'kovksie pesni*.

56. www.kulichki.com/mitki/russian/music/pesni.html. The translation is mine.

57. "Na sopkakh Man'chzhurii" (track 6), *Mit'kovskie pesni. Na more tanki grokhotali.* The website "The Anthology of Famous Songs" documents the various versions of the song. It mistakenly credits the Mitki CD as its source for the words of the prerevolutionary version of "In the Hills of Manchuria." Khvostenko only sings a few strophes from that version. http://retro.samnet.ru/phono/onesong/na_sopkakh.htm.

58. As the St. Petersburg artist Yuri Krasev put it in an interview, Kurekhin, like the Yufit's Necrorealist group and Timur Novikov's New Academicians, was interested in an aesthetic of exacerbation or exaggeration (*usilenie*) (Andreeva, *Timur. Vrat' tol'ko pravdu!*, 122).

59. Girard, *Violence and the Sacred*, 277–78.

60. Shinkarev, *Maxim and Fyodor: Young Russians Search for the Meaning of Life*, 24; Shinkarev, *Sobstvenno literatura*, 21.

61. Shagin, *Mit'kovskie pesni s kartinkami*, 14.

62. Shuliakhovskaia, "Mit'ki i seks."

63. See Florensky's illustration "The Fundamental Work 'The Mitki and David Bowie' Has Yet to Be Written" for a visual representation of the dichotomy between the dowdy Mityok and the hip David Bowie. Shinkarev, *Mit'ki. Risunki Aleksandra Olegovicha Florenskogo*, 54.

64. Shinkarev, *Mit'kovskie pliaski*, 21.

65. Shagin makes this statement in 1995, in the liner notes for the Mitki's first CD, *Mitki Silence* (*Mit'kovskaia tishina*).

66. Shinkarev, *Sobstvenno literatura*, 282; and Shinkarev, *Mit'ki. Risunki Aleksandra Olegovicha Florenskogo*, 115, 117.

67. *Vladimir Shinkarev*, edited by Kushnir, 171.

68. See especially two early moments in Roeg's film, where the camera lingers on the pages from the book, with the poem and painting on facing pages (*The Man Who Fell to Earth*, 17:00, 21:00–23:00).

69. Thian, "Moss Garden: David Bowie and Japonism in Fashion in the 1970s," 131–32, 135.

70. For a description of Grebenshchikov's performance, see Ryback, *Rock Around the Bloc*, 212. About Bowie and Ronson, see Buruma, "The Invention of David Bowie," 287. Such scrapbooks are kept and displayed at the Museum of the Realia of Russian Rock Music, located within the Museum of Nonconformist Art (10 Pushkinskaia, in St. Petersburg).

71. For a vivid description of this recording session, and of Fripp's considerable contribution to it, see Rüther, *David Bowie and Berlin*, 131–34.

72. Quoted in Buruma, "The Invention of David Bowie," 282–83.

73. Butler, *Undoing Gender*, 52–53.

74. Butler, *Notes toward a Performative Theory of Assembly*, 34.

75. Rekshan, *Kaif polnyi. Pochti documental'naia rok-simfoniia*, 19.

76. Dolinin, *Ne stol' otdalennaia kochegarka*, 51. Dolinin's remark about supervising Shagin and Shinkarev's work in boiler rooms comes from an interview I conducted with him on February 11, 2017.

77. Shinkarev, *Sobstvenno literatura*, 329. For a full translation of this section of Shinkarev's *Mitki*, see the Appendix of this volume.

78. Brodsky, *Less Than One*, 478.

79. Brodsky, *Nativity Poems*, 2–3. The translation of this poem is by Glyn Maxwell.

80. Butler, *Undoing Gender*, 25–26.

## Chapter 3. Fire Water

1. "Chto prines Rossii svobodnyi rynok alkogolia. 'Obshchee delo'" (discussion originally televised on July 4, 2009, Channel 1), www.youtube.com/watch?v=-VUnRslEk4M (accessed October 6, 2016).

2. Shinkarev, *Mit'ki. Risunki Aleksandra Olegovicha Florenskogo*, 77.

3. Ibid., 132.

4. Kuznetsov, "Voistinu oppan'ki!," 24.

5. Levintov, *Vypivka i p'ianka*, 98.

6. Babor, *Alcohol: No Ordinary Commodity*, 82.

7. For more on the perception of Leningrad/St. Petersburg as a "brewer" city, see Levintov, *Vypivka i p'ianka*, 266–67.

8. Interview in St. Petersburg with Iosif Gurvich (April 10, 2006). For more information about government control of the sale and production of alcohol, see Gurvich's *Upotreblenie alkogolia v Rossii* (15–26), parts of which draw on his earlier research.

9. Kharms's sketch cycle "Accidents" ("Sluchai," in Daniil Kharms, *Polet v nebesa: stikhi, proza, dramy, pis'ma*, 353–430), written during the thirties, has arguably influenced a great deal of Shinkarev's other writing as well, such as his absurdist novella *Maksim i Fedor*. Shagin himself is fascinated by Kharms's work and wrote a sketch inspired by it with Stalin as a character (www.kulichki.com/'mitki/kharms/). Viktor Tikhomirov wrote a series of similarly irreverent Kharmsian sketches about former Soviet leaders ("Legendy o revoliutsii," *Zolot na vetru*, 145–50). For an overview of Kharms's work in the context of the OBERIU movement in the Soviet Union, see Ostashevsky, *OBERIU: An Anthology of Russian Absurdism*.

10. Shinkarev, *Sobstvenno literatura*, 348.

11. Hetko, "Mitki and Kharms," 52–54.

12. Shinkarev, *Mit'ki. Materialy k istorii dvizheniia. Konets mit'kov*.

13. "Beer Line" (1990–93). Reproduced in *Mitkat. Suomessa 'Mitki' in Finland*, 15.

14. Shagin, *Bezzavetnye geroi*, 14. This drawing by Shagin can be found on the Internet as well: www.bochkavpechatleniy.com/social/blog/60512/20324.

15. Shagin, *Bezzavetnye geroi*, 59.

16. www.liveinternet.ru/community/moscow_mitki/post65920791/.

17. *Mit'ki. Pro zaek*, 96.

18. Reproduced in Shuliakhovskaia, "Mit'ki i seks."

19. Shinkarev, *Sobstvenno literatura*, 274–75.

20. Reproduced in Shuliakhovskaia, "Mit'ki i seks."

21. Shinkarev, *Sobstvenno literatura*, 275.

22. Ibid., 274–75.

23. Gurevich, "Prel'stitel' (popytka kritiki)," 292.

24. Shinkarev, *Sobstvenno literatura*, 348, 349.

25. "Mit'ki bez portveina. Chto obshchego mezhdu filosofiei mit'kov i programmoi anonimnykh alkogolikov?"

26. Travis, *The Language of the Heart*, 5.

27. Iakimovich, "P'ianstvo kak predmet iskusstva i filosofii."

28. Bakhtin, *Sobranie sochinenii*, Tom 4 (2), 139.

29. Sapego, *Mit'ki*, 34.

30. Shagin himself uses this idiom in his memoir to describe an episode of youthful immoderate drinking among a group of friends in celebration of his graduation from high school: "I tilted back [*vypil iz gorla*] [a bottle of strong red wine from the south], finishing it in front of everybody" (ibid., 32).

31. Shenkman, "Moskva mit'kovskaia."

32. Sapego, *Mit'ki*, 31–34.

33. Ibid., 32.

34. Ibid.

35. Ibid.

36. V. Koshvanets, "Tost za demokratiiu." Originally published July 27, 1986, in *Leningradskaia Pravda*. Reprinted in Sapego, *Mit'ki*, 36–38.

37. Sapego, *Etiketki.*

38. Shinkarev, *Sobstvenno literatura*, 259 (Russian: "Oni dolzhny ustroit' mit'ku dostoinuiu ottiazhku, da ne odnu").

39. Gilmore, *Stories Done: Writings on the 1960s and Its Discontents*, 167.

40. Russian: "Nado napravliat' libido na chto-nibud' poleznoe—kartiny risovat', naprimer." http://mitki.kulichki.net/sex/.

41. Russian: "Chto s nim delat', s p'ianen'kim?" (ibid.)

42. Russian: "Erotika mit'kov napriamuiu sviazana s alkogolem" (ibid.)

43. Sapego, *Mit'ki*, 85.

44. Shinkarev, *Sobstvenno literatura*, 260.

45. Ibid., 340.

46. www.1tv.ru/sprojects_edition/si5761/fi1585.

47. From an interview in Viktor Tikhomirov's documentary *Andrei Bitov. Zelenyi chemodan.*

48. Aleksandr Florenskii, *Neskol'ko slov iz perioda moego geroicheskogo p'ianstva*, illustrations 2, 3, 7, 18.

49. Ibid., illustration 16.

50. Ibid., illustration 29.

51. Russian: "Zhidkost'—eto veshchestvo, prinimaiushchee formu sosudov, v kotorykh nakhoditsia. Alkogol' ne imeet formy, no on diktuet nashe povedenie" (Sapego, *Mit'ki*, 26).

52. Levintov, *Vypivka i p'ianka*, 11.

53. Sapego, *Mit'ki*, 84.

54. Russian: "Vnutrennost' tserkvi, a za oknom—more."

55. Interview with Aleksandr Florensky conducted in St. Petersburg (April 25, 2005).

56. Raikhel, *Governing Habits*, 165.

57. "Dmitrii Shagin: Smysl tvorchestva."

58. Interview with Aleksandr Florensky conducted in St. Petersburg (October 16, 2004).

59. Travis, *The Language of the Heart*, 270.
60. Butler, *Notes toward a Performative Theory of Assembly*, 181–82.
61. Shinkarev, *Mit'ki. Materialy k istorii dvizheniia. Konets mit'kov*, 379.

## Chapter 4. Mosaic Authorship

1. For a more detailed discussion of Arendt's concept in relation to the subject of this book, see Boym, *Another Freedom: The Alternative History of an Idea*, 159–61, and the next chapter.
2. A. Borovsky, "The Trophy Unconscious" ("Trofeinoe bessoznatel'noe"), in O & A Florensky, *Russkii trofei / Russian Trophy*, 2.
3. Lotman, *Vnutri mysliashchikh mirov*, 189.
4. O & A Florensky, *Olga Florensky, Taxidermy. Alexander [sic] Florensky, Modest Architecture. O & A Florensky, A Moveable Bestiary*, 112.
5. The photo was taken shortly before the original installation of the exhibit, which took place in the St. Petersburg park known as the Summer Garden. "Florenskie Pavel [*sic*] i Ol'ga: 'Peredvizhnoi bestiarij v Letnem sadu,'" www.33plus1.ru/Decor/Art/Russian/MIF/florenskie_bestiarii.htm.
6. Iuganov and Iuganov, *Slovar' russkogo slenga*, 151.
7. Shagin, "Spasenie sestrionki," in *Mit'ki. Pro zaek*, 99–100.
8. In her interesting essay about orthography, Olga Florensky herself takes note of the Mitki's fascination with handwritten script as an expressive device and discusses the interplay between typefaces and writing styles that arose from her work on the animation of the small film studio Troitskii Bridge's *Mitkimaier*, the satirical cartoon about the Mitki (Florenskaia, *Psikhologiia bytovogo shrifta*, 5, 20). The film was in fact an outgrowth of the Florenskys' compilation of a book project titled "The Mitki Alphabet," a pictorial listing of major members of the group, each represented by a satirical collage composition of a letter from the Russian alphabet and a droll rhymed couplet about him or her. Some people in the production of the volume also worked for Troitskii Bridge and suggested making the film. The film's evolution from an orthographic project points to the general prominence in the group's aesthetics of alphabetic semiotics and the miscellany format. For an account of the film's genesis, see A. Florenskii, "Mit'kovskaia azbuka," in the Florenskys' collection *Dvizhenie v storonu knigi*, 336–37. While plans for the publication of "The Mitki Alphabet" as a book fell through, different illustrations from the series are available on the Internet.
9. Florenskaia, "Taksidermiia, ili zachem cheloveku iskusstvennye zhivotnye," in O & A Florensky, *Olga Florensky, Taxidermy. Alexander [sic] Florensky, Modest Architecture. O & A Florensky, A Moveable Bestiary*, 25.
10. Shinkarev, *Mit'ki. Materialy k istorii dvizheniia. Konets mit'kov*, 279.
11. Tupitsyn, *The Museological Unconscious*, 97.
12. Shinkarev, *Mit'ki. Materialy k istorii dvizheniia. Konets mit'kov*, 417–18.
13. Olga Florenskaya [*sic*], Facebook, photo album "Studia ruchnoi pechati B&F" (accessed October 4, 2016).
14. O & A Florenskie, "Istoriia pro Mobi Dik," on Aleksandr Florensky's Facebook page, July 5, 2011.
15. Ibid.

16. O & A Florenskie, *Dvizhenie v storonu knigi*, 257.
17. Shinkarev, *Mit'ki. Materialy k istorii dvizheniia. Konets mit'kov*, 196.
18. O & A Florenskie, *Dvizhenie v storonu knigi*, 7.
19. Ibid., 266.
20. Shinkarev, *Maksim i Fedor. Papuas iz Gondurasa. Domashnii ezh. Mit'ki*, 349.
21. Interview with Aleksandr Florensky conducted in New Haven, Connecticut (July 10, 2015).
22. Bitov, "'Nichego' Vladimira Shinkareva," in Sapego, *Mit'ki*, 16.
23. O & A Florenskie, *Dvizhenie v storonu knigi*, 306.
24. A full version of this narrative, drawn from various apocryphal sources, can be found in Natalia Gorbacheva's *Sviataia Kseniia i Diveevskie blazhennye*, 72–75. For documentation of the emergence of the legend of Kseniya, and the ways in which its fanciful details reflected largely nineteenth-century interests and preoccupations, see Kizenko's article "Protectors of Women and the Lower Orders."
25. Gorbacheva, *Sviataia Kseniia i Diveevskie blazhennye*, 73.
26. Florenskaia, "Ob Aleksandre Florenskom," in O & A Florenskie, *Dvizhenie v storonu knigi*, 173.
27. Shevstova, "Sviataia blazhennaia Kseniia Peterburgskaia," 85–86.
28. Gorbacheva, *Sviataia Kseniia i Diveevskie blazhennye*, 76.
29. O & A Florenskie, *Dvizhenie v storonu knigi*, 92.
30. A typical statement of the Marquis de Custine about the relation of Russians to the capital city comes from his impressions of St. Petersburg shortly after arriving there in 1839: "Men stay silent in Russia, but the stones speak, in pitiful accents. No wonder the Russians fear and neglect their old buildings, for these bear witness to the history that they would prefer, more often than not, to forget." Marquis de Custine, *Letters from Russia*, 45.
31. Shinkarev, *Sobstvenno literatura*, 322.
32. Groys, *Art Power*, 96.
33. Olga Florenskaya [*sic*], Facebook, *Classic Death*, www.facebook.com/florenskaya.olga/media_set?set=a.782052005167835.1073741842.100000891272646&type=3 (accessed October 4, 2016).
34. Quoted in Kharkhordin, *The Collective and the Individual in Russia*, 24.
35. Ibid., 91.
36. Olga Florenskaya [*sic*], Facebook, "September in Roccasecca," www.facebook.com/florenskaya.olga/media_set?set=a.1246837915355906.1073741858.100000891272646&type=3&pnref=story (accessed October 4, 2016); Aleksandr Florensky, Facebook, "Georgian Beauties," www.facebook.com/oflorensky/media_set?set=a.862356247146804.1073741893.100001173116446&type=3 (accessed October 4, 2016).
37. See Florenskaia's discussion of this series in O & A Florenskie, *Dvizhenie v storonu knigi*, 42.
38. Jonquet, *Gilbert & George: Intimate Conversations with François Jonquet*, 314–15.
39. Stepanova, "Chelovek ne mozhet zhit' bez chuda (o vozmozhnosti poznaniia iskusstva)," 851; Stepanova, "Konstruktivizm," 855.

40. NAMEGALLERY, Facebook, April 6, 2017, www.facebook.com/NAME GALLERY/.

41. NAMEGALLERY, Facebook, March 14, 2017, www.facebook.com /NAMEGALLERY/.

42. Butler, *Undoing Gender*, 28.

43. Ibid., 48.

44. A partial facsimile of this text can be read on Kostya Mitenev's April 21, 2015, Facebook posting ("Manifest 'neprimknuvshikh' [Assotsiiatsiia], Leningrad, 1980"): www.facebook.com/photo.php?fbid=10153222941011462&set=a .10151454936046462.1073741825.829176461&type=3&theater.

45. O & A Florenskie, *Dvizhenie v storonu knigi*, 18.

46. Ibid., 112.

47. Forrester, "The Poet as Pretender," 41.

48. www.facebook.com/events/171813042508251 5/.

49. Bartky, *Femininity and Domination*, 15.

50. Frontinskii, "Shtrikhi k portretu Olega Grigorieva," in Skobkina, *Geroi leningradskoi kul'tury*, 161.

51. Grigoriev, *Vinokhranitel'. Stikhotvoreniia*, 316–17.

52. Shinkarev first quoted this verse in his novella *Maksim i Fedor* (*Sob stvenno literatura*, 8).

53. Florenskaia, "Eshche pro Olega Grigorieva," in Grigoriev, *Vinokhranitel'. Stikhotvoreniia*, 495.

54. *Mit'ki. Materialy k istorii dvizheniia. Konets mit'kov*, 280.

55. Ibid.

56. Deleuze and Gattari, *Anti-Oedipus: Capitalism and Schizophrenia*, 62.

57. Gurevich, "Prel'stitel' (popytka kritiki)," 294.

## Chapter 5. Satire, Sex, and Chance

1. "Predislovie V. Krivulina," in Tikhomirov, *Zoloto na vetru*, 326.

2. Shinkarev, "Vyshel—vse tvoe," in Tikhomirov, *Zoloto na vetru*, 4–5.

3. Tikhomirov, "Daesh' impotentsiiu!," in Sapego, *Mit'ki*, 322. As if to underscore what he felt was the continued relevance of this piece, Tikhomirov also posted this essay on his Facebook page: "Daesh' impotentsiiu!" February 13, 2016, www.facebook.com/notes/виктор-тихомиров/даешь-импотенцию/10204018426341217.

4. Deleuze, "The Dice Throw," in Iversen, *Chance*, 71.

5. Boym, *Another Freedom*, 159–60.

6. Nabokov, "Good Readers and Good Writers," 4.

7. Wilde, "The Decay of Lying," in *Intentions*, 4.

8. Tikhomirov, *Zoloto na vetru*, 332.

9. The earlier, unfinished version of this painting can be seen on Tikhomirov's Facebook page: "Karavai, kotoryi razlomil daikon A. Kuraev, beseduia s khudozhnikom" (A loaf of bread broken open by the deacon A. Kuraev while speaking to the artist), Facebook, October 20, 2015, www.facebook.com/photo .php?fbid=10207179498920022&set=gm.1080084275344302&type=3&theater.

10. Butler, *Gender Trouble: Feminism and the Subversion of Identity*, 24–25.
11. Lévy, *Collective Intelligence*, 71.
12. Ibid., 81.
13. Tikhomirov, *Zoloto na vetru*, 343.
14. Ibid., 146.
15. Bakhtin, "Satira," 27.
16. "'Preodolenie volka' v musee snovidenii Z. Freida." http://www.museum.ru/N25447.
17. Tikhomirov, *Zoloto na vetru*, 147.
18. Ibid., 149–50.
19. Gura, *Simvolika zhivotnykh v slavianskoi narodnoi traditsii*, 177–99.
20. "Chem khoroshi eti sovetskie fil'my, chto spravedlivost' pobezhdaet." Interview with Viktor Tikhomirov, conducted in St. Petersburg, Russia (April 13, 2006).
21. Shinkarev, *Mit'ki. Materialy k istorii dvizheniia. Konets mit'kov*, 198.
22. Ibid., 200.
23. Rozanov, *Apokalipsis nashego vremeni*, 616.
24. Elena Mal'gina, "Ivan Okhlobystin: 'Ia by ikh zhiv'em v pechku zapikhal!" *NGS Novosti* (December 11, 2013), http://news.ngs.ru/more/1551208/.
25. Tikhomirov, *Chapaev Chapaev*, 100.
26. Ibid., 188.
27. Tikhomirov, "Otechestvennyi mir—2. Bez gomoseksualizma i nekrofilii," *Mit'ki gazeta* 2 (1992): 19.
28. Yurchak, *Everything Was Forever, Until It Was No More*, 249.
29. Ibid., 246.
30. Berlant and Edelman, *Sex, or The Unbearable*, 6.
31. Tikhomirov, *Evgenii Telegin i drugie*, 13.
32. Ibid., 186, 198.
33. Ibid., 22–23.
34. Zhitinskii, *Puteshestvie rok-diletanta. Muzykal-nyi roman*, 154.
35. Tikhomirov, *Evgenii Telegin i drugie*, 53.
36. *Sokurov* (dir. Tikhomirov), 12:30, 16:00–18:30.
37. Lotman, "Dinamicheskaia model' semioticheskoi sistemy," 87.
38. Fedorov, "Muzei, ego smysl i naznachenie," 111, 82.
39. Lévy, *Collective Intelligence*, 70.
40. Shinkarev, *Mit'ki. Materialy k istorii dvizheniia. Konets mit'kov*, 203.

## Conclusion

1. Quoted in Masha Gessen's article about the trial, "Ia prishla v etot sud, chtoby eshche raz vysvetit' absurdnost' neftegazovogo syr'evogo pravosudiia."
2. Prigov, *The Organs of Power*, 146. An alternate translation of this poem can be found in Gessen's *Words Will Break Cement: The Passion of Pussy Riot*, 39.
3. Interview with Irina Vasilieva, conducted in St. Petersburg, Russia (April 22, 2005).
4. Nabokov, *Eugene Onegin*, 32.
5. Valieva, "Ot sostovatilia," in her collection *Sumerki Saigona*, 5.

6. Rekshan, *Leningradskoe vremia, ili ischezaiushchii gorod*, 104.
7. Shinkarev, *Mit'ki. Materialy k istorii dvizheniia. Konets mit'kov*, 293.
8. Bakhtin, *Sobranie sochinenii*, Tom 6, 143.
9. Savitskii, *Andeground*, 154.
10. Shinkarev, *Sobstvenno literatura*, 329–30.
11. Mirzoeff, "The Subject of Visual Culture," in Mirzoeff, *The Visual Culture Reader*, 10.
12. Evgenii Orlov, "Preface," in Schlatter and Maitre, *The Space of Freedom*, 9.
13. Komaromi, "The Material Existence of Soviet Samizdat," 615.
14. Shinkarev, *Sobstvenno literatura*, 133.
15. Ibid., 213.
16. Sinyavsky, *V teni Gogolia*, 501.
17. For a discussion of Kurekhin's methods, see Yurchak, "A Parasite from Outer Space: How Sergei Kurekhin Proved That Lenin Was a Mushroom," and my article "Hijacking Authority: Academic Neo-Aryanism and Internet Expertise," 95–96.
18. Shinkarev, *Sobstvenno literatura*, 227; Tikhomirov, "V ozhidanii Kurekhina," 237.
19. "S: Sveta iz Ivanova," in Lur'e, *Azbuka protesta*, 114–17.
20. For a discussion of the administrative paradigm of "verticality," and its importance to the "Russia United" party in recent times, see Boris Makarenko's "Post-Crimean Political Order," in Maria Lipman and Nikolay Petrov's edited volume *The State of Russia: What Comes Next?*, 6–27. As Makarenko notes: "The disconnect between the Center and the regions can become the main axis of conflict in non-competitive political systems, which explains why the Kremlin paid particular attention to strengthening of the 'power vertical.' 'Verticality' in relations between higher and lower echelons of government is reaching its maximum level, despite the restoration of gubernatorial elections" (18).
21. "V: Vlast'," in Lur'e *Azbuka protesta*, 26.
22. This event took place on August 23, 1989.
23. Shinkarev, *Sobstvenno literatura*, 227.
24. Ellison, *Invisible Man*, 581.
25. Quoted in Komaromi, "The Material Existence of Soviet Samizdat," 611.
26. Ibid., 615.
27. Yurchak, *Everything Was Forever, Until It Was No More*, 244.
28. Shinkarev, *Sobstvenno literatura*, 232.
29. Sedgwick, *Epistemology of the Closet*, 130.
30. Makarevich and Pirog, "Unusual Perspective / Fantastic Possibilities," 282.
31. Groys, *Art Power*, 3–4.
32. Bessant, *Democracy Bytes*, 130, 168.
33. Ol'ga Florenskaia, "Klassicheskaia smert," http://progallery.org/exhibitions/last/exhibition/1652_klassicheskaya_smert.html.
34. See especially Duncan, "Taking the Smooth with the Rough."
35. Andrei Bitov, "'Nichego' Vladimira Shinkareva," in Sapego, *Mit'ki*, 14–15.
36. Shinkarev, "Installiatsiia 'Kot ob"elsia i lezhit v tsvetakh."

37. Gurevich, *Khudozhniki leningradskogo andegraunda. Biografishekii slovar'*, 147.

38. Shinkarev, *Mit'ki. Materialy k istorii dvizheniia. Konets mit'kov*, 278.

39. Avrich, *Kronstadt 1921*, 229, 241. "Libertarian socialists" is Paul Avrich's term, and the phrase "the inner world of the toilers" comes from the rebels' political manifesto "What We Are Fighting For" (*za chto my boremsia*).

40. Eikhenbaum, "O Chekhove," 468.

41. For a discussion of this post, and a link to it, see Gessen, "The New Face of Russian Resistance."

# Bibliography

## Works by the Mitki

### Texts and Exhibit Catalogs

Florenskaia, Ol'ga. *Psikhologiia bytovogo shrifta*. St. Petersburg: Krasnyi Matros, 2004.

Florenskie, O & A. *Dvizhenie v storonu knigi. Teksty s kartinkami, rasstavlennye strogo v khronologicheskoi posledovatel'nosti*. St. Petersburg: Retro, 2001–2.

Florenskii, Aleksandr. *Neskol'ko slov iz perioda moego geroicheskogo p'ianstva*. St. Petersburg: MITKILIBRIS, n.d.

Florensky, O & A. *Olga Florenskaya, Taxidermy. Alexander [sic] Florensky, Modest Architecture. O & A Florensky, A Moveable Bestiary*. St. Petersburg: MITKILIBRIS, 2000.

Florensky, O & A. *Russkii trofei / Russian Trophy*. St. Petersburg: MITKILIBRIS, 2006.

*Krasnaia strela. Sankt-Peterburg-Moskva. Vystavka k 300-letiiu Severnoi stolitsy*. Moscow: Art Servis Tsentr, 2003.

*Mitkat. Suomessa 'Mitki' in Finland*. Turku, Finland: Aboa Velus & Ars Nova, 2007.

*Mit'ki-Arkhitipy*. St. Petersburg: MITKILIBRIS, 2002.

*Mit'ki. Pro zaek*. Moscow: Vagrius, 2001.

*Mit'ki. Retrospektivnaia vystavka k 10-letiiu dvizheniia*. St. Petersburg: Gosudarstvennyi russkii muzei, 1994.

Sapego, Mikhail, ed. *Mit'ki*. St. Petersburg: Amfora, 2008.

Sapego, Mikhail, ed. *Pro razvedchika Riabova*. St. Petersburg: Krasnyi Matros, 1999.

Shagin, Dmitrii. *Bezzavetnye geroi*. St. Petersburg: Obraztsovaia tipografiia, 1998.

Shagin, Dmitrii. *Dyk!* . . . St. Petersburg: Krasnyi Matros, 2002.

Shagin, Dmitrii. *Mit'kovskie pesni, s kartinkami*. St. Petersburg: Kompozitor Peterburg, 2005.

Shinkarev, Vladimir. "Installiatsiia 'Kot ob"elsia i lezhit v tsvetakh." In *Vystavka "Napisannaia kniga." Rukopisnai grafika*, 73. St. Petersburg: Muzei Anny Akhmatovoi v Fontannom dome, 2004.

Shinkarev, Vladimir. *Maksim i Fedor. Papuas iz Gondurasa. Domashnii ezh. Mit'ki*. St. Petersburg: Novyi Gelikon, 1996.

Shinkarev, Vladimir. *Maxim and Fyodor: Young Russians Search for the Meaning of Life*. Translated by Andrew Bromfield. London: Seagull Publishing House Limited, 2002.

Shinkarev, Vladimir. *Mit'ki*. St. Petersburg: Krasnyi Matros, 1998.

Shinkarev, Vladimir. *Mit'ki. Materialy k istorii dvizheniia. Konets mit'kov*. St. Petersburg: Amfora, 2010.

Shinkarev, Vladimir. *Mit'ki. Risunki Aleksandra Olegovicha Florenskogo*. Moscow: IMA Press, 1990.

Shinkarev, Vladimir. *Mit'kovskie pliaski*. St. Petersburg: Krasnyi Matros, 2005.

Shinkarev, Vladimir. *Sobstvenno literatura. Proza, stikhi, basni, pesni*. St. Petersburg: Grand, 2000.

Shinkarev, Vladimir. *Vsemirnaia literatura*. St. Petersburg: Krasnyi Matros, 2000.

Tikhomirov, Viktor. *Chapaev Chapaev*. St. Petersburg: Amfora, 2010.

Tikhomirov, Viktor. *Evgenii Telegin*. St. Petersburg: Krasnyi Matros, 2017.

Tikhomirov, Viktor. "V ozhidanii Kurekhina." In *Geroi leningradskoi kul'tury. 1950-e–1980-e*, edited by Larisa Skobkina, 237. St. Petersburg: Tetra, 2008.

Tikhomirov, Viktor. *Zoloto na vetru*. St. Petersburg: Grand, 1999.

*Vladimir Shinkarev*. Edited by Isaak Kushnir. St. Petersburg: OOO "P.R.P.," 2006.

### Films and Music

*Andrei Bitov. Zelenyi chemodan*. Directed by Viktor Tikhomirov, 2001. https://www.youtube.com/watch?v=GsGiGuzKYAg.

*Andrei Kuraev. Priamaia rech'*. Directed by Viktor Tikhomirov, 2016.

*Chapaev-Chapaev*. Directed by Viktor Tikhomirov, 2014.

*Mit'ki: Polet Ikara*. Directed by Viktor Tikhomirov, 2000.

*Mit'ki ne khotiat nikogo pobedit', ili Mit'kimaier*. St. Petersburg: Studios "Troitskii Most" and "48 Chasov," 1992 and 1997. https://www.youtube.com/watch?v=hybEBNWtZmY.

*Mit'kovskaia tishina*. CD. Moscow: CD-Land, 1995. Catalogue # AM 052.

*Mit'kovskie pesni*. CD. Moscow: "Soiuz," 1996. Catalogue # SZCD 0632-96.

*Mit'kovskie pesni. Na more tanki grokhotali*. CD. Moscow: "Soiuz," 1997. Catalogue # SZCD 0739-97.

*Sokurov*. Directed by Viktor Tikhomirov, 2004.

*Trava i voda* (*Grass and Water*). Directed by Viktor Tikhomirov, 1992.

## Secondary Sources

Andreeva, Ekaterina, ed. *Timur. Vrat' tol'ko pravdu!* St. Petersburg: Amfora, 2001.

Avrich, Paul. *Kronstadt 1921*. New York: W. W. Norton, 1970.

Babor, Thomas, et al. *Alcohol: No Ordinary Commodity. Research and Public Policy.* Oxford: Oxford University Press, 2003.

Bakhtin, Mikhail. *Problems of Dostoevsky's Poetics.* Translated by Caryl Emerson. Minneapolis: University of Minnesota Press, 1984.

Bakhtin, Mikhail. "Satira." In *Sobranie sochinenii,* Tom 5, 11–38. Moscow: "Russkie slovari," 1995.

Bakhtin, Mikhail. *Sobranie sochinenii,* Tom 4 (2). Moscow: Iazyki slavianskoi kul'tury, 2010.

Bakhtin, Mikhail. *Toward a Philosophy of the Act.* Translated by Vadim Liapunov. Austin: University of Texas Press, 1999.

Baranov, A. N. "Zhargon v kontekste postmodernizma (Mit'kovskii rimeik Novogo Zaveta)." Appendix to *Slovar' russkogo slenga. Slengovye slova i vyrazheniia 60–90-kh godov,* edited by I. Iuganov and F. Iuganov, 283–302. Moscow: Meta Tekst, 1997.

Barthes, Roland. *Image-Music-Text.* Translated by Stephen Heath. London: Fontana Press, 1977.

Bartky, Sandra Lee. *Femininity and Domination: Studies in the Phenomenology of Oppression.* New York and London: Routledge, 1990.

Baudrillard, Jean. *Simulacra and Simulation.* Translated by Sheila Faria Glaser. Ann Arbor: University of Michigan Press, 1994.

Beckett, Samuel. *Waiting for Godot: A Tragicomedy in Two Acts.* New York: Grove Press, 1956.

Berlant, Lauren, and Lee Edelman. *Sex, or The Unbearable.* Durham, NC: Duke University Press, 2014.

Bersani, Leo, and Adam Phillips. *Intimacies.* Chicago: University of Chicago Press, 2008.

Bessant, Judith. *Democracy Bytes: New Media, New Politics, New Generational Change.* London: Palgrave Macmillan, 2014.

Bitov, Andrei. "The Mitki on the Cusp of Time and Space" ("*Mit'ki* na granitse vremeni i prostranstva"). In *Mit'ki,* edited by Mikhail Sapego, 7–12. St. Petersburg: Amfora, 2008.

Boym, Svetlana. *Another Freedom: The Alternative History of an Idea.* Chicago: University of Chicago Press, 2010.

Brodsky, Joseph. *Less Than One: Selected Essays.* New York: Farrar, Straus and Giroux, 1986.

Brodsky, Joseph. *Nativity Poems.* New York: Farrar, Straus and Giroux, 2001.

Buruma, Ian. "The Invention of David Bowie." In *Theater of Cruelty: Art, Film, and the Shadow of War,* by Ian Buruma, 279–91. New York: New York Review of Books, 2014.

Butler, Judith. *Gender Trouble: Feminism and the Subversion of Identity.* New York and London: Routledge, 1990.

Butler, Judith. *Notes toward a Performative Theory of Assembly.* Cambridge, MA: Harvard University Press, 2015.

Butler, Judith. *Undoing Gender.* London: Routledge, 2004.

Chemiakin, Mikhail. *Mihail Chemiakin.* Vol. 1, *Petersburg Period, Paris Period.* Oakville, Ontario: Mosaic Press, 1986.

Custine, Marquis de. *Letters from Russia.* Translated by Robin Buss. London: Penguin Books, 1991.

Davis, Angela Y. "The Truth Telling Project: Violence in America." In *Freedom Is a Constant Struggle: Ferguson, Palestine, and the Foundations of a Movement*, by Angela Y. Davis, 81–90. Chicago: Haymarket Books, 2016.

Debord, Guy. *The Society of the Spectacle*. Translated by Donald Nicholson-Smith. New York: Zone Books, 1994.

Deleuze, Gilles, and Félix Guattari. *Anti-Oedipus: Capitalism and Schizophrenia*. Translated by Robert Hurley, Mark Seem, and Helen R. Lane. Minneapolis: University of Minnesota Press, 2008.

"Dmitrii Shagin: Dlia kartiny Repina nastupila temnaia polosa." *Izvestiia* (October 11, 2013) http://izvestia.ru/news/558619. Accessed July 17, 2014.

"Dmitrii Shagin: Smysl tvorchestva." *Vechnyi zov* (May 2007): 4–5.

Dolinin, Viacheslav. *Ne stol' otdalennaia kochegarka. Vospominania. Rasskazy*. St. Petersburg: Izd. Imeni N. I. Novikova, 2007.

Duncan, Pansy. "Taking the Smooth with the Rough: Texture, Emotion, and the Other Postmodernism." *PMLA* 129:2 (March 2014): 204–22.

Eikhenbaum, Boris. "O Chekhove." In *Formal'nyi metod. Antologiia russkogo modernizma*, Tom 2, edited by Sergei Oushakine, 464–70. Moscow-Ekaterinburg: Kabinetnyi uchenyi, 2016.

Ellison, Ralph. *Invisible Man*. New York: Vintage Books, 1980.

Elman, Richard. *Uptight with the Stones*. New York: Charles Scribner's Sons, 1973.

Evdokimov, Rostislav. *Zapiski lzhesvidetelia*. Moscow: NP "Posev," 2016.

Fedorov, Nikolai. "Muzei, ego smysl i naznachenie." In *Russkii ksomizm. Antologiia*, edited by Boris Groys, 32–136. Moscow: Ad Marginem Press, 2015.

Forrester, Sibelan. "The Poet as Pretender: Poetic Legitimacy in Tsvetaeva." *Slavic and East European Journal* 52:1 (Spring 2008): 37–53.

Frontinski, Oleg. "Shtrikhi k portretu Olega Grigorieva." In *Geroi leningradskoi kul'tury. 1950-e–1980-e*, edited by Larisa Skobkina, 160–61. St. Petersburg: Tetra, 2008.

Gessen, Masha. "Ia prishla v etot sud, chtoby eshche raz vysvetit' absurdnost' neftegazovogo syr'evogo pravosudiia." *Nove vremia / The New Times* (March 30, 2013).

Gessen, Masha. "The New Face of Russian Resistance." *NYR Daily* (June 14, 2012) http://www.nybooks.com/daily/2017/06/14/the-new-face-of-russian-resistance/.

Gessen, Masha. "Retrofitting Totalitarianism." *Public Books* (2015) http://www.publicbooks.org/nonfiction/retrofitting-totalitarianism.

Gessen, Masha. *Words Will Break Cement: The Passion of Pussy Riot*. New York: Riverhead Books, 2014.

Gilmore, Mikal. *Stories Done: Writings on the 1960s and Its Discontents*. New York: Free Press, 2009.

Girard, René. *Violence and the Sacred*. Translated by Patrick Gregory. Baltimore, MD: Johns Hopkins University Press, 1984.

Gorbacheva, Natalia. *Sviataia Kseniia i Diveevskie blazhennye*. St. Petersburg: Palomnik, 2007.

Gordon, Lois. *Reading Godot*. New Haven, CT: Yale University Press, 2002.

Grigoriev, Oleg. *Vinokhranitel'. Stikhotvoreniia*. Illustrations by Aleksandr Florensky. St. Petersburg: Vita Nova, 2008.

Groys, Boris. *Art Power*. Cambridge, MA: MIT Press, 2008.
Groys, Boris. "A Style and a Half: Socialist Realism between Modernism and Postmodernism." In *Socialist Realism Without Shores*, edited by Thomas Lahusen and Evgeny Dobrenko, 76–90. Durham, NC: Duke University Press, 1997.
Gura, A. V. *Simvolika zhivotnykh v slavianskoi narodnoi traditsii*. Moscow: Indrik, 1997.
Gurevich, Liubov. *Khudozhniki leningradskogo andegraunda. Biografishekii slovar'*. St. Petersburg: "Iskusstvo—SPb," 2007.
Gurevich, Liubov. "Prel'stitel' (popytka kritiki)." *Postscriptum. Literaturnyi zhurnal* 2 (1995): 291–311.
Gurvich, Iosif, ed. *Upotreblenie alkogolia v Rossii. Istoriia, statistika, psikhologiia*. St. Petersburg: Fakul'tet psikhologii S. Peterburskogo gosudarstvennogo universiteta, 2008.
Hamel, Christine. *Puschkinkult in weißen Nächten. St. Petersburger Seelensprünge*. Wien: Picus Verlag, 2003.
Hetko, Eli. "Mitki and Kharms." Bachelor's thesis, Wesleyan University, April 2011.
Hetko, Eli. "We Could Be Antiheroes: How David Bowie Became the Loathed Adversary of a Soviet-era Youth Movement." *Slate Magazine* (January 15, 2016) http://www.slate.com/articles/news_and_politics/roads/2016/01/mitki_the_soviet_era_youth_movement_that_loathed_david_bowie.html.
Iakimovich, Aleksandr. "P'ianstvo kak predmet iskusstva i filosofii." *Vodka. Gallereia M. Gel'mana, 22 maia–20 iiunia 1997 gg. Moskva, Mit'ki, Avdei Ter-Oganian, Vladimir Arkhipov*. http://www.guelman.ru/gallery/moscow/vodka/.
Iuganov, I., and F. Iuganov, eds. *Slovar' russkogo slenga. Slengovye slova i vyrazheniia 60–90-x godov*. Moscow: Meta Tekst, 1995.
Iversen, Margaret, ed. *Chance: Documents of Contemporary Art*. London: MIT Press, 2010.
Jameson, Fredric. "Postmodernism and Consumerist Society." In *The Anti-Aesthetic: Essays on Postmodern Culture*, edited by Hal Foster, 111–25. Port Townsend, WA: Bay Press, 1987.
Jonquet, François. *Gilbert and George: Intimate Conversations with François Jonquet*. London: Phaidon Press, 2004.
Kan, Aleksandr. *Kurekhin. Shpiker o kapitane*. St. Petersburg: Amfora, 2012.
Karpinski, L. V. "Pochemu stalinizm ne skhodit so stseny?" In *Inogo ne dano*, edited by Iu. N. Afanas'ev, 648–70. Moscow: "Progress," 1988.
Kharkhordin, Oleg. *The Collective and the Individual in Russia: A Study of Practices*. Berkeley: University of California Press, 1999.
Kharms, Daniil. *Polet v nebesa. Stikhi, proza, dramy, pis'ma*, edited by A. A. Aleksandrov. Leningrad: Sovetskii pisatel', 1991.
Kizenko, Nadieszda. "Protectors of Women and the Lower Orders: Constructing Sainthood in Modern Russia." In *Orthodox Russia: Belief and Practice Under the Tsars*, edited by Valerie Kivelson and Robert H. Greene, 105–24. University Park: Pennsylvania State University Press, 2003.
*Kollazh v Rossii. XX vek*. St. Petersburg: Palace Editions, 2005.

Komaromi, Ann. "The Material Existence of Soviet Samizdat." *Slavic Review* 64:3 (Autumn 2004): 597–618.

Kushnir, Aleksandr. *Sergei Kurekhin. Bezumnaia mekhanika russkogo roka*. Moscow: Bertel'smani Media Moskau, 2013.

Kuznetsov, Luka. "Voistinu oppan'ki!" *Krasnyi shchedrinets. Iumor, satira, parodii, absurdistika* 3 (1986): 19–24.

Lacan, Jacques. "The Mirror Stage as Formative of the *I* Function as Revealed in Psychoanalytic Experience." In Écrits*: The First Complete English Edition*, 75–81. Translated by Bruce Fink. New York: W. W. Norton, 2006.

Levintov, Aleksandr. *Vypivka i p'ianka*. Moscow: Eksmo, 2005.

Lévy, Pierre. *Collective Intelligence: Mankind's Emerging World in Cyberspace*. Translated by Robert Bononno. Cambridge, MA: Perseus Books, 1997.

Likhanova, Tat'iana. "Konets mit'kov." *Novaia gazeta* (November 15, 2010) http://novayagazeta.spb.ru/articles/6245/. Accessed October 5, 2017.

Likhanova, Tat'iana. "Mityok-Raskol'nikoff [*sic*]." *Novaia gazeta* (March 24, 2008) http://novayagazeta.spb.ru/articles/4150/. Accessed September 24, 2016.

Lipman, Maria, and Nikolay Petrov, eds. *The State of Russia: What Comes Next?* London: Palgrave Macmillan, 2014.

Lipovetsky, Mark. *Charms of Cynical Reason: The Trickster's Transformation in Soviet and Post-Soviet Culture*. Brighton, MA: Academic Studies Press, 2011.

Lotman, Yuri. "Dinamicheskaia model' semioticheskoi sistemy." In *Readings in Soviet Semiotics: (Russian Texts)*, edited by L. Matejka et al., 76–93. Ann Arbor: Michigan Slavic Publications, 1977.

Lotman, Yuri. *Vnutri mysliashchikh mirov*. St. Petersburg: Azbuka, 2016.

Lur'e, Vadim, ed. *Azbuka protesta. Narodnyi plakat*. Moscow: O. G. I. Polit.ru, 2012.

Lyotard, Jean-François. *The Postmodern Condition: A Report on Knowledge*. Translated by Geoff Bennington and Brian Massumi. Minneapolis: University of Minnesota Press, 1984.

Makarevich, Igor, and Gerald Pirog, "Unusual Perspective / Fantastic Possibilities." In *Beyond Memory: Soviet Non-Conformist Photography and Photo-Related Works of Art*, edited by Diane Neumaier, 279–91. New Brunswick, NJ: Rutgers University Press, 2004.

*The Man Who Fell to Earth: A Film by Nicolas Roeg*. DVD. Anchor Bay Entertainment, 2003. Catalogue # DV11477.

Masiagin, V. P., and S. A. Iakimov. *Ofitsery baltiiskogo flota*. St. Petersburg: Izmailovskii, 2003.

Matveeva, Anna. "Nikto ne znaet pro seks." *Artgid* (February 28, 2013) http://artguide.com/posts/307-nikto-nie-znaiet-pro-sieks-337.

Mihailovic, Alexandar. "Hijacking Authority: Academic Neo-Aryanism and Internet Expertise." In *Digital Media Strategies of the Far Right in Europe and the United States*, edited by Patricia Simpson and Helga Druxes, 83–102. Lanham, MD: Lexington Books, 2015.

Mirzoeff, Nicholas, ed. *The Visual Culture Reader*. London: Routledge, 2002.

"Mit'ki bez portveina. Chto obshchego mezhdu filosofiei mit'kov i programmoi anonimnykh alkogolikov?" *Novaia gazeta* 48 (June 8, 2004) http://2004

.NovayaGazeta.Ru/nomer/2004/48n/n48n-s25.shtml. Accessed September 14, 2004.

Monastyrskii, Andrei. *Slovar' terminov moskovskoi kontseptual'noi shkoly*. Moscow: AD MARGINAM, 1999.

Nabokov, Vladimir. *Eugene Onegin: A Novel in Verse by Aleksandr Pushkin*. Vol. 3, *Commentary: Six to End*. New York: Pantheon Books, 1964.

Nabokov, Vladimir. "Good Readers and Good Writers." In *Lectures on Literature*, 1–7. New York: Harvest Books, 2002.

Nemerov, Alexander. "The Flight of Form: Auden, Breugel [*sic*], and the Turn to Abstraction in the 1940s." *Critical Inquiry* 31:4 (Summer 2005): 790–810.

Ostashevsky, Eugene, ed. *OBERIU: An Anthology of Russian Absurdism*. Evanston, IL: Northwestern University Press, 2004.

Peltz, Judith, ed. *Poetischer Sankt Petersburg-Führer*. Darmstadt: Wissenschaftliche Buchgesellschaft, 2002.

Pivovarov, Viktor. *Vliublennyi agent*. 2nd ed. Moscow: ArtGuide Editions, 2016.

Pleshakov, Constantine. *The Tsar's Last Armada: The Epic Voyage to the Battle of Tsushima*. New York: Basic Books, 2002.

"Prezentatsiia issledovaniia Vladimira Shinkareva 'Konets mit'kov'." *Zelenaia lampa* (November 11, 2010) http://www.greenlamp.spb.ru/2010/11/11/. Accessed July 14, 2017.

Prigov, Dmitrii. *Napisannoe s 1975 po 1989*. Moscow: Novoe literaturnoe obozrenie, 1997.

Raikhel, Eugene. *Governing Habits: Treating Alcoholism in the Post-Soviet Clinic*. Ithaca, NY: Cornell University Press, 2016.

Rekshan, Vladimir. *Kaif polnyi. Pochti documental'naia rok-simfoniia*. Leningrad: izd. "Financy i statistika," 1990.

Rekshan, Vladimir. *Leningradskoe vremia, ili ischezaiushchii gorod*. St. Petersburg: Amfora, 2015.

Remnick, David. "Letter from Moscow: Post-Imperial Blues." *New Yorker* (October 13, 2003): 79–86.

Richards, Keith. *Life*. New York: Little, Brown, 2010.

Ronen, Omri. "Leksicheskii povtor, podtekst i smysl v poetike Osipa Mandel'shtama." In *Slavic Poetics: Essays in Honor of Kirill Taranovsky*, edited by Roman Jakosons et al., 367–87. The Hague: Mouton, 1973.

Rosenfeld, Alla, ed. *Moscow Conceptualism in Context*. Munich: Prestel Verlag, 2011.

Roth, Michael. "Leo: Two Prominent Thinkers Consider New Forms of Intimacy." *Bookforum* (April/May 2008) http://www.bookforum.com/inprint/015_01/2249.

Roudinesco, Elisabeth. *Jacques Lacan: An Outline of a Life and History of a System of Thought*. London: Polity Press, 1999.

Rozanov, Vasilii. *Apokalipsis nashego vremeni*. Moscow: Eksmo, 2008.

Rüther, Tobias. *David Bowie and Berlin*. Translated by Anthony Mathews. London: Reaktion Books, 2015.

Ryback, Timothy W. *Rock Around the Bloc: A History of Rock Music in Eastern Europe and the Soviet Union*. New York: Oxford University Press, 1990.

Sapego, Mikhail, ed. *Etiketki*. St. Petersburg: Krasnyi Matros, 2007.

Savitskii, Stanislav. *Andeground. Istoriia i mify leningradskoi neofitsial'noi literatury*. Moscow: Novoe literaturnoe obozrenie, 2002.

Schlatter, N. Elizabeth, and Joan Maitre, eds. *The Space of Freedom: Apartment Exhibitions in Leningrad, 1964–1986*. Richmond, VA: University of Richmond Museums, 2007.

Sedgwick, Eve Kosofsky. *Between Men: English Literature and Homosocial Desire*. New York: Columbia University Press, 1985.

Sedgwick, Eve Kosofsky. *Epistemology of the Closet*. Berkeley: University of California Press, 2008.

Shekhter, Tat'iana. "Andegraund kak novaia khudozhestvennaia real'nost'." In *Iz padeniia v polet. Nezavisimoe iskusstvo Sankt-Peterburga. Vtoraia polovina XX veka*, edited by Sergei Koval'skii, 50–55. St. Petersburg: Muzei Nonkonformistskogo Iskusstva, 2006.

Shenkman, Ian. "Moskva mit'kovskaia." *Ogonek* 50 (December 2002) http://www.ogoniok.com/archive/2002/4778/50-42-43/.

Shevstova, V. V. "Sviataia blazhennaia Kseniia Peterburgskaia." In *Nebesnye pokorviteli Sankt-Peterburga*, edited by O. S. Nadporozhskaia, 83–99. St. Petersburg: "Neva," 2003.

Shklovsky, Viktor. "Iskusstvo kak priem." In *Formal'nyi metod. Antologiia russkogo modernizma*, Tom 1, edited by Sergei Oushakine, 130–46. Moscow and Ekaterinburg: Kabinetnyi uchenyi, 2016.

Shuliakhovskaia, Natalia. "Mit'ki i seks." http://mitki.kulichki.com/sex/.

*Sindrom Tsusimy. Sbornik statei*. St. Petersburg: Almanakh Tsitatel', 1997.

Sinyavsky, Andrei [Abram Terts]. *V teni Gogolia*. London: Overseas Publication Exchange, 1975.

Smelov, Boris. *Boris Smelov: Retrospective*. St. Petersburg: Gosudartsvtennyi Ermitazh, 2009.

Solomon, Andrew. *The Irony Tower: Soviet Artists in a Time of Glasnost*. New York: Knopf, 1991.

Sontag, Susan. "Notes on Camp." *Partisan Review* (Fall 1964): 515–30.

Steinholt, Yngvar B. "You Can't Rid a Song of Its Words: Notes on the Hegemony of Lyrics in Russian Rock Songs." *Popular Music* 22:1 (January 2003): 89–108.

Stepanova, Varvara. "Chelovek ne mozhet zhit' bez chuda (o vozmozhnosti poznaniia iskusstva)." In *Formal'nyi metod. Antologiia russkogo modernizma*, Tom 2, edited by Sergei Oushakine, 851–52. Moscow and Ekaterinburg: Kabinetnyi uchenyi, 2016.

Stepanova, Varvara. "Konstruktivizm." In *Formal'nyi metod. Antologiia russkogo modernizma*, Tom 2, edited by Sergei Oushakine, 853–59. Moscow and Ekaterinburg: Kabinetnyi uchenyi, 2016.

Thian, Helene Marie. "Moss Garden: David Bowie and Japonism in Fashion in the 1970s." In *David Bowie: Critical Perspectives*, edited by Eoin Devereaux, Aileen Dillane, and Martin J. Power, 128–46. London: Routledge, 2015.

Travis, Trysh. *The Language of the Heart: A Cultural History of the Recovery Movement from Alcoholics Anonymous to Oprah Winfrey*. Chapel Hill: University of North Carolina Press, 2009.

Tsvetaeva, Marina. *Stikhotvoreniia. Poemy. Proza*. Moscow: Eksmo, 2014.

Tupitsyn, Victor. *The Museological Unconscious: Communal (Post)Modernism in Russia*. Cambridge, MA: MIT Press, 2011.

Valieva, Yulia, ed. *Sumerki Saigona*. St. Petersburg: Zamizdat, 2009.

Volkov, Solomon. *St. Petersburg: A Cultural History*. New York: Free Press, 1995.

Wilde, Oscar. *Intentions*. New York: Boni and Liverwright, n.d.

Woodhead, Leslie. *How the Beatles Rocked the Kremlin: The Untold Story of a Noisy Revolution*. New York: Bloomsbury, 2013.

Yurchak, Alexei. *Everything Was Forever, Until It Was No More: The Last Soviet Generation*. Princeton, NJ: Princeton University Press, 2006.

Yurchak, Alexei. "A Parasite from Outer Space: How Sergei Kurekhin Proved That Lenin Was a Mushroom." *Slavic Review* 70:2 (Summer 2011): 307–33.

Zhitinskii, Aleksandr. *Puteshestvie rok-diletanta. Muzykal-nyi roman*. Leningrad: Lenizdat, 1990.

Žižek, Slavoj. "Why Are Laibach and NSK Not Fascists?" In *Primary Documents: A Sourcebook for Eastern and Central European Art since the 1950s*, edited by Laura Hoptman and Tomas Pospiszyl, 285–87. New York: Museum of Modern Art, 2002.

# Index

Page numbers for illustrations and captions are in italics.

Abramovic, Marina, 41
Akvarium (rock group). *See* Grebenshchikov, Boris
alcoholism: affective dimensions of, 15, 96–97, 99–100, 101, 111, 117; alcohol and sexual politics, 114–16, 118, 145; the Mitki and Alcoholics Anonymous, 15, 102, 104, 108–9, 120, 124; restriction on hard liquor, 100
Arefiev, Aleksandr, xvi, xvii, 6, 9, 10, 147, 148, 150, 206, 207
Arefiev circle of artists. *See* Arefiev, Aleksandr
Auden, W. H., 4, 35–40, 71, 73, 90–91
Avrich, Paul, 218, 238n39

Babel, Isaak, 169, 188
Babor, Thomas, 231n6
Bakhtin, Mikhail, conception of: carnival, 205, 227n13; dialogue, 50–51, 57; the grotesque body, 54, 118, 226n62; polyphony, 57, 203; Rabelais, 54, 110, 232n28; satire, 179, 186, 236n15; self-renunciation, 65, 227n141
Baranov, A. N., 228n35
Bartelik, Marek, 223n10
Barthes, Roland, 49, 50, 226n53
Bartky, Sandra Lee, 158
Bashlachev, Aleksandr, 45
Baudrillard, Jean, 34, 35, 132, 226n25
Beckett, Samuel, 40–42, 226n38
Beckmann, Max, 43
Benjamin, Walter, 169, 183, 213
Bergman, Ingmar, 45
Berlant, Lauren, 194, 236n30
Bersani, Leo, 9, 64, 224n14, 227n11
Bessant, Judith, 216, 237n32
Bitov, Andrei, 3, 48, 117, 126, 127, 144–45, 162, 216, 217, 226n50, 232n47, 234n22, 237n35
blockade, Leningrad, 5, 112–13
Borovsky, Aleksandr, xiii, 129, 233n2
Bowie, David: *Alladin Sane*, 60; "Heroes," 58, 92; interest in Kabuki theatre and *onnagata* tradition, 92; in *The Man Who Fell to Earth*, 30, 210; perception of, among the Mitki, 14, 60, 71, 88, 89, 113, 172, 227, 230n63; *Ziggy Stardust and the Spiders from Mars*, 41, 60
Boym, Svetlana, 166–67, 185–86, 233n1, 235n5
Brexit, 23
Brezhnev, Leonid, 6, 18, 63–64, 68, 114, 200
Brodsky, Joseph, 7, 69, 87, 94, 228n24, 230n78, 231n79
Brueghel the Elder, painter of *The Fall of Icarus*, 35–37, 71, 73, 84, 228n31

Buruma, Ian, 230n70, 230n72
Butler, Judith, 57, 59, 61, 64, 93–94, 125, 156, 157, 173, 227n68, 227n3, 230nn73–74, 231n80, 233n60, 235n42, 236n10

Cammell, Donald (*Performance*), 30
Cervantes, Miguel de, 33, 48
Cézanne, 9, 27, 43
Chemiakin, Mikhail, 10, 224n16
Chivers, C. J., 224n26
Clapton, Eric, 125
Cocteau, Jean, 45
Conrad, Joseph, 30
Cooperative of Experimental Graphic Art (TEII), xv, 27, 202
Corinth, Lovis, 43
Crimean War, 4
Custine, Marquis de, 147, 225n7, 234n30

Dadaists, 4, 209
Dante Alighieri, 56
Daumier, Honoré, 31
Davis, Angela, 13, 224n20
Debord, Guy, 15, 224n23
Defoe, Daniel, 48
Deleuze, Gilles, 34, 162, 166, 235n56, 235n4
Dolinin, Viacheslav, xii, 93, 230n76
*Don't Change the Meeting Place* (*Mesto vstrechi izmenit' nel'zia*), 9, 37, 99
Duchamp, Marcel, 67
Dugin, Aleksandr, 136, 147, 210

Edelman, Lee, 194, 236n30
Eikhenbaum, Boris, 66, 218–19, 238n40
Ellison, Ralph, 213, 237n24
Elman, Richard, 225n8
Erofeev, Venedikt, 43
Evdokimov, Rostislav, 5, 22, 223n3, 225n40

Fanailova, Elena, 11
Fedorov, Nikolai, 198, 236n38
Florensky, Aleksandr, xvi, 2, 8, 10, 16, 23, 24, 37, 38, 70, 74, 86, 99, 108, 121, 123, 124, 145, 147, 162, 204, 213, 218, 229n42, 229n49, 232n55, 233n2, 233n8, 234n21, 234n36; drawings for Shinkarev's *Mitki*, 61, 62, 76, 77, 78, 90, 98, 100, 106, 122, 230n36; *Drawings about Jerusalem*, 139–40, 142, 143, 144; *A Few Episodes from the Period of My Epic Drinking*, 117–18, *119*; "Some kids stuck needles into a masochist . . ." (Mazokhistu na lavke vtykali deti ne ot toski . . .), 158–59, *160*, 161. *See also* O & A Florensky
Florensky, Katya, 16, 22, 153, 159, 161, 162. *See also* O & A Florensky
Florensky, Olga, xvi, 2, 6, 8, 10, 14, 16, 22, 40, 70, 74, 80, 81, 84, 118, 145–46, 162, 204, 211, 218, 229n51; as a totem of both the feminine and transgressive gender ambiguity for the Mitki, 75–76, 114–15, 129–30
Florensky, Olga, literary work: essay about Oleg Grigoriev, 159, 161; poetry, 7, 146–48, 153, 157–58; *The Psychology of Everyday Script* (*Psikhologiia bytovogo shrift*), 131, 238n8
Florensky, Olga, graphic work: *Bluebeard*, 148, *149*, 150; *Classic Death*, 151, 216–17, 234n33; *Heroes of Russian Aviation*, 87–90, *89*; *The Letter И*, *85*; *Moby Dick*, 132, *133–35*, 136–39; *September in Roccasecca*, 147, 153, 234n36; *A Story about the Miracle of Miracles* (*Rasskaz o chude iz chudes*), 154–55; *Taxidermy* installation, 126, 128–29, 131, 158. *See also* O & A Florensky
Forrester, Sibelan, 157, 235n47
Fox, James, 30
Fripp, Robert, 92, 230n71
Frontinski, Oleg, 158, 235n50

gender: homophobia, 189, 193, 214; homosociality, 60, 68, 80, 123, 172, 191; indeterminacy, 7, 54, 71, 75–76, 80, 95, 145–46; instantiations of masculinity and femininity, 64, 73, 78, 84, 114, 184; LGBTQ community, 188, 192, 214; misogyny, 172; performativity, 93, 144, 147, 154, 161, 166, 218; queerness, 60, 66, 92, 194; sexual trauma, 105–6, 176–77
Gessen, Masha, 8, 224n13, 227n2, 236nn1–2, 238n41
Gilbert & George, 154, 156, 234n38
Gilmore, Mikal, 232n39
Girard, René, 87, 88, 230n59
Goethe, Johann Wolfgang von, 43–45, 150
Gogol, Nikolai, 10, 57, 210, 224n18, 237n16
Golubev, Vasili, ix, 2, 63–64, 200; *The Mitki Send Brezhnev Off to Afghanistan*, 64
Gorbachev, Mikhail, 15, 23, 63, 65, 100, 102, 108, 112, 113, 114, 117, 210

Gorbacheva, Natalia, 234nn24–25, 234n28
Gordon, Lois, 41–42, 226nn40–41
Grebenshchikov, Boris, 41, 45–47, 92, 226n39, 230n70
Greenberg, Clement, 21–22
Grigoriev, Oleg, xvi, 10, 114, 158–61, 235nn50–51, 235n53
Groys, Boris, 8, 38, 50, 56, 151, 162, 215, 216, 224n11, 226n30, 234n32, 237n31
Guattari, Félix, 34, 162
Guelman, Marat, 16, 155
Gura, A. V., 236n19
Gurevich, Liubov, 9, 33, 51, 53, 88, 107, 162, 218, 224n15, 226n61, 231n23, 235n57, 238n37
Gurvich, Iosif, xiv, 100, 231n8

Hašek, Jaroslav, 48
Hetko, Eli, 101, 227n5, 231n11
House of Hope on the Hill (Perekyulya, Russia), xii, 15, 125
Housman, A. E., 35–36

Iakimovich, Aleksandr, 232n27
Icarus, in the work of the Mitki, xvi, 14, 24, 35–36, 39, 71, 73, 81, 84, 90, 102, 154, 159, 216, 229n49, 229n51
Imperial Academy of Fine Arts, 26, 27
"Itinerant" painters (*Peredvizhniki*), 27
Iuganov, I. and F., 233n6
Iversen, Margaret, 235n4

"Jack of Diamonds" (*Bubnovyi valet*) school of painting, 51
Jagger, Mick, 29–31, 41
Jameson, Fredric, 19, 32, 224n31, 225n14
Jonquet, François, 234n38

Karpinski, Lev V., 65
Kesey, Ken, 4, 75
Kharkhodin, Oleg, 234n34
Kharms, Daniil, 101, 177, 231n9, 231n11
Khvostenko, Aleksei, 49, 86–87, 230n57
Kirchner, Ernst, 43
Kizenko, Nadieszda, 234n24
Klimova, Ekaterina, 19
Komaromi, Ann, 209, 227n1, 227n8, 237n13, 237n25
Kovalsky, Sergei, 223n1, 223n7
*Krasnyi shchedrinets*, 61, 62, 63, 99
Kseniya, Saint ("The Blessed"), 122, 144–47, 234n24
Kuraev, Andrei (Russian Orthodox priest and author). *See* Tikhomirov, Viktor
Kurekhin, Sergei, 41, 45, 87, 92, 202, 210, 226n39, 230n58, 237n17
Kushnir, Aleksandr, 226n39
Kushnir, Isaak, 230n67
Kuznetsov, Andrei ("Kuzya"), 2, 74–75
Kuznetsov, Luka (art historian), 61, 63, 64, 66, 99, 227n10, 231n4

Lacan, Jacques, 55, 226n65
Laibach, 67, 228n20
Laing, R. D., 16
Lenin, Vladimir Ilyich, 70, 177–78, 179, 182, 196
Leningrad Higher School of Industry and Art. *See* Mukhin School
Leningrad Underground, 5–6, 7, 10, 11, 13, 15, 18, 23, 36, 45, 63, 74, 90, 92, 93, 96, 99, 159, 202, 205, 206
Leskov, Nikolai, 154, 169
Levintov, Aleksandr, 100, 101, 120, 231n5, 231n7, 232n52
Lévy, Pierre, 22, 174–75, 178, 198, 236n11, 236n39
Lianozovo group of nonconformist painters, 4, 18
Lifshitz, Mikhail, 13, 224n21
Likhanova, Tatiana, 224n22
Lipman, Maria, 237n20
Lipovetsky, Mark, 22, 187, 225n39
Losev, Lev, 59, 61
Lotman, Yuri, 57, 128, 198, 227n67, 233n3, 236n37
*lubki*, Russian wood engravings, 19, 71, 117, 159, 164, 180
Lur'e, Vadim, 237n19
Lyotard, Jean-François, 8, 35, 56, 66, 224n11, 227n17, 228n19

Makarenko, Anton, 152
Makarenko, Boris, 237n20
Makarevich, Andrei, 46
Makarevich, Igor, 215, 237n30
Mandelstam, Osip, 7, 10, 37
Mandelstam, Roald, 10, 40, 147, 150
Masiagin, V. P., 228n21
Matveeva, Anna, 164
Medvedev, Dmitri, 11, 12, 32
Mirzoeff, Nicholas, 208, 209, 237n11
Mitin, Aleksei, xii, 24
Mitki, 2, 24, 212; *Mitkimaier*, 70–72, 74–75,

Mitki (*continued*)
233n8; interest in Japanese culture, 87–88, 91–92, 94–95; *Sisters, or a Woman's Lot*, 82. *See also* Florensky, Aleksandr; Florensky, Olga; Golubev, Vasili; Kuznetsov, Andrei; Shagin, Dmitri; Shinkarev, Vladimir; Tikhomirov, Viktor; Vasilieva, Irina
Monastyrsky, Andrei, 4, 18–20, 21, 132, 225n36
Moscow Conceptualists, 18–21, 41. *See also* Monastyrsky, Andrei
Mukhin School (*Mukhinskoe uchilishche*), 27

Nabokov, Vladimir, 93, 169, 197, 201, 235n6, 236n4
Naumenko, "Mike," 46
Navalnyi, Alexei, 12
navy, Russian and Soviet, 4, 8, 68–69, 84, 87, 94, 102, 122, 193, 218
necrorealism. *See* Yufit, Evgeni
*Neue Slowenische Kunst*. *See* Laibach
Novikov, Timur, xv, 193–94, 202, 212, 230n58
Novodvorskaya, Valeriya, 17

O & A Florensky, 16, 19, 150–56, 233n4; *Internal Space* installation, 158; *Moby Dick*, 137; *Movement in the Direction of IYE*, 140–42; *Russian Trophy* installation, 151–52
Okhlobystin, Ivan, 188, 189, 236n24
Orthodox Church, Russian, 108, 122, 123, 135, 145, 147
Ostashevsky, Eugene, 231n9

Paul, Jean (Johann Paul Friedrich Richter), 69
Pavlensky, Piotr, 5
Pechstein, Max, 45
Peltz, Judith, 225n7
*Peredvizhniki*. *See* "Itinerant" painters
Peter the Great, 26, 68, 102, 122
Pharaoh Amenhotep III, 26
Phillips, Adam, 9, 224n14, 227n11
Pivovarov, Viktor, 18, 224n29
Plato, 32
Pleshakov, Constantine, 229n53
postmodernism: affective dimensions of, 35, 39, 50, 66; in relation to the desire for the Other, 8, 68; as sequence of identical images, 19, 224n31, 225n14; as tool for demystification and destabilization of orthodoxies, 8, 22, 26, 34, 38, 51, 215–16, 217, 224n11, 226n30
Prigov, Dmitri, 20, 199, 213, 236n2
Prilepin, Zakhar, 11
protest: performative dimensions of, and as performance art, xv, 12, 17, 31, 47, 201, 203, 204, 206, 208, 209, 213, 216, 219; in relation to ideological ambiguity, 4, 22, 200, 207, 211, 218
Pushkin, Aleksandr, 18–19, 48, 101, 144, 177, 194–95, 213, 217
Pussy Riot, 4–5, 17, 31, 59, 63, 199, 214, 216, 227n2, 236n2
Putin, Vladimir, 4, 7, 8, 10, 12, 17, 32, 59, 97, 178, 181, 205, 207, 211

Raikhel, Eugene, 121–22, 232n56
Rekshan, Vladimir, xiii, 28, 93, 201–2, 230n75, 237n6
Remnick, David, 8, 224n12
Repin Institute. *See* Imperial Academy of Fine Arts
Richards, Keith, 25, 29–31, 41, 210, 225n9
Robert, Hubert, 152
Roeg, Nicholas, 30, 91, 230n68
Ronen, Omry, 37
Rosenberg, Harold, 21–22
Rosenfeld, Alla, 224n10
Rouault, Georges, 29
Roudinesco, Elisabeth, 226n64
Rousseau, Henri, 51
Rozanov, Vasili, 79, 189, 193, 236n23
Runyon, Damon, 37
Rüther, Tobias, 230n71
Ryback, Timothy W., 230n70

*samizdat*, xv, 6, 14, 58, 59, 61, 65, 90, 92, 98, 99, 156–57, 161, 162, 209, 213, 227n1, 228n33, 237n13
Sapego, Mikhail, 85, 86, 140, 161, 204–5, 226n50, 229n54, 232n29, 232n32, 232nn36–37, 232n42, 232n51, 232n53, 234n22, 235n3, 237n35
Sassoon, Siegfried, 35–36
Satarov, Georgy, 218–19
Savitskii, Stanislav, 237n9
Schiller, Friedrich, 150, 186
Schlatter, N. Elizabeth, 223n1, 223n7, 237n12

Sedgwick, Eve Kosofsky, 51, 52, 61, 63, 65–66, 80, 191, 192, 214–15, 226n57, 227n7, 227n9, 227n15, 229n48, 237n29
Shagin, Dmitri, xv, 2, 6–15, 24, 25–57, 59–63, 67–71, 73–76, 84, 88, 91, 93, 94–95, 96–99, 102, 105–17, 120–25, 127, 129–31, 136, 144–45, 147–48, 159, 161, 170, 177, 200, 209, 214, 224n22, 225n6, 225n11, 226n26, 228n25, 228nn30–32, 229n46, 230n61, 230n65, 230n76, 231n9, 231nn14–15, 232n30, 232n57, 233n7; autobiographical prose, 105–6, 111–13; poetry, 35–40, 41, 79–80, 87; style of painting, 43, 48
Shagin, Dmitri, graphic work: "Beer," 102, *103*; *Brothers on the Bridge*, *104*; *The Little Boat* (*Korabliushechka*), 71, 72, 81; *The Mitki Write a Letter [to the Oligarchs]*, *203*, 204–5, 207; panel for *Sisters, or a Woman's Lot*, *82*; *Seizure of the Mitki's Studio*, 207, *208*
Shagin, Vladimir (artist, father of Dmitri Shagin), xvi, 6, 111, 206
Shagin, Tatiana (wife of Dmitri), 10
Shakespeare, William, 28, 192
Shekhter, Tatiana, 92, 93, 228n34
Shenkman, Ian, 232n31
Shevchuk, Yuri, 7, 25, 171, 223n7
Shinkarev, Vladimir, 2, 5–23, *24*, 25–57; on social media, 21–23
Shinkarev, Vladimir, literary work: "Alcohol," 121–22; "A Cat Overate and Lies among the Flowers," 217–18; *The End of the Mitki* (*Konets mit'kov*), xvi–xvii, 11, 13, 19, 31–42, 45, 47–52, 54–57, 58, 73, 125, 131, 135–36, 140, 162, 185, 202, 207, 218; *Maksim i Fedor*, 235n52; *Mitki*, xv–xvi, 6, 7, 11, 14, 21, 32, 33, 35, 36, 37, 39, 48–52, 55, 57, 59, 60–62, 64–65, 69, 73–74, 81, 90, 98, 99, 105, 106, 116, 135, 142, 144, 150, 210, 212, 214, 221, 223n8, 227n4, 228n30, 229n41, 230n77; *Mitkovian Dances* (*Mit'kovskie pliaski*), 20, 90, 224n34, 230n64
Shinkarev, Vladimir, graphic work: *Dancing Alone*, 81, *83*; *Goethe, "The Sorrows of Young Werther,"* 43, *44*, 45; "Rainbow Arch, don't drink our beer!," 102, *103*
Shklovsky, Viktor, 40, 226n36
Shuliakhovskaia, Natalia, 106, 229n44, 230n62, 231n18, 231n20
Sinyavsky, Andrei, 10, 224n18, 237n16
Situationists, 4, 35
Smelov, Boris, 10, 110, 224n17
Sokurov, Aleksandr. *See* Tikhomirov, Viktor
Solomon, Andrew, 18
Sontag, Susan, 32, 76, 183, 225n16, 229n41
Sorokin, Vladimir, 11, 178
Stalin, Iosif, 17, 18, 65, 67, 106, 178, 179, 186, 194, 196, 231n9; cult of personality, 6, 13, 34, 68, 151, 174, 176, 177
Steinholt, Yngvar B., 226n47
Stepanova, Varvara, 154, 155, 234n39
*Stiob*, 20, 87, 196
St. Petersburg: alcohol and, 110–11, 120; art world of, 10, 18, 93; city views, xii, 26, 198, 225n7, 234n30; real estate interests, 205

TEII (Tovarishchestvo Eksperiemental'nogo izobrazitel'nogo Iskusstva). *See* Cooperative of Experimental Graphic Art
Thackeray, William Makepeace, 51
Thian, Helene Marie, 230n69
Tikhomirov, Viktor, 2, 164–98, *168*; *Andrei Kuraev. Priamaia rech'*, xvii, 169, 170–72, 197, 198, 235n9; *Bread and Onion*, *171*; *Chapaev Chapaev*, 169, 170, 174, 183–84, 186–92, 236n25; *Eugene Telegin and Others* (*Evgenii Telegin i drugie*), 18, 194–96, 224n30, 236n31; *Gold on the Wind* (*Zoloto na vetre*), 182; *Grass and Water* (*Trava i voda*), xvi, 174, 176; *Nestor Makhno Throws an Unneeded Woman Overboard*, *173*; panel for *Sisters, or a Woman's Lot*, *187*; *Sokurov*, xvi, 174, 196, 236n36; views on homosexuality, 192–93, 197; "Wolf, you won't get away from us!," *181*
Tikhomirov, Vladimir, 207
Tolokonnikova, Nadezhda, 39, 63, 199, 227n2. *See also* Pussy Riot
Tolstoy, Lev, 6, 43, 106, 127, 185, 186, 196
Travis, Trysh, 109, 124, 232n26, 233n59
Trezzini, Domenico, 26
Tsoi, Viktor, 7, 46
Tsvetaeva, Marina, 157, 158, 164, 197
Tupitsyn, Victor, 132, 233n12

Valieva, Yulia, 202, 236n5
Vasilieva, Irina, xii, 8, 19, 201, 236n3

Vasiliev Island, 26, 28, 29, 122
Visconti, Luchino, 9, 74; *Rocco and His Brothers* (*Rocco e i suoi fratelli*), 91
Volkov, Solomon, 4, 66, 223n2, 227n16

Wilde, Oscar, 169, 235n7
Woodhead, Leslie, 46, 226n46
Wright, Richard, 213

Yashke, Vladimir, 2
Yufit, Evgeni, 193, 196, 197, 214, 230n58
Yurchak, Alexei, 193, 213, 214, 228n28, 236n28, 237n17, 237n27

Zhitinskii, Aleksandr, 196, 226nn47–48, 236n34
Žižek, Slavoj, 67, 139, 228n20

www.ingramcontent.com/pod-product-compliance
Lightning Source LLC
LaVergne TN
LVHW010607100826
845148LV00014B/2884
*9780299314941*